P9-BZZ-290

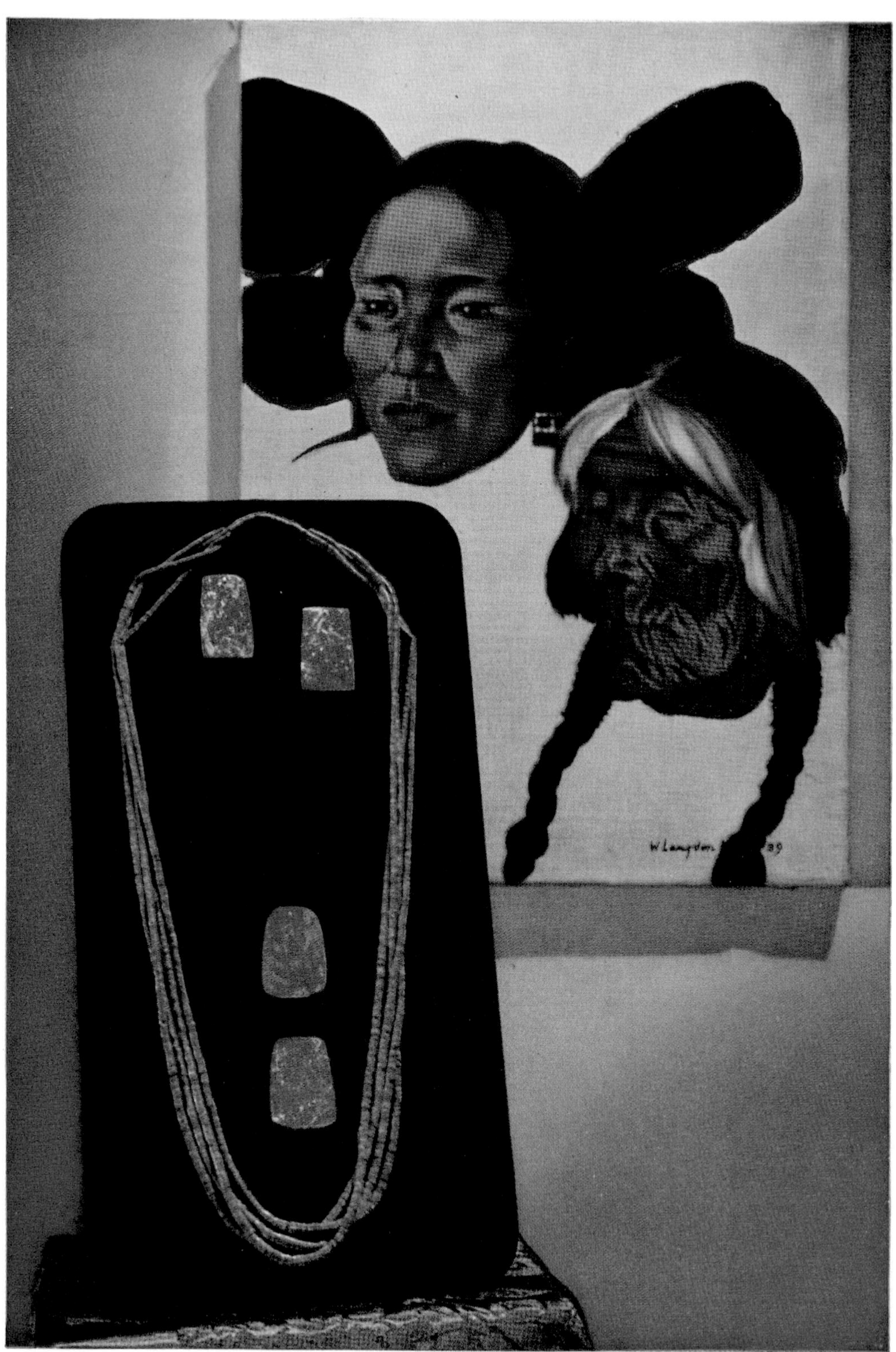

EKTACHROME BY NATIONAL GEOGRAPHIC PHOTOGRAPHER B. ANTHONY STEWART

*National Geographic on*

# INDIANS OF THE AMERICAS

*a Color-illustrated Record*

**Hopi Heads Symbolize the Beauty and Antiquity of a Priceless Turquoise Necklace**

A thousand years ago some lucky Indian of ancient Pueblo Bonito prized this necklace of 2,500 hand-drilled beads. Found buried with four ear pendants under 15 feet of New Mexico sand, it was an outstanding discovery of the National Geographic Society's Pueblo Bonito Expeditions of 1921–1927. The background painting by W. Langdon Kihn, illustrator of Part I of this volume, portrays later dwellers in the region. Girl's hairdo represents a squash blossom; old wife wears her hair in braids.

*National Geographic on*

# INDIANS OF THE

*A Volume in the*
*National Geographic* Story of Man *Library*

Illustrated with full-color reproductions of 149 paintings by

**W. LANGDON KIHN and H. M. HERGET**

and eight contemporary Indian painters; 117 photographs in natural color by JUSTIN LOCKE, LUIS MARDEN, KIP ROSS, RICHARD H. STEWART, and others; 128 black-and-white photographs, maps, drawings, and diagrams.

Foreword by **JOHN OLIVER LA GORCE**
President, National Geographic Society, 1954–57


First through sixth printings: 330,000 copies
Seventh printing, with revisions, 1965: 75,000 copies
Manufactured in the United States of America
Library of Congress Catalog Card Number 61-15830

**WASHINGTON, D. C.**

**THE**

# AMERICAS

*a Color-illustrated Record*

**MATTHEW W. STIRLING**

Director, Bureau of American Ethnology, Smithsonian Institution, 1928–57, and Leader of National Geographic Society-Smithsonian Expeditions to Mexico, Panama, and Ecuador.

With contributions by HIRAM BINGHAM, Leader of National Geographic-Yale University Peruvian Expeditions; O. F. COOK, former botanist, U. S. Department of Agriculture; ANDREW ELLICOTT DOUGLASS, Leader of National Geographic Tree Ring Expeditions; CLIFFORD EVANS, Associate Curator, Division of Archeology, U. S. National Museum; NEIL M. JUDD, former Curator, Division of Archeology, U. S. National Museum, Leader of National Geographic Pueblo Bonito Expeditions; DONALD B. MARSH, Bishop of the Arctic; PHILIP AINSWORTH MEANS, late authority on Andean civilizations; SYLVANUS GRISWOLD MORLEY, Director of Carnegie Institution Chichén Itzá Project, 1924–40; FROELICH G. RAINEY, Director, University of Pennsylvania Museum; FRANK H. H. ROBERTS, JR., former Director, Bureau of American Ethnology; DOROTHY DUNN, HELGA LARSEN, BETTY J. MEGGERS, and others.

NATIONAL GEOGRAPHIC SOCIETY

NATIONAL GEOGRAPHIC PHOTOGRAPHER GUY STARLING

**Dr. La Gorce Shows His Weapon Collection to a Sioux Visiting the Society's Headquarters**

THIS IS THE INDIAN OF THE AMERICAS: The Navajo artist bent over his work of silver; Tarascan girls at a village fountain; the Eskimo battling a polar bear; the bow-and-arrow stalker in Guiana jungles; the ancient Maya priest decked in writhing quetzal plumes.

Here he is hunting, warring, here at play laughing, here sacrificing a human as a jagged obsidian blade descends in a grim pagan rite. From Indians crouched about a Texas hearth 37,000 years ago to those working riveting hammers in mid-20th century America, Indian life crowds upon these pages.

Indians dancing, worshiping, scalping, planting, raiding, clowning, mourning. Indians founding empires, feasting in golden halls, grubbing for roots. The Indian as medicine man and canoe builder, astronomer and horse thief, as food giver, warm friend . . . and deadly foe.

These things are revealed not in the words of armchair scholars but of doing men: the scientist who goes to live among a primitive jungle tribe or joins in a thrilling whale hunt; the professor who scales Andean cliffs to discover a lost city; the bishop who covers two and three-quarters million square miles of arctic diocese.

Since its birth in 1888 the National Geographic Society has contributed much to knowledge of the American past. Research expeditions have carried The Society's flag to Mexico, Panama, Peru; from Cape Horn to the bleak northland tundra of Southampton Island. Here are expedition leaders' exciting accounts: Matthew W. Stirling discovers the New World's oldest dated work of man, throws light on La Venta, or Olmec, culture, explores Panama's past by dugout and helicopter; Neil M. Judd reconstructs ancient life at Pueblo Bonito; Andrew Ellicott Douglass tracks down the "missing link" in the tree ring chronology of the Southwest; Hiram Bingham relives his historic discovery of Machu Picchu.

Two notable artists commissioned by The Society created an incomparable pictorial record under the guidance of Franklin L. Fisher, late Illustrations Editor of the *National Geographic Magazine*. W. Langdon Kihn is represented by 103 paintings of the North American Indian, H. M. Herget by 37 paintings of the Maya, Aztec, and Inca empires. Works of eight contemporary Indian artists are also included.

Explorers, scientists, writers, artists, photographers, cartographers, the wealth of Society materials all have contributed to this comprehensive volume. Its contents are as new as the latest find, as up-to-date as the remarkable carbon-14 dating technique which brings scientific accuracy to bear on prehistoric eras where only conjecture served before.

The Society's appreciation goes to each contributor, to Dr. Stirling for his counsel through the book's long months of preparation, and to Melville Bell Grosvenor, my successor as Editor of the *National Geographic Magazine,* whose conception and able direction were most valuable. Special thanks are due Merle Severy, who skillfully compiled and edited the text; Andrew Poggenpohl, who arranged the illustrations; and other members of the *National Geographic Magazine* staff for their part in creating a work in which every member of The Society may take pride.

JOHN OLIVER LA GORCE

KODACHROME BY JUSTIN LOCKE

**Huehueteotl, Ancient God of Fire,** looks down the ages at a modern Indian miss. This wrinkled, hunchbacked, leering god, wearing an incense burner as a hat, was discovered in 1941 at Cerro de las Mesas in Veracruz. Huehueteotl is one of many archeological treasures brought to light in Mexico by nine National Geographic Society-Smithsonian Institution expeditions led by Dr. Stirling.

# • CONTENTS

## Part III • INDIANS TODAY, FROM AMAZON TO ARCTIC

PART I

# INDIANS OF NORTH AMERICA

# A HISTORICAL PANORAMA

BY MATTHEW W. STIRLING

PAINTINGS BY W. LANGDON KIHN

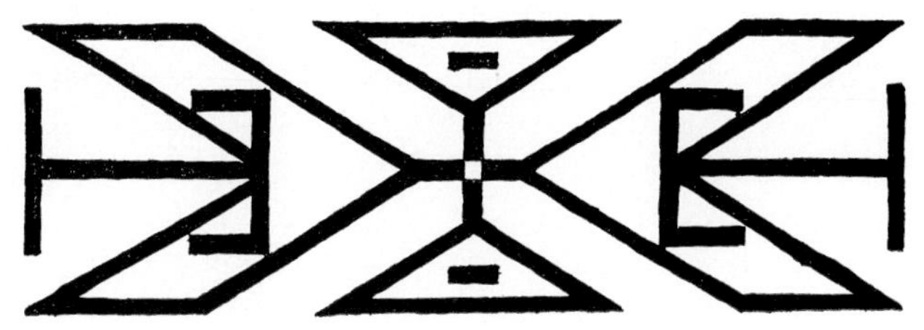

PAINTING BY W. LANGDON KIHN

**Fierce, Stalwart, Free Stood the American Warrior.** Chief One Bull fought Custer. Resplendent in Sioux trappings at 91, this nephew and adopted son of Sitting Bull evokes the Indian's indomitable spirit.

## CHAPTER I

# AMERICA'S FIRST SETTLERS THE INDIANS

"ARE THESE THINGS not a dream?" wondered battle-scarred conquistadores as they gazed upon temples, causeways, magnificent cities of the Aztecs. Many a Spanish don following Cortés to Mexican shores in 1519 expected to find naked savages living in primitive state.

Imagine their surprise to discover a flourishing people whose civilization outglittered their own. Palaces filled with gold, silver, and jade art made their heads swim. Tenochtitlán's canals eclipsed those of Venice. Cholula's great pyramid outbulked those along the Nile.

The quill of Bernal Díaz del Castillo, soldier-chronicler of Cortés's conquest of New Spain, scratched to a stop. How could he describe "things that had never been heard of or seen before, not even dreamed about"?

In Peru the conquerors came upon wonders equally staggering. The Chimu capital of Chan-Chan surpassed Assyria's Nineveh, Ur of the Chaldees, Babylon, even mighty Carthage. The imperial highway of the Incas, knifing three thousand miles down the ice-crested Andes, tunneling through living rock, spanning dizzy river chasms, marching mile after mile across burning desert, made Rome's Appian Way seem a garden path. Spanish eyes popped to see terraced irrigation systems soar into the clouds.

Even 20th century man, smug with the awareness of his own technical accomplishments, marvels at ancient Peruvian walls. Twenty-ton cut stones were fitted without mortar so that even today, countless earthquakes later, a slip of paper cannot be edged into the joints. Skyscraper towns rose in North American Pueblo lands centuries before New York's skyline took on its jagged look.

Today's surgeons are astounded by delicate brain operations successfully performed by Indians of the Andes in pre-Columbian days when Old World doctors were still prescribing ground unicorn horn and lioness milk. Indeed, aboriginal American knowledge of calendar, astronomy, and mathematics put medieval Europe's savants to shame. Ancestors of the Maya used the zero a thousand years before the Arabs.

Half the world feeds on the potato. Millions owe their subsistence to corn, and manioc, and beans—all foods first cultivated by American aborigines. The traditional Thanksgiving turkey dinner is all Indian. Rarely do we sit down to *any* meal without paying homage to the Indian.

Drink hot chocolate, munch peanuts or chew gum at a ball game, light a cigarette and you are indebted to the Indian. Speed along the highway and you are riding on rubber from the Indian. Speed too fast and the doctor will ease the pain of your injuries with cocaine—also In-

**Sioux Mass for Attack as Custer Marches to His Fate.** Surprise, confusion grip the tepee camp stretched three miles along tree-lined Little Bighorn River. Cooking fires still burn; women hustle children away from flying hoofs and brandished weapons. It is June 25, 1876. On this crucial day Sioux and Cheyenne, embittered by white encroachment on their sacred treaty-protected hunting grounds in the Black Hills of Dakota, lashed out, annihilated a cavalry column led by famed Indian fighter General George Armstrong Custer. The event rocked the nation.

At daybreak Custer's Crow scouts spied the smoke of Sioux fires, but did not realize that 12,000 to 15,000 Indians were gathered there. Custer split his 7th U.S. Cavalry into three wide-spreading columns, then rode at the head of some 225 troopers down barren ravines toward the Sioux camp.

PAINTING BY W. LANGDON KIHN

Here whooping Indians rally as dust marks Custer's approach. While Sitting Bull "made medicine" to invoke aid of the gods, Chiefs Crazy Horse and Gall led more than 2,500 warriors to the attack. Custer made his stand on a grassy knoll behind his dead horses. The Indians squirmed near, then made a last howling charge. They took no prisoners, left the bodies where they fell. Several miles away, Reno's and Benteen's men in the other two columns, unaware of Custer's fate, beat off attacks a second day before the Indians, sighting a relief column, melted into the hills. Crazy Horse surrendered next spring, but Sitting Bull and Gall escaped into Canada, to return later under amnesty.

To re-create the scene of Custer's fight, artist W. Langdon Kihn went over the Montana battlefield, now a National Monument, with Sitting Bull's nephew, One Bull (page 12), who fought that day.

JOSEPH K. DIXON

**Returning Deerslayer Treads a Wooded Path.** Plains Indians once lived in eastern woodlands. When white men drove them from the prairies some again took to forests in western mountains. Their buffalo herds slaughtered, they used canvas from the trader instead of hides to cover tepees.

dian. White man conquered the tropics with the aid of the Indian's quinine.

Who is our benefactor? The man profiled on the Indian Head nickel? The fearless mounted warrior of the movies—tall, eagle-nosed, wearing a feather headdress, living in a tepee?

This man is an American Indian, true. But so is the short, flat-nosed Wai Wai living in a palm-thatched Guiana hut. And the stocky Eskimo, builder of Arctic igloos.

We picture the whooping, hard-riding Sioux. We see the war-painted brave crouched behind a ledge, ready to ambush a covered wagon train with tomahawk, bow and arrow. We label our conception "*the* American Indian," forgetting that accident placed this single type of aborigine astride our path of westward expansion. Sharp conflict fixed the image in our national memory. Bowing to stereotype, today's Eastern States Indian dons the Western Plains headdress his fathers never knew, so people will know he's Indian.

Of course, none are true Indians in the sense Columbus took them to be—inhabitants of India. Nor are they "redskins." Fondness for painting themselves with red ocher or red vegetable paints led the American aborigines to be called redskins by early explorers, fur traders, and colonists.

Thus arose the erroneous idea that the Indian's skin is naturally red, or copper-colored. Actually it is brown, sometimes shading almost to white.

If not real Indians, or redskins; if not the Lost Tribes of Israel, or refugees from sunken Atlantis, who are these people? Whence did they come?

Roll back the centuries to when the last great ice sheet still covered much of the northern portion of the globe, to perhaps 40,000 years ago. Let imagination carry you to bleak Alaskan shores. Before you a land bridge extends through the fog to what is now East Cape, Siberia. Over this bridge comes a venturesome Asiatic wanderer, a prehistoric Columbus of name unknown. He carries a stone-tipped spear. Perhaps tracking an animal has led him first to set foot on American soil.

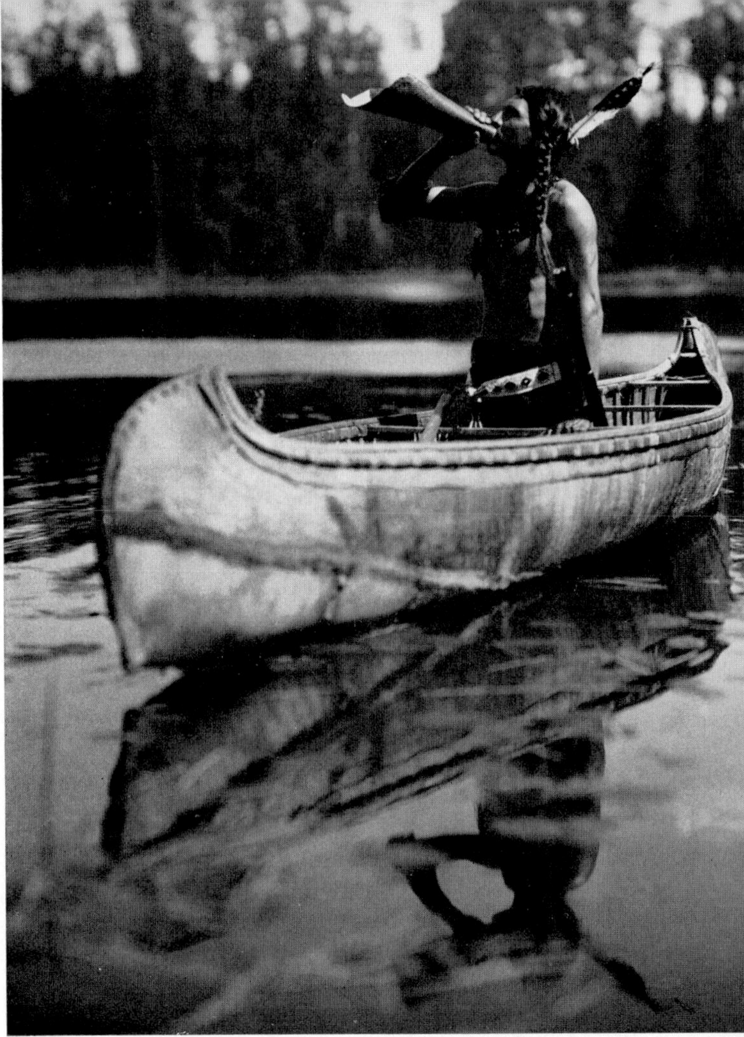

ROLAND W. REED, © R. F. WILLIAMS

**Luring Moose from Forest Depths,** a Chippewa hunter simulates their mating call. When a bull appears phantom-like at water's edge, a lucky shot means feasts of venison.

Years whirl by. Glaciers melt. The sea rises to engulf the bridge. A strip of water separates the two continents. But migrants still come. They cross the ice, or paddle over in skin boats, just as Eskimos sometimes do today.

These first comers push southward into more hospitable climes and more productive lands. To roving hunters in quest of game, this vast virgin territory seems a paradise. No human enemies bar their way. Deer, elk, bison abound. The giant ground sloth with its sluggish habits proves an easy victim. The mighty mammoth and American camel—also to become extinct—provide meat for the hunter. He leaves ingeniously flaked stone knives and projectile points at camp sites to be found centuries later together with the bones of his prey.

Through many centuries Asiatic people, responding to population pressure from the south and west, found this natural route into the Americas, just as successive streams of European immigration later penetrated inland from the Atlantic seaboard. So completely did these Asiatics establish themselves that, when the Europeans arrived, the two continents and practically all adjacent islands were occupied from the Arctic coast to Tierra del Fuego.

Wherever early white explorers went, they found signs of Indian achievement. The Indian was not only a skilled agriculturist, astronomer, engineer, builder of great empires. He was an adept weaver

## Gallant Ally, Bitter Foe

Sacagawea, loyal Shoshoni girl who trekked 4,000 wilderness miles with Lewis and Clark, symbolizes the Indian's helping hand. At right, high on Columbia River banks 200 miles from the Pacific, she stands, infant on back, beside her husband Charbonneau, the interpreter, as Dalles Indians show the expedition leaders a way through the white water in 1805. Friendly, too, were the nomadic Cree of northern woodlands (bottom right). They trapped furs for the trader, their birchbark canoes served the explorer, their women often married French voyageurs. But relentless pressure from European settlers prodded most tribes into war. Some groups, after defeat, resented reservation life and broke out to return to ancestral lands. One such revolt occurred in 1872 when Modoc (below) entrenched themselves in a natural lava fortress in northern California. There they made a bitter last stand, held out for four months, inflicted heavy losses on attacking U. S. troops.

PAINTINGS BY W. LANGDON KIHN

of textiles and basketry, and a maker of artistic pottery without aid of the potter's wheel.

True, although the Indian devised a hand loom, he was deficient in mechanical inventions. For example, he never discovered the keystone arch nor the practical use of the wheel. But he made up for this in the higher arts.

He was an excellent orator and dramatist. His poetry is filled with fine imagery, a deep appreciation of nature, and it reflects his often beautiful religious philosophy. Singing and dancing were highly developed. Works in sculpture, modeling, painting by aboriginal American artists take their places beside the masterpieces of all time.

The Indian was fond of games of chance and skill. Not only man-to-man competition in foot racing and wrestling, but sports requiring team play and mass participation were widespread. Lacrosse (page 22), a game since taken over by the white man, was a favorite among woodlands tribes east of the Mississippi. Maya youth played ball in the court at Chichén Itzá (page 203).

The European explorers also found an amazing range of cultures—from complex urban social organizations down to the most primitive, where the only recognizable unit was the family. Whatever his environment or stage of social development, the Indian learned Nature's secrets and found how best he could turn them to his ends.

Thus wandering bands of primitive Shoshoni, living in the parched deserts of the Great Basin, found food in the region's sparse and spiny plants, in grasshoppers, and fly larvae scraped from the surface of alkaline lakes. They made nets to trap the fleet jack rabbit and, for lack of better material, built their rude shelters of brush.

The diversity in aboriginal culture is illustrated most strikingly by languages. North of Mexico alone, at the time of the conquest, there were more than 50 unrelated linguistic stocks, and 700 distinct dialects. These dialects differed from one another as English differs from German or French, and the linguistic stocks have no common vocabulary or grammatical structure. This shows that many peoples of different origin had been isolated for long periods.

All these native American languages were capable of expressing abstract thought and subtle shades of meaning, their vocabularies were extensive, and the grammatical structure intricate and systematic. However, phonetic writing had never developed in the New World.

The principal linguistic stocks north of Mexico are the Eskimauan, which includes the entire Arctic coast from Alaska to Greenland; Athapascan, which includes Alaska and most of interior Canada west of Hudson Bay, and reappears in Arizona, New Mexico, and western Texas; Algonquian, which spans southern Canada from the Rocky Mountains to the Atlantic, thrusting south of the Great Lakes to Tennessee; the Iroquoian, which includes the St. Lawrence Valley and Lake Erie and Lake Ontario regions, south to northern Georgia.

The Shoshonean stock includes the Great Basin and northern Texas; the Siouan takes in most of the Great Plains and parts of the Carolinas and Virginia. The Muskhogean stock extends over most of Mississippi, Alabama, Georgia, and Florida.

Many lesser stocks dot the map of North America, the Pacific coast region being astonishingly diverse in this respect. And the linguistic situation south of the border is just as complex.

The varieties in physical type were not so great nor so striking as the cultural differences. All American Indians can be classified generally as of Mongoloid stock, to which the people of eastern Asia also belong. All have straight or slightly wavy black hair and brown

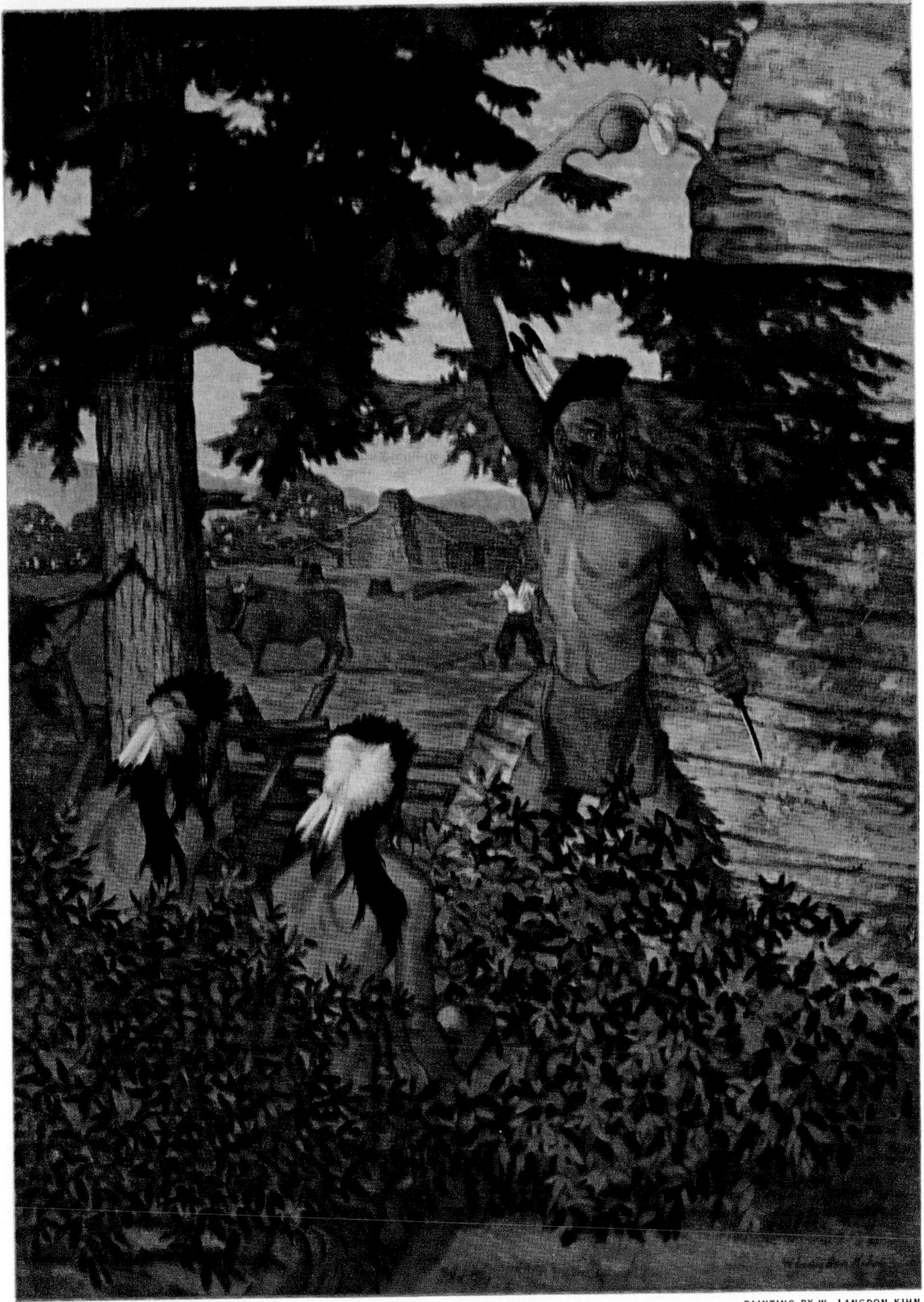

PAINTING BY W. LANGDON KIHN

**A War Whoop Rings Out.** The Iroquois leader, hideous in war paint, signals the attack. The farmer drops plow for gun. Seldom could the isolated settler and his family survive the surprise raid. One tragic dawn in 1704, savages fell upon sleeping Deerfield, Massachusetts, killing 49 villagers, taking 111 others captive to French Canada. The colonial era was not one of continuous border warfare but of periodic outbreaks when Indians went on the warpath to defend their lands or to take scalps and thus gain prestige. Many massacres by Indians were to avenge attacks made upon them.

## Lacrosse, Council Fires, Missionaries Shaped Iroquois Life

An Iroquois brave leaps high to catch the stuffed deerskin ball. Villages, even tribes competed in lacrosse, as much the national game of Indians east of the Mississippi as baseball is with modern Americans. But when they met in war council, in full regalia, tribal representatives of the five-nation Iroquois Confederacy might argue for grimmer conflict, perhaps against an old chief's plea for peace (right).

Christian peace was the message Jesuit missionaries early sought to bring to these warlike tribes of northeastern forests. Alone and unarmed (lower right), they wrote a heroic chapter in American history. Many a pioneer priest suffered unspeakable tortures. Yet they systematically learned the Indians' own beliefs the better to convert them, and despite hostility and every hardship continued to work among them for more than a century.



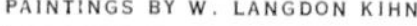
PAINTINGS BY W. LANGDON KIHN

64
65
67
66
63
68
69
H
70
81
62
71
72
75
77
78
79
61
60
F
G
73
59
76
80
H
74
42
D
7
6
5
57
58
43
41
A
16
15
56
44
39
40
4
17
55
14
8
18
19
45
46
38
3
47
E
13
A
2
37

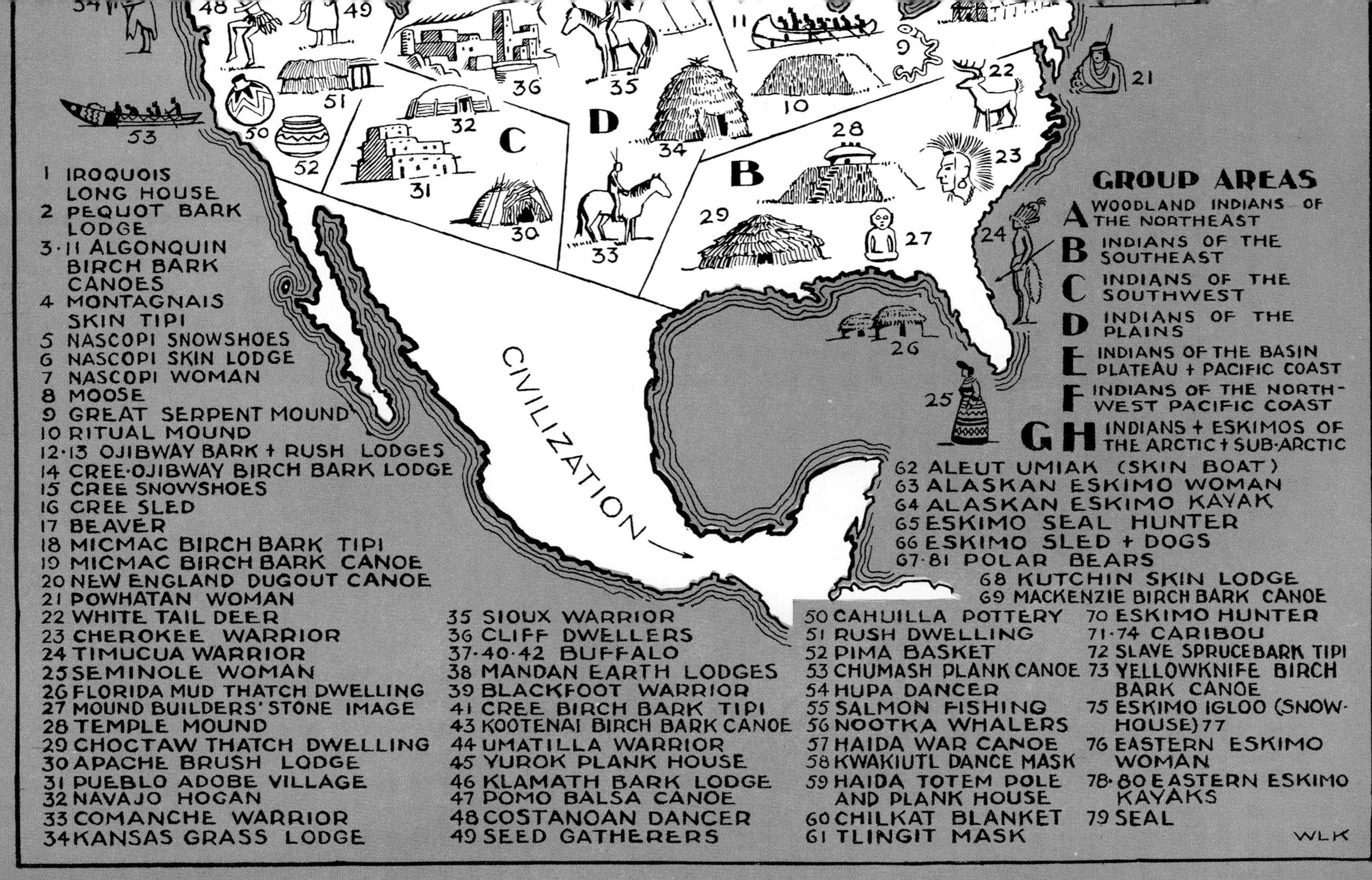

GROUP AREAS
A WOODLAND INDIANS OF THE NORTHEAST
B INDIANS OF THE SOUTHEAST
C INDIANS OF THE SOUTHWEST
D INDIANS OF THE PLAINS
E INDIANS OF THE BASIN PLATEAU + PACIFIC COAST
F INDIANS OF THE NORTH-WEST PACIFIC COAST
GH INDIANS + ESKIMOS OF THE ARCTIC + SUB-ARCTIC
CIVILIZATION
1 IROQUOIS LONG HOUSE
2 PEQUOT BARK LODGE
3·11 ALGONQUIN BIRCH BARK CANOES
4 MONTAGNAIS SKIN TIPI
5 NASCOPI SNOWSHOES
6 NASCOPI SKIN LODGE
7 NASCOPI WOMAN
8 MOOSE
9 GREAT SERPENT MOUND
10 RITUAL MOUND
12·13 OJIBWAY BARK + RUSH LODGES
14 CREE·OJIBWAY BIRCH BARK LODGE
15 CREE SNOWSHOES
16 CREE SLED
17 BEAVER
18 MICMAC BIRCH BARK TIPI
19 MICMAC BIRCH BARK CANOE
20 NEW ENGLAND DUGOUT CANOE
21 POWHATAN WOMAN
22 WHITE TAIL DEER
23 CHEROKEE WARRIOR
24 TIMUCUA WARRIOR
25 SEMINOLE WOMAN
26 FLORIDA MUD THATCH DWELLING
27 MOUND BUILDERS' STONE IMAGE
28 TEMPLE MOUND
29 CHOCTAW THATCH DWELLING
30 APACHE BRUSH LODGE
31 PUEBLO ADOBE VILLAGE
32 NAVAJO HOGAN
33 COMANCHE WARRIOR
34 KANSAS GRASS LODGE
35 SIOUX WARRIOR
36 CLIFF DWELLERS
37·40·42 BUFFALO
38 MANDAN EARTH LODGES
39 BLACKFOOT WARRIOR
41 CREE BIRCH BARK TIPI
43 KOOTENAI BIRCH BARK CANOE
44 UMATILLA WARRIOR
45 YUROK PLANK HOUSE
46 KLAMATH BARK LODGE
47 POMO BALSA CANOE
48 COSTANOAN DANCER
49 SEED GATHERERS
50 CAHUILLA POTTERY
51 RUSH DWELLING
52 PIMA BASKET
53 CHUMASH PLANK CANOE
54 HUPA DANCER
55 SALMON FISHING
56 NOOTKA WHALERS
57 HAIDA WAR CANOE
58 KWAKIUTL DANCE MASK
59 HAIDA TOTEM POLE AND PLANK HOUSE
60 CHILKAT BLANKET
61 TLINGIT MASK
62 ALEUT UMIAK (SKIN BOAT)
63 ALASKAN ESKIMO WOMAN
64 ALASKAN ESKIMO KAYAK
65 ESKIMO SEAL HUNTER
66 ESKIMO SLED + DOGS
67·81 POLAR BEARS
68 KUTCHIN SKIN LODGE
69 MACKENZIE BIRCH BARK CANOE
70 ESKIMO HUNTER
71·74 CARIBOU
72 SLAVE SPRUCE BARK TIPI
73 YELLOWKNIFE BIRCH BARK CANOE
75 ESKIMO IGLOO (SNOW-HOUSE) 77
76 EASTERN ESKIMO WOMAN
78·80 EASTERN ESKIMO KAYAKS
79 SEAL
WLK

**Proud, Fearless Mohawk Chief** wears silver earrings bartered from white traders. He dons eagle headdress only on formal occasions, as when he sits with the Federal Council of the Iroquois. The Mohawks, early established in the Mohawk Valley, New York's gateway to the West, got firearms from Dutch traders about 1614 to help them gather furs. Possessing these weapons spurred the warlike tribe's rise to power. They extended their sway from the Susquehanna to the St. Lawrence. They terrorized Algonquian enemies, striking deep into French Canada.

The Mohawks sided with British against American in the Revolutionary War, were driven from their ancestral home, and later settled on Canadian lands assigned to them by the Crown. Today more than 13,000 Mohawks live in the Provinces of Ontario and Quebec. Some 400 others dwell in New York City, where they help build Manhattan's skyscrapers (page 421).

eyes. Complexion is generally dark.

The principal differences are in facial features, head form, and stature. The Indians east of the Mississippi and in the Great Plains were usually tall and stalwart in build, often exhibiting the aquiline nose we so commonly associate with the typical Indian face. This type also prevails in western and southern South America.

On the other hand, the Indians of Middle America and the Amazon Basin are shorter in stature and darker in complexion, with broader and flatter noses.

Seven times as many people live in New York City today as occupied all North America north of Mexico when Columbus arrived. Ethnologists estimate the total population of this area was then about 1,150,000.

Of this number 918,000 lived within the limits of the present United States (including 72,000 in Alaska), 220,000 in Canada, and 10,000 in Greenland. The greatest concentrations were in the southeastern United States and in California, areas whose mild climate and abundant food supply could support large populations.

After these enterprising people had discovered America, populated it, and developed their interesting and diverse cultures, all that remained was for the Europeans to discover the Indians.

## NORTHEASTERN WOODLANDS INDIANS

When Norsemen visited the New England coast during the first two decades of the 11th century, their all too brief descriptions of the savages, or *skraellings,* indicate an Algonquian people whose Northeastern Woodlands culture changed but little during the next few centuries.

The Norsemen described the Indians as swarthy, ferocious in aspect, with ugly hair, big eyes, and broad cheeks. They were clad in skin clothing, armed with bows and arrows, and used stone axes. They navigated the rivers in birchbark canoes and eagerly traded their furs for strips of red flannel to bind their heads.

They expressed keen surprise at the Vikings' iron tools and were terror-stricken at the bellow of Thorfinn's bull, brought over for breeding.

The Norsemen also described "self-sown wheatfields," but it is impossible to say whether these were fields of cultivated maize or of wild rice.

No records have been preserved of subsequent Norsemen visits to America, but possibly the Basques, Normans, and Bretons explored this region by mid-15th century in search of fishing grounds. At any rate, soon after John Cabot sighted Cape Breton in 1497, Basques established

**This Seneca Warrior,** stern and dignified, suggests a James Fenimore Cooper character. Indians of the Eastern Woodlands, together with many northern Plains tribes, were fine physical specimens. The metal blade on this brave's war club and silver band around his head came from white men, probably in exchange for furs such as adorn his garments.

In mid-17th century the Seneca burst out from ancestral lands in the Lake Seneca region of western New York, spread their conquering mantle westward to Lake Erie and south along the Allegheny River into Pennsylvania, and became the most populous nation of the Iroquois Confederacy. Today some 7,700 Seneca are listed on the census rolls of New York State.

PAINTINGS BY W. LANGDON KIHN

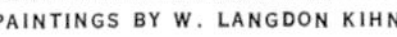

PAINTINGS BY W. LANGDON KIHN

## Prowess as Hunter, Fisher, Warrior Spelled Prestige for the Red Man

With his last arrow, a snowshoed Penobscot Indian (above) takes aim at the moose he has trailed through wintry woods. His quarry, largest of the deer family, has bogged down, weak from wounds and plowing through heavy drifts. No longer can forest monarch stand off or escape the hunter relentlessly closing in with reinforced bow. Indians of the Penobscot River Valley in Maine lived near the sea during summer; in winter they moved inland to hunt game. On the success of the chase hung the tribe's survival.

Great Lakes Indians (top left) spear fish through holes in the ice. Bundled in Eskimolike furs, they chopped openings in the ice with stone hatchets and erected shelters over them. The man crouching under the tent at right dangles a lure with one hand and waits patiently, spear in the other. A woman with a basket makes her rounds, collecting the catch.

Indian tribes often went to war to defend hunting and fishing rights, so vital to their existence. Drums beat, painted braves (left) chant war songs as they dance after smoking the pipe of battle. The leader carries a war banner of eagle feathers. A scalp adorns the third man's lance. Among the Chippewa any brave could instigate a raid by sending a messenger with tobacco to ask warriors to join the party. Those willing smoked the pipe, then assembled for a feast given by the leader. They danced every night until the eve of departure, when a dog-meat feast closed the festivities. Chippewa warred mainly against their hereditary enemies, the Sioux, driving them onto the Plains.

**Beneath a Towering Elm, William Penn and the Delawares Pledge Eternal Peace**

Benjamin West's painting captures the feeling of brotherly love in 1683 when the founder of Pennsylvania forged a bond of friendship with the Indians at Shackamaxon, now a city park in Philadelphia. Penn's men trade bolts of cloth and chests of goods for land under this compact, to remain in force "as long as water flows and the sun shines and grass grows."

Voltaire called Penn's treaty the only one "never sworn to and never broken." It and others made by the fair-dealing Penn long spared the infant Quaker commonwealth the terrors of Indian warfare suffered by other English colonies along the eastern seaboard.

COURTESY OF PENNSYLVANIA ACADEMY OF THE FINE ARTS

a permanent fishing settlement on Newfoundland. By 1578 some 150 French vessels were trading with the coastal Indians from Newfoundland to the mouth of the Potomac.

The Spaniards, meanwhile established in Florida, cast covetous eyes on the fur trade of the northern Atlantic coast. In 1565 Pedro Menéndez de Avilés wrote from St. Augustine that more than 2,000 buffalo skins had been canoed down the Potomac to Chesapeake Bay by Indians, and there traded to the French.

Thus, when English colonists arrived at Jamestown and Plymouth, the whites were already a familiar story to Indians of the Atlantic seaboard.

The first European settlements in the northeast were confined to a comparatively narrow coastal strip, but their presence was felt by tribes of the interior long before the white man appeared in person. The pressure created by the arrival of the French, the English, and the Dutch forced the westward withdrawal of the contact tribes. This caused conflicts with those whose territory was invaded. When these people were forced back in turn, established tribal territory again was dislocated. Finally the Siouan tribes living in the western Great Lakes region were pushed out from shaded woodlands into the sunlight of open plains. Their mode of existence changed with their new environment.

The conquest of the New World by the Spaniards is a story of the quest for gold. The conquest of northeastern North America is a story of French and English rivalry for control of the fur trade. Since furs were to be had only through friendly native allies, the European rivals soon took sides with the Indians.

When Champlain sought to colonize the St. Lawrence region early in the 17th century, it was only natural that he made friends with the Algonquians who occupied that territory. This alliance inevitably brought the French into conflict with the Iroquois, hereditary enemies of the Algonquians.

What Champlain had no means of knowing was that the agricultural and semisedentary Iroquois possessed a genius for political and military organization which, combined with their warlike traditions, was destined to give them the upper hand in conflict with native rivals.

When the English undertook to aid the Iroquois in their struggle, they allied themselves with the side that represented the balance of power. So it came about that North America is now basically English instead of French.

In contrast to English practice, the Roman Catholic French desire to convert the natives to Christianity was a leading factor in stimulating exploration. In 1615 Champlain sent missionaries into the St. Lawrence territory, first the Récollets, a Franciscan order. Then in 1625 the Jesuits came, pursuing their calling under almost unbelievably difficult conditions, with an unselfish courage and perseverance unsurpassed in the history of religion (page 23).

Because the Jesuits made a particular point of studying the natives and recording their customs, we have for the St. Lawrence and Great Lakes region a thorough knowledge of the aboriginal tribes before they had become greatly altered by contact with the Europeans.

Of all the North American tribes none were fiercer, more intelligent, more independent than the Iroquois (pages 21-23). Surrounded by Algonquian enemies, they lived in palisaded villages east and south of Lake Erie and Lake

Ontario, where they controlled the region between the Hudson and Ohio Rivers.

At the beginning of American history, they were only a weak remnant on the verge of extermination by their Algonquian neighbors. But at this critical juncture the Dutch furnished them with firearms, and so they were able to hold their own.

Increasing their strength further under the leadership of Dekanawida and Hiawatha, an Iroquois confederation was established among the Mohawk, the Onondaga, the Seneca, the Oneida, and the Cayuga. This confederation, known to the French as the "Long House" and to the English as the "Five Nations," was a unique experiment among American Indians and strongly influenced our own democratic type of government. Typical in many ways of Northeastern Woodlands culture were the customs and beliefs of the Iroquois.

The good Fathers found the Indians difficult to convert, for the entire background and philosophy of Christianity ran counter to native Indian beliefs.

*(Continued on page 41)*

## AMERICA THROUGH 16TH CENTURY EYES →

In the century after Columbus made his historic landfall, Europe knew only that a totally new world existed beyond the rim of the western ocean. What its people were like, how they lived, remained to be learned.

Thus the first pictures to be published of America stirred intense excitement. Imagine the effect today if The National Geographic Magazine were to publish authentic photographs of people on another planet, their settlements, their way of life.

The two artists who first depicted America were Jacques le Moyne de Morgues and John White. They painted what they saw on these shores at different places and times, but their work appeared almost simultaneously, in 1590 and 1591, when the Walloon engraver Theodore De Bry reproduced the paintings in two volumes that were to launch his vast publishing project, *Grands et Petits Voyages*.

Le Moyne, in 1564, took part in an ill-fated attempt to establish a French Huguenot colony in Spanish Florida. The Spanish a year later stormed the Huguenots' Fort Caroline, and Le Moyne with a few others barely escaped to a French ship.

White, as one of Sir Walter Raleigh's colonists, made three voyages from England to "Virginia," in 1585, 1587, and 1590. On the second he went as governor of the settlement on Roanoke Island; when he reluctantly sailed away for supplies, he left his daughter and his granddaughter, Virginia Dare, first English child born in the New World. He never saw them again, for when he returned the "Lost Colony" had disappeared, leaving the single enigmatic word "Croatoan" carved on a tree.

At no small peril both Le Moyne and White went boldly among the brown-skinned natives they found in this incredible new land. Le Moyne was commissioned to chart all Florida; his map (page 59) was accurate about places the French visited, but he accepted many unreliable names and positions from the Indians.

John White described Indian celebrations around fires on Virginia's shore (opposite), when warriors had "escaped any great danger by sea or lande, or be returned from the warr . . . in token of joye." His water colors showed the Indians living in neat towns, raising corn, pumpkins, and *uppowoc* (tobacco), and hunting deer in the adjoining forest. "When they go to battle they paynt their bodyes in the most terrible manner that they can devise," White said of the "lordes of Virginia."

Le Moyne spoke approvingly of the Florida Indians' storing their crops in public granaries. He painted their chiefs adorned with elaborate tattoos and headdresses. At times he was prone to exaggerate: his "crocodrilles," or alligators, are fantastic in size. Yet despite that fancy which sometimes clouds the detailed reporting in both men's drawings, these remain important documents of New World life.

ENGRAVINGS BY THEODORE DE BRY

**"When They Be Returned from the Warr . . . They Make Merrie about the Fyer."** John White depicts the Indians' "manner of prainge with rattels" and singing—"a strange custome, and worth the observation."

**"Howses of the Towne of Secota Have Gardens . . . Wherin Groweth Tobacco (E)."** Indians dance around curiously carved posts (C), feast in the street (D), hunt and cavort in this neatly arrayed town on the Pamlico River (L) in present North Carolina. Crouching in a hut (F), a watchman "maketh continual cryes and noyse" to frighten marauding "fowles and beastes" from ripening corn. Space was left between rows (H), "otherwise one stalke would choke the growthe of another." Pumpkins (I) grow near by.

ENGRAVINGS BY THEODORE DE BRY

**"The Towne of Pomeiooc . . . Compassed Abowt with Poles Stucke Faste in the Grownde."** Only the chief and his nobles occupied houses, which were built of poles tied together and covered with mats. These turned up to admit light. The chief's dwelling (B) and the temple (A) were the largest, "builded rownde and covered with skynne mattes." Feasts and celebrations were held in the middle of the village. When streams were too distant, Indians dug ponds for water (C). Open towns like near-by Secota (opposite) were described by White as "commonlye fayrer" than those huddled inside palisades, such as Pomeiooc.

**"The Chieffe Applyed to by Women Whose Husbandes Have Died in Warr or by Dysease."** Lamenting widows seek sustenance, vengeance for their fallen warriors, permission to remarry after a proper time. Le Moyne's colonists (right) shoulder muskets and halberd.

**"The Manner of Makinge Their Boates in Virginia is Verye Wonderfull."** John White saw Indians fell trees by building fires close to the roots (upper right), then burn off tops and boughs. Lacking iron tools, they hollowed out trunks by fire and scraping with shells.

ENGRAVINGS BY THEODORE DE BRY

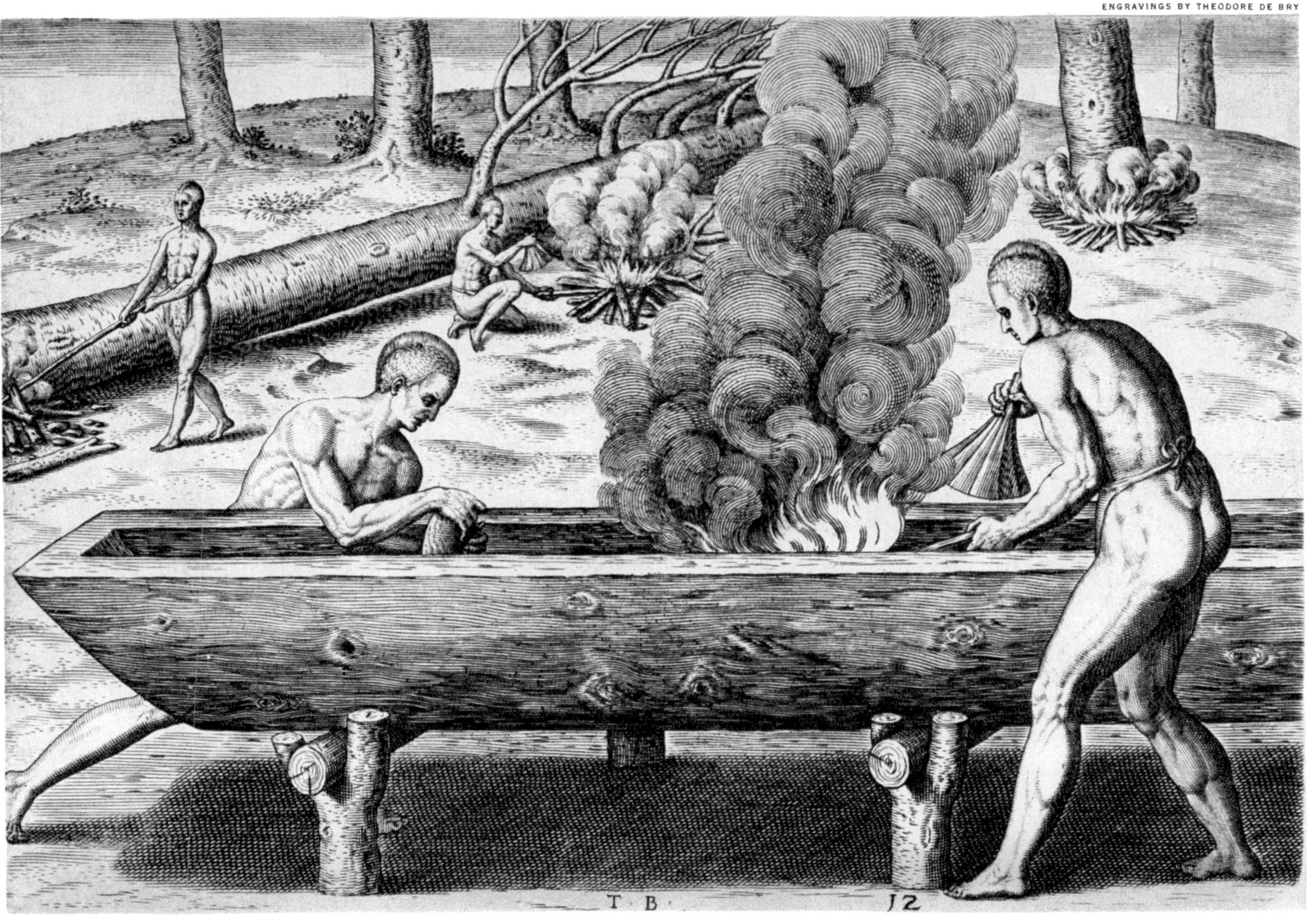

**"Broylinge Their Fishe over the Flame . . . They Take Good Heed that They Bee Not Burntt."** Two shadlike fish sizzle atop a wooden grill, two beside the fire. New catch includes garfish and small hammerhead shark. Virginia's Indians ate their fish at once; Florida's cured them for later use.

**"Their Manner of Killynge Crocodrilles."** As the reptile comes openmouthed to attack, the Indians shove a pointed pole down its throat, turn it over and assault its soft underbelly with clubs and arrows. From riverbank huts (left) Indians watch for their prey.

ENGRAVINGS BY THEODORE DE BRY

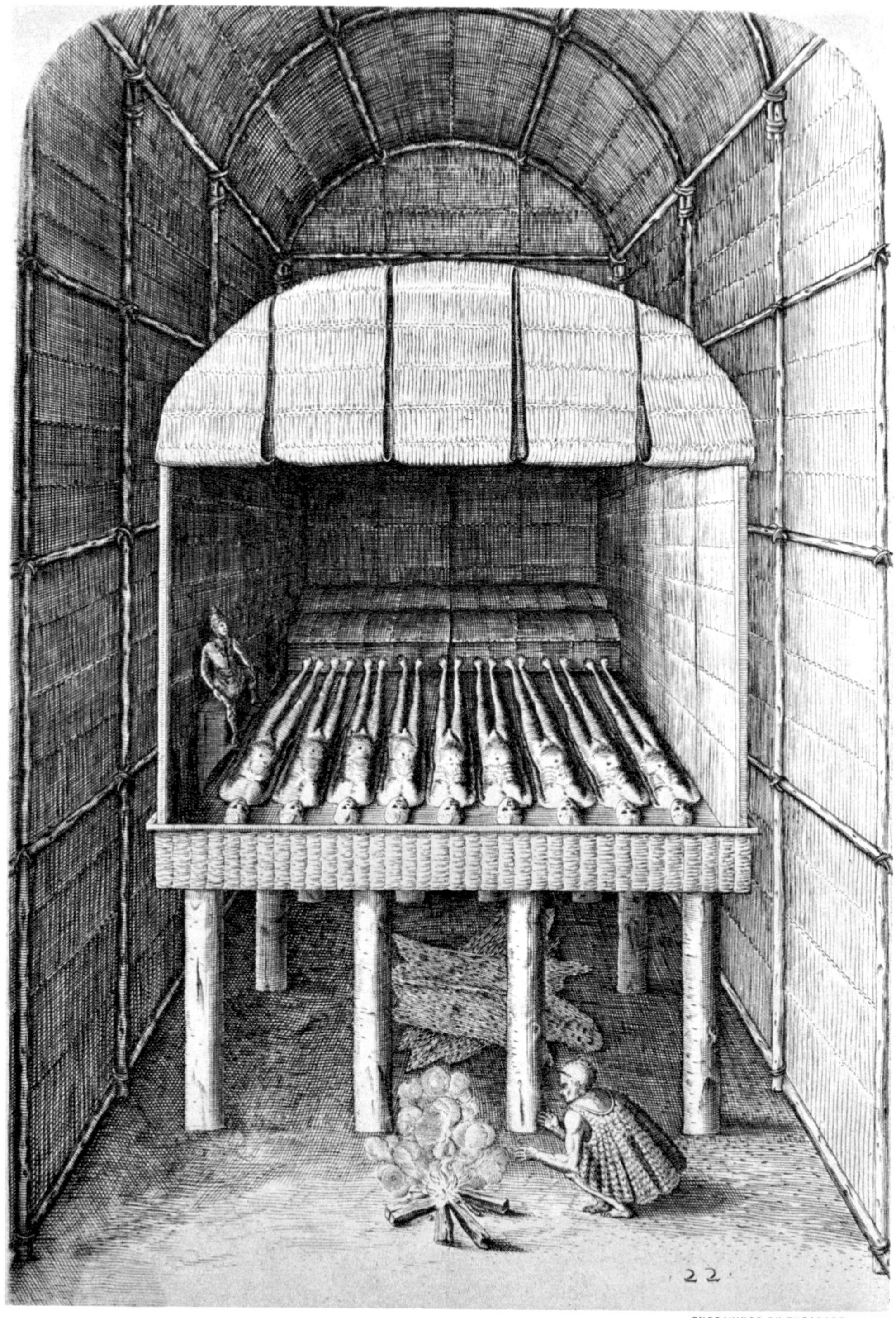


ENGRAVINGS BY THEODORE DE BRY

**"The Tombes of the Weroans or Cheiffe Lordes."** John White describes Virginia Indians preserving bodies of departed chiefs for veneration. They were drawn and skinned; their flesh, "clene taken from the bones," was dried in the sun. The skeleton, covered with its own tanned skin, was placed on a scaffold, the flesh in mats at its feet. Beside it the Indians "sett their idol Kiwasa [left] . . . for they are persuaded that the same doth kepe the dead bodyes . . . that nothinge may hurt them." Priest keeping vigil sleeps on deerskins beneath scaffold.

The fundamental idea of Christianity —immortality, with conduct during life determining the soul's reward or punishment—was incomprehensible to the aborigines, who gave little thought to the hereafter and did not mix ethics with religion. Moral principles of good and evil were not sharply defined and any such spirit abode as a "happy hunting ground," or an Indian hell, was foreign to native thought until missionaries implanted the idea.

Dreams or visions, induced by fasting or drugs, wherein he regularly saw and spoke with individuals known to be dead, amply proved to the Indian that soul and afterlife existed. Offerings placed with the dead manifested this belief. The souls of the dead, however, were usually feared and often extreme measures were taken to prevent their return.

Among the Huron, the body was placed in a flexed position in a bark coffin erected upon a scaffolding in the woods near the village, along with offerings of food and ornaments. Every 12 years, at the great feast of the dead, all bodies of tribal members who had died in the interim were removed from their original burial scaffolds by relatives. With demonstrations of affection, the bones were cleaned and wrapped with the finest robes, then conveyed to the village where they were displayed for a short time together with new offerings. From here the bones were carried to a huge common burial pit in which on the designated day all bones of the tribal dead were deposited with great ceremony (page 51).

Neither did Indians clearly comprehend the idea of a personified ruling deity. The loosely organized democratic tribes were unacquainted with a highly centralized type of government. Therefore the political analogy of a ruling god held no meaning for them.

The Indian's religion was entirely practical and designed to help him, not in the future, but in the immediate present. Thus when he thought himself plagued by an evil spirit, the obvious way to rid himself of his difficulty was to propitiate that spirit with offerings. His attention thus was fixed equally upon friendly and unfriendly forces. The missionaries, of course, interpreted this attitude as worship of the Devil.

Underlying all this was the mystic conception of an impersonal supernatural force which permeates all nature and animates all phenomena which control the destiny of man. This force, akin to the life principle, is called *manito* by the Algonquian, *pokunt* by the Shoshoni, and *orenda* by the Iroquois. Early white travelers, not comprehending the real nature of this idea, usually translated it as "The Great Spirit."

Among the American aborigines were many secret societies and groups which appeared in public only in elaborate masks and costumes in which they represented various deities, some of whose powers they supposedly acquired through this sacred paraphernalia. Characteristic is the Iroquois Society of Faces, which is still active (page 54).

The Indian's imagination peopled forest and lake with strange beings. Hunters having odd experiences attributed these to encounters with weird semihuman "faces," which occasionally appeared to them in dreams. These faces were supposedly empowered to cure various diseases. The man who dreamed of a face was instructed in his dream to carve a likeness of it as a mask, thus making him a healer while wearing it and singing the proper curing songs. If not treated respectfully and given occasional offerings of tobacco and ashes, the faces would produce the diseases they could cure.

The variety of faces is large. Some are black, some red, some white; some are young, and some old. Most are deformed and twisted. One with a broken and twisted nose had a mountain fall on his

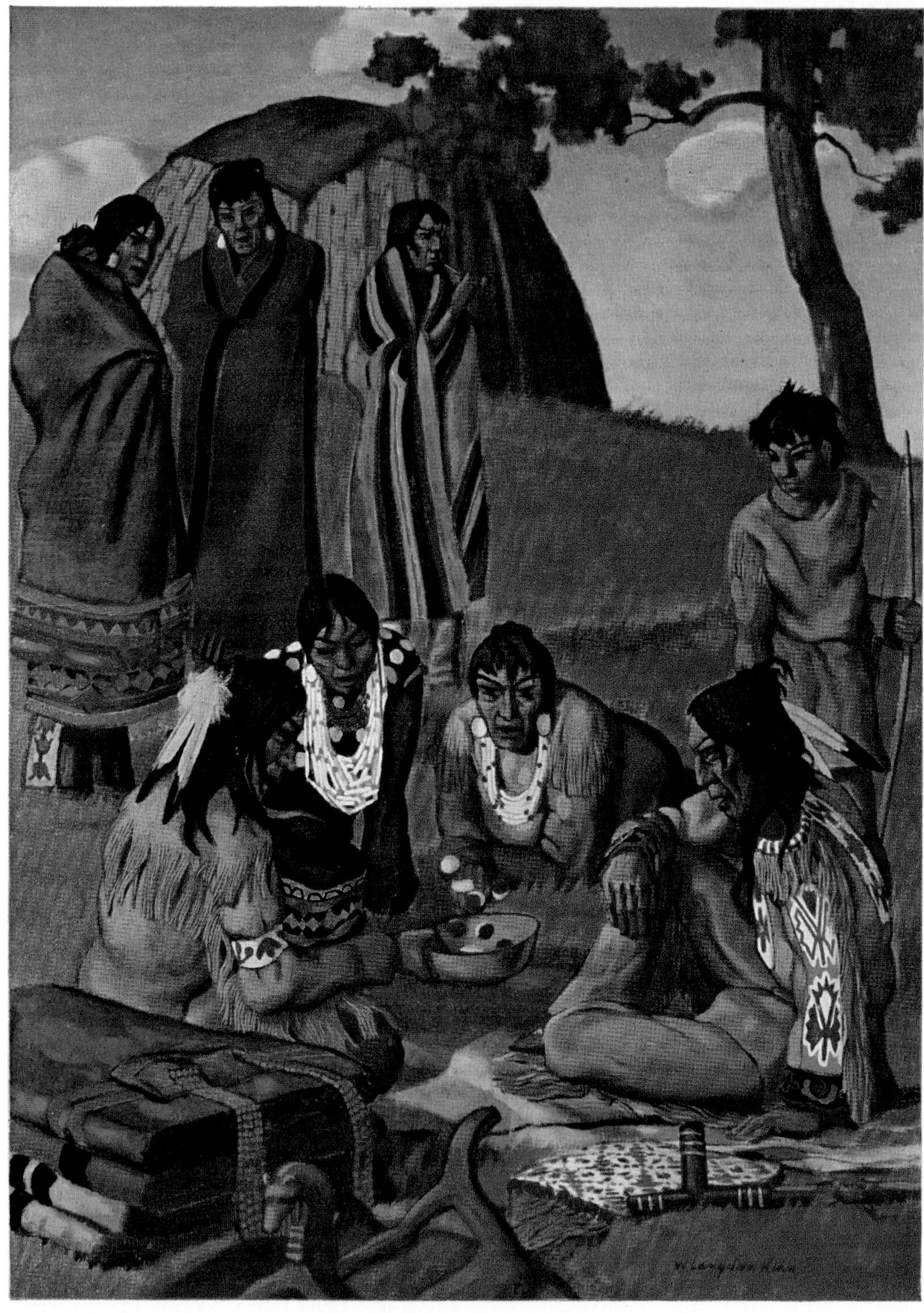

**Singing Menominee Gamblers** stake blankets, pipes—even wives—on a flip of the red-and-white disks. They bet, then the man who is to "shoot" begins a song in which the others join. Suddenly the player strikes the bowl; the dice fly upward. How they land determines how many small wooden counters he wins. The final winner of all counters takes the stakes, including the saddle (foreground), perhaps even the watching wife. In some tribes losers became slaves of the winner.

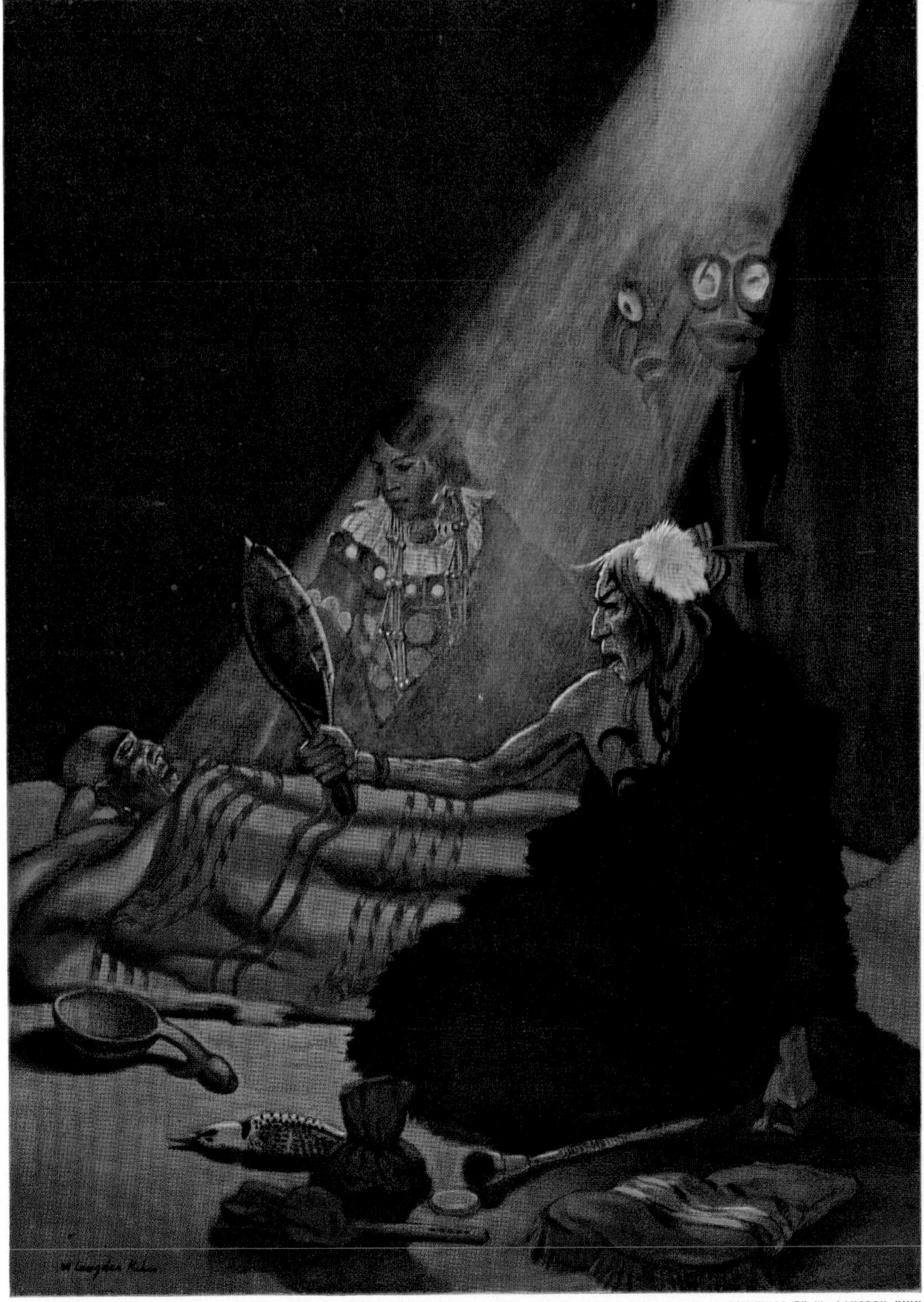

PAINTINGS BY W. LANGDON KIHN

**Making Medicine Against Death,** an Iroquois shaman in fur cape shakes his shell rattle and chants a curing song. A beam of sunlight, coming through the smoke hole in the top of the lodge, lights the face of the dying warrior, whose wife grieves by the bedside. Ritualistic objects litter the floor. Fantastic masks with human hair are set on the lodgepole to frighten away spirits causing the illness. As controller of supernatural forces the medicine man played a powerful role in tribal life.

PAINTING BY W. LANGDON KIHN

**Master Canoe Makers Were the Chippewa.** Stakes outline the craft's shape. The builders place thick, pliable sheets of birch bark inside, bend edges upward and fasten them to wooden gunwales. Next they install bent cedar ribs (right foreground), fasten thwarts to brace the canoe, then sew the bark with strings from spruce roots. Spruce gum makes seams watertight. In versatility, the portable bark canoe outshone the ponderous dugout (page 46). Territory of the Chippewa, once one of the largest Indian tribes north of Mexico, extended from Lake Huron westward to the Dakotas.

face. Other disease spirits owe their misshapen features to their constant conflict with the Life God, who bested them in these encounters.

In spring and fall, when sickness is common, the Society of Faces go en masse through all homes of the community, shaking their turtle-shell rattles, making weird cries, and talking with a curious nasal twang. Thus they frighten away the invading disease spirits.

Both the Iroquois and the Algonquians believe in a masked cannibal called "Long Nose," who kidnaps children. Youngsters are never disciplined by corporal punishment. Fear that Long Nose will carry them off in his huge pack basket usually insures their good behavior.

The fabric of the Indian's religion was woven about his intimate observations of Nature. Each day he saw the sun rise in the east and set in the west, obliterating the stars which guarded the heavens at night. He noticed the regularity of the waxing and waning of the moon. He watched the procession of the equinoxes with the accompanying complex phenomena of the seasons: regular migrations of animals, birds, and fish; the annual growth cycles of plants and trees; heat and cold, rain and sunshine, lightning, wind, and snow.

At times Nature was lavish with her favors; often she denied man his wants. Now and then disease struck with unseen weapons and laid him low. All these things required explanation so that man might know how to produce more favors from Nature and make life more tolerable.

Lacking knowledge of physics, astronomy, and meteorology, the Indian personalized the various striking features of Nature. Among the Iroquois, the alternation of the seasons symbolized the perpetual struggle between the Life God and "Stony Coat," the god of ice and winter, whose function was to destroy. The adventures of these supernatural beings with Indian culture heroes form the intricate substance of a rich mythology wherein are explained, often in allegorical language, all things the Indian has pondered.

Since the Indians considered that the coming of each kind of food was brought about by supernatural causes, it was the custom to offer the first of each type obtained to the particular spirit supposed to control it.

A joyous occasion was the annual gathering of sap from budding maple trees in early March. With the rigors of winter behind them and the full prospects of spring and summer ahead, this was a happy season—a time of renewed activity, the "commencement" season (page 47).

The Menominee have a charming legend which explains the story of maple sugar. When man was new he did not know how to obtain the sap. One day the old grandmother, Nokomis, showed Manabusha, the great culture hero and friend of man, how to tap the trees and collect the sap. But the sap came out in the form of pure, thick syrup.

"This," thought the wise Manabusha, "is bad. The people will not have enough work if sugar is made so easily. It must be more difficult, to keep them occupied so they will not fall into idleness."

So Manabusha climbed to the top of the highest tree. With his hand he sprinkled water like rain over the trees, diluting the syrup so that it would flow from the trees in a watery sap.

Thereafter the Indians had to work hard to make sugar. Wood must be cut, bark vessels made, and the sap collected and boiled for several nights to reduce it to usable form.

By introducing the iron kettle, the French showed the Indians how to reduce further the sweet liquid, which the natives regarded as a beneficial medicine.

The *Jesuit Relations* tells how an early Father, hearing that a pagan Indian was near death, visited his wigwam to administer the rites of the Church. After baptizing him from a bark vessel standing in the room, he inquired of the wife what medicine the patient had been taking. The woman pointed to the vessel, and the priest discovered that he had performed the baptism with sweet maple sap.

"Fortunately," wrote the good Father, "I was able to secure water and perform the ceremony over again before the patient died."

The agricultural Indians of the Northeastern Woodlands used simple but effective methods of cultivation. Champlain tells that in place of plows they used a hardwood instrument shaped like a spade. The gardens were planted in May. They placed three or four kernels of Indian corn, or maize, and a few beans in rows at intervals of about three feet and heaped small hills of dirt over them. When the seed sprouted, the bean vines would climb the cornstalks, at the same time keeping the ground about the hills free from weeds.

Pumpkins and squash usually were planted in open areas fringing the corn patch, where vines would not be too much shaded by the tall corn plants. The Iroquois believed that the guardian spirits of the three plants were sisters who desired to remain together.

The Iroquois name for maize means "our life." This veneration for corn was typical of all agricultural tribes of America, who regarded it as their principal means of subsistence. Many varieties of beans and corn were cultivated and there were numerous methods of preparing them as food. The aboriginal New England dish of succotash, a mixture of maize and beans, still retains its Indian name.

Garden care was mainly a woman's job, the men being too busy hunting at cultivating and harvesting time (pages 48-49).

Indian women have been described as drudges, beasts of burden, chattels, as virtual slaves of their husbands, and their existence a continuous round of backbreaking work, of childbearing, and dutiful waiting on their husbands' every whim. Such a picture is not characteristic.

In the old days Indian women worked hard, took pride in their work, lived, loved, and gossiped much as women do in all parts of the world. Since much of

PAINTINGS BY W. LANGDON KIHN

**When the Maple Sap Ran,** Woodlands Indians tapped trees and brought the sap to a large trough. Women (above) hang kettles of green birch bark over embers to reduce the sap to syrup, which they pour into molds to harden. The family's right to certain groves of sugar maples carried from generation to generation.

**With Fire and Stone Adzes,** Massachusetts Indians (left) skillfully shape a dugout canoe by eye. The sturdy dugout predominated south of the limit of available birch. The Pilgrims at Plymouth met these Indians, living in bark-covered Quonset huts. Soon afterward they were virtually wiped out by the white man's smallpox.

their work was out of doors, their life was a healthy one.

The husband had no real authority over his wife's person and, while custom differed among tribes, the woman as a rule could leave her husband when she wished. Marriage, too, involved mutual consent as in our society. So-called wife purchases, when analyzed, are found to consist either of mutual exchange of gifts by the families or as compensation to the bride's family for loss of her services.

**Four Scalps on Warpath!** the painted warrior boasts to his somber-faced brother. Crimson-dyed horsehair, like a plumed Roman helmet, adorns the scalplock of this member of the Sauk and Fox.

This combined tribe, originally of Great Lakes canoe and farming peoples, migrated to Kansas after the Black Hawk War of 1832, in which Abraham Lincoln served as captain of volunteers. There they adopted the horse and prairie ways.

War, to the Indian, was as much a game as a way to wield power or to wreak vengeance on an enemy. Killing a foe merited less than taking unnecessary risks in battle. Touching an enemy with finger or coup stick in the midst of combat was the warrior's proudest feat.

Eagle feathers worn in certain ways, as by the man at right, were badges of honor denoting rank or prestige. His bear-claw necklace is punctuated with trader's beads.

**Wild Rice, Cultivated Corn,** crops that sustained Indian life, were harvested by women. Corn, gift of the American aborigine, ranks as one of the world's great bounties. It saved Jamestown and Plymouth from famine, grew wherever there was good soil and enough water.

Below, Iroquois women husk the tasseled ears which earlier they had gathered in baskets on their backs. Corn was roasted or boiled while green, parched and pounded into meal when dry. Indians ate mush, hominy, and corn dumplings. They knew corn soup, succotash, and popcorn. From dried husks they made moccasins, masks, and dolls. Corncob fires, nearly smokeless, warmed tepee and lodge.

Chippewa wives (lower left) reap wild rice, flailing the kernels into baskets in their birchbark canoe. Rice grew along shores in the Lake Superior region. Shortly before harvest time, women paddled through the fields tying rice stalks into looped bundles to protect the ripening grain from the birds, wind, and rain.

PAINTINGS BY W. LANGDON KIHN

Among such groups as the Iroquois, women had an important voice in tribal councils (page 23), and the right to nominate candidates for the chieftaincy of clan or tribe. A mother could even forbid her son to go on the warpath.

Indeed, records show that often white women taken captive in Indian raids later refused an opportunity to return to pioneer life. They had found living among the Indians more pleasant.

Misconceptions of the Indian woman's role arose when visitors saw the wife busily working while the man, if home, reclined lazily, seemingly with nothing to do. They overlooked the fact that his were the more strenuous pursuits: hunting, fishing, warfare, the clearing of land.

By ingenuity the Indian learned to hunt game over winter's heavy snow and in summer travel the waterways of his Woodlands home, a region of lakes and rivers. The snowshoe and canoe were two of his most useful inventions.

Snowshoes varied in form and construction, depending upon whether they were to be used in the woods or in the open, on hard or soft snow, but all were constructed on the same principle. A strip of ash was steamed and bent into shape and webbed with a netting of rawhide strips, moose intestine, twine, or sinew. When caught by a sudden snowstorm, the Indian quickly made an emergency pair by bending a frame of green willow and webbing it with bark strips.

The dugout canoe, hollowed from a log by fire and stone adzes, was used by most tribes south of the St. Lawrence (page 46). More ingenious and practical was the portable bark-covered canoe, widespread in the Woodlands region (page 44). Birch, spruce, or elm bark, and occasionally moose hide, covered a light cedar frame. Somewhat fragile, the craft was so light that one man could easily carry it across even a long portage. Early explorers adopted the birchbark canoe and with it penetrated to distant parts of the country.

The birchbark canoe was as necessary to the Woodlands Indian as the automobile is to us today. The nomadic Algonquian tribes of the northeast continually transported themselves and their equipment by this means. These wandering groups, seeking food, established themselves at different places as the seasons varied.

Hunting, fishing, and seed-gathering were their principal means of obtaining food. In a region where game still is relatively abundant, it was much more so before the coming of the white man and his firearms. Deer, moose, and caribou were plentiful; geese, ducks, and swans abounded, as did many other forms of bird and animal life.

Yet the Indian was often hard pressed to obtain enough food throughout the year. In summer he found it difficult, with his stone-headed arrows, to stalk and kill larger animals. When chance afforded, moose, deer, and caribou were driven into the water and shot from canoes while they swam. In winter, hunters with snowshoes ran down the heavy beasts floundering through the snow (page 29). It was also easier then to track down rabbits and other small game.

Fishing was highly important to a people living in a region of rivers and lakes. Quantities of fish were obtained through weirs and fish traps set across the streams, particularly when salmon were migrating in the coastal rivers, and in spring when sturgeon moved from lakes into streams. Spearing, shooting with bow and arrow, and jigging with lures and barbless hooks were also practiced.

In winter, fish were speared through holes cut in the ice (page 28). In summer, the usual spear-fishing method was for two men to go out in a canoe at night. The man in the stern paddled while the other speared fish attracted by the light of a bark torch in the bow. Fish were preserved by smoking and drying.

PAINTING BY W. LANGDON KIHN

**A Huron Family Buries Its Loved Ones.** Skulls and bones on their backs, mournful Indians journey to the feast of the dead held every 12 years by the Huron, a tribe which lived southeast of Georgian Bay, in Ontario, Canada. Bodies were taken from scaffolds and carried, often many miles, to a common burial pit and there laid to rest amid cries of lament. "Nothing has ever better pictured for me the confusion there is among the damned," wrote the Jesuit Brébeuf of the assembled nation's din. By firelight, tribesmen scattered corn over the remains and burial offerings, and covered the pit with fur robes. Visitors received gifts, and the ceremony ended with a feast.

# IMPACT OF THE WHITE MAN

During the waning days of Indian domination, great and valiant heroes emerged. Many foresaw that the white man's encroachment, if allowed to continue, meant disruption of the native manner of living and eventual extermination of the Indian.

The Eastern Woodlands area had its share of such men. Some, like Cornplanter, famous Seneca chief, believed that the Indian should make friends with the white men, save himself by imitating them, and subsist in open competition with them. In his old age Cornplanter regretted having taken this course.

Others believed that it was impossible for the Indian to make such basic changes, and that his only salvation was to resist and repel the invader. A famous exponent of this theory was Metacom, known to the English as King Philip. He was a Wampanoag, the son of Massasoit, whose friendly acts made possible the success of the Plymouth Colony.

For ten years Metacom quietly organized the Indians of New England, and in 1675, declared war upon the whites. During the ensuing year 52 of 90 English towns were attacked, and 12 completely destroyed. But for the treachery of some followers, Metacom would have driven the whites from New England. He was killed when colonists night-raided his Rhode Island swamp hideaway on August 12, 1676, ending "King Philip's War."

More than a century later the final desperate stand of Indian against white man in the northeastern United States was made under the leadership of Tecumseh (page 55). One of the ablest of all Indian warriors, he was noted for his humane character. Among other acts, he persuaded his tribe, the Shawnee, to abandon torturing prisoners, a basic practice of Indian warfare at the time.

Tecumseh vigorously opposed the white man's advance and denied the U. S. Government's right to purchase land from a single tribe on grounds that the vast woodland was common hunting territory belonging to all tribes. When the Government ignored his contention, he

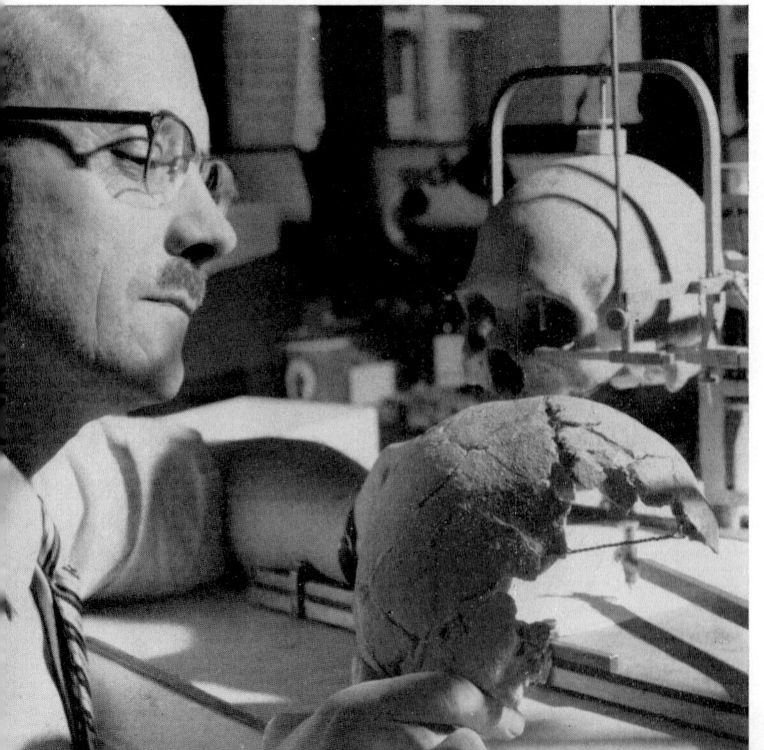

**America's Oldest Inhabitant**

Twelve or more millenniums ago a pre-Folsom man roamed our western plains. He was quenching his thirst near present-day Midland, Texas, when ravenous animals may have pounced upon him. Dr. T. Dale Stewart of the Smithsonian Institution pieced the ancient man's skull together. Here he compares it with the strikingly similar one of a modern Indian.

The skull, oldest human remains yet found in the Americas, was dated by measuring its fluorine absorption compared to that of fossil bones of now extinct animals found at the same water-hole site. Tests revealed them to be about the same age.

Hearths at Lewisville, Texas, suggest habitation 37,000 years ago.

SCIENCE SERVICE

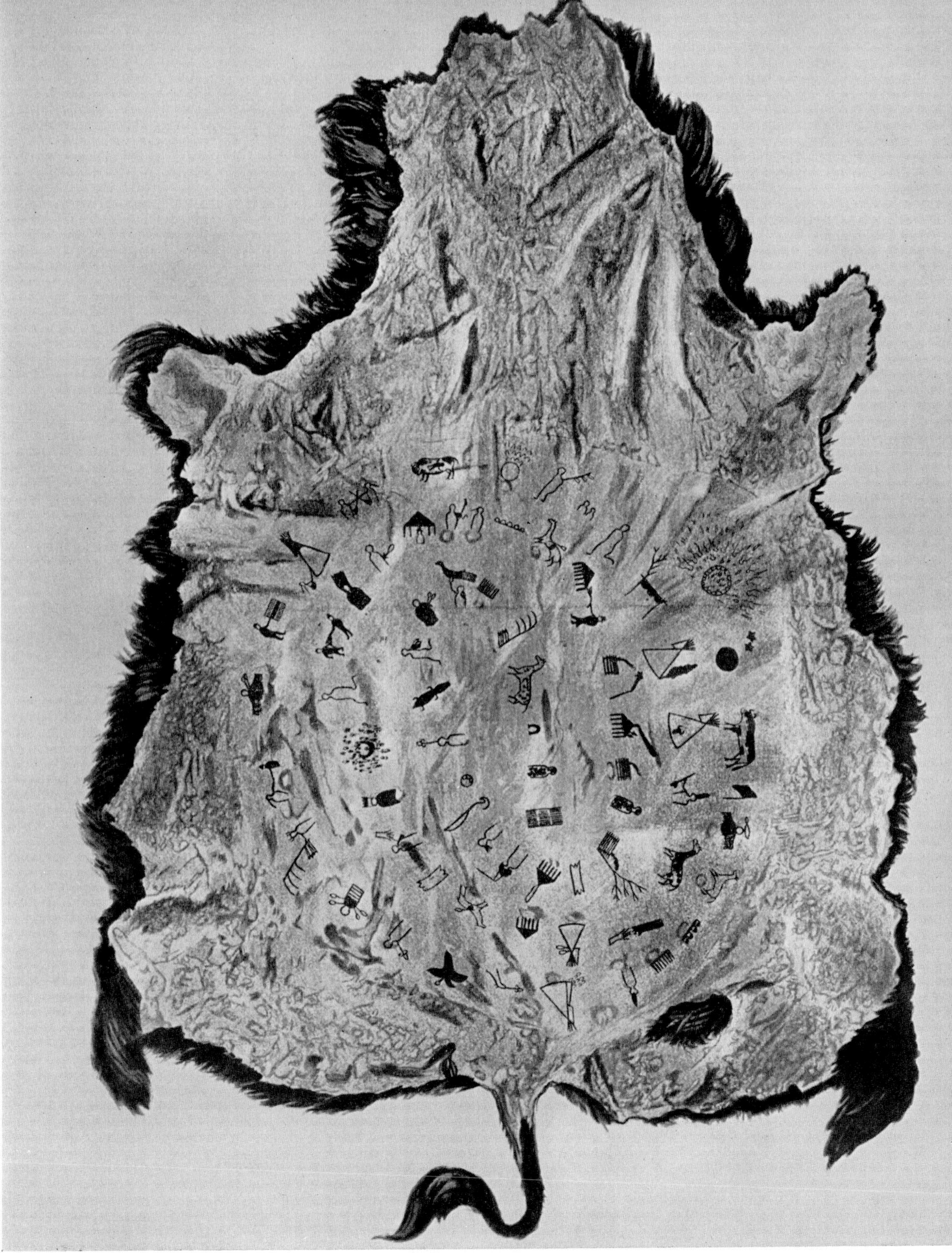

BUREAU OF AMERICAN ETHNOLOGY

**Buffalo Robe Calendar** records 71 winters among the Dakota Sioux. Lone Dog, the artist, noted the passing years with symbols of important events spiraling counterclockwise out from center. His winter count begins in 1800 with 30 parallel lines in three columns at center. Each line stands for a Dakota slain by the Crows that year. Directly above, a spotted figure marks a smallpox epidemic. A horseshoe indicates shod mounts stolen from white men by the Dakotas, whose horses lacked shoes. Meteorite shower (left) is 1833–34, when "the stars fell." A cow (right) denotes 1868–69, when Texas longhorns entered Dakota country. Blacked-out sun attended by stars shows the eclipse of 1869.

formed a great confederacy of practically all Indians east of the Mississippi in hope of making the Ohio River the permanent boundary line between the two races. Tecumseh's purpose was defeated when followers precipitated the Battle of Tippecanoe in 1811, before plans of organization were complete.

The warrior then allied himself with the British against the Americans and was commissioned a brigadier general in the British Army, commanding 2,000 Indian allies. In 1813 he protected Proctor's retreat, following Perry's victory at Lake Erie, forcing Proctor to make a stand against the Americans near Chatham, Ontario. In the battle that followed, the Americans under Harrison won and Tecumseh was killed.

He had a premonition of this disaster and laid aside his British uniform, dressing in native costume for the fight. The death of Tecumseh removed the last serious obstacle in the path of white expansion and sealed the doom of native life in the eastern United States.

Another Indian whose career paralleled Tecumseh's was Thayendanegea, known to the whites as Joseph Brant. One of the first prominent Indians to read and write English, he was a Mohawk chief, born in 1742, active in border wars of the 18th century.

He fought with the British in Pontiac's war of 1763. Later he was commissioned a British colonel and, with his native troops, took an active part in famous raids against American settlements in 1779. His sister became the wife of Sir William Johnson.

As with many other peoples, most noted Indians owe their prominence to military activities. This should not, however, produce an unbalanced picture of Indian life. Warfare against the whites was inevitable because of the pressure of white expansion.

The Indian's method of fighting differed vastly from the mass tactics of the Europeans. His tech-

**Nightmares in Wood,** these carved masks represent supernatural beings seen in dreams by men of the Iroquois Society of Faces. Shaking huge turtle-shell rattles, members of the secret cult danced through the village to drive out demons of disease. The society still flourishes, but today when Iroquois don their grotesque masks to go from house to house chasing spirits they ride in automobiles.

PAINTINGS BY W. LANGDON KIHN

nique was to scatter forces, placing emphasis on concealment, surprise, and ambush. Not until the colonists adopted Indian fighting methods could they cope with them.

Two practices connected with warfare in the Northeastern Woodlands area have been prominent in literature. One was the torturing of prisoners, the other the taking of scalps. Both customs appear to have originated with the Iroquois and to have spread from them. European rivals in the northeast offered bounties to their Indian allies for enemy scalps, Indian or white. With this stimulus, the practice of scalping spread rapidly and widely. Bounties for the scalps of hostile Indians in the West were offered as late as the middle of the last century.

Probably no misunderstanding led to so much ill feeling and bloodshed between Indians and whites as the difference in their concepts concerning land ownership.

In America, the land within tribal boundaries was regarded as belonging to the tribe. Neither the Indian individual nor the family possessed vested rights in land, although each family might appropriate or have assigned to it, for cultivation or gathering, that required for its own needs. Thus it was impossible for any chief, family, or any section of a tribe legally to sell or give away any part of the tribal holdings.

Naturally any such treaties and transfers of rights had no significance to the early Indians. The first white settlers either were not aware of this fact or found it convenient to ignore it. Inevitably the Indians considered themselves ousted when the white men took possession of their lands.

Typical of the Indian attitude was the speech Toohulhulsote, a Nez Percé, made when the whites tried to

**Tecumseh, Shawnee Chief,** foresees death and discards British uniform and medal for native buckskins. A brigadier general in the War of 1812, he has accused the British of cowardice in retreating before the Americans. He will persuade his allies to stand on the Thames River, Ontario, and himself perish in that battle.

Born in 1768 near present Springfield, Ohio, Tecumseh early gained renown in border wars of the Northwest Territory. His father and two brothers died fighting the whites. Tecumseh's own death in 1813 shattered the last hope of a united Indian stand against the juggernaut of white expansion.

Paradoxically, a bronze bust of Tecumseh spells luck for midshipmen at the U.S. Naval Academy.

force his people to leave their home in the Wallowa Valley for a distant reservation.

"The earth," he said, "is our mother, and her body should not be disturbed by the hoe or the plow. Men should subsist by the spontaneous productions of Nature. The sovereignty of the earth cannot be sold or given away."

"We never have made any trade. Part of the Indians have given up their land. I never did. The earth is part of my body, and I never gave up the earth. So long as the earth will keep me, I wish to be let alone."

Early explorers, accustomed to European ideas of regal descent and individual political power, applied such terms as king, queen, or princess to members of the simply organized democratic village tribes of eastern America. This was absurd.

The idea of a legal executive head, though entirely foreign to these Indians, was fostered by the colonists because it helped them to do business, particularly to buy land.

Inherited rank was also an alien idea, for the most part. Even the so-called "chief" among many tribes was recognized as leader only because of his personal exploits or recognized ability. He had no actual authority, his rule being purely advisory but backed by custom. In certain groups, such as the Iroquois and some Pueblo tribes, it was the rule to select chiefs from a particular clan, although in practice such positions were usually elective.

The outstanding instance of despotism was among the Natchez and neighboring tribes of the lower Mississippi. However, submission to the chief's will was apparently voluntary and based upon religion.

Among the Natchez a caste system developed based on heredity, and on the northwest coast a caste distinction did

**History in the Flesh.** Jacob Lone Tree, eight-year-old Winnebago Indian, reads of doughty deeds of his Great Lakes ancestors. His classmate is fascinated to find a real Indian boy with savage roach cut in a Wisconsin school. The Winnebago fought under Tecumseh in the War of 1812.

UNITED PRESS

U.S. ARMY, OFFICIAL

**Yakima Chief Visits Warrior Son.** In tribal regalia father rides out to inspect son's iron steed on a firing range near Yakima, Washington. Indians fought bravely in two world wars and in Korea.

arise, based on property. But among American Indians generally, ideas of caste and individual wealth were absent.

The breakdown of native culture was inevitable once the white man had entrenched himself in the New World.

The first disaster was the introduction of smallpox, measles, and chicken pox, diseases to which the Indians had developed no resistance. Whole tribes were swept away, others decimated. The white man's alcohol likewise did much to break down Indian pride and spirit.

More devastating in the long run was the psychological effect of the contact of two conflicting cultures.

Tribal organization was based on kinship, which carried with it the obligation of mutual assistance and protection.

Typically, inheritance was reckoned through one side of the family, the mother's, and children came under the mother's clan. Our system of bilateral descent, conversely, puts children directly under parental authority and removes the feeling of oneness with the clan.

The new culture also obliterated the basic occupations of tribal life. The division of labor between the sexes was so strongly fixed by custom that when the encroachment of the white man destroyed the game, fenced off hunting grounds, and removed the possibility of aboriginal warfare, the balance was completely destroyed. The woman's work remained, but the man, left with nothing to do, could only loaf about. No longer was there place for the hunter, warrior, weaponmaker.

The woman, besides tending household and fields, also was a potter, usually the weaver of textiles and baskets, and the dresser of skins. These skilled arts, which permitted full development of the individual, vanished with the coming of metal kitchen utensils and machine-woven cloth. Readjustment has been slow and painful.

Today the blood of the American Indian flows in the veins of many of our leading citizens. His contributions to civilization, toward the betterment of mankind are met on every hand, but his story as a separate people now is a subject of history and a record of the past.

# SOUTHEASTERN INDIANS

POCAHONTAS, DAUGHTER OF POWHATAN, holds a special place in American legend. How she persuaded her warlike father to spare the life of Capt. John Smith when he was held captive by the Indians is a story known to everyone. She was then a girl of 12. The year, 1608.

This episode (page 62), questioned by some because Smith did not mention it in his writings until years later, fits with what we know of the character of both Pocahontas and her father.

Her real name was Matoaka ("playful"). John Smith says she was called Pocahontas because "the savages did think that, did we know her real name, we should have the power of casting an evil eye upon her." This belief was widespread.

Powhatan, whose real name was Wahunsonacock, was founder of the Powhatan confederacy, typical of Algonquian tribal groups along the south-central Atlantic seaboard. These Indians were at their peak when Smith and his followers first entered Chesapeake Bay.

About this same time the Iroquois confederacy began in the North. But whereas the Iroquois tribes banded together through mutual consent, the Powhatan confederacy was based on conquest, treachery, and personal despotism.

With the arrival of the Jamestown colonists in 1607, Powhatan began to receive a bitter dose of his own medicine. The English, by superior force of arms, seized the Indians' winter supplies of corn, reducing them to near starvation.

In 1613, the colonists, knowing Powhatan's affection for Pocahontas, decoyed her aboard a ship and held her hostage to prevent Powhatan warring against them. During her captivity she was

**Le Moyne's Map** presents a 16th century European conception of the American "Province of Florida." Whalelike sea monster cruises offshore; Appalachian streams yield gold, silver, and copper. Indian hearsay named and located most villages, rivers, lakes, and forests.

LIBRARY OF CONGRESS

# CHAPTER 2

converted to Christianity, met and married John Rolfe, "an honest Gentleman, and of good behavior." In 1616 she and Rolfe voyaged to England where she was received as a princess, had her portrait painted (basis of the Kihn portrait, page 61), and was presented to the King and Queen. As a result of this marriage Powhatan kept peace with the English.

The Jamestown colonists were surprised to receive from England a royal gift for the old reprobate, consisting of a crown, scarlet cape, elaborate bedroom set, pitcher, basin, and other costly items, with orders to hold a coronation.

Hearing of the English King's fine present, Powhatan considered it a trap, and replied that if the English wished to make him a present they would have to bring it to him. This was no simple undertaking, since Powhatan was on a hunting trip almost a hundred miles away by canoe and wilderness trail.

But the English had their orders and, after a long and toilsome journey, they reached the forest camp of the suspicious chief. The cumbersome bed was hauled up on the stream bank, the basin and pitcher set beside it.

Powhatan was persuaded to accept the scarlet cloak, "but a fowle trouble there was to make him kneele to receave his crowne. He, neither knowing the majestie nor meaning of a Crowne, nor bending of the knee, indured so many perswasions, examples, and instructions, as tired them all."

The English finally resorted to strategy. Two stout soldiers grasped Powhatan by the shoulder and bore down heavily, pressing him behind the knees so that he was forced to kneel. Three others pushed the crown onto his head. This was the signal for firing a ceremonial volley, at which the terrified "king" leaped up and attempted to flee for his life.

He was restrained, however, and when convinced he was to be put to no further compulsions, gave to Captain Newport his old moccasins and mantle. The mantle still is in the Ashmolean Museum in Oxford, England, but there is no record of what happened to the luxurious bedroom suite left under the Virginia trees.

Through Powhatan's affection for his daughter Pocahontas, open warfare was deferred for some time. In 1622, however, four years after Powhatan's death, Opechancanough, his brother, attacked the now scattered colonists, killing 347 men, women, and children.

Another more devastating attack followed 22 years later. But retaliation was so severe that in 1646 the colony's Assembly reported the Indians to be "so routed and dispersed that they are no longer a nation, and we now suffer only from robbery by a few starved outlaws."

More successful in resisting the white men were the warlike Calusa, who occupied southern Florida. These were the first Southeastern Indians to meet the Europeans, a century before Jamestown, possibly more.

Among gold-seeking Spanish adventurers in the Antilles soon after Columbus were slavers, who found it easy to decoy trusting natives onto their ships and then sail off with them. But the Indians made poor slaves.

Some of these slavers must have visited the Florida coast well before the first recorded visit, that of Ponce de León in 1513. Maps of the peninsula were published in Europe before this date. More convincing evidence is the murderous reception Florida Indians gave Spanish mariners. Such conduct would be unlikely at their first meeting with whites.

Of powerful physique, these Calusa were the fiercest fighters in the New World. Ponce de León, seeking the "Fountain of Youth," was attacked by 80 canoes and forced to withdraw after an all-day battle. Eight years later they beat off his colonizing expedition of 1521, grievously wounding him with an arrow.

These near-naked warriors dismembered slain enemies, apparently sacrificed captives en masse, even were said to be cannibals. Killing and plundering, they drove back all European attempts to enter their country until foreign epidemic diseases thinned their ranks. By late 18th century they had ceased to exist as a tribe. The few survivors were absorbed among the late-arriving Seminole.

The Calusan linguistic stock, together with its north Florida neighbor, the Timucuan, was related to Muskhogean,

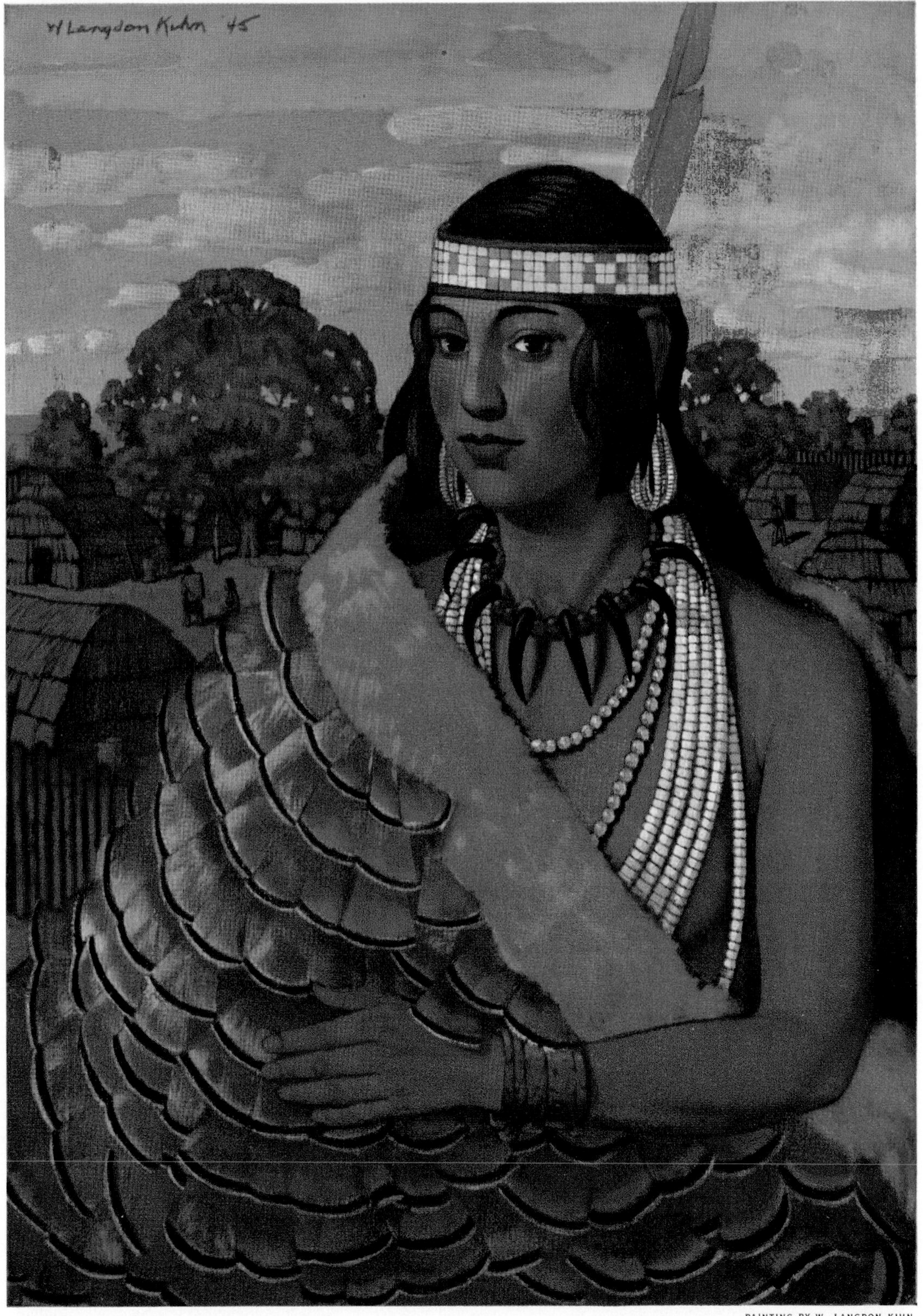


PAINTING BY W. LANGDON KIHN

**Pocahontas, Powhatan's "Dearest Jewell and Daughter,"** proudly wears a turkey-feather robe. With features from a portrait of 1616, this shows the Indian "princess" before she "renounced idolatree."

C:S.
King Powhatan comānds C:Smith to be ſlayne, his
daughter Pokahontas beggs his life his thankfullneſs
and how he ſubiected 39 of their kings. reade ỹ hiſtory.


BUREAU OF AMERICAN ETHNOLOGY

**Pocahontas Saves Capt. John Smith.** His head rests upon a stone, the executioners' clubs are about to descend, when Pocahontas intervenes, begs for his life, places her head upon Smith's. Relenting, Powhatan adopted Smith into the tribe. So went Smith's own account, which appeared with this drawing by an unknown artist in his *Generall Historie of Virginia, New England, and the Summer Isles*, published in 1624. Today a few Pamunkey descendants of the once-feared Powhatan confederacy maintain tribal life near Richmond, Virginia. They have occupied this same reservation since 1677.

leading stock of the entire Southeast (group area map, page 24).

Typical Muskhogean-speaking peoples were tribes comprising the great Creek confederacy, which occupied the territory now Georgia and Alabama; the Choctaw, who lived in central and southern Mississippi (page 68); the Hitchiti of western Georgia; and the later Seminole.

Southeastern tribes in general were agriculturists. Each household had its garden plot a hundred feet square or more. They used wooden hoes and planting sticks to weed and cultivate these gardens, and made forest clearings by girdling the larger trees and felling the smaller ones with stone axes. They planted four varieties of corn, the principal crop.

They also raised pumpkins, beans, squash, sunflower seeds, tobacco, and gourds from which many utensils were made. They ate wild fruits, roots, and berries, supplemented by fish and game.

A custom of Southeastern Indians which impressed early travelers was their ceremonial use of "black drink." This strong tea, made by boiling leaves of the shrub *Ilex cassine* in water, was purgative, emetic, and a caffeine stimulant.

The Creeks drank the sacred beverage before council meetings to "invigorate the mind and body and prepare for thought and debate." It also played a role in their busk, or green corn ceremony, a New Year's celebration.

The Creeks conceived the new year as beginning in July or August with the ripening of the first crops, particularly maize. This celebration lasted eight days in large centers, four in smaller towns. The sacred number 4, or its multiples, was prominent in rituals.

The ceremony, centering in the plaza, was punctuated by singing, drinking the black drink, and dancing in which both men and women took part.

Climax was the lighting of the sacred fire, four logs aligned with the cardinal points. All other fires had earlier been put out and the hearths swept clean. Now new fires were laid and kindled from the sacred fire.

Preparing for the busk, the Creeks provided themselves with new clothing, new pottery and other household equipment. Houses were swept, sprinkled with clean sand, and the whole town put in order. Left-over food, clothing, equipment was burned; old pottery broken and cast away.

This material renovation symbolized the moral and spiritual renovation, the new life which was to begin the new year spotlessly pure. This concept, reminiscent of ancient Mexico, probably came from the Temple Mound cult, so widespread through the Southeast.

The Mound Builders have long been the subject of romantic, speculative writings picturing them variously as ancient, non-Indian, and highly civilized. Who were these mysterious builders of great earthworks which our own ancestors found buried in the forests from Great Lakes to Gulf of Mexico?

The roots of this culture sink deep into the past. Javelin points found in the Southeast are similar to those that occur in the high Plains together with remains of now extinct mammoth, camel, and giant bison. While no such association has yet been discovered in the East, the makers of these flaked stone points

**Temple Mound Artistry** is revealed in this realistically carved stone pipe found near Spiro, Oklahoma. Tobacco burned inside the hollow head; smoke was drawn through an aperture in the rear.

NATIONAL GEOGRAPHIC PHOTOGRAPHER B. ANTHONY STEWART

## Ritual Made Life Go Round in Mound-building Days

Stocky, pearl-decked Hopewell women beat a rhythmic tattoo as priests perform a harvest ritual atop the mound (right). Tribal dignitary in foreground wears copper-covered antlers, holds a ceremonial mask in one hand, a spear in the other, tipped with obsidian. The burial mound, erected over the ashes of prominent dead, is in its primary stage. Succeeding mantles of earth will give it a tall domed shape. In southern Ohio the Burial Mound, or Hopewell, culture reached its zenith 300 B.C.–A.D. 100. Temple Mound period followed.

The chief of a Temple Mound tribe (lower right) greets his elder brother, the sun, and shows him his course across the heavens. Temples and chief's lodge were built on great flat-topped earth mounds. Probably inspired by Mexican example, this sun-worshiping cult flourished in rich agricultural lands of the Southeast from the 9th through the 17th centuries. The Spanish explorer De Soto, on his way to discover the Mississippi River in 1541, saw Temple Mound building at its peak.

Not all ceremonies took place atop mounds. Excavations near Macon, Georgia, reveal a peculiar council chamber hollowed out of red clay; only domed roof shows above ground. In this ceremonial earth lodge, about A.D. 1015, Macon warriors (below) plan an ambush of their enemies. They sit fifty strong around the circle. Before each seat a receptacle holds pipe, tobacco, magical charms. Raised platform represents an eagle, sacred to Southeastern forest dwellers. Kneeling figure wears a roach headdress. Powwow follows strict ceremonial procedure, for rite makes might. These may have been ancestors of the historic Creeks.

PAINTINGS BY W. LANGDON KIHN

COLONEL ALBERT W. STEVENS

**Ohio's "Great Serpent" Slithers Through a Smiling Countryside.** Indian mounds in animal or bird form dot the upper Mississippi and Great Lakes area. Largest, this remarkable effigy mound loops 1,330 feet from coiled tail at left to head at right. Some scientists see jaws open to seize an egg. Others say oval is aboriginal way to portray snake's heart; the body once continued beyond.

were probably contemporary with western hunters of 20,000 years ago.

The first Southeasterners of whom we have adequate knowledge came into the region about 7000 B.C. This is revealed by carbon-14 dating at Russell Cave in Jackson County, Alabama. This method determines the age of organic remains by measuring the amount of radioactive carbon they contain.

These first sparse residents were a long-headed hunting, fishing, and food gathering people who lived in scattered villages along rivers and the seacoast where shellfish were available.

During this period, the Eastern Archaic, people did not dispose of their garbage, but let it accumulate where they lived. As the refuse piled higher, they continued to build their houses on it.

They buried their dead in this same refuse pile, together with offerings of bone, stone, or shell implements, spears, animal-teeth necklaces, red body paint, basketry, and other objects for the departed's use in the hereafter. Crude clay bowls appear after pottery making was introduced to the region about 1200 B.C.

The early Burial Mound period—second major era of Southeastern prehistory—commences about 1000 B.C., when a wave of new people came into the lower Mississippi Valley from the west and spread rapidly to the north and east.

Rather than displacing the Archaic people, these newcomers merged with them, profoundly changing their way of life. They brought agriculture, probably with corn the leading crop. Tubular smoking pipes show that tobacco was in use. Polished stone celt replaced the grooved ax of the Archaic. Copper tools and ornaments came in from the mineral-rich Lake Superior region.

A new and elaborate cult of the dead is reflected in the burial mounds built over conical log tombs of important persons. This cult reached its highest development in the Ohio Valley in the so-called Hopewell period (page 65).

About A.D. 800 this Burial Mound culture gave way to a new civilization brought in from the southwest by a round-headed people who deformed their skulls. Bow and arrow replaced the spear. Their pottery showed more variety in form and decoration.

This is called the Temple Mound period, from the great ceremonial centers these people built. Around a rectangular court stood huge flat-topped mounds (page 65). These served not for burials, but as elevated foundations for mat or thatch temples dedicated to sun worship, a concept derived from Mexico. Ritualistic objects, traded from afar, were the most elaborate of the entire mound-building era.

A sacred fire burned perpetually in a clay-lined fire pit tended by old men. The fire was believed to be of solar origin. If allowed to go out, disaster would befall the tribe, and only human sacrifice would appease the deity.

As in Mexico, these temples were destroyed at intervals and new ones built.

## Peaceful Pursuits Contrast with Grim Taensa War Trophies

Priests leave their temple past skulls mounted on poles (bottom right). The Taensa temple, crowning a Mississippi earth mound, contains the bones of departed chiefs, despotic representatives of the sun on earth. Inside, four old men tend a perpetual fire in the sun god's honor. Stylized eagles perch atop the thatch.

Corn was staff of life for the Choctaw of the Louisiana bayou country (below). Expert agriculturists, they practiced head binding, and used hickory bow and blowgun.

Rifle makes a successful deer hunt for the Seminole family (right) whose dugout glides through placid waters of Florida's Everglades. Roseate spoonbill wings overhead. But peace was a luxury for the Seminole. Their name, first used about 1775, means "runaway" or "separatist" in Creek. They migrated from Georgia and Alabama to Florida, raided Georgia, harbored runaway slaves. This led Andrew Jackson to invade Spanish Florida in 1818; it was annexed a year later. Attempts to remove the tribe west in 1835 sparked the costliest Indian war in U.S. history, decimated the 5,000 Seminole. Although seven generals failed to conquer the tribe completely, most survivors were sent to Oklahoma. Today some 1,150 live in Florida.



PAINTINGS BY W. LANGDON KIHN

As many as a dozen temples successively enlarged a single mound site.

What dramatic and colorful ceremonies must have taken place at Cahokia in southern Illinois, at Etowah in Georgia, and Moundville in Alabama, when this Temple Mound period reached its peak between 1550 and 1650! It marked the highest development achieved by Indians north of Mexico.

Representative of this culture were the Natchez of Mississippi and the related Taensa (page 68).

The Natchez government was a true theocracy. The supreme god lived in the sun. His kinsman came to earth, taught the people religion, organized their society, then turned himself into a stone to be revered in their temple.

Members of the ruling Sun clan had a divine right to extravagant honors from the commoners, or stinkards, as they were called. The children of noblewomen inherited their mother's rank, but children of common women fell one grade below their father's. A man could raise his status by certain means, but only to the lower grade of nobles.

Ceremonies at the death of a "Sun" lasted several days and were conducted with great pomp. The climax came when a score or more persons were put to death so that their spirits might accompany their lord in the other world. Victims—mainly the Sun's wives—were given tobacco pills to numb their senses, then strangled by a cord.

Others volunteered for sacrifice to honor their leader. Parents gained merit by offering children under three.

Natchez power was shattered in early 18th century wars with the French, who in 1731 sold 450 survivors into slavery. The mound-building period was at an end.

After 1700 the Southeastern tribes scattered widely and shrank in numbers. The final blow came in the 1830's when the Government forcibly removed most of the survivors west of the Mississippi, ending the real aboriginal life of once the most populous native region in the United States.

An abundance of colorful accounts by explorers and missionaries reveals native customs changing under Spanish, French, English, and American rule. Yet in no section of the States is it harder to trace tribes than in the Southeast. Tribes merged, split, were exterminated. Others, like the Shawnee, wandered widely.

Linguistic diversity, too, illustrates the multiple origin of the region's natives.

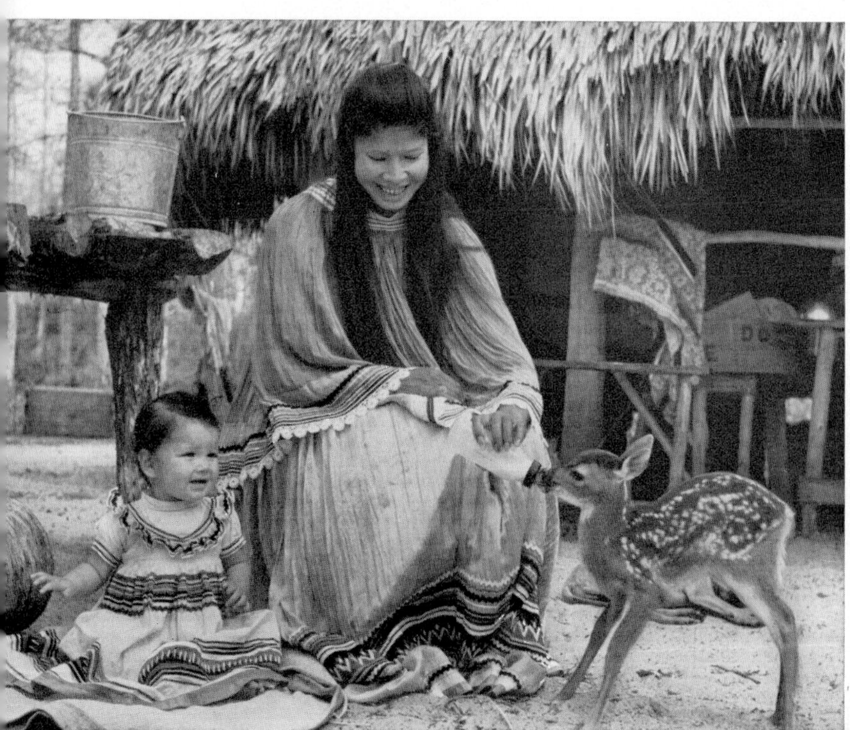

**Mealtime in the Everglades**

Seminole women (right) prepare food on a split-log table in Florida's Big Cypress Reservation. The Seminole preserve more of their original ways than any other Indian group in the Southeast. But enameled kitchenware on table and in palm-thatched storage attic behind symbolizes white man's influence. Flowing dress and pompadour hairdo, now so typically Seminole, were adapted from the Gibson Girl costume of the 1890's. Gay decorations, such as adorn the child's dress at left, came in with the sewing machine. Bottle and nipple feeding spotted fawn came from the general store.

NATIONAL GEOGRAPHIC PHOTOGRAPHER WILLARD R. CULVER

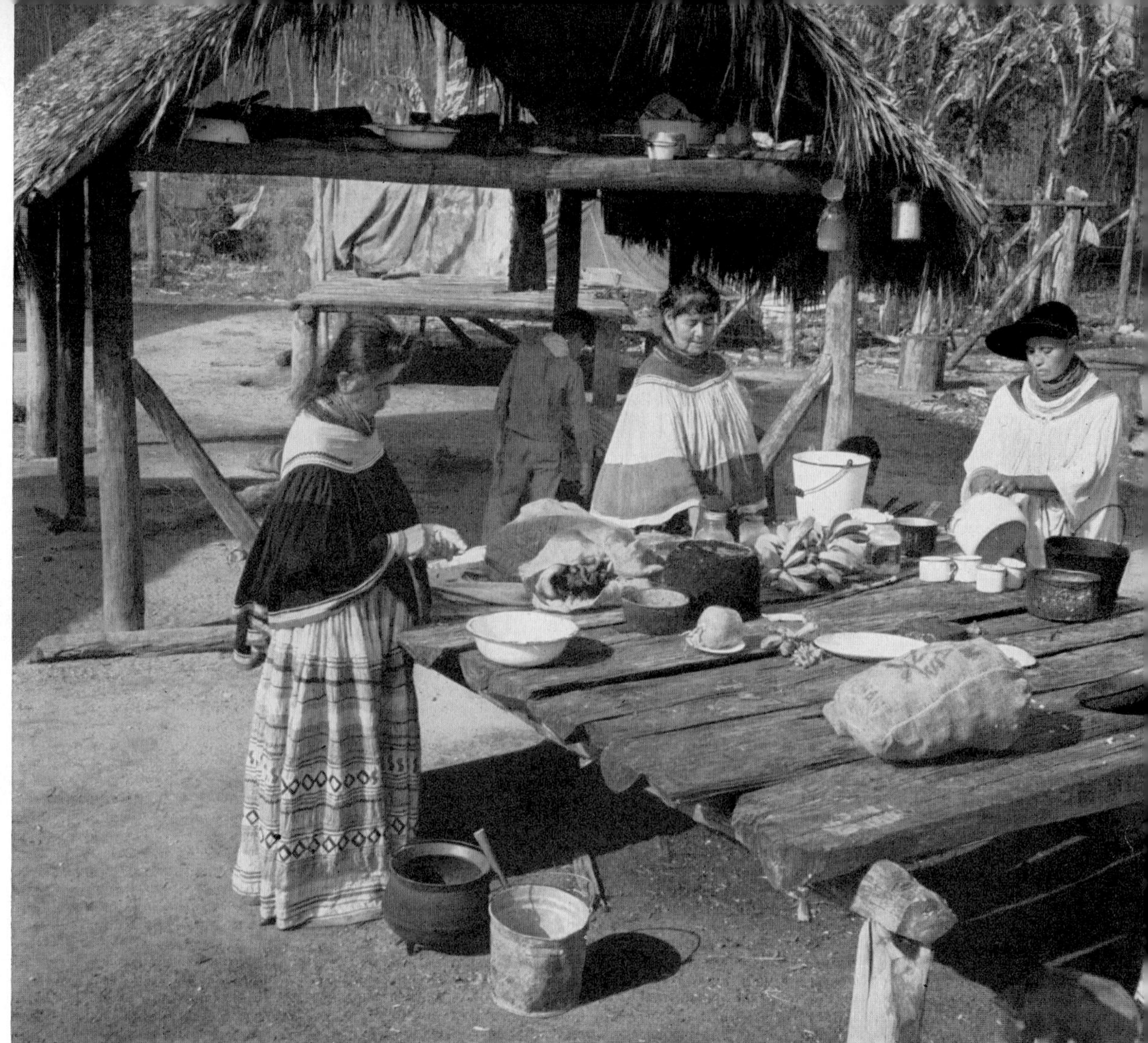

There was not only the dominant Muskhogean, and offshoots of Algonquian stock, but the Caddoan, which reflects southern Plains culture.

The Iroquoian language was represented mainly by the important Cherokee tribe of the southern Appalachians, and by the Tuscarora confederation of North Carolina. The far-flung Siouan stock included the Biloxi of Mississippi, the Cheraw and Catawba of the Carolinas, and several central Virginia tribes.

The Yuchi of the upper Savannah River spoke a language unrelated to any other. Along the Mississippi, the Attacapan, Chitimachan, Tunican, and Natchezan were also small independent groups.

Remnants of Creeks, Hitchiti, and Yuchi from Alabama and Georgia, joined by runaway Negro slaves, became the Seminole tribe, which did not exist before the American Revolution. In the early 1800's they overran Florida, relentlessly pursued by United States troops.

When the tribe resisted Government efforts to remove them to Oklahoma, fighting culminated in the Second Seminole War. Begun in 1835 by Osceola, famous Seminole leader, it lasted nearly eight years, cost the Government 1,500 soldiers, and resulted in most Seminole being moved west of the Mississippi.

A few escaped to the swamps. Today their colorful descendants live in the Everglades, the only Southeastern group to retain much of their native culture.

PAINTING BY W. LANGDON KIHN

**Eagle Calf, Montana Blackfoot Indian, Dons War Bonnet of Ermine Tails, Owl and Eagle Feathers**

## CHAPTER 3

# INDIANS OF OUR WESTERN PLAINS

FOUR HUNDRED YEARS AGO the nomad rulers of an empire of grass that rolled, almost treeless, across North America from Mississippi River to the Rocky Mountains, saw their first horses.

In July, 1541, a Wichita tribe in central Kansas stood dumbstruck as 30 pale-skinned warriors in shining armor, astride great pawing war beasts, rode into a tepee village they called "Quivira" or "Eldorado" and, in angry frustration, looked vainly about for objects of gold. Coronado had come as far north as he would go into a seemingly endless and empty continent.

Although the Spanish knew it not, the lonely expanses stretching north, east, west, and south would someday rank among the richest agricultural lands on earth. They belonged then, however, to aboriginal peoples on the verge of giving up farming for hunting. Over the next three centuries the horse would shape a new way of life for Plains Indians. To them it was a far more important "find" than any such throne of gold as the Spaniard sought.

The picture of human occupation of the Great Plains during the centuries immediately before the discovery of America by Europeans is obscure. We do know, however, that various agricultural peoples encroached on the Plains from the south and from the Northeastern Woodlands. As they moved into the open prairies, they saw huge buffalo herds, elk, and antelope, and the possibility of obtaining food by hunting became obvious.

Gradually most of them began to leave their permanent villages during the hunting season to follow the buffalo. They brought back quantities of dried meat and hides.

When Coronado's horsemen crossed the Plains, they met hunting parties using large wolflike dogs as beasts of burden. The dogs carried 40- to 50-pound packs or were hitched to the travois, basically two light poles that dragged on the ground behind (page 94).

Crude as was this primitive device, it marked the beginning of nomadic life for the Plains Indian. Dogs as burden bearers and the sledlike travois are traits that probably came from the far north.

Not for almost a century after Coronado did the horse appear out of the south in any numbers. But when it came it worked a revolution. As a mount, it enabled the Indian to hunt buffalo farther afield and with far greater prowess. As a beast of burden, it outcarried man and dog combined. In the languages of most Plains tribes, having no word for this new animal, they called the horse "big dog."

By 1750, Indian and horse had met all across the Plains. When the great era of white westward movement began about the middle of the last century, the nomadic, warlike life of mounted prairie tribes was at full flower.

These were the Indians met by trappers and explorers on their way to the Rockies, Mormons on their trek to Great Salt Lake, covered wagoners on the Oregon Trail, California-bound forty-niners.

ROLAND W. REED, ©R. F. WILLIAMS

**From a Crag, Piegan Braves Scout a Montana Plain**

Oddly, most of these tribes had, like the white man, come to the Plains from elsewhere and in quite recent times. As late as 1700, for example, the Cheyenne and Arapaho were still farmers living in permanent villages in present-day Minnesota.

The Dakota, or Siouan tribes, living still farther east in the Woodlands, were feeling strong pressure behind them from the Chippewa, who had been given guns by the French. Driven by the Chippewa, the Dakota forced the Cheyenne and Arapaho westward across the Missouri and finally to the base of the Rockies. The Dakota themselves, and some of the Chippewa, moved out onto prairie lands.

Similar pressure from the Ohio River region forced other Woodland tribes onto the Plains. The expanding white settlement along the Atlantic seaboard set up a pressure impetus that traveled from tribe to tribe, spreading them three-quarters of the way across the continent.

Northern and eastern parts of the Plains were peopled that way, many tribes keeping habits of ancestors who came from forests east of the Mississippi. Among these were the Kansa, the Missouri, the Iowa, the Osage, and the Quapaw. Southern tribes, such as the Wichita and Pawnee, seem to have occupied their lands for a much longer time. Their tribal territories remained much as they were when Coronado came.

Some Plains tribes evidently brought with them from the northeast knowledge of the conical tent. With buffalo-hide covering in place of bark, the tent or tepee—simple, knockdown, and portable—proved extremely useful to earth-lodge peoples when they began following the buffalo for part of the year. With the introduction of the horse, the Indian could increase the size of his tent as well as his hunting range.

Most characteristic dwelling of the Plains Indians, however, was the earth lodge (page 91). Before Coronado, the central Plains were dotted with earth-lodge villages of agricultural peoples. Remains of these settlements may still be seen from North Dakota through Kansas.

The earth lodge was airy, clean, and admirably suited to the severe winters of the northern Plains. Early white settlers merely modified this Indian dwelling in building their long-lasting sod houses on the prairie.

Grass houses of the Caddo, Wichita, and Waco were very similar (page 87), although the walls were steeper and lacked a sod covering, made unnecessary by the milder climate of the southern Plains.

Typical of the farming earth-lodge tribes were the Mandan, whom the French explorer La Vérendrye visited in 1738. They then had six villages, each protected by encircling palisades and a deep ditch. The French were much impressed by these fortifications, which they saw must be impregnable to other Indians.

The Mandan were probably the earliest

arrivals of the village-dwelling tribes of the upper Missouri. Later the Hidatsa, or Minataree as they are sometimes called, moved in from the east. Although they spoke a different tongue, they generally adopted Mandan ways.

Still later, an offshoot of the Hidatsa moved westward across the Plains, gradually abandoned the earth lodge, and took up the nomadic life of the tepee. Ranging near the headwaters of the Cheyenne and the Yellowstone in the eastern Rockies, they became known as the Crow. In similar fashion, the Comanche, Kiowa, Arapaho, and Cheyenne have definite traditions of splitting off from agricultural earth-lodge peoples.

From the south, a Pawnee group drifted northward to become earth-lodge neighbors of the Mandan. These were the Arikara, one of the most warlike of upper Missouri tribes.

The artist George Catlin described the chief Mandan village in 1833: "In ranging the eye over the village from where I am writing, there is presented to the view the strangest mixture and medley of unintelligible trash (independent of the living beings that are in motion) that can possibly be imagined.

"On the roofs of the lodges, besides the groups of living, are buffaloes' skulls,

**Bison Butt Down Indian Horses in Snorting Fury.** Daring braves pick off stampeding prey as one unseated hunter teeters atop horse and charging beast. Buffalo gave Plains Indians food, clothing, shelter, buffalo-chip fuel. Their sinew was turned against them as part of the hunter's bow. Lewis and Clark saw "immence hirds . . . not less than 10 thousand buffaloe within a circle of 2 miles." George Catlin, Pennsylvania artist-ethnologist who recorded this hunt, lived among the Indians in the 1830's.

LIBRARY OF CONGRESS

skin boats, pots and pottery, sleds and sledges—and suspended on poles, erected some 20 feet above the doors of their lodges, are displayed in a pleasant day, the scalps of warriors, preserved as trophies; and thus proudly exposed as evidence of their warlike deeds.

"In other parts are raised on poles the warriors' pure and whitened shields and quivers, with medicine bags attached; and here and there a sacrifice of red cloth, or other costly stuff, offered up to the Great Spirit, over the door of some benignant chief, in humble gratitude for the blessings which he is enjoying.

"Such is a part of the strange medley that is before and around me; and amidst them can be seen in the distance, the green and boundless, treeless, bushless prairie; and on it, and contiguous to the palisade which encloses the village, a hundred scaffolds on which their 'dead live,' as they term it."

The Mandan and other settled tribes on the Plains—Caddo, Pawnee, Arikara, and Hidatsa—knew how to make pottery. Probably this art came into the Plains from the Eastern Woodlands.

Spanish explorers compared the Caddo's ware with the best in Spain. In 1833, the German traveler, Prince Maximilian, wrote of the Missouri pottery: "The clay is of a dark slate color and burns a yellowish red, very similar to what is seen in the burnt tops of the Missouri hills. This clay is mixed with flint or granite,

## Plains Indians Danced to the Sun, Gambled on the Turn of a Moccasin

Arapaho Sun Dancers, headed by seven-foot White Owl (left), face the sacred medicine bundle on its four-legged stand at the start of one of the most solemn ceremonies of the Plains tribes. To them, as to the Aztecs, the sun reigned supreme. Dancers gazed open-eyed at their fiery deity. The central pole symbolized an enemy. This was to be struck with feather-tipped coup sticks, here held in the mouth.

In former times self-torture played a prominent part in the Sun Dance. Celebrants pierced breast or back with wooden skewers attached to the pole by thongs, then writhed until the flesh gave way and dropped them to the ground. Another test was to attach buffalo skulls to the thongs and drag the heavy skulls around the dance ground. The deeper the skewers, the more valiant the dancer. Often they were imbedded so firmly that other dancers had to sit on the buffalo heads to tear the skewers loose.

Gambling often gripped the Indian with an intensity rivaling religious fervor. Below, Sioux warriors watch the man manipulate the moccasins. High stakes swung on this sport, which resembled the old pea-and-shell game. The gamblers wear beaded shirts fringed with ermine tails. Milk teeth of the elk adorn the dress of the wife, whose baby naps in a portable cradle ornamented with bright beads. Ladderlike frames propped behind the men are lazy-backs, back rests which took the place of chairs. Beds line the tepee's dew cloth beneath painted, feathered war trappings. Center fire drives away wintry chill.

PAINTINGS BY W. LANGDON KIHN

reduced to powder by the action of fire.

"The workwoman forms the hollow inside of the vessel by means of a round stone which she holds in her hand while she works and smooths the outside with a piece of poplar bark. When the pot is made, it is filled and surrounded with dry shavings, and then burnt, when it is ready for use."

Fortunately for our knowledge of the Mandan, not only Catlin and Maximilian but such travelers as Lewis and Clark, Brackenridge, and Bradbury visited them early in the 19th century, for in the spring of 1837 they were struck by a smallpox epidemic (page 90). When the disease abated, only 23 men, 40 women, and 60 or 70 children were left of the 1,800 souls that before had composed the nation. Those few that recovered, disfigured almost beyond recognition, were soon absorbed in other tribes. The Mandan ceased to exist as a nation.

The white man's coming struck the Plains Indian hard in many such ways. So, too, did the tough, far-ranging Indian of the open prairie strike a deep impression, often terror, in the hearts of white travelers, and lastingly etch his image in the Nation's imagination.

His powerful physique, feathered warbonnet, and prominent hooked nose still remain as mind's-eye features of all American Indians. His body paint ran to dramatic vermilions, yellows, and black. His hair sometimes hung in two braids,

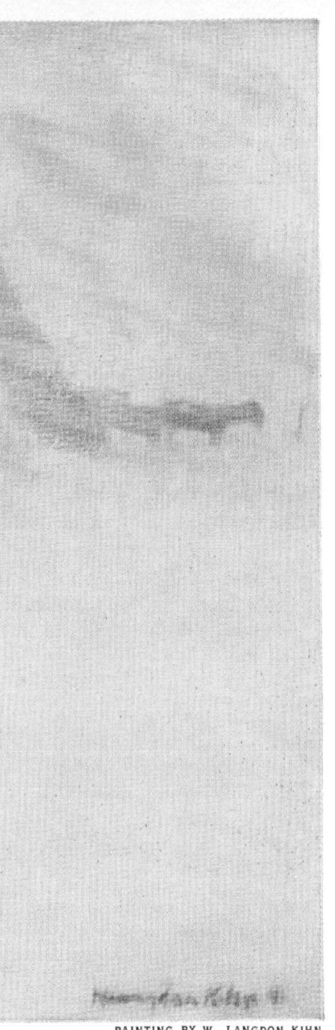

PAINTING BY W. LANGDON KIHN

**Snow Masks Horse Thief**

Covered by a howling, driving blizzard, the intruder readies his rawhide lariat as he stealthily approaches a mount tied near its owner's tepee. Stealing horses was an honorable pursuit among the Plains Indians. The successful thief not only got the horse, but his fellow tribesmen's acclaim for exposing himself to danger.

If caught, he was killed, just as white men killed horse thieves in early days of the West. Chief honor—a greater coup—came from taking a mount tied near a tepee, far riskier than taking one hobbled in an open field.

sometimes in a forelock down over the nose, and sometimes stood stiffly erect, as in the forelock of the Crow.

The Plains Indian loved war regalia. A party of Plains warriors, bronzed and painted, naked except for breechcloth, weapons, and ornaments, riding at full gallop with bodies low to their horses' withers, eagle feathers flying, and the terrifying war cry ringing across the prairie, made a spectacular impression upon enemies. And the Indian knew it.

I have talked with old warriors and seen the reminiscent gleam come into their eyes when describing old encounters. They spoke with undisguised admiration of their foes' appearance as they galloped past. Brilliant uniforms and martial music of bygone European armies never glamorized warfare more than the feathers, paint, and war cries of the Plains Indian.

The mounted Indian usually rode bareback; nowhere in the world did more expert horsemen develop. Their roving equestrian life engendered a warlike spirit. Transcending its original primary purpose of vengeance or protection, warfare developed into a glorified game, a way of gaining honor and prestige, excitement and adventure.

Like any game, it acquired definite rules and a scoring system. The ultimate object became exposing oneself to risk and danger rather than killing enemies, which was secondary.

Score was kept by "counting coup"—a point system for brave exploits. Highest honor came from touching an enemy in combat with the hand; next was to touch him with bow or a coup stick carried for the purpose. It gave greater honor to spear and dismount a foe than to shoot him with bow and arrow or gun.

Also important were such feats as capturing an enemy's gun, taking a scalp, or stealing horses from another tribe. Witnesses were desirable, but seldom did a man falsify his achievements.

The warrior painted a pictorial record of his exploits on his tepee or on the bare side of his buffalo robe. On certain occasions he could boast publicly of his deeds. If he had four coups or more, he was an "ace," and might then hold tribal positions of honor and leadership. He could wear certain feathers or paint his face in certain ways, and others knew at a glance what honors he held.

"Family connections" had nothing to do with an individual's standing in his group. Leadership or the so-called chieftaincies came not through inheritance but as reward for personal achievement. Indians did not even inherit family names. Even so, Plains tribesmen regarded names

**Blackfeet Bring in Furs to Trade.** Pitching their tepees outside the fort's log stockade, tribesmen unload rich pelts from back-packs, horses, and travois. The trader will barter for them in dry goods, tobacco, trinkets, vermilion for face paint, sometimes rifles. Favorite swap was rum for beaver.

PAINTING BY W. LANGDON KIHN

It was at fur-company posts such as this, scattered across the Great Plains during the 19th century, that Indians and whites met when the West was growing up. Often, peace pipes extinguished, war parties attacked these outposts. Defenders swept the circling band with fire from corner blockhouses.

as valuable property, often possessing magical virtues. They could be sold, pawned, given away, or discarded at will. A boy usually took a new name on reaching manhood. A girl kept her first name throughout life. Marriage did not change it.

Frequently Indian names suggested by some exploit or incident sound curious to our ears. A prominent Kiowa gloried in the name "Stinking Saddle Blanket." To the Indians this implied that he was a man who rode so hard and far on the warpath that he did not have time to change his saddle!

Loose or mistaken translations of Indian names into English often produced curious results. The name of the famous Chippewa chief "Hole in the Day" should have been translated "Rift in the Sky." The well-known Dakota Sioux warrior "Young Man Afraid of His Horses" actually was "Young Man Whose Very Horses Are Feared."

Sitting Bull, the Hunkpapa Sioux leader, was so called because the hieroglyph of his name appeared to represent a seated buffalo. Actually, his name meant "The Bull in Possession."

Indians are far from devoid of a sense of humor.

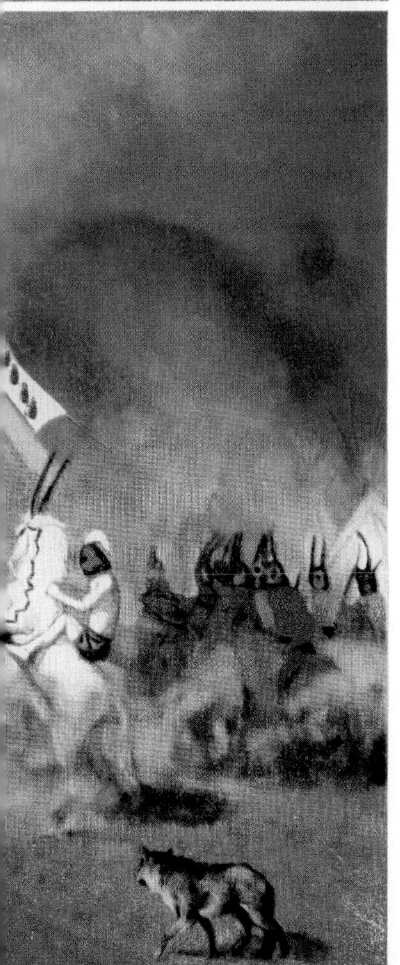

**Covered Wagons Dare Indian Domain.** Banded together for mutual protection, a gold rush train crosses Sioux and Cheyenne country under the eye of Indian scouts. Soon comes the attack. The pioneers, hastily barricaded behind tight circle of wagons, will repel it, or leave their bones to bleach on the prairies.

The High Plains became part of the United States with the Louisiana Purchase of 1803. Next spring, Lewis and Clark "hoisted Sail and Set out in high Spirits" from St. Louis, explored the mighty Missouri, crossed the Continental Divide, boated down the Columbia River—the first Americans overland to the Pacific. Half a century later the westward movement was at full flood; between 1843 and 1857 some 350,000 pioneers undertook the long trek. Their stirring tales of hostile tribesmen made the Plains Indian *the* American Indian in most people's minds.

**Sioux Rainmakers Ride Under Darkening Skies.** Storm clouds give thunderous answer to the ghostly Sioux Horse Dance, performed beneath an arching rainbow. Riders paint themselves the color of their horses. Man and mount wear hornlike feathers.

Four black horses represent the west; white, the north; sorrel, the east; buckskin, the south. Four virgins lead the procession wearing scarlet-dyed buckskin dresses. Wreaths of green sage crown scarlet-painted faces. Single eagle feathers hang from their braids. Beyond the black-hooded horsemen, six grandfathers sing.

Artist and spectators were drenched, but the downpour missed the performers, who carried out the ceremony in bright sunshine. The big, circular tepee encampment is typical of those Lewis and Clark saw when passing through Sioux, or Dakota, lands in 1804.

PAINTINGS BY W. LANGDON KIHN

A Blackfoot, noted among his fellow tribesmen for stinginess, carried the name, "Johnny Belches When He Eats." He was much embarrassed by whites laughing at him when they heard it. Whereupon he formally requested the tribal council to bestow a new name on him.

Custom required him to furnish a feast for the gathering. So Johnny purchased, at minimum cost, a small, undernourished steer. The council met and, after keeping Johnny in suspense for a couple of days, finally called him in to announce that his cause was just. They had given him a new name.

Henceforth he was to be known as "Johnny Does Not Belch When He Eats."

Not only warfare could enhance a brave's prestige, but also generosity in aiding the needy. The man who gave away valuable horses, for example, was greatly admired.

Since the buffalo hunt was vital to the tribe, success as a hunter was a principal means of gaining prestige and honor. Buffalo hunting, however, was organized under strict leadership and regulation. When scouts reported buffalo in the vicinity, the village authorities assigned roles to the hunters, who remained under military discipline while the hunt lasted.

**Blackfoot War Party Skirts the Skyline**

Bands of feather-bonneted warriors often displayed themselves to foes before attacking. War was a game, and risk its spice. The Indian full knew his dramatic impression; he heightened it by warpaint and trappings. His fondness for pintos, or "painted" piebald horses, gave the Wild West its characteristic steed. Natural-born riders, the Plains Indians took the Spaniard's horse, and proved their prowess as mounted hunter and fighter beyond compare.

A swirl of warriors (left) marks the attack. They peel off, strike at the flanks, circle tighter and tighter, presenting the most fleeting of targets. Always best in a running fight, the Plains warrior guided his mount with his knees, leaving hands free for bow and arrow, lance or gun. He could hang alongside his horse's neck, body out of sight; he could shoot under the horse's belly, or swing onto or off his mount at full gallop. Near-naked, bareback riders swooped in to pick up dead or wounded tribemates, sparing them from enemy scalping or mutilation.

JOSEPH K. DIXON

Three methods of organized hunting prevailed. In the "surround" system, used principally in the south, horsemen stampeded the buffalo in a circle and shot them one by one from the edge of the herd (page 75).

In the northern Plains, where heavy winter snows often covered the ground, Indians built a strong corral with a narrow entrance, from which long winglike fences extended outward in a V shape. The animals were herded into the wings of the funnel. Men stationed along the sides kept them converging until they entered the enclosure where they could be easily killed.

Blackfoot and Crow hunters practiced a third basically similar method. Long converging wings led to the edge of a cliff. The animals were driven over and killed by the fall (page 95).

When the buffalo were scattered, the hunter frequently covered himself with an animal skin and stalked his quarry against the wind. Both lance and bow and arrow were used.

The short recurved bow of western tribes, made of wood or horn and backed with buffalo sinew, was extremely powerful. Observers often reported arrows passing entirely through a bison's body.

In early times flaked stone points tipped the arrows. Later, triangular iron points were introduced by the trader.

Bow and arrow proved more effective for short-range work on horseback than the single-shot rifle. Not until the very end of the 19th century did the bow give way completely to the handgun and repeating carbine.

To the women fell the task of preparing products of the hunt. Buffalo meat was cut into strips, hung on wooden frames, dried and smoked. Pounded with dried berries and wild cherries and mixed with fat, the dried meat became pemmican, a concentrated, nutritious food for long journeys.

Buffalo hides were staked out on the ground for the women to scrape, dry, and later make soft and pliable by dressing with buffalo brains, liver, and fat. The

## Caddo Lodge, Blackfoot Tepee Housed Dwellers of the Plains

Grass huts of the sedentary Caddo tribe look as if they belonged on Samoa. Actually, these beehive dwellings (right) were typical of the southern Plains. They resembled the earth lodges to the north, but without heavy sod covering the thatch. Their rafter poles were bent in a rain-shedding dome, lashed at top as in the frame in the background. Some lodges had leather-hinged doors, others walls that stopped short of the ground.

Caddo warriors tattooed their bodies and shaved their heads, save for a roach on the scalp and long braid behind. This agricultural tribe boasted the finest potters of the Plains.

Admirably suited to wandering Blackfoot ways was the easily transported tepee (below). This restless, aggressive tribe, without pottery art, canoes, or agriculture, adopted the white man's horse and gun, spread over immense territory from Montana north into Saskatchewan, Canada. Women not only made and erected the tall tents, they owned them. If a brave had trouble with his wife, he couldn't order her out of the tepee, but had to leave himself.

A tepee began with three or four poles, depending on the tribe. These poles, lashed together about three feet from the small ends, were raised like a big tripod. Ten to 20 more poles then were laid up in a cone, with their tops locking one another. Such a frame stood firmly against high winds. The buffalo skin covering laced down the front, leaving a door flap at bottom. Two outside poles adjusted a smoke hole and ventilator opening at the top according to the direction of the wind.

High-peaked Moorish-type saddle on horse is a "woman's saddle." Men mostly rode bareback, or used a pad saddle with short stirrups.

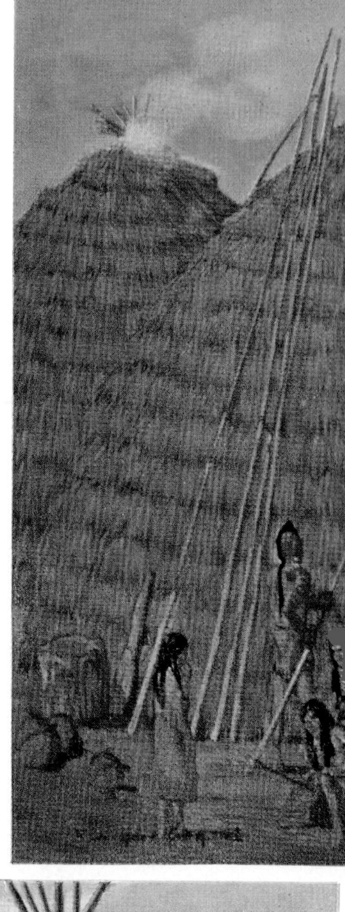

PAINTINGS BY W. LANGDON KIHN

hides could then be worked into tepee covers, robes, or dresses.

The dressed side of buffalo robes was often decorated by painting or simple geometric designs formed of dyed porcupine quills. When the white traders came, colored glass beads gradually replaced quillwork in clothing. Great Plains beadwork can usually be dated by the various types of beads brought in by traders at different times.

Before the coming of the whites, the Indian man's normal costume was a small skin apron attached to a belt. With traders also came the breechcloth, worn by passing it between the legs and tucking it under the belt, fore and aft, so that it hung down a little at each end. This, with moccasins, was the dress for ordinary occasions.

Long skin leggings, reaching from ankle to thigh and fastened to the belt, might be added, but apparently only extreme northern tribes wore shirts, introduced by Canadian Indians.

Plains Indians placed rawhide soles on their soft leather moccasins. This contrasted to Eastern Woodlands practice, where one-piece moccasins of soft leather were made. Southwestern and Mexican Indians wore sandals.

While near nudity characterized the men, women were more fully clothed. In most Plains tribes they wore a full-length sleeveless dress of elkskin or buckskin, the upper portion draping over the shoulders in the form of a cape. They also wore knee-high leggings, held by garters. Women of the Osage, Pawnee, and Cheyenne, on the other hand, wore a two-piece costume like that of eastern Indians, consisting of a skirt and cape.

Favorite "costume jewelry" was the milk teeth of the elk, perforated and attached by sinew or thread (page 77).

Except for fur caps sometimes used in

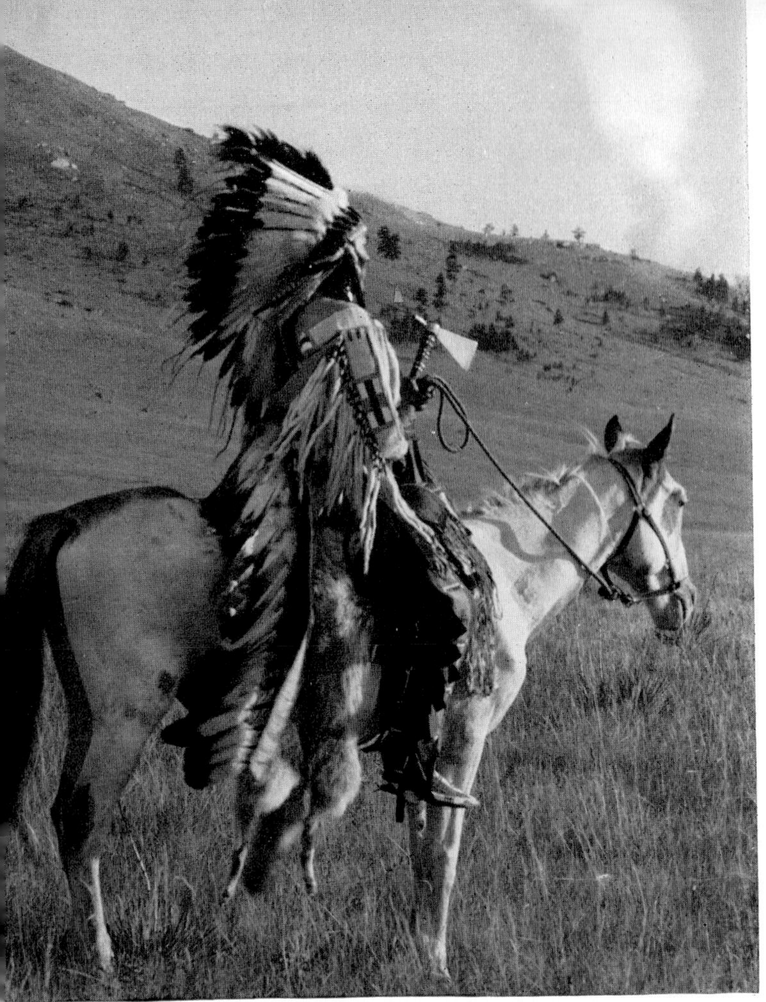

JOSEPH K. DIXON

**Smoke in the Sky!** A war-party leader in full regalia, gripping steel tomahawk and rope rein, reads signals rising above the ridgeline. Smoke codes by day, signal fires by night carried messages long distances through clear skies of the Plains. Near tribal campgrounds, lookout points were manned constantly.

A simpler, more graceful, or more practical dwelling was never devised by man. A large tepee encampment of the western Plains around the middle of the last century was one of the most picturesque sights offered in the North American continent.

In tepee-dwelling tribes, the organized camp circle was a prominent feature. Each band, or family group, pitched its tepees in an assigned segment of the circle. The council tent stood in the center.

At regular intervals around the circle were the tepees of the police, appointed by the council to enforce regulations. These warriors were selected from men's societies or clubs, military or ceremonial in nature and generally named for animals. Many tribes organized their societies by age grades. A man "graduated" from one to another as he grew older. Some northern Plains tribes had similar women's societies which performed ceremonies helping to obtain game.

far-northern reaches of the Plains, no headgear was worn by either men or women.

In addition to producing clothing, the woman made, erected, and was responsible for transporting the tepee, which was considered her property.

The size, form, and construction of the tepee often varied with different tribes. A typical tepee took 10 or 12 buffalo hides to cover. These were rid of hair and tanned on both sides, then skillfully tailored to fit tightly over the conical framework of smooth, barkless poles. Among the Crow and Blackfoot, tepees were sometimes 50 feet in diameter.

Characteristically, political organization among Plains tribes was loose, so loose it is not always easy to say what constitutes a tribe.

There were seven divisions among the Dakota: the Yankton, Teton, Sisseton, Yanktonai, Mdewakanton, Wahpeton, and Wahpekute. All self-governing and independent, these groups were yet bound by a common language, thought of themselves as one people, and did not war with one another. The name Dakota means, in Sioux language, "Friends."

Like the Dakota units, the three independent Blackfoot groups—the Piegan, Blood, and Blackfoot—felt close affinity.

Yet the Hidatsa, an earth-lodge people, did not consider themselves strictly related to the tepee-dwelling Crow, even though both groups spoke the same language. Their customs differed too much.

Complicating the tribal picture were the many Plains languages.

Most prominent linguistic stock was the Siouan, whose dialects include Mandan, Hidatsa, Assiniboin, Crow, Dakota, Iowa, Kansa, Osage, Omaha, Oto, and Ponca. These languages reached the Plains from the east.

From the north came the Algonquian languages of the Cree, Plains Chippewa, Atsina, Blackfoot, Cheyenne, and Arapaho. From the northwest came Athapascan, represented on the Plains by the Sarsi and the Kiowa Apache.

On the western High Plains the Shoshonean stock includes the Northern and Wind River Shoshoni, the Bannock, the Ute, and the Comanche. The Caddoan dialects spoken by the Arikara, Pawnee, Caddo, and Wichita came from the south.

Perhaps it was this linguistic diversity, combined with nomadic habits, that led the Plains Indians to develop the most effective sign language ever devised. By graceful signs and gestures of fingers and hands they communicated as fluently as by oral speech.

So realistic were the gestures, so adept these sign talkers that even the uninitiated, with little practice, could follow the trend of conversation. Sign language became of great use to white trappers and traders, and later to military men.

Religious concepts of the Plains Indians were similar to those of American Indians in general. Most Plains tribes revered the sun as the pre-eminent deity, a concept evidently coming from the south. The most characteristic and widespread ceremony of the Plains was the Sun Dance (page 76).

The sky, the moon, the earth, and the wind were also personified as gods. Lesser supernatural beings were the ruling spirits of the buffalo and the bear, lightning, thunder, rain, and whirlwind. Numberless mythological beings were honored in a lengthy series of myths.

The term *wakonda* in the Siouan languages expresses the idea of supernatural force. Every man's goal was to acquire contact with some supernatural being. Prolonged fasting in some lonely place sometimes induced a vision in which he spoke with some animal, human in character. The animal who gave the revelation was thenceforth regarded as protector of the individual, who always carried with him on any dangerous or important undertaking a bundle containing skin or feathers or some other part of such an animal, together with additional objects related to the vision. A man not fortunate enough to have a vision of his own might purchase a bundle from a medicine man.

Some famous bundles became the property of societies or tribes and were made the central feature of ceremonies. Although these bundles acquired high value, they could be sold or transferred. Sacred songs, prayers, even entire ceremonies might be sold or borrowed.

Among the Skidi Pawnee, the two most important sky gods were the Morning Star and Evening Star. They represented respectively the male and female principle, and as such they were regarded as parents of the first human. There were two sacred bundles, the Skull bundle and the Morning Star bundle.

Human sacrifices were sometimes offered to the Morning Star. The ceremony, evidently southern in origin, represented a renewal of life on earth.

Sacrificial rites were held at irregular intervals, usually when the Morning Star appeared to some warrior in a dream, or when the star seemed unusually bright, or a comet arched near it in the sky.

For the ritual, a beautiful maiden was captured from a neighboring tribe, to be sacrificed as bride of the Morning Star.

Often the captive would be held for several months without knowing her fate, until the proper season for the ceremony arrived. During this time she was given every comfort and treated with the greatest respect, as befitted the prospective bride of a god (opposite).

When the day to begin the ceremony arrived, the priest came to the chief's lodge and spread out the contents of the medicine bundle as an altar. The girl was brought into the lodge, undressed, and her entire body painted red. She and her male captor then were dressed in costumes from the Morning Star bundle. Preliminary ceremonies lasted three days, with everything done to allay the girl's fears.

On the afternoon of the fourth day, a scaffold was erected outside the village, consisting of five symbolically painted horizontal bars lashed between two uprights. The right half of the girl's body was painted red, the left half black, and a fan-shaped eagle-feather headdress was attached to her hair.

She was led to the scaffold, the procession being timed to the star's rising. If the girl mounted the

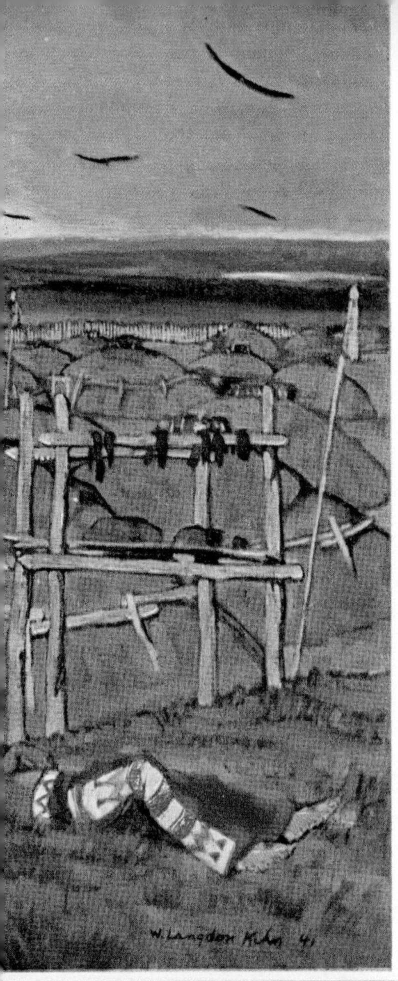

## Smallpox Took Grisly Toll, Human Sacrifice But Few

Vultures circle, mourners wail from the domed roofs of their earth lodges. These are the only signs of life in the Mandan village (left), where the air hangs heavy with the stench of death. Epidemic smallpox, contracted from two diseased white men on a Missouri River trading boat, wiped out the Mandan in 1837. Indians, who had not known smallpox before the coming of the whites, had scant resistance and no way of combating it. The scourge spread like wildfire from village to village, tribe to tribe—to Arikara, Assiniboin, Blackfoot, Pawnee.

Among the Pawnee, the Skidi band (below) was the only Plains tribe to practice human sacrifice. In the smoke of a grass fire, a medicine man bathes the nude body of a young maiden, readying her for sacrifice as bride of the Morning Star. Soon she will be painted red and black, lashed to a sacred scaffold, and killed amid elaborate ritual (page 89).

Both Mandan and Pawnee built their strong, roomy earth lodges 30 to 60 feet in diameter, banking sod atop grass thatch over an ingenious post-and-rafter frame. Doorway tunnels usually faced east, direction of the rising sun, chief deity of many tribes. Skins curtained the openings. To harden floors, the earth was tamped and flooded with water; then dry grass was piled on it and set afire. Couches lined the wall. Covered with buffalo robes, they served as seats by day, beds by night. A fire burned in the center, beneath the smoke hole. Miniature cellars stored corn, dried meat, skins, extra clothing, and personal effects.

PAINTINGS BY W. LANGDON KIHN

**Shoshoni Women Garbed as Men Parade Enemy Scalps.** Drums thud. Scalps flutter like battle pennants atop tall poles. A war party has come home triumphant, bearing fresh scalps, trophies of great daring. Symbolizing victory, women bring forth all the tribe's old scalps, dried and mounted on hoops. In the scalp dance alone did women lead a tribal ritual or don warrior's apparel. These victory fetes took place among many tribes, even though scalp taboos and beliefs differed widely. Sometimes scalps were placed on buffalo chips and left on the battleground as sacrifice to the sun god. The Dakota destroyed theirs after a year in an impressive ceremony, releasing enemy spirits from earthly ties.

PAINTING BY W. LANGDON KIHN

Having served their ceremonial purpose, scalps might adorn a warrior's trappings or become bridle pendants. They might go into sacred medicine bundles, or they might simply be thrown away. Contrary to popular notion, a warrior's honors were measured not by his tally of scalps, but by counting coup (page 79). An Indian who killed or first struck an enemy (the higher honor) not always did the scalping; he might leave it to another in his party. Scalping was not practiced by all North American Indians, nor was it necessarily fatal. Some Plains tribes sought to overpower foes and scalp them alive, sending them mutilated back to their people as a gesture of defiance, a goad to new battle.

**Blackfoot Hunters Stampede Bison Over Cliff's Edge**

High above a circular tepee camp, a great herd is decoyed into a funnel of logs, rocks, and brush by mounted Indians disguised with buffalo robes. Suddenly blanket-waving beaters spring up (right). With a sound like thunder, the terrified bison sweep toward the mesa's rim; the decoys ride clear as best they can. Those animals not killed by the fall make easy targets for Indians waiting below.

Before the professional white hunter all but wiped out the American buffalo, vast herds darkened the Plains. Some experts estimated them to number more than sixty million. They roamed with the seasons and the grass, feeding always into the wind, wary yet vulnerable to Indians, cunning, swift, brave.

Buffalo sustained the Plains Indian; their pursuit became a way of life. Their flesh gave food, their blood drink. Buffalo chips fed prairie campfires. The hides housed the Indians, clothed them, gave them cooking vessels, shields, saddles, and warm robes.

Unlike the pig's squeal, not even the bison's beard was wasted: it decorated clothing, bows, and lances. Thick woolly bison hair stuffed "medicine balls." The ribs gave scrapers, arrowheads, and dice. Hoes were fashioned from shoulder blades; leg bones became knives, awls, and hammers. The skull made a fetish, porous hip bones saw use as paintbrushes, the horns yielded cups, bowls, spoons. Sinew made bowstrings and backed bows. From the scrotum came rattles; from the bladder, water bags. Even the tail found use as whip or fly swatter.

**Back-pack and Dog Travois Carried the Buffalo Hunter's Loads Before the Horse Came**

Coronado met bands, such as these wandering Kiowa (left), crossing the Kansas prairie in 1541. They left their villages to follow bison herds in long migrations, loading food and camp gear into women's packs and onto the light-poled travois dragged by their Huskylike dogs.

The first horses astounded the Indians. A century later the Spaniard's mounts were coming in numbers to the Western Plains. Escaped stallions sired wild herds that thrived on the endless grasslands. Horses swiftly changed Indian life. Wider hunting range, greater load-carrying capacity caused many tribes to abandon sedentary agriculture entirely for nomadic hunting.

In all their roving, Plains Indians strangely never used the great river highways that were to carry white explorers westward. Lacking canoe and keelboat, the Indians used only the bullboat for crossing larger streams. This crude craft consisted of buffalo hide stretched over a circular frame, an unwieldy bowl hard to paddle.



PAINTINGS BY W. LANGDON KIHN

scaffold of her own will, it was considered an especially favorable omen. She was lashed by the wrists to the scaffold, and as soon as the star appeared over the horizon, two men came from the east with flaming brands and touched her lightly on her armpits and groin. Four other men touched her symbolically with war clubs.

The man who had captured her then ran forward with the sacred bow and arrow from the Skull bundle and shot her through the heart. Simultaneously, another man struck her on the head with the club from the Morning Star bundle.

Then the Skidi Pawnee priest opened her breast with a flint knife and smeared his face with blood from her heart, while her captor caught some of the falling blood on dried meat. Every male in the tribe pressed forward to shoot an arrow into the girl's body, fathers or uncles pulling bows for boys too small to shoot by themselves. Then for three days, the entire village feasted and danced.

One of the most romantic episodes in Plains Indian history took place in 1818 in connection with this ceremony. The hero was a young Pawnee chief named Petalasharo, handsomest and most daring man in the tribe.

The girl had been lashed to the scaffold preparatory to the final act, when Petalasharo stepped forward, dramatically declaring that he intended to rescue the girl or lay down his life in the attempt. He leaped on the scaffold, cut the girl's bonds, and carried her through the astonished crowd to where two horses had been led. Placing her on one, mounting the other, he rode swiftly away. When safe from pursuit, he presented her with food, the horse she was riding, and sent her to her people, some 400 miles away.

Then Petalasharo returned to his village. His prominence and previous honors were such that no attempt was made to punish him. Probably most of his tribesmen admired the unprecedented feat. Thereafter other chiefs opposed human sacrifice in the Skidi Pawnee rituals.

As the white man pressed westward in ever-increasing numbers, taking up lands, building military posts and railroads, slaughtering the buffalo, the Plains Indian realized that unless this advance was checked he was doomed. The end of the buffalo herds meant the end of his free wandering life on ancestral hunting grounds.

Treaties failing, he felt armed resistance to be his only hope. Not accustomed to organized warfare, the Indian probably did not realize the futility of his stand. Yet his success against insuperable odds was remarkable. In his favor were his familiarity with the terrain, his fine physical condition, warlike tradition, excellent horsemanship, and above all, the fact that he was fighting to preserve a deeply loved homeland and ancestral way of life.

ROLAND W. REED, © R. F. WILLIAMS

**Nomads at Trail's End**

White hunters, railroads, settlements doomed the bison and Plains Indian life, yet not until 1890 did fierce Sioux give up their battle against hopeless odds. Their image lives on. The Plains Indian, tall, hawk-nosed, with feather warbonnet, symbolizes all American Indians today. His features adorn currency and monuments. As fighter for liberty, he personifies an American ideal.

The white man's disregard of the strict rules by which the Indian fought put the latter under a handicap. Yet in the end it was disease and decimation of food supply rather than bullets and the numbers of his enemies that brought the Indian's inevitable downfall.

Gradually forced to adopt a way of life as a Government ward in reservations, the Plains Indian accepted his fate reluctantly, contesting every step of his further constriction. Such was the last outbreak of the Sioux and their allies, who slaughtered Custer's men on the Little Bighorn in Montana in 1876 (page 14).

But resistance was crushed, the Indian's spirit broken. Like a caged panther, his unused muscles grew soft and his eyes glowed with the memory of the freedom of a day which even he came to realize was forever gone.

With the passing of the hunt and the warpath, the rich ceremonies built around them lost their meaning. Indians who knew the old life were still stirred by the old emotions. But younger generations, raised in a new world, have found themselves between two cultures.

PAINTING BY W. LANGDON KIHN

**Blue of the Sky, Red of the Desert Color Navajo Life.** Proudly this young mother, bedecked in silver and turquoise, comes to a tribal ceremony by covered wagon. The industrious Navajo, largest and one of the most adaptable of United States tribes today, herd sheep on dry New Mexico and Arizona tablelands, weave bright blankets, rugs, and work silver with traditional artistry.

## CHAPTER 4

# INDIAN TRIBES OF PUEBLO LAND

FRANCISCO VÁSQUEZ DE CORONADO in 1540 led his band of gold-hungry explorers into the rocky country near the headwaters of the Little Colorado River in what is now western New Mexico.

The conquistadores were fired by reports of Cabeza de Vaca and Fray Marcos de Niza, who had preceded them into that sun-seared land. Had not Fray Marcos himself seen from a distance the very city the guides said they were now approaching? Had he not stated that it appeared even more magnificent than rumors foretold?

Finally the great moment arrived. From a rise across the shallow valley, Coronado and his fellow Spaniards viewed the first of Seven Cities of Cíbola, drab against a background of arid hills.

The Spaniards were not impressed. Says Pedro de Castañeda, chronicler of the expedition:

"When they saw the first village, which was Cíbola, such were the curses that some hurled at Friar Marcos that I pray God may protect him from them. It is a little, crowded village, looking as if it had been crumpled all up together. There are ranch houses in New Spain which make a better appearance at a distance."

The conquistadores were in search of gold. They could not see or understand the other riches which lay behind these adobe walls, the wealth of a people who had intimate acquaintance with Nature and with Mother Earth, a people to whom religion and poetry were one. In the environment seemingly so unproductive to the Spaniards, this race saw beauty with which to build their arts and ceremonies.

Wealth of a material sort these Indians neither had nor cared about. In the turquoise adorning their house entrances they saw the depths of clear waters and the sky's infinite space, and thus it represented pure beauty. That turquoise might possess value of another sort never occurred to them. Among their possessions little else attracted the Spaniards.

Coronado's expedition was a failure, so far as its main purpose was concerned. Other fabled "cities of Cíbola" proved as disappointing as the first. No mines were discovered, no golden Inca halls.

The expedition's unfavorable reports discouraged further penetration for 40 years. Then, in the wake of later explorers, Spanish settlers drifted into the territory. As colonization mounted, the Pueblo Indians rebelled and drove out the white men in 1680.

The Spanish conquerors soon returned. Again in 1696 the Pueblos rose to expel the invaders, but after much bloodshed the uprising was put down. Since then the Pueblos, peacefully for the most part, have lived in their native manner down to the present day—remarkably unchanged after four centuries of white contact.

In probing the vast area we now call the Southwest, the Spaniards saw ruins of imposing settlements, apparently the work of an ancient people, long vanished. With the start of American occupation

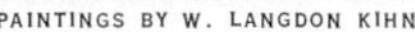
PAINTINGS BY W. LANGDON KIHN

**Navajo Fire Dance Climaxes the Night Chants.** Fire dancers, bodies painted white with clay to ward off heat, race around a blazing bonfire. Each clutches a burning brand, strikes the dancer ahead. Wildly they circle closer and closer to the leaping flames. One of the most impressive Indian ceremonies in North America, the Navajo Night Chants draw tribesmen from far and near. The many rituals, jugglery acts, prayers and songs under the stars combine the gaiety of a social gathering, the solemnity of a religious ceremony, the spectacle of tribal drama. Typical of Southwest ritual, clowns burlesque the priests, dance out of step, jest with blanket-wrapped onlookers. Left above: A Yaqui dancer, member of a fierce Mexican border tribe, pushes aside his mask.

**Coronado Takes Hawikuh, Pueblo of the Zuni.** Toledo blades, armor glint in the sun as conquistadores loot and kill in this "village of about 200 warriors . . . three and four stories high. The people of the whole district had collected here," says Castañeda's chronicle of 1540. "When they refused to have peace on the terms the interpreters extended to them, but appeared defiant, the Santiago [war cry] was given, and they were at once put to flight. The Spaniards then attacked the village, which was taken with not a little difficulty, since they held the narrow and crooked entrance." Coronado himself fell under a barrage of stones, was snatched from death by lieutenants. But Spanish fury conquered the pueblo in less than an hour. The troops found food they needed, but no gold, neither here nor in any of the legended Seven Cities of Cíbola. They departed, and the Zuni remained unmolested for 40 years.

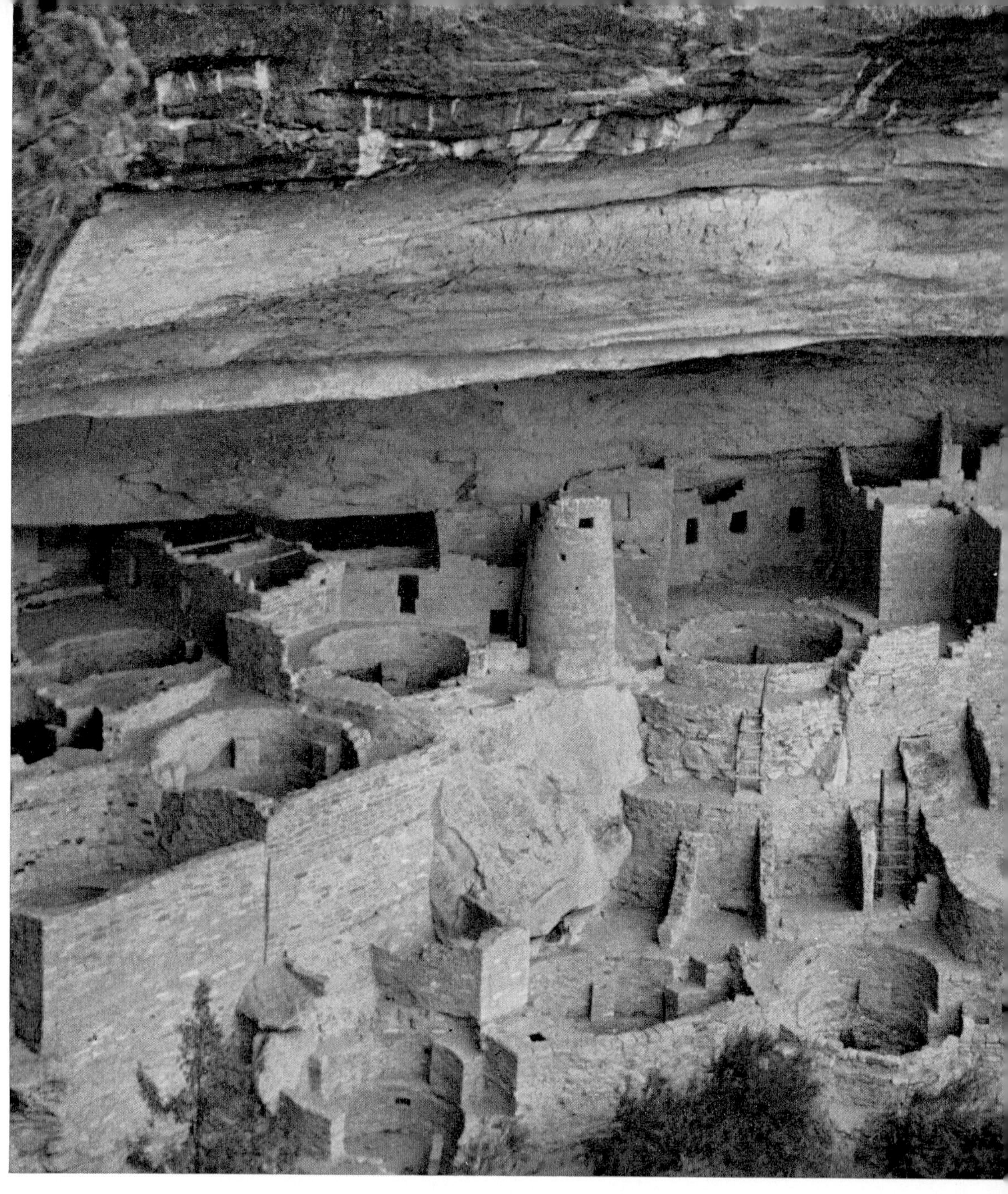

about mid-19th century, some of these ruins were mapped. The world at large began to hear of them. "Cliff dwellers" became a household word.

These strange cities, it was said, might be 20 or 30 thousand years old! Perhaps a highly civilized non-Indian race built them, then grew effete and was vanquished by barbarians. Or perhaps the people were dwarfs, for their windowless dwelling places (actually storage granaries) were so small!

Thus fancy ran free until, after 1880, the spades of archeologists began to uncover the true prehistory of the Southwest. We now know that the "cliff dwellers" were early Pueblo agriculturists who built their amazing strongholds on cliffs for safety from hostile nomads. More is known today of the American

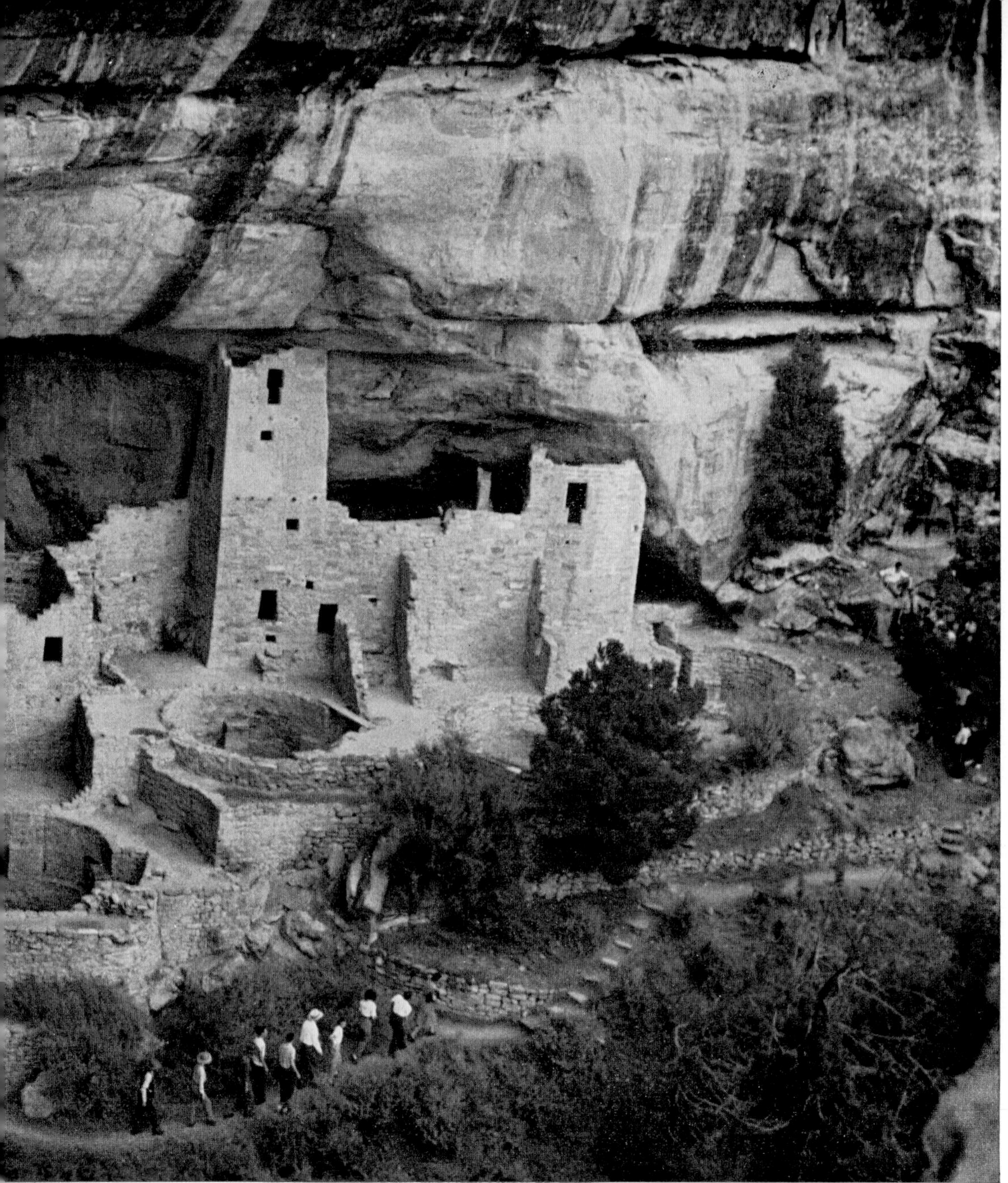

NATIONAL GEOGRAPHIC PHOTOGRAPHER WILLARD R. CULVER

**Cliff Palace Crowds Below Mesa Verde's Rim**

Largest of prehistoric cave villages in Mesa Verde National Park, Colorado, this ancient eight-story apartment house once sheltered at least 400 Indians from enemies and the elements. Here chanting black-eyed women ground corn on stone metates, while men clambered up perilous cliffside paths to till mesa-top fields and hunt game. Flat roofs are gone, but masonry walls of the 200 family rooms, 23 kivas, and storage bins have withstood seven centuries' wear. Two cowboys discovered the forgotten pueblo in 1888.

Pueblos than of any comparable archeologic area in the world. In the tree-growth rings of wooden house beams, preserved in the dry stillness of the centuries, science has found a calendar that can date these sites more certainly than do cornerstone numerals carved by Romans date their edifices (Chapter 16).

The vast stage that mounted this Indian drama extends from southern Utah

PAINTINGS BY W. LANGDON KIHN

**Mesa Verde People Watch White-Painted Priests Emerge.** Cliff dwellers cluster on stepped rooftops beneath their four-story tower as masked members of a tribal society come forth for a public ceremony. Secret rites have concluded in the sacred kiva below. This circular windowless chamber, banned to women, represents the universe. The ceiling is the sky, the floor the earth. A hole at floor center symbolizes the passageway by which man first came from the underworld. The artist here recreates Cliff Palace (page 102) as it must have appeared in its stone-age heyday, long before the white man came to America. By Coronado's time these cliff villages were silent ruins. Archeologists believe a 24-year drought in the late 13th century, plus hostile nomads, spelled disaster to a great culture. This pueblo depended on crops grown above it on Mesa Verde—"green table" in Spanish.

and Colorado to northern Sonora and Chihuahua in Mexico. Its arid heartland is Arizona and New Mexico (group area map, page 24).

Centuries before Cabeza de Vaca and his cavaliers heard of the Seven Cities of Cíbola, there were people here of considerable culture. These first human occupants we know much about were the Basket Makers. But thousands of years before their arrival, much more primitive men hunted the mammoth, the camel, and the giant bison. Theirs was a different land and a different climate, as the last great glaciers thawed to the north. Of those Folsom and pre-Folsom people only scattered traces have been found, although more are discovered each year.

The Basket Makers first arrived about the start of the Christian era to occupy uplands of present-day New Mexico, Utah, and northern Arizona. These long-headed pioneers used spear throwers and lived in caves, probably also in brush shelters erected in the open. They knew no pottery, but made coiled baskets, fine square-toed sandals of woven cord, and twined yucca-fiber bags with colored decorations. So precious was good textile material that they hacked off their own hair for weaving.

Eventually these enterprising people either invented pottery making or, more likely, learned it from Mexican neighbors, and made the bow and arrow their principal weapon. They learned to make pit homes, artificial caves, digging out a cellar hole which they lined with mud or stones and roofed with a dome of poles covered with mats, brush, plaster, and earth. A smoke hole pierced the roof center and the room was entered through a tunnel in the side. In such subterranean homes they warded off winter cold.

About A.D. 500 a people shorter in stature invaded the country of the Basket Makers. The newcomers had round heads made even broader by their custom of lashing babies to hard cradleboards, which flattened the backs of their skulls. They wore round-toed sandals, and discovered or brought with them the use of cotton. With the Basket Makers, among whom they apparently settled, these were the ancestors of today's pueblo-dwellers.

At first they lived in circular pit houses

**Turquoise Adorns a Zuni**

Marked as a man of wealth, he represents the most numerous Pueblo tribe, which dwells near an arm of the Little Colorado River in western New Mexico.

Turquoise to him mirrors water and sky—sheer beauty. His ancestors, in the seven cities Coronado sought, made it into beads, rings, mosaics. Only in this century have Indian artisans mounted it in silver. Feathers plucked from the captive eagle embellish prayer sticks.

much like those of the Basket Makers, but gradually they began to build structures above ground with thick pole-and-plaster walls. Sometimes they joined these dwellings, making a house of several rooms.

In time these people built multi-unit community structures. Slabs of translucent selenite often served as window glass. Ceremonial chambers were circular in form, whereas at present they are usually rectangular.

Their agriculture became more intensive, their ceremonies more elaborate, their arts more specialized and localized as the culture advanced. Its greatest flowering came in the period from about A.D. 1050 to 1400. Early in this era the Pueblos built great apartment dwellings like Pueblo Bonito (page 111) and Chettro Kettle of Chaco Canyon. These are the most impressive structures ever erected by aborigines north of Mexico.

Just as these peaceful agriculturists were achieving their highest advance, warlike enemies appeared—fierce nomads from north and east. For protection many apartment dwellers deserted the open lands to build their pueblos on ledges and high open caves, such as the imposing Cliff Palace and Spruce Tree House of Mesa Verde (page 104).

Archeological evidence of these nomad invaders is scant. Even during the Spanish period they form a shadowy background, always elusive, always hostile to the settled Pueblo peoples. But these were the forebears of the second great group of Southwest Indian tribes. Among them were the Ute, the Kiowa, and the Comanche, who formed a link with the buffalo hunting tribes of the Great Plains; the Navajo, and the Apache, whose warlike exploits extended into fairly recent times under their famous chief Geronimo (page 115).

**Fleet Hunters Run Down Rabbits.** Prehistoric Hopi, forebears of present Pueblos, stun the nimble prey by hurling boomerang-like sticks. A line of Indians drives jackrabbits toward a net wall raised on open ground. As the trapped quarry frantically seek escape, barefoot runners race in, curved missiles ready. Hunting nets such as this have been found, well preserved, in northern Arizona caves. Similar roundups corralled antelope and turkeys. Then as now, the Hopi also farmed industriously.

**Pima Woman Retains the Basket Makers' Skill.** Seated in shade before a square adobe village house and domed igloolike hut, a Pima wife weaves willow strips, cattail, and devil's-claw into coiled basketry of ancient design. Chin tattooing enhances her beauty to her husband. He wears his hair even longer than hers, tying it off in a dangling bun. Nearly 2,000 years ago, the Hohokam, ancestors of these *rancheria* peoples, came to Basket Maker land.

PAINTINGS BY W. LANGDON KIHN

**Towering Walls Guard the Havasupai,** isolated deep in a gorge branching from Grand Canyon. Only two trails thread the sheer red sandstone cliffs, but today the remote tribe boasts telephones! Its 300 members farm hemmed-in gardenland turned green by the beautiful stream flowing through the canyon. From it comes the tribal name, Havasupai, "People of the Blue-green Water." Of old, they migrated in winter to the parched mesa above to hunt and gather pine nuts; now most remain year-round in their village (page 409).

These people are primarily hunters and seed gatherers who live in temporary villages or shelters. Most practice agriculture of sorts, probably learned from the Pueblos, for, despite hostility, the sedentary peoples and the nomads exchanged customs across the years.

Whence these wanderers came, anthropologists still can only guess. Linguistic evidence shows it must have been from afar. Navajo and Apache, for example, speak tongues of far-flung Athapascan stock, traceable to Canada.

No "vanishing Americans," the Navajo, largest of Indian tribes in the United States, number more than when the Spaniards came. Over 75,000, they occupy a huge territory in northeastern Arizona and northwestern New Mexico. With the Apache, they comprise over half the Southwest's present-day Indian population.

Contrasting both to the Pueblos and to the nomads are the tribes living along the Gila and lower Colorado Rivers in southwestern Arizona.

These stem from the same period as the early Pueblos, when another people, the Hohokam, invaded the semi-desert region south and west of the land of the Basket Makers. Like the Basket Makers, they were longheaded. They lived in square houses of poles and brush plastered with mud, and surrounded their villages with adobe walls. Expert farmers, the Hohokam built elaborate irrigation systems which made the desert bloom (page 112).

Just as prehistoric Pueblos

were direct ancestors of the modern Pueblo peoples, so were the Hohokam probable ancestors of present-day Pima, Papago, and other farm-village or *ranchería* tribes. Most speak dialects of Sonoran stock from Mexico, related to Aztec.

These cultural middlemen live, like the nomads, in single-family dwellings. But these are clustered in true villages. Like the Pueblos, they practice agriculture. Domestic crops, however, are supplemented with the nomad's wild plants: the mesquite bean, screw bean, yucca, agave, and the fruit of the giant saguaro cactus.

This two-way influence is also apparent in the Havasupai who, deep in precipitous Havasu Canyon (opposite), in the western end of Grand Canyon National Park, till their fields and live in what is probably the most isolated Indian settlement in the United States.

Until recently the Havasupai moved in winter to the high plateau, where firewood is plentiful and they could gather piñon nuts and hunt deer. They dwelt in Navajo-like hogans. Today they no longer make this migration, and mainly live in cottages (Chapter 20).

These, then, are the three native groups—nomads, village tribes, and Pueblos—that today occupy the Pueblo land of the Southwest. Mutually influenced to a considerable extent, their tribal patterns yet remain quite distinct.

Most dominant culturally, despite numbering only about 20,000 in all, are the Pueblo Indians. They live in 26 towns, most of them near the upper Rio Grande in New Mexico. Here compact communal houses of adobe brick, stone, or clay and rubble crowd together, each consisting of two or more set-back stories. This is the characteristic architecture responsible for the name the conquistadores gave the Indians—*pueblo*, the Spanish word for town.

To the east stand Picuris, Jemez, San Ildefonso, San Juan, Santa Clara, Nambe, Tesuque, Santo Domingo, San Felipe, Santa Ana, Chochiti, Zia, Taos, Sandia, and Isleta.

West of these, but still in the Rio Grande drainage, are the pueblos of Acoma and Laguna. Farther west, on the headwaters of the Little Colorado River, is the pueblo of Zuni.

In northeastern Arizona, also in the drainage of the Little Colorado, stand the seven Hopi villages. In this same group is the pueblo of Hano, settled in early historic times by immigrants from the Rio Grande region.

Despite the cultural homogeneity, no single tongue prevails among the various Pueblo tribes. There are several languages, of wholly different stocks. Zuni and affiliated villages, for instance, have one all their own.

Today, Taos and Zuni are the skyscrapers of Pueblo land. Taos dwellings reach five stories. Each of the five is smaller by the width of a room than the one below it, producing a rectangular terraced pyramid (page 414). At Santa Clara and Jemez, buildings face the four sides of a court, climb in terraces at front, end with a perpendicular wall in the rear. The great ruin in Chaco Canyon in New Mexico (page 111) varies this style by terracing back from a semicircular court.

Sometimes buildings climb away from both sides of a street, as at Acoma. The upper tiers are entered by ladders projecting through holes in the roof, although now side doors are becoming more common. Too, there is a growing tendency to build individual houses, after the European fashion.

Fireplaces usually are built in a corner of the room, and a hood over them carries the smoke to the chimney. In another corner, parallel with the wall, are the slab-lined mealing bins, with their stone metates for grinding corn (page 117). Tortillas are often baked on a stone slab as they were centuries ago (page 120).

## From Pueblo Bonito to Zuni Stretches a Ghostly Line

High on the rim of Chaco Canyon in what is now northwestern New Mexico, ancient Pueblo hunters look down upon the fortress city their people built in the desert, centuries before Columbus. Four stories tall at outer wall, its apartments terrace back from an inner court, like a half-cut cheese. Smoke drifts from cooking fires. Ladders jut from roof holes of kivas, where tribal men's societies chant their rites.

Shown here at highest development, Pueblo Bonito shelters more than 1,200 inhabitants in some 800 rooms. Its wealth brings traders from afar. Envious nomad barbarians from the north attack. Eventually they will conquer, and this great communal city will crumble into rubble, covered by windblown sands until archeologists of National Geographic Society expeditions dig it free in the 1920's (Chapter 16).

Pueblo culture, however, survived, absorbing from and changing the nomads who came against it. Zuni, one of 26 modern pueblos, traces its heritage back to the ancient builders. Its rites (below) evoke the spirits of long-dead ancestors. In the famed Zuni Shalako, priests chant beside giant *kachina* images, "Behold us maned with buffaloes' dead manes and beaked with beaks beyond man's memory of birds." By Indian belief, spirits enter the images to honor the dead, provide game for hunters, and bless the hall, here festooned with blankets and skins.



PAINTINGS BY W. LANGDON KIHN

The material culture of the Indians has changed much more during American occupation than it did under the Spaniards. Yet, though these communities depend on farming, resistance to the introduction of farm machinery has been marked, because such devices interfere with the basis of traditional ceremonials.

At Isleta the newly erected town council house remained unfinished pending a long-drawn-out controversy as to whether an old-style or tin roof should be used. Eventually advocates of the tin roof won out. Now many houses of the eastern pueblos have tin roofs.

Factory-made stoves have now generally replaced the picturesque earthen dome-shaped oven, an Old World invention borrowed from Mexico during early historic times. Window frames with glass panes are also in general use.

The white man's alcohol, however, has met resistance in the Pueblo community. The Pueblo Indians were among the earliest advocates of prohibition in this country. Because the governing bodies saw the bad effect of alcohol on their people, the pueblos banned it. Off-reservation drunkenness remains a problem. Today at practically all the pueblos strict prohibition is still in force.

The standard drink of Pueblo aborigines was *atole,* a thin gruel of cornmeal. Now coffee has become the universal beverage, with bottled carbonated drinks a close second.

Although the potter's wheel was unknown in aboriginal America, early pottery of the Southwest was so good it could hold water indefinitely and be placed directly on the cooking fire.

The art so degenerated after the introduction of cheap metal kitchen utensils that the technically poor ware can be used only for decorative or ritual purposes. But the tourist demand for native

**Ancient Engineers Bring Water to the Desert.** Stone-age Hohokam carve irrigation canals to turn parched lands along the Gila and Salt Rivers of Arizona green with crops. Village houses, mud plaster over poles and brush, stand behind thick adobe walls, with ladders the only way across. Archeologists found ruins of one city nine miles from the nearest river. Its water flowed through a canal seven feet deep, 30 feet wide at top. Overall, Hohokam canals watered about 200,000 acres. Some have been restored to use today.

**Medicine Men Work With Tribal Faith.** Navajo "medicine," even today, invokes ancient curing ceremonies (lower left). Sunlight stabs down from the smoke hole in the hogan's roof, illuminating a kneeling woman. While a helper behind feathered prayer sticks shakes his rattle and chants, a masked shaman stalks across a beautifully wrought sand painting. Its curiously elongated figures, drawn in varicolored sands, are mythological beings. The "doctor" touches various symbols, then various parts of the patient's body. When the ritual ends, the sand painting is destroyed. With it, so the Navajo believe, goes the illness.

As corn dancers parade in Tewa pueblo of San Ildefonso (below), clowns caricature the solemn priests. A gray-painted jester cavorts in front of the sacred wand, decorated with feathers, sash, foxskin, and other sacred emblems. A chanting chorus keeps time to a beating tom-tom, an appeal to the gods for bountiful crops. Clowns often take part in Pueblo ceremony. They relieve the ritual's intense seriousness and keep onlookers from growing too sad. They safely break the most rigid taboos and play practical jokes on spectators.



PAINTINGS BY W. LANGDON KIHN

art products has sparked a revival, and frequently in artistic form and decoration the modern ware compares favorably with the ancient products.

At Zuni, black, white, and red pigments are used. In Hopi pottery making, yellow and black appear in designs revived from an earlier day. The famous ware of Santa Clara and San Ildefonso (page 117), however, utilizes a new technique, whereby patterns of dull black are produced on a glossy black surface.

Basketry, practiced in the Southwest long before pottery making, is now practically a lost art among the Pueblos, except the Hopi. The best Southwest basket makers of the present are the Pima (page 107) and the Apache.

So also, when machine-woven textiles were brought in by white traders, weaving was virtually abandoned, except in the Hopi and Zuni pueblos and by the Navajo. Of these, the Hopi male weavers are probably the most skillful, while the Navajo women have won greater fame.

The Navajo probably learned weaving from the Pueblos in the early 18th century and made a specialty of it after the introduction of sheep from Mexico. The finest Navajo weaving was done during the 19th century from yarn obtained by unraveling *bayeta*, a woolen trade cloth introduced by the Spaniards. These beautifully woven blankets were usually of two colors in simple broad stripes. The now-rare Navajo bayeta blankets are in demand by collectors.

About 1850, American traders introduced vegetable-dyed yarn imported from Saxony. This eliminated laborious unraveling of textiles for dyed thread, and greatly increased blanket production. When, in the 1870's, the Navajo began to produce rugs instead of ponchos, this spurred the art. About 1880 came brilliant and cheaper aniline-dyed Germantown yarns.

The modern era of Navajo weaving begins after 1890, when traders introduced the aniline dyes that enabled weavers to use native wool and produce rugs cheaper. As a result, Navajo weaving has become a major asset to the tribe's economy.

Of Navajo blankets the question is often asked, "What does this design mean?" Despite much talk of symbolism, and the explanations many an enterprising native artisan will obligingly give a prospective customer, the answer generally should be "Nothing." One might as well ask the meaning of designs on wallpaper or a patchwork quilt.

True, identifying names are given to certain designs or design elements, but the Indian potter, weaver, or jeweler, except where ritual objects are concerned, thinks of the decorative value of his creation, not of any secret meaning.

In the old days rarely was any pattern other than plain stripes used, with no significance apart from decorations intended. Modern times have brought complex and bizarre figures, many introduced by traders. Even designs from sand paintings (page 112) are used, an unthinkable heresy to Navajo priests of old. It is not even uncommon to see on a beautifully woven rug the words "Ivory Soap" or "Kleenex," copied from a cardboard box!

Designs have been borrowed, too, in silver working, another alien craft that has taken root among the Navajo. Except for a few scattered copper objects received in trade from Mexico, the Indian tribes of Pueblo land formerly knew nothing of metals or metalworking.

Finally, about the middle of the 19th century, a Mexican silversmith entered Navajo country. Soon the craft spread. Along with borrowed patterns, the first silver used by the Navajo consisted of coins obtained from Americans. Later, Mexican pesos—of a purer grade of silver and hence easier to work—were used exclusively. From these beginnings the Navajo have developed an art that has brought them world fame (page 417).

The dramatic topography of the Southwest had a profound effect upon the religious ideology of the tribes who made the region their home. It is a land of tremendous distances, of fantastic formations, of red cliffs and square-cut buttes.

The clear air is occasionally invaded by black storm clouds, the clamor of thunder, and the quick stab of lightning. The deep blue of the sky is painted at dawn and at sunset with colors which defy the brush of the painter.

As all this appeals to the modern artist and poet, so did it stimulate the imagination and poetic instincts of the Indian. In the rising thunderclouds he saw the advancing forms of the *kachinas,* bearing rain for his cornfield. In the rumble of the thunder he heard the beating of the wings of a mythical bird; the whirlwind was a wandering spirit.

To the Pueblo Indian, his people lived in the center of the universe. All nature was created for him and explained in rich mythology. His complete belief produced a deep affection for those deities who made life pleasant for him, particularly those directly concerned with his sustenance: the corn mother, the squash maidens, the rain gods who brought life-giving moisture, the hunting gods who helped him find game. He willingly performed lengthy ceremonies to please them.

PAINTING BY W. LANGDON KIHN

**Geronimo, Dread Apache Raider,** led the rebel Chiricahua off an Arizona reservation in 1881. For five years he struck white settlements, killed, burned, then vanished, often into Mexico's Sierra Madre. His surrender to General Nelson Miles ended the U.S. Army's most famous Indian hunt. In 1909, at 80, he died in Oklahoma, his name destined to be an American paratroop cry.

## Snake Dancers, Potters, Weavers Characterize Pueblo Life Old and New

Rattlesnake gripped in teeth, a Hopi Snake Society dancer in full paint and regalia stamps across the ceremonial court at Walpi (below). A second priest distracts the reptile with feather whip, while the team's third member stoops to pick up another rattler. Hopi believe the venomous snakes, set free, will carry news of the ritual to pleased rain gods. Cloudbursts often follow!

At San Ildefonso (right) smoke billows from hot ashes as two women tong hand-shaped pottery from the primitive firing hearth. The craft is age-old, but the two-tone black decorative technique is new, developed here and at Santa Clara.

Hopi men, master Pueblo weavers, produce belts and sashes on an old-style lap loom (bottom right). The wife bends patiently, grinding corn meal. Kachina doll hangs beside deerskin, bringing luck to a dwelling differing little from Coronado's day. Basket of corn meal rests beside water jar in the wall niche.



PAINTINGS BY W. LANGDON KIHN

Most conspicuous among the Pueblos is the kachina cult, concerned primarily with the control of weather, particularly the bringing of rain. The kachinas are supernatural beings, said to have been created at the time the first ancestors of man emerged from the underworld. Others say they represent spirits of man's early ancestors, residing in the west in some prominent mountain.

There are many varieties of kachina, each having its own curious features and costume and each concerned with some aspect of nature connected with the health and welfare of man.

The religion of the Indian is intimate and omnipresent. He feels himself as much a part of the supernatural world as are the nature gods of his own creation. No crisis of life, no activity affecting the welfare of individual or tribe is too trivial to have its place in religion, its special rite.

Ceremony attends the individual at birth, at marriage, during sickness, and at death. It precedes planting and harvest. War expeditions, journeys—all are fitted into the religious pattern. Nothing is haphazard, nothing left to fate.

The major part of a ritual is held in secrecy in the underground ceremonial chamber, or *kiva,* with only the initiated present. Many rites, often lasting several days, end in public performances.

In the Indian's poetic mind the kiva represents the universe, a sort of primitive planetarium. The roof and walls are the firmament, the floor is the earth. Around the walls are benches for members of the secret society, and beyond these are imaginary "cloud seats" where the gods watch ceremonies in their honor.

In the center of the floor a small hole represents the *sipapu,* the sacred place where emerged the ancestral twins from whom all mankind descended. Near

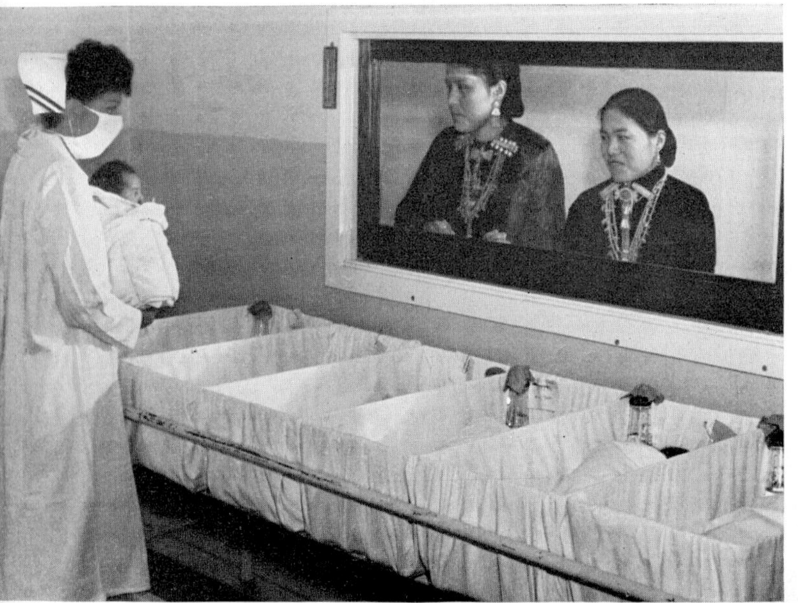

JERRY MC LAIN

**Navajo Nursery** in an up-to-date Indian hospital is a far cry indeed from the ancient cradleboard (right). Not entirely forgotten, such tight-lashed conveyances of Indian offspring once uniformly flattened the backs of round Pueblo heads. Unlike white men's children, virtually all Indian babies are born with plentiful straight black hair.

H. ARMSTRONG ROBERTS

JACK BREED

**Sand-painted Circle Will Spirit Away Boy's Illness,** so Navajo believe. The medicine man gestures swiftly; awestruck patient hides face behind bony knee. Through the strange symbols of colored sand and meal the priest summons forth healing spirits to remove the foreign substance in the sufferer's body, introduced perhaps by some witch. Itchings and skin diseases are considered by the Navajo's Pueblo neighbors to be malignant acts of the ant spirit. Thus, at Acoma, one prominent symbol is the horned toad, eater of ants. Pueblo sand paintings and curing rites resemble those of the Navajo. Few white men may witness these ceremonies, photographers almost never.

this is a larger opening covered with a plank, upon which the dancers stamp to signal denizens of the underworld that a ceremony is under way.

Masks and other sacred paraphernalia must be meticulously cared for between ceremonies by special keepers, lest ill luck and death descend on the village. Because of this fear Pueblo Indians are reluctant to part with ritual objects. Duplicates can be made and sold, however, since they acquire power only through elaborate ceremony.

An Acoma Indian described to me, with great emotion, the passing of the Scalp Society, formerly one of the most important in the pueblo. To be eligible for membership, an Acoma had to kill an enemy in combat and take his scalp.

American occupation made scalp-lifting impossible. Finally only a single aged member remained to care for the sacred materials. The headmen met in grave conference. Disaster threatened the community should the old man die, leaving the society's objects untended. They decided the society itself must be brought to an end before too late.

Thereupon the old man, carefully purifying himself, spent days in the kiva praying, making offerings, devitalizing the sacred masks and other objects of the ancient Scalp Society.

At last, the task completed, the aged scalp priest in the early morning hours carried the emasculated equipment of his beloved society up through the door of the kiva where it had been stored since before the conquistadores. All other villagers stayed hidden indoors.

Three times he descended from the rock with portions of his precious load, the last time just as the rising sun cast its ruddy hue on the summit of the Enchanted Mesa to the north. Then, bearing his burden to a point in the desert known only to himself, he buried all beneath the sands.

The sun was well above the horizon when he wearily climbed the age-old rock to enter the apparently deserted city. For him this was the end—he was unfrocked by his own will that his people might go on.

As the dwellers reappeared from their doorways and the unnatural silence ended, the old priest descended the ladder into the kiva. But now all was changed. Until this moment he had always sat in the presence of the gods. He looked at the "cloud seats" around the painted walls. He felt nothing there. The kiva was empty.

Undoubtedly the most famous of all North American ceremonies is the Hopi Snake Dance, held in alternate years at most Hopi villages. For nine days, the Antelope Society and the Snake Society pray and dance for rain.

The dance at Walpi is considered most authentic. Certainly it is most colorful. At Walpi the snakes are gripped solely by the mouths of the celebrants, no hands, and the snake is held as near the middle as possible to allow its head more freedom of movement (page 116).

Ancient priests probably would roll over in their graves if they were to see the ceremony's modern setting. Visitors converge on the mesa. Indian vendors sell soda pop and chewing gum. Native policemen busily impound cameras and lay down rules to spectators. So famed has the dance become that it is scarcely possible to crowd everyone in.

Snakes are there, ready in ceremonial

**Maize, Mainstay of Pueblo Life**

With pronged wooden digging stick, a prehistoric Acoma farmer (above) cultivates his sun-baked field. Squash grows among the cornstalks. Behind rises the famous Rock of Acoma, a sandstone mesa 357 feet above the surrounding plain. Built upon it is Sky Village, oldest continually occupied settlement in the United States. This same tribe was raising corn, squash, and beans before the coming of the Spaniards, who introduced other crops, cattle and sheep.

Laguna breadmakers (left) turn blue cornmeal dough into *piki*, crisp, wafer-thin, and palatable as the tortillas of Mexican meals. The women feed their stove dry mesquite sticks. They then spread a thin paste of cornmeal and water, with a dash of wood-ash lye, over the hot stone slab. Indians of the Southwest concoct many different dishes of this basic bread, rolling it around meat, nuts, beans, and chili peppers. Today most use metal tops on their stoves. Except for the women's silver-mounted jewelry, this scene could be prehistoric.

PAINTINGS BY W. LANGDON KIHN

crocks in the kiva. Days before, members of the Snake Society go out in pairs to gather them, the first day to the north, the second day to the west, the third to the south, the fourth to the east. Most are rattlesnakes.

On the eighth day the first dance is held outside the kiva. On the ninth day the snakes are brought out to a bower on the plaza. Then the priests, first of the Antelope and then of the Snake Societies, come from their kivas and parade four times around, stamping a foot drum each time to notify the gods below that the ceremony has begun. The priests line up facing each other.

Three at a time, Snake Society priests go to the bower. One receives a snake, grasps it in his teeth. He dances down the plaza, while the second celebrant distracts the snake with a feather whip. Then the snake is dropped, to be picked up by the third priest. As each dancer drops his snake, he returns to the bower for another, and repeats the performance.

Spectators are ignored, unless it is to lash out at them with a snake to move them back, or in anger at one's wary kick at a loose snake.

Finally, when all the snakes have been danced with, the chief Snake priest pours cornmeal in the outline of a six-segmented circle, representing the four corners of the world, its zenith, and its nadir. The snakes are thrown into the circle, and women scatter more cornmeal on them.

Then, at a signal, the Snake priests rush in and with each hand grasp as many snakes as they can hold. With squirming burdens, they run from the pueblo down to the plain below, where the snakes are carried toward the four quarters of the compass and set free as messengers to bear news of the ceremony to the rain gods.

Why are the priests not bitten? The Hopi are neither immune, nor have the fangs or poison glands been removed. Chief secret of the dangerous dance is the Indians' skill in handling and distracting the snakes. Too, for several preceding days the snakes have been handled; this takes the edge off their aggressiveness. In the kivas, the snakes are allowed to strike, thus draining their venom. Dancers are sometimes bitten, but I have never known of serious results.

The ceremonial life of the village-dwelling tribes is less elaborate than that of the Pueblos. Their religious ideas center on the interpretation of dreams, particularly

**Nomad and Pueblo Share a Starkly Beautiful Land**

Nature's palette paints a vivid Southwestern scene as the Navajo sheepherder (above) pauses to let his flock browse high above the winding river. Sheep adopted from Spanish *rancheros* in the 18th century helped the Navajo wanderer wrest a living from his harsh, yet radiant land. Sheepherding gave rise to the Navajo weaving industry. Now atomic-age wealth in oil and uranium further bolsters the tribal economy.

Ornate silverwork adorns the Zuni women (left), who display "squash blossom" necklaces, common in Pueblo land. Coming first from Spanish Mexico, these actually represent pomegranates, a fruit early Indians had never seen. Circular or oval "concha" silver ornaments mounting native turquoise are also Zuni designs copied from the Navajo, who knew no metal craft before the mid-19th century. Zuni women have worn the same hand-woven black dress since pre-Columbian days.

PAINTINGS BY W. LANGDON KIHN

among such western tribes as the Yuma, Cocopa, and Mojave.

All Yuman tribes cremate the dead, thus releasing the spirit, otherwise believed to remain in the body. When an individual died in a house, the house and all his personal property were burned.

The cremation, held in the open, presents a wild, barbaric scene. As the flames of the funeral pyre rise, mourners wail and cry, tear their hair and scratch their faces. Women rip off their dresses and throw them in the flames. Others throw in offerings, often money, asking the departing spirit to take these to their own dead relatives and friends. Mourners then fast for four days.

Several village tribes hold a strange memorial service for the dead. The annual *Károk* of the Yuma climaxes in the public burning of images of the dead, also their personal effects. The names of the dead are never again spoken.

Today the white man's iron rails bisect the great American Southwest. Automobiles roar across the land on arrow-straight roads. But behind these narrow ribbons the great canyons remain unchanged from the days of the Basket Makers. Thunderheads rise with the same magnificence they displayed when Pueblo Bonito was in flower. The machine age has come to the desert, but it has touched the Indian more lightly than many realize.

The rain priests still make their elaborate calculations; the masked dancers perform their age-old ceremonies. When the rainstorm follows, soaking the parched cornfields, the Indian, gazing beyond the gasoline haze of the highway, offers quiet thanks, serene in the knowledge that above, below, and in the four world quarters his own gods still rule.

PAINTING BY W. LANGDON KIHN

**Chief Joseph, the Xenophon of American Indians,** led his Nez Percé warriors, women, and children through the Northwest in a 1,000-mile march comparable to the ancient Greek's retreat of the Ten Thousand. With U.S. troops ahead, behind, on his flank, this "greatest of Indian strategists" outfought them several times, finally was cut off, forced to surrender only 50 miles from Canada. The "Pierced Noses" lived in the Snake and Columbia River basins in present Idaho, Oregon, Washington.

CHAPTER 5

# INDIANS OF THE FAR WEST

BETWEEN THE WASATCH RANGE of Utah and the foothills of the Sierra Nevada the traveler gazes down from his high-flying plane upon what seems to many a panorama of complete desolation —the Great American Desert.

Mile after mile of saline flats and sagebrush plains unfolds west of Great Salt Lake, where a century ago hundreds of covered wagon pioneers left their bones and those of their oxen to whiten along torturing trails.

The Great Basin was an implacable enemy to white men then. Even now, though crossed by railroads, airlines, and highways, much of it seems unfit for man or beast. Yet from this forbidding, inhospitable waste, before the white man's arrival, some 10,000 Indians wrested a living and in their way prospered.

They did this without agriculture, or tools save crude implements fashioned from sticks and stones, without even adequate clothing or shelter from the severe cold of winter or summer's blazing heat. Rarely in human annals can be found as striking an example of man's adapting to an unfriendly environment.

In long-past geologic ages the Great Basin was a region of lakes and lush forests. And so it was when man first entered the scene, we have learned through scattered excavations in caves and near old lake terraces. Now carbon-14 dating at Lewisville, Texas, suggests an antiquity for aboriginal Americans of 35,000 B.C. and beyond.

With passing centuries rainfall became scanty, winters extremely cold, summers hot. Food grew scarce through the parched and withered land. The Indian had to utilize every form of it he could get. Big game was scarce. Even bison, which had ranged most of Utah and northern Nevada until A.D. 1500, had retreated from the Great Basin.

Forests gone, the Indian used sagebrush to make rude shelters, often merely roofless semicircles, which served as windbreaks and gave only scant protection against rain and snow.

White travelers who had encountered the colorful Plains and Pueblo tribes expressed scorn for Indians of the Great Basin, who belong almost exclusively to one linguistic stock, the Shoshonean. Exaggerated descriptions pictured them as living at the level of animals, always half starved, hibernating without food like bears in caves, whence they emerged in the spring, crawling on hands and knees to eat grass.

To the disgust of early observers the Shoshoni ate crickets, lizards, snakes, gophers, and roots. However, since one's diet is largely a matter of custom, a Shoshoni might be just as annoyed at seeing a white man eat crab or lobster.

Nuts of the pine tree, or piñon, were the basic food. In southern areas, seeds of the mesquite bean, ground into flour, and the agave or century plant, roasted in stone-lined pits, also were favored.

Skillful basket weavers, the Great Basin tribes collected roots and the seeds of wild rye and other grasses in large conical carrying baskets and processed them in basketry trays (page 131).

Food collecting was often a community effort. When Mormon crickets or long-horn grasshoppers swarmed, the Indians encircled an area with converging fire. The singed insects accumulated in enormous piles in the center.

Group drives caught the abundant jack rabbits, good for food, and whose skins made winter robes. Nets of twisted grass were strung in a quarter-mile arc. Entire families spread out in a line, beat the brush and drove the rabbits before them into the barrier. The fast and wary antelope also were corralled and dispatched with bow and arrow.

The quest for food so preoccupied Great Basin tribes, living in widely scattered groups, that they had little time for dances or courtship. Most marriages resulted when families gathered at rare intervals to sing, dance, and gamble for a week

**White Deerskins, Yellow Water Lilies, Gay Beads Marked Indian Life on Pacific Slopes**

Hupa tribesmen (right) usher in the new year in the Trinity River Valley of northwest California by parading treasured albino deerskins on high poles. Chief dancers in the 10-day September ritual wear crowns of sea-lion tusks, carry sacred obsidian knives. Shell beads adorn dancers' necks; headdresses are of wolf pelt. Hupa hunters masked man odor by bathing and smoke, got within easy bowshot of game, disguised as deer. So well did they play the part that panthers sometimes pounced on them.

Oregon's Klamath Indians (below) harvest seedpods of the yellow water lily in long dugout canoes, sun-dry, pound, and winnow them into *wokas*, a highly prized food. The supply was enormous; Klamath Marsh alone had 15 square miles of solid water-lily growth. The hardy Klamath never took the warpath against whites, but raided other tribes for female slaves.

A Yakima girl (lower right) rides in beaded finery behind the high, decorated pommel of a Spanish-type saddle. Otterskins wrap her long braids; beaded cape is elkskin, her earrings are shell. The Yakima lived along the Columbia, Yakima, and Wenatchee Rivers in Washington.

PAINTINGS BY W. LANGDON KIHN

or two when food was plentiful. Since the two sexes were not always equal in number, a man might have two or more wives, a woman more than one husband. Taking sisters or brothers as plural spouses was considered a wise precaution against jealousy.

Not until about 1840 did white immigration into the Far West begin in earnest. Starting with caravans on the Oregon Trail, and the Mormon settlements around Great Salt Lake, it reached its peak in the California gold rush. The most direct routes traversed the heart of the Great Basin.

Tens of thousands of gold seekers crossed the desert during the rush years. Hollow-cheeked and red-eyed from heat and acrid dust, they cursed this "useless" country, scorned the "Diggers," as they contemptuously called the root-gathering natives. But when rich lodes of gold and silver were struck in western Nevada, miners stampeded back across the Sierras into the Basin.

With recently acquired horses and guns the Indians, particularly the Ute, put up stern resistance for a while. Then in 1869 the golden spike driven at Promontory Point, Utah, joined the last sections of the transcontinental railroad. Ranchers came. Grazing livestock reduced the edible plants. White settlers began cutting down for fuel the piñon trees, the red man's most important source of food. The aborigines had lost their sun-scorched kingdom.

In this period there grew to manhood in Mason Valley, Nevada, a Paiute of lowly origin who became known as Wovoka, "the Cutter." He never left his little native valley. Although industrious and of good character, he was distin-

**Chumash Mariners Return from Sea.** Bearskin-clad captain orders his craft carried above reach of tide or storm along California's Santa Barbara coast. With flint tools and patient skill, Chumash tribesmen built the New World's only planked canoes. Lacking big trees for dugouts, they split planks from driftwood. These they shaped and smoothed. Along the edges they drilled holes, "sewed" the planks together with fiber cords, calked the seams with asphalt. Keel, endposts, and a thwart amidships formed the frame; shells and paint gave decoration. Double-bladed paddles propelled the light craft, 12 to 25 feet in length, carrying 2 to 13 fishermen. Sail power was unknown to pre-Columbian Indians of North America.

**Indian Nets Chinook from the Churning Columbia.** Salmon, migrating upriver to spawn and die, leap up the thundering green-white curtain of Celilo Falls. Braced on ancestral fishing stand, clad only in breechclout, this Indian scoops up fish just as modern Indians in dungarees and crew shirts were later to do, by treaty right, from similar platforms at the same site. Lewis and Clark in 1805 portaged around the falls, noted stacks of salmon "neatly preserved." Salmon was the Columbia River Indians' chief food and commodity of trade.

Now reservoir waters backed up by the new Dalles Dam have buried Celilo Falls. The U. S. Government has paid the Yakima and other tribes more than $26,000,000 for the loss of their traditional fishing grounds.

PAINTINGS BY W. LANGDON KIHN

guished neither in intellect nor aggressiveness. Yet in his early thirties he became one of the most influential Indians in North America. From Gulf of Mexico to Canadian border pilgrims came to his little dome-shaped tule hut. Wovoka was originator and prophet of the Ghost Dance movement, which excited great unrest among Western tribes.

About 1888 Wovoka, already a medicine man of repute, had his great revelation. While he lay ill with fever, an eclipse of the sun awed the Indians. Wovoka believed that his soul had traveled to the spirit world and there consulted with the Indian god who revealed to him that the Indians would regain their ancient inheritance and be rejoined by departed relatives and friends.

Wovoka said he was given a set of songs and dances for the Indians to practice to ready themselves for the great day of deliverance. He attributed no supernatural powers to himself, but considered that he had been chosen as prophet to herald the coming restoration.

The new movement spread like wildfire from Nevada to tribes east of the Rockies, and culminated in the killing of Sitting Bull and the massacre at Wounded Knee (South Dakota) in 1890.

Among the American Indians many such messianic movements arose in the wake of white domination, including the great Pontiac Conspiracy (1763–65).

First to describe aboriginal life in the Plateau area north of the Great Basin were Lewis and Clark, who arrived at the headwaters of the Missouri in 1805. There they noted many traits of buffalo-hunting Plains tribes among the northeastern Shoshoni, who had adopted the tepee, the rawhide container, and danced the characteristic Sun Dance.

Obtaining horses from the Shoshoni, Lewis and Clark pushed on through western Montana territory of the Flatheads. The name of this Salishan tribe was bestowed, not because they deformed their heads, but because, unlike their neighbors to the west, they left their skulls as Nature formed them—flat on top. Living on fish and game, the Flatheads built their houses underground, roofed with cedar-bark mats laid over poles and covered with earth.

Lewis and Clark found similar men's and women's pit houses among the Nez Percé, accommodating from 10 to 15 persons each, and community dwellings housing as many as 50 families. Each village had a large ceremonial or dance house.

The semi-dugout house in various forms appeared among tribes farther west—the Wallawalla, the Palus, the Umatilla, the Tenino, the Yakima (page 127), and the Klikitat. Typical of the Northwest, it extended well into California.

The Nez Percé tribes, occupying the valleys of the Snake River and the Columbia as far as The Dalles, were so named because French trappers reported that tribes in the vicinity pierced the nose to receive a shell ornament. The Nez Percé, so far as is now known, were never given to the practice!

They were courageous fighters. Rebelling at an order restricting them to a small reservation in Idaho, Chief Joseph, renowned among American Indian leaders (page 124), won several victories over United States troops, then led his people in 1877 in a masterful 1,000-mile retreat through Idaho and Montana.

Joseph's speech at the time of his surrender expresses the hopelessness that came to tribe after tribe as they retreated before the inexorable tide of the white man's advance.

"I am tired of fighting," he said. "Our chiefs are killed. Looking Glass is dead. Toohulhulsote is dead. The old men are all dead. It is the young men who say yes or no. He who led the young men is dead. It is cold and we have no blankets. The little children are freezing to death.

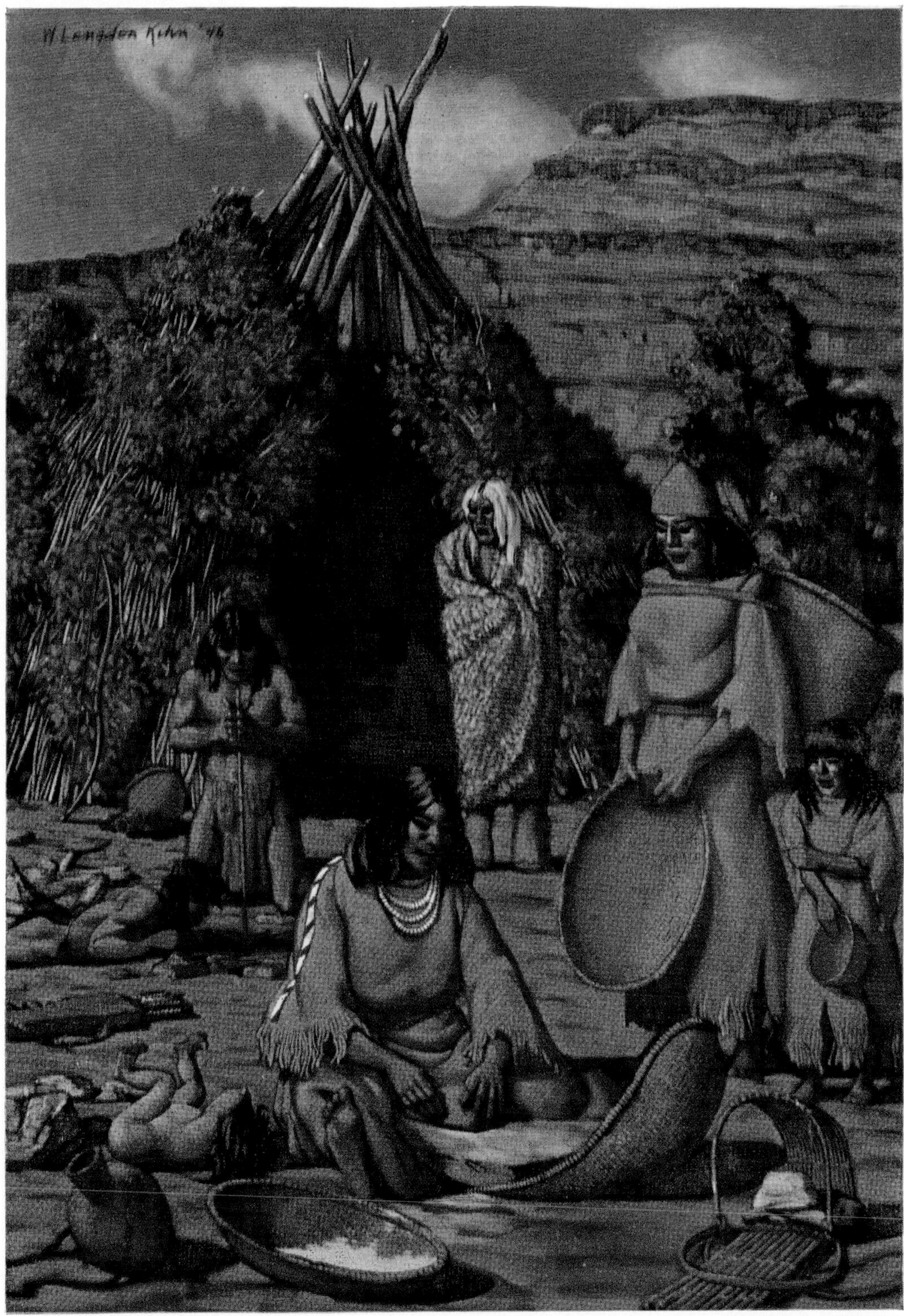


PAINTING BY W. LANGDON KIHN

**Paiute Subsist on a Lean Land.** Roaming the arid reaches of the Great Basin, the Paiute lived a primitive existence unchanged for centuries. As these women are doing, they gathered and ground wild seeds into meal. Their few utensils, even water containers and cooking vessels, were baskets. Men kindle fire by friction before the crude brush hut. Child's hooded cradle lies in right foreground.

My people, some of them, have run away to the hills and have no blankets, no food. No one knows where they are —perhaps freezing to death. I want to have time to look for my children and see how many of them I can find. Maybe I shall find them among the dead.

"Hear me, my chiefs. I am tired. My heart is sick and sad. From where the sun now stands I will fight no more forever."

Unlike the forest-dotted, low-lying region east of the Mississippi, the Far West is a land of tremendous topographic diversity. Death Valley, lowest point in the United States, and Mount Whitney, one of the highest, are within sight of each other. Burning sands give way to verdant meadow and towering evergreen forest.

The Indians there were as diversified as the setting, whose rugged barriers circumscribed their movements.

Tribes living in the Columbia River region had, in their salmon runs, better food sources than tribes of the inhospitable Great Basin (page 128). Best off from the standpoint of abundant natural resources and genial climate were tribes dwelling between the Sierra Nevada-Cascade Range and the Pacific Coast.

Here, in one of the most complex ethnological areas in the New World, tribes of two chief linguistic stocks, Hokan and Penutian, lived under nearly perfect conditions for primitive man. Deer, elk, rabbits, and squirrels abounded. Marshes and lakes teemed with waterfowl, rivers and ocean with fish, and along the coast there were clams, mussels, abalones, crabs, and crayfish.

Tribes of extreme southern California—the Mohave, the Yuma, the Kamia, and the Diegueño—learned from tribes of northern Mexico and Pueblo tribes of the Southwest how to grow maize, beans, squash, and to make good pottery. Yet in the "Promised Land" of central California, now one of the world's most productive regions, agriculture was as unknown as famine.

Acorns were the Indian staff of life. These were gathered in the fall, ground and leached, then made into a thick soup cooked by hot stones dropped into a tight-woven basket.

In keeping with the mild climate, clothing was simple. Only in cold weather did the men wear as much as a skin wrapped around the hips. Women wore double aprons of fringed buckskin, shredded bark, grass, or fiber cordage: a small apron suspended from the waist in front, a larger one behind. As footwear, central tribes wore deerskin socks; southern tribes, sandals of twisted agave fiber.

California tribes produced no cloth. The nearest approaches to it were finger-woven fiber bags and twined

**Indian Converts Dance Before Spanish Mission**

Now extinct, the Costanoan tribe lived along the California coast from Monterey to the Golden Gate. They were early converts of the Mission of St. Francis, which gave the city of San Francisco its name. The original chapel founded by Spanish priests in 1776 still stands within the city, well-preserved. It is known today as Mission Dolores.

An artist with Russia's first round-the-world expedition, which touched here in 1805, sketched the scene which Mr. Kihn painted above. Indians, after Sunday Mass, dance in ancient tribal fashion while two friars look on. Vulture feathers made the dark ceremonial bonnets worn by the dancers.

robes made of twisted rabbitskin strips. As basket weavers, however, these tribes were without peer.

Basket weaving reached its peak among the Pomo, who produced the finest feathered baskets and practiced a wide variety of weaving techniques. The peace-loving Pomo were also chief minters for a large area, making currency from clamshells and magnesite. They counted, using a unit of 100 fours.

Many California tribes had hereditary chiefs. More powerful still were the medicine men. Some specialists in the cure and prevention of snake bite handled live rattlesnakes in their ceremonies. The bear doctor was feared, for he had the power to kill enemies by turning himself into a grizzly bear.

As among Indian tribes in general, the medicine man claimed his power from a vision, produced by fasting or drugs, in which he met and conversed with some animal who taught him how to contact the spirit world. His cure often was to suck out of the patient the invading object causing the disease. This might be a piece of flint, a live lizard, or a spider. He could cause death just as well, it was believed, by mixing poison with some part of his intended victim, such as a hair or a nail paring.

An old Indian woman of my acquaintance had a bag filled with toenail and fingernail parings she had saved all her life, fearing lest they fall into the hands of a person who might harm her.

The California Indians first became known to the white man in 1542 when Juan Rodríguez Cabrillo sailed among the channel islands and along the Santa Barbara coast. There he encountered the Chumash Indians, in many respects the most advanced of California's tribes.

Villages in this, the most densely populated section of California, consisted of dome-shaped communal houses accommodating 40 or 50 persons. Built of willow poles covered with tule mats, these large circular dwellings were unique in two respects. They were partitioned into rooms, and in these rooms were platform beds supported on posts.

Fine basket weavers and skillful wood carvers, the Chumash also made beautifully formed and polished pots and animal, bird, and fish carvings in soapstone. Most remarkable were their planked ocean-going canoes (page 129).

California Indians farther north were first described by Francis Fletcher, chaplain of Sir Francis Drake's *Golden Hind,* which put in north of San Francisco in 1579. These were undoubtedly the coastal Miwok.

The natives received the Englishmen with elaborate ceremonies and loud wailings. The women tore out their hair and lacerated their bodies until they were covered with blood. Drake was crowned with an elaborate feather crown; yards of shell beads were placed around his neck. The puzzled Englishmen did not realize that the Indians considered them ancestors returned from the dead.

The first Franciscan mission in California was founded at San Diego in 1769. By 1823, twenty other missions stood north along the coast to beyond San Francisco. The Indians met the priests

**Paiute Prophet Wovoka Spellbinds His People.** In the campfire's eerie light, chanting men and women, wild eyes riveted on the figure at center, circle slowly, keeping time to ritual songs taught them by the prophet. Frenzy mounts. Swaying dancers crumple to the ground, sprawl in prolonged trances. Devotees ready themselves to be delivered from bonds, restored to their heritage, reunited with loved ones. Stemming from Wovoka's fevered revelation of 1888, the cult spread swiftly from tribe to tribe. Its message of hope fired deep longings of the Indians, defeated, confined to reservations, their culture, their ancestral way of life gone. It triggered the Sioux uprising of 1890.

PAINTINGS BY W. LANGDON KIHN

**"Big Heads" Dance to Save the Earth.** Arrayed in savage splendor, secret cult members meet before their round house for one of a vital series of ceremonies held October to May. They believed the world would disintegrate if dances ceased. This cult, originating among southern Wintun Indians, flourished in central California, and took the name of the Kuksu, or "Big Head," Dance. Pincushion-like headdresses measure four feet across; feathers or poppies tip the slender rods. Dancers carry flag, bird-bone whistle, magic staff, gourd rattle, and bow and deer-head quiver. Stamping on a foot drum, they will perform inside the ceremonial lodge. Boys became cult novices at an early age.

in peace, were forcibly converted to Christianity, made dependents of the missions (page 133), and held there by Spanish troops from near-by presidios. Discipline and strange tasks as well as the new religion drastically changed their lives.

In 1834 the Mexican Government took over the missions, making token provision for tribes settled around them. But the Indians had already lost the self-assurance that went with their own culture and had not learned to adapt to the new. Their health and spirits had begun to fail. They soon lost their restored lands, their numbers fell, and the mission tribes were on the way to extinction.

The 1849 gold rush concentrated in the north and along the Sierras where the missions had not penetrated. In early gold-rush days the Indians' lot was hard. Miners hunted them like wild game for sport. The Modoc, the Shasta, and other of the more warlike tribes resisted, but opposition was short-lived (page 18).

Following the mining came the State's amazing agricultural development. As the white population increased, many tribes became extinct; of others only a handful of survivors remains.

To white men California is a paradise gained. To the Indians, a paradise lost.

PAINTING BY W. LANGDON KIHN

**Memories of Past Days' Glory Show in This Niska Chief's Face** as he wears the carved totem of his clan. A cannery worker in modern-day British Columbia, he poses in old-time regalia, holding dyed-feather wands, the eagle of his mythological origin crowning his head. Denim work shirt peeks from under blue wool blanket adorned with red-flannel design, rows of pearl buttons, wisps of swan's-down.

## CHAPTER 6

# INDIANS OF THE NORTH PACIFIC COAST

MOST ARISTOCRATIC of all Indians north of Mexico were the tribes which dwelt on our wild and beautiful North Pacific coast. Theirs was a civilization rivaled, above the Rio Grande, only by the Pueblo Indians of Arizona and New Mexico.

Their realism in dance and impersonation was matched by the skill of those who designed the masks and costumes. With their famous totem poles, Northwest Coast carvers and painters produced what many modern critics consider the finest art work ever developed by the American Indian.

Their art found further expression in the skillful weaving of baskets and blankets, stonework, and in the working of native copper and, later, silver. Yet of two developments usually considered as signs of an advanced culture—agriculture and pottery making—they had neither.

Unlike the vast majority of their North American kinsmen, these tribes did not develop democracy. Rather, they set much store by wealth, family connections, and possessing slaves. Social-climbing and crushing one's rivals in wealth and prestige became prime goals. In their celebrated *potlatch* ceremonies they carried "keeping up with the Joneses" to fantastic extremes.

Interestingly, the great impetus to this late-flowering culture came from the white man. In prehistoric times the amount of property a man could accumulate limited his ability to advance his status. But with the coming of the white man's fur trade and steel tools, the Indian's rather simple social system became greatly elaborated.

Like the introduction of the gun among Eastern Woodlands tribes, and the horse to the Plains, the fur-trade wealth pouring into the Pacific Northwest brought into high relief already existing cultural traits. Yet nowhere else did white influence have such spectacular effect. From Puget Sound to the Copper River Delta in southern Alaska, Indian culture burgeoned like the flare of a skyrocket before finally spluttering out.

Who were these fascinating tribes? Northernmost was the Tlingit, who came into contact with the Eskimo and the Ahtena Indians. Visited by Russians in 1741, they were the first Northwest Indians to encounter European civilization.

Next came the Haida, who extended from southern Prince of Wales Island down through the Queen Charlotte Islands; and the Tsimshian, who lived in the basins of the Nass and Skeena Rivers.

South of the Skeena River to the northern coast of Vancouver Island dwelt the Kwakiutl, whose territory was almost split in two by a Salishan tribe, the Bellacoola, who lived along Dean Channel and the Bella Coola River.

Southernmost tribe was the Nootka,

**In the Frog Clan's Carved and Painted House, Tlingit Spin and Weave**

While her companion rolls mountain goats' hair into thread, the weaver copies designs from the pattern board to her right. Unseen warp is of cedar-bark threads. On this simple crossbar "loom," without using shuttle, heddle, batten, or other such aid, Chilkat Tlingit produced masterpieces of finger weaving. A finished example is draped over the chief. Festive cedar-bark collar is worn by man at right. Drab trade goods supplanted the gay Chilkat blanket, but its weaving has been revived among this southeastern Alaska tribe.

settled along the deep-indented west coast of Vancouver Island.

Heavy rainfall and the tempering climatic influence of the Japan Current characterize the region. Forests of gigantic evergreen trees mantle rugged mountains that rise abruptly from the sea and march inland in an almost unbroken succession of ranges to the Rocky Mountains. A jagged chain of islands, separated by a maze of sea channels, skirts the entire coast.

In this crumpled realm of forest, mountain, and ocean, these warlike tribes, among the few in North America to wear body armor, jealously kept their independence and spoke unrelated languages. Yet their homeland constituted one of the most distinct cultural areas in North America (group area map, page 24). Their influence extended as far north and west as the Aleutians, as

far east as the Mackenzie River, and as far south as California.

Theirs was a maritime culture. Villages hugged the seacoast or main waterways, where the sea pushes fingers far into the mountains in sunken valleys, or fiords, and the great rivers cut their way through the barrier which isolates the coastal region from the interior. Fish and whales were the buffalo of Northwest tribes; seaweed, roots, and berries their maize; the gigantic ocean-going cedar canoe their horse.

Basic unit of exchange was the woolen trade blanket. The value of any object was expressed in blankets. In earlier times blankets of sea-otter fur were apparently used, but the complex financial system of these wealth-minded Indians probably did not develop until after the advent of the trade blanket.

For high-denomination bank notes, the Indians used curious large shield-shaped plaques of copper, painted and engraved, whose value spiraled higher and higher through sale and resale.

**Aleut Women Weave Watertight Baskets, Split Strands with Fingernails**

Beside the weaver, a tub of water keeps straw moist. Bearded man descends notched log ladder, of a kind used by Siberian tribes. Entrance to this barabara, or Asia-type pit house, was through a roof hole. Roof was sod over dry grass supported by driftwood poles. In this typical Aleutian Islands community house, each family had its matted-off quarters. As many as 150 people lived in a single underground dwelling up to 240 feet long, heated and lighted with seal- or whale-oil lamps of stone. Modern Aleuts live in frame houses.



PAINTINGS BY W. LANGDON KIHN

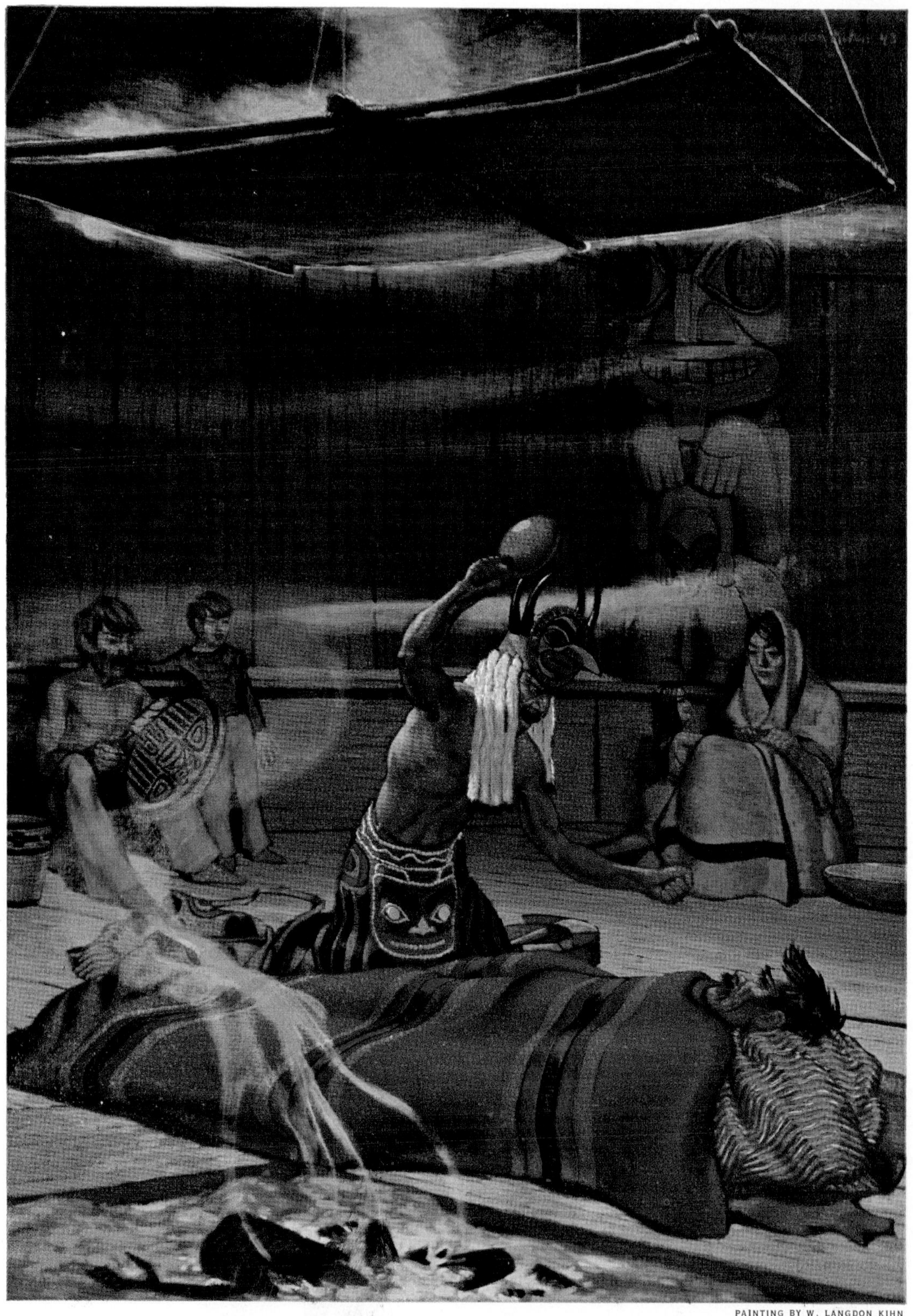

PAINTING BY W. LANGDON KIHN

**Shaman Wears Spirit Helper's Headdress,** his earthly apprentice beats a drum. The Tlingit medicine man shakes his rattle, conjures away the malady. Bark mat below smoke hole shields fireplace from rain.

Purchase of a well-known copper constituted one of the most elaborate of Northwest Coast ceremonies. Coppers were always sold to rivals. If an offer to sell a copper was refused, this was an admission that the rival group could not raise sufficient wealth to make the purchase, and the group was correspondingly humiliated. Therefore, when a man accepted such an offer, all members of his group had to back him to the limit with loans of blankets. His wealth represented the holdings of the group.

Once the offer was accepted, details of the purchase were arranged in advance. The public sale, however, resembled an auction, with lavish display of the blankets offered in payment. The intended purchaser first made a low offer, at once accepted by the owner, who had to show how little he cared for money. But his friends vigorously protested and demanded more, citing previous sales. This continued until the agreed-on price was finally reached and the property transfer took place.

Each copper had a name, and its history and value were well known. In 1893 one copper worth 5,000 blankets was called "Making the House Empty of Blankets." Another valued at 6,000 blankets was named "Steelhead Salmon"—it glides out of one's hands like a salmon. A third copper worth 7,000 blankets was called "All Other Coppers Are Ashamed to Look at It."

Not only the sale of coppers, but the building of houses, the erection of totem poles, memorial services, the naming of children of important families, or their initiation into secret societies served as occasions for the big winter ceremonials of Northwest Coast tribes. Feasting and singing, spectacular costumed performances, and formal distribution of property marked these events.

Potlatch, the general name for such rites, is taken from the Chinook jargon, general trade language of the region, and is a corruption of the Nootka word *patshatl,* meaning "giving."

Details of the potlatch differed among the several tribes, but the underlying idea was always the same—to acquire rank and social status for the giver of the ceremony and his descendants. Not only did the giver gain much prestige by stripping himself of possessions, but he actually became potentially richer than before. Self-esteem dictated that when others gave potlatches they must return to him an even greater gift than the one they had received.

This complex ritual developed out of the widespread aboriginal custom of exchanging gifts as goodwill tokens. The obligation of a return gift gave rise to the white expression, "Indian giving."

Chiefs also rivaled one another in destroying property. At a formal feast to which a rival was invited, a chief might burn blankets, destroy a canoe, kill a slave, or break a copper. If the rival was not able to destroy quickly an equal or greater amount of property, his name was "broken," his prestige lost.

No modern diplomats were ever more sensitive to protocol than the prestige-seeking Northwest Coast Indians. Seating at formal feasts was carefully arranged according to rank, and aristocrats were ever alert to see that the family's prestige was maintained.

If a dignified person should slip and fall in the mud and thus be made to appear ridiculous, he could prevent any further reference to the incident by giving a small face-saving potlatch.

Similarly if his group received an accidental favor from the opposing group, such as the rescue of a drowning child, a potlatch would be given at once—not to express gratitude, but to prevent his group from being laughed at for loss of dignity.

Vengeance potlatches were given by an individual insulted by a member of a rival group, if the person delivering the insult was of equal rank. One ignored, as well as he could, insults from a person whose clan wealth was greater. Insults from individuals of lower social status were beneath notice. Since blood cannot be extracted from a turnip, where would be the profit in potlatching such a one?

The basic social fabric out of which these complex ceremonial systems developed was one of three social grades: aristocrats, commoners, and slaves.

The aristocrat inherited status through his mother's line, and was respected in proportion to the number and elaborateness of the potlatches he gave.

While the individual who had not inherited caste could gain approval by giving potlatches, aristocrats never accepted him as a social equal. They regarded him a newly rich social climber.

Derelictions of any individual reflected on the entire family group. Thus, when parents were too lazy or devoid of pride to give potlatches, or left orphaned children, a paternal uncle ceremonially adopted the youngsters to save the family name, thereby giving them the same status as his own children.

Slaves, obtained by war, purchase, or through debt, had no rights, were not permitted to marry, and were regarded as much the property of their owner as was his canoe. As a rule, these menials were badly treated, and might even be sacrificed at potlatches to the greater glory of their owners. Later, when white occupation made it difficult for the Indian to kill slaves, he made the same gesture of relinquishing property in a less dramatic way by freeing the slave.

All Northwest Coast tribes are divided into two or more groups which control marriage and descent. Among the Haida, everyone is born either a Raven or an Eagle. One must always marry in the opposite group; so when a man is a Raven, his wife and children are Eagles, since descent is reckoned only through the mother's family line.

While the southern Tlingit are divided into Ravens and Wolves, the Tsimshian have four groups: Eagles, Wolves, Ravens, and Killer Whales.

Among the Kwakiutl, the principal object of marriage was to acquire, through the wife, the clan crest and privileges for the expected children. This was achieved through a property exchange.

The husband paid the wife's father an agreed amount of property at marriage. The wife was then given to him as first installment on the return payment. When a child was born, the clan privileges were formally given, along with material property.

With this payment, the marriage was considered annulled, since the father had redeemed the payment made on his daughter. She could now stay with her husband or leave, as she chose. Sometimes the husband made a new payment so that he might retain a claim on her.

The ceremony in which the marriage money plus interest was returned to the son-in-law, along with delivery of the clan crest, was usually a part of one of the big winter potlatches. Dramatizations of mythological episodes in the clan tradition accompanied the ceremony.

Dr. Franz Boaz, when among the Kwakiutl some 70 years ago, heard of a man punishing his father-in-law who had delayed repaying the purchase money and evaded giving his name to the son-in-law.

The son-in-law carved an image representing his wife and invited the populace to a feast. Placing a stone around the image's neck, he threw it into the sea. Thus he humiliated his father-in-law and indicated that he regarded the daughter as worthless.

Each clan was in effect an extended family, headed by a hereditary leader. Among the Tsimshian, Haida, and Tlingit, the heir was eldest son of the chief's eldest sister. Among the other tribes he was son of the chief. As symbol of the group, the chief had custody

PAINTING BY W. LANGDON KIHN

**A Tense Moment for the Nootka.** Will the harpoon stay fixed in the sounding whale? Soon sealskin floats will be attached. One blow from the giant flukes will smash the frail canoe, or it may be towed for days before lances finish the beast. Bolder Nootka leaped with spears on wounded whales' backs. The successful hunt meant flesh and skin for food, intestines for oil containers, sinew for rope, blubber to be eaten or made into oil. Seals and porpoises were harpooned from canoes in similar manner.

**Celebrants Arrive in Totem Pole Town for the Potlatch Ceremony.** Richly attired clansmen, actors in masks crowd painted cedar canoes paddled by mustached slaves. Townspeople emerge from wooden community houses to cluster in welcome along water's edge beneath a forest of storied poles.

PAINTING BY W. LANGDON KIHN

From Oregon to Alaska, the potlatch was winter's main social event. Hooded men impersonated legendary animals. Dancing, singing, feasting led up to extravagant giving or destruction of property in which the host impoverished himself and clan in a frenzied bid for prestige or to break a rival.

**Bellacoola Girl in Party Dress** wears ermine-trimmed raven headdress, carries raven rattle as proud symbols of her clan. Silver bracelet represents a bear. Swan's-down, sign of good will, clings to her button blanket, will float off like snow when she dances. Decorating woolen trade blankets with mother-of-pearl buttons was popular among Northwest tribes in the 1880's and 1890's. The Bellacoola still dwell on ancestral lands in British Columbia.

of the tribal wealth, lands, and produce.

Every foot of territory throughout the area, including coastal water, was "owned." This implied, rather than ownership of the land itself, the right to hunt, fish, and exploit products of the soil.

Usually the first seasonal harvest of stream and forest was given to the chief as token of his custodianship. When fish or berries came in season the chief would call on the group to build a fish trap or to hold a community berry gathering. The resulting food supply he used to give a general feast, during which he formally announced his hereditary right to the use of the spot, then told the group to go ahead and use it for themselves.

Violation of rights to such "owned" places was a frequent cause of wars. The desire to obtain prestige through war honors and to acquire captives for slaves was another motive. But revenge for real or fancied injuries was the most common reason these bellicose aborigines took up their bows and arrows, spears, copper knives, and stone-headed clubs and went into battle.

As protective armor troops wore wooden helmets and sleeveless shirts either of rawhide in several thicknesses or of vertical wooden rods, tightly bound with stout twine.

The heads of slain enemies were generally taken as trophies. In later times, the Tlingit collected scalps, taking all the head hair and the ears. The much-valued war honors, unlike other honors,

**Shaiks, Chief of the Tlingit,** carries a Killer Whale staff of office. "Bear teeth" in his cedar headdress are abalone shells. Human hair adorns hat and staff. His mustache belies the common misconception that American Indians had no facial hair. Most tribesmen zealously plucked it out. Hairs were coarser, scantier than among whites, but some tribal elders and, in the Pacific Northwest, young men as well, wore mustaches and beards.

PAINTINGS BY W. LANGDON KIHN

had to be earned and could not be transmitted through inheritance.

Captives did not always supinely accept their fate. A totem pole at one Tsimshian village has carved on it the figure of a woman holding a severed head. This commemorates an occasion when the Haida raided the Tsimshian and took a number of captives. One woman escaped and returned to her people. However, she first went to the trouble of killing and beheading her captor, bringing his head with her as souvenir.

The fact that this is recorded on a totem pole shows that it is over-simplification to say that totem poles were purely heraldic in nature and represented only the owner's mythologic genealogy. They might record any notable experience of the owner, such as being the first of his group to see a white man, or being converted to Christianity. One man carved on his pole a representation of the Tsar of Russia, to commemorate the sale of Alaska to the United States. Several Tlingit poles bore the likeness of Abraham Lincoln wearing top hat and beard.

There was nothing sacred or religious about totem poles. They represented the owner's claim to fame and were a means of displaying to the public his prestige and social standing. Sometimes, as a touch of vanity, the figure of the owner is shown holding a valuable possession to indicate his wealth. Again, a rival might be depicted in ridiculous light.

For example, a man of the Raven clan gave a potlatch to a rival of the Killer

Whale group, bestowing the usual gifts. The latter became a drunkard and could not return the gifts as required by social law. So the Raven man carved on his totem pole the figure of a Raven biting the dorsal fin of a Killer Whale. The impoverished Killer Whale representative could do nothing to offset the affront.

The wood-carving art of the North Pacific Coast was already fully developed by mid-18th century, as shown by the smaller objects collected by Captain Cook, Capt. George Dixon, Malaspina, and other explorers. But totem-pole descriptions begin to occur in travelers' writings only about the year 1790, by which time a few poles were standing in some Haida villages in the Queen Charlotte Islands. The custom probably did not originate much before this period.

The totem pole doubtless evolved from the practice of carving the front house post. With carving facilitated by iron tools introduced by the Russians about 1750, it is easy to see how the desire of the Haida or Tsimshian aristocrats to outdo one another in making bigger and better house posts would result, first, in a house post reaching above the roof of the house, and, finally, in one being erected as a detached mast.

Among the interior villages of the Tsimshian, poles sometimes more than 50 feet high were placed in a row, well in front of the houses. With the introduction of commercial paints, a rich palette of colors replaced the simple red, black, and white of the earliest poles.

Reaching its peak development between 1840 and 1880, totem-pole art rapidly declined when the native cultures began to break down as a result of ever-increasing contact with the whites.

Some specialists, to whom this carving art appears Asiatic in inspiration, have suggested that it may have been introduced by Polynesian or Asiatic crews of early European voyagers. Many such sailors, it is known, settled among the Indians.

Northwest Coast carvers and painters produced highly realistic designs. Some images or masks were actual portraits. Mostly, however, they preferred grotesque representation of semianimal or semihuman mythological beings.

A curious stylization developed wherein the artist dissected his subject, representing features symbolic of the creature he wished to portray.

The faces of a man, a killer whale, and a beaver, as carved on a totem pole or a box, might all look essentially alike. Erect ears on top of the head, however, showed beaver and killer whale to be animals. They were further distinguished by characteristic symbols: the dorsal fin of the killer whale, and the flat cross-hatched tail and long incisor teeth of the beaver.

Some of the carved masks used in dramatic performances were elaborate affairs, with movable parts attached to strings cleverly operated by the performers. Uncanny jugglery and sleight of hand also were part of these presentations, probably unequaled in their electrifying realism and dramatic power among American aborigines.

With performers elaborately costumed and masked to represent animals and legendary beings, these theatrical displays by secret societies dealt with mythological subject matter, supernatural "seizures," and miraculous restorations. Nevertheless they were more social than religious. A feature of many was the initiation of new members into the society.

In a typical initiation, the novice, captured by his hereditary spirit animal and taken to the forest, later was returned, apparently dead. Ceremonial attendants restored him to life. Such ceremonies usually lasted four days. Two described by mid-19th century travelers well illustrate the vividness of these displays.

"During the song and dance, which at first seemed to present nothing peculiar, a well-known slave . . . suddenly ceased dancing and fell down on the ground, apparently in a dying state, his face covered with blood.

"He did not move or speak, his head fell on one side, his limbs were drawn up, and he certainly presented a ghastly

**Haida Raise a Totem Pole**

Clan dignitaries, guests in ceremonial robes assemble as men strain at the ropes to erect a lofty memorial to a departed chief. Downward from the Eagle clan totem at the crest, the figures represent the chief himself, the Thunderbird, and one of the chief's ancestors. Projections on other poles symbolize fins of the Killer Whale.

Totem poles are not idols, but proclamations of prestige. Hollowed at back for easier handling, these painted masts represent months of carving by well-paid professionals. Standing them alone was a late development. Earlier poles formed part of the house framework, and were pierced by door openings.

Christianized Haida abandoned their villages around 1880, zealously cut down poles or sold them. At Tsimshian settlements on the upper Skeena River the totem-pole custom persisted until after 1900. Poles of recent vintage erected outside their proper region are imitations.

PAINTING BY W. LANGDON KIHN

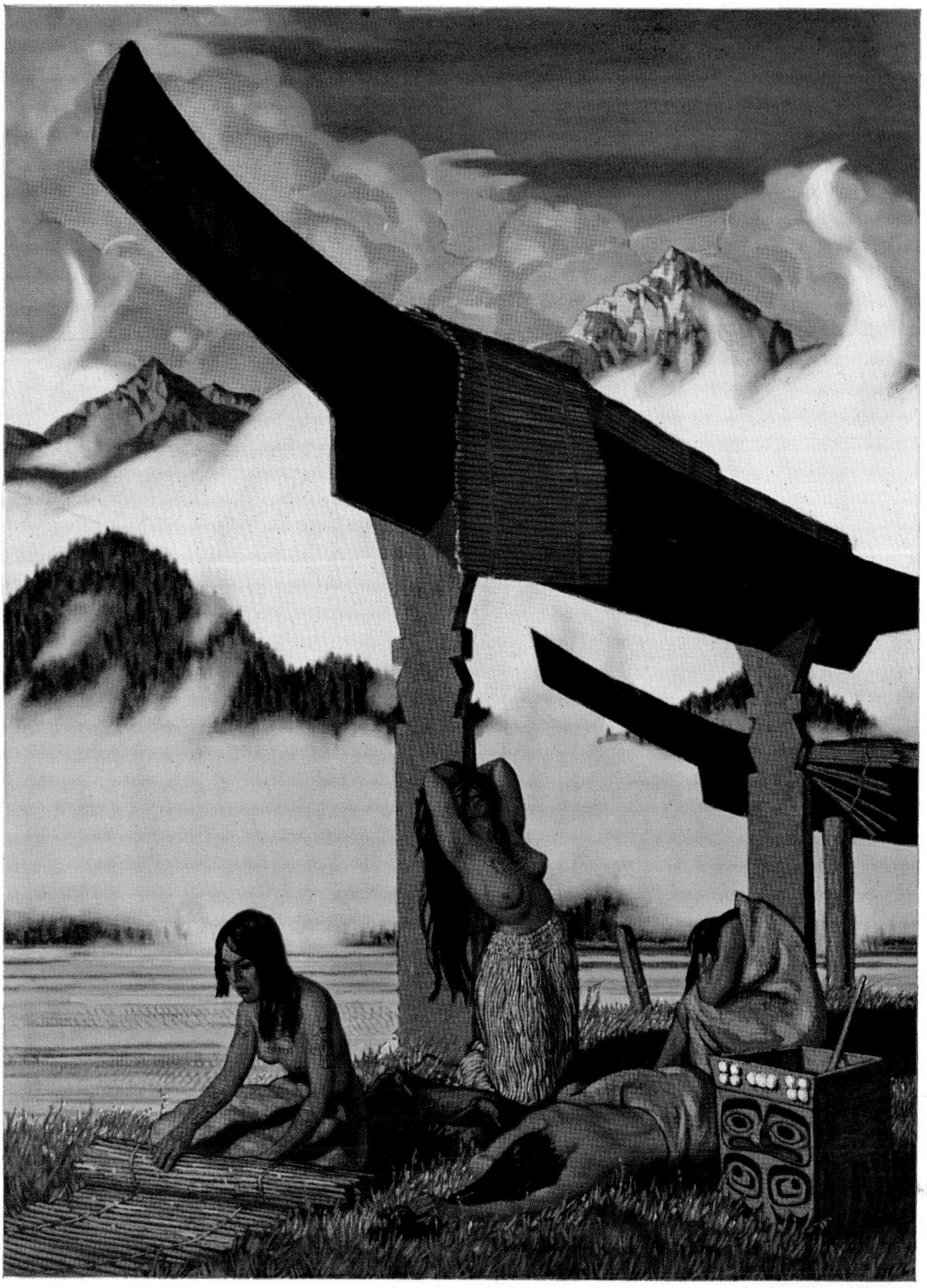

PAINTING BY W. LANGDON KIHN

**Tattooed Widows Wail for a Chief Buried in a Canoe,** his head toward the sea, his canoe rendered unfit for use. Earth burial was viewed with horror. Some tribes placed burial boxes on carved posts or hid them in caves; others cremated, burying only shamans. Slaves were sometimes sacrificed at funerals. Missionaries with great difficulty persuaded Northwest Coast Indians to adopt the white man's cemetery. Now one sees totemic animal symbols accompanied by Biblical verses on white-marble tombstones.

spectacle. While the dance raged furiously around the fallen man, the doctor, with some others, seized and dragged him to the other side of the fire round which they were dancing, placing his naked feet very near the flames.

"After this a pail of water was brought in, and the doctor, who supported the dying man on his arm, washed the blood from his face; the people beat drums, danced, and sang, and suddenly the patient sprang to his feet, none the worse for the apparently hopeless condition of the moment before.

"While all this was going on, I asked the giver of the feast whether it was real blood upon the man's face, and if he were really wounded. He told me so seriously that it was, that I was at first inclined to believe him, until he began to explain that the blood which came from the nose and mouth was owing to the incantations of the medicine man, and that all the people would be very angry if he did not afterwards restore him. . . .

"On the morning of December 13, another strange ceremony began, by the king's firing a pistol, apparently without a moment's warning, close to the ear of Satsat, who dropped down instantly as if shot dead on the spot.

"Upon this all the women set up a most terrible yelling, tearing out their hair by handfuls, and crying out that the prince was dead, when the men rushed in, armed with guns and daggers and inquiring into the cause of the alarm, followed by two of the natives covered with wolfskins, with masks representing the wolf's head. These two came in on all fours, and taking up the prince on their back, carried him out, retiring as they had entered.

"The celebration terminated with a shocking and distressing show of deliberate self-torment. These men, each with two bayonets run through their sides, between the ribs, walked up and down in the room, singing war songs, and exulting in their firmness and triumph over pain."

Details of costume differed somewhat among the various Northwest Coast tribes. Men as a rule wore their hair comparatively short, keeping it out of the eyes with a fur or cloth headband. Women wore their hair in two braids, and used ear and nose ornaments made of bone, wood, and abalone shell. Tlingit women beautified themselves by wearing, in slits in their lower lips, 3- or 4-inch wooden disks shaped like pulley wheels.

While the Kwakiutl and others painted their faces, the Haida practiced tattooing, favoring elaborate designs representing their family crests.

Two methods of deforming the head were practiced by Northwest Coast Indians. The Kwakiutl bound the head in infancy so that the skull grew upward and back in an elongated fashion. The Nootka placed a pad on an infant's forehead, flattening the front of the skull and causing it to slope backward from the eyebrows with "beautifying" effect.

Unlike most other American tribes, Northwest Coast Indians went barefoot the year round, wore raincoats (cedar-bark ponchos) in the wet season, and the old men went about entirely nude in summertime. Also, many men sported luxuriant mustaches.

Women once wore an apron made of shredded cedar bark, suspended by a belt of the same material (opposite). But the most conspicuous wearing apparel for both men and women was the blanket, woven from a mixture of mountain-goat wool, cedar bark, dogs' hair, and feathers. The weaving technique was about the simplest on the continent, but the results often were works of art (page 138).

A less elaborate blanket was made of soft cedar bark, the weft being simply turned across the warp. These blankets were usually trimmed with fur. Others were made of tanned sea-otter skins.

The earliest known blankets had simple designs, purely geometric in character. Complicated heraldic designs probably were not adopted until the general culture began to elaborate after contact with the whites. In this respect, the evolution of intricate patterns from simple beginnings parallels the known development of Navajo weaving.

With the coming of the white traders, woolen blankets gradually replaced the native types except for display purposes. Nowadays men wear shirt and trousers and women wear a dress under the blanket.

Whaling was an important industry of the Nootka of Vancouver Island and the Quileute and Makah who lived along the west coast of the Olympic Peninsula.

The Nootka pursued the whale in seagoing dugout canoes (page 143), frequently far from land. A whaling party usually numbered three to ten canoes, each about 30 feet long and manned by a crew of eight.

The whale-hunt leader, who inherited his position, acquired a helping spirit by praying in a special forest shrine containing wooden figures and the skulls of previous whale chiefs. To gain fortitude he wore clothing made from stinging nettles or thorny rose bushes. Wearing special adornments, such as scalps, was believed to bring additional supernatural power, for the whale was thought too powerful to be taken by human effort alone.

Whalers approached within a yard of the whale before thrusting the broad-pointed harpoon. They drove it as close to the head as possible to avoid the dangerous tail swipe of the wounded mammal. A long line of whale sinew was fastened to the detachable harpoon head. Inflated sealskin floats on the line served as drags and also marked the whale's position when it sounded.

Sometimes a whale would tow a canoe three or four days before it tired sufficiently to be killed with long lances. A daring lancer sometimes leaped on the whale as it was harpooned, drove his spear into its back, and stayed with the animal as it submerged. A respected, heritable Nootka name means "Stepping on a Whale."

Although tribes north along the coast were glad to make use of any whale carcass cast up on their shores, it was only with the Kodiak islanders and Aleuts that we again find expert whalers.

Aleut whaling ceremonies resembled those of the Nootka, but their boats—the closed kayak and the large, open umiak —were Eskimo. Also, they smeared the stone blades of their whale lances with poison from roots of the monkshood, which grows abundantly in the islands. A whale struck by such a lance died within two or three days and the carcass would wash ashore. Only whaling leaders knew the secret of preparing poison and they made the populace believe it got its magic potency from the fat of corpses.

The warlike inhabitants of the bleak and foggy Aleutian Islands, when first encountered by Russians in the 18th century, showed a combination of traits reflecting influences from the Eskimo, the eastern Siberian tribes, and tribes of the American Northwest.

In common with Northwest Coast people, the Aleuts had a social class system with slaves, wore rod armor in combat, and lived in large wooden communal houses (page 139).

The Aleut language is related to Eskimo, and like the Eskimo, the Aleut's principal weapons were javelins or harpoons, propelled by a throwing stick. Their aboriginal costume was Eskimo-like. The men wore long shirts of feathered birdskins, while women's similar garments were made from fur-seal or sea-otter skins. Light transparent raincoats with pointed hoods were made from strips of seal intestines, decorated at

PAINTING BY W. LANGDON KIHN

**Salmon Steak Broils Over an Indian Campfire.** Winter's fillets dry on racks beneath massive canoe cedars flanking Alaska's Chilkat River. Fishing's easy harvest prevented famine, allowed leisure for winter's rich ceremonial life. Each spring salmon choked the rivers; also eulachon, or candlefish, source of the oil Indians lavished on dried meats, berries, other foods. Eulachon oil was foremost trade item of central Northwest Coast tribes with neighbors north and south and Athapascan tribes of the interior. Hudson Bay traders called these trade routes "grease trails."

the seams with feathers, and weatherproofed by hood and wrist drawstrings.

Because of the abundant food supply—sea mammals, fish, birds, birds' eggs, mollusks, berries and roots—the Aleutians were about as densely populated as any section of aboriginal America.

In 1740 there were probably 25,000 natives in the islands, but the effect of white contact was disastrous to them. In 1834, according to the missionary Veniaminoff, fewer than 2,500 remained. The smallpox epidemic in 1848 reduced them to about 900.

When the Japanese invaded the western islands in World War II, mystery surrounded the fate of those Aleuts living on Attu. When the Americans reoccupied this island, all natives were gone. After the war, they were returned from Japan and resettled on Atka.

Time has brought many changes to the Aleutians and to the entire Pacific Northwest. The colorful cedar dugout has given way to the gasoline launch. The salmon cannery has set a new tempo of life. The hunter pursues deer and wild duck with rifle and shotgun. The sea otter, which once gave the Northwest Coast Indian his standard of value, is now almost extinct.

Some aged men and women still recall the old way of life. But the potlatch is gone, and the cherished coppers, and only a few rotting totem poles yet stand where many once were proudly raised.

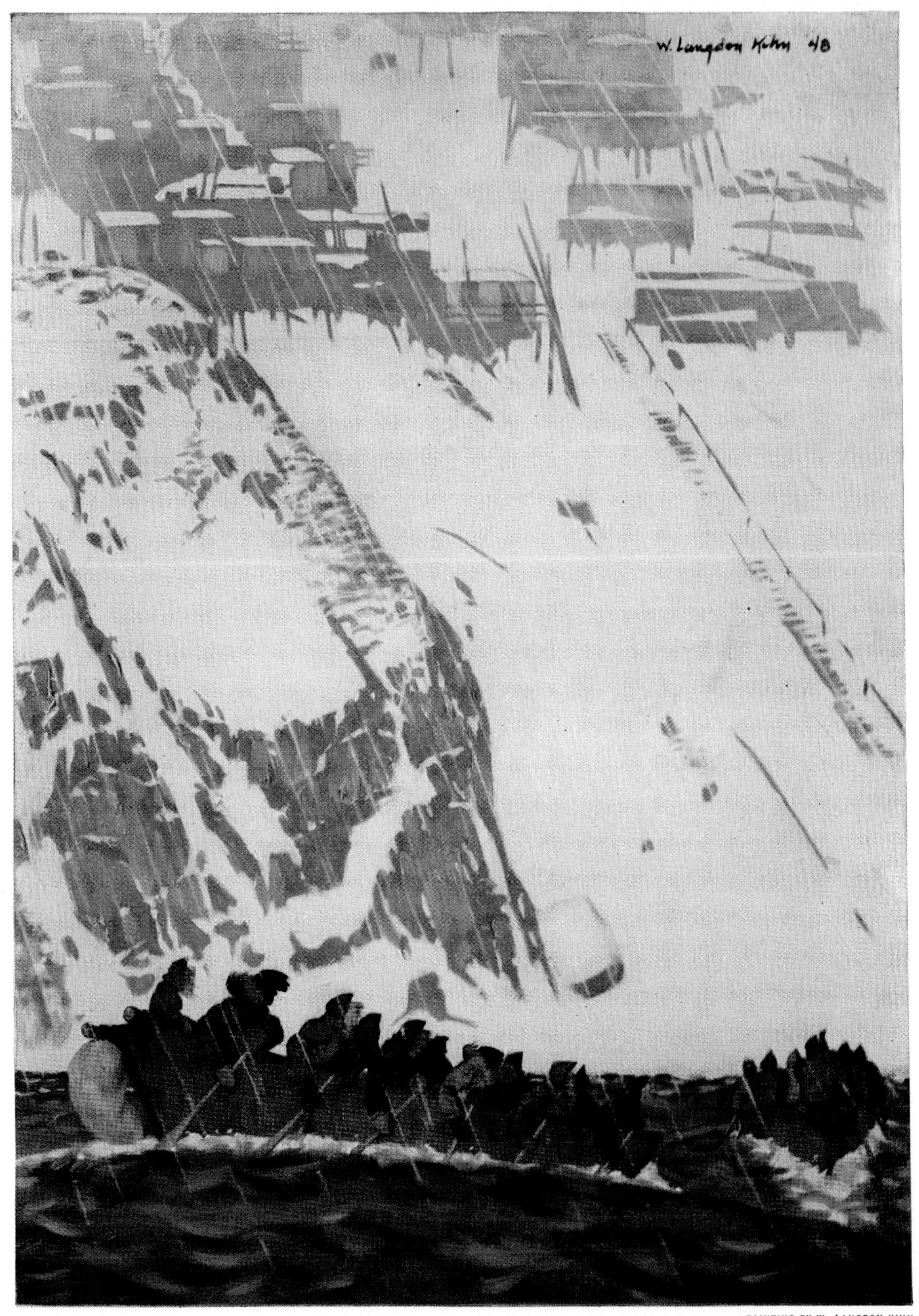


PAINTING BY W. LANGDON KIHN

**King Islanders Paddle Home to Cliffside Village.** These Bering Sea Eskimos venture in big walrus-skin umiaks across storm-swept waters to work as stevedores or trade ivory carvings in white man's Nome.

## CHAPTER 7

# NOMADS OF THE FAR NORTH

"I STEPPED FORWARD and took each of them by the hand . . ." wrote a young Scotsman in 1793, high in the Canadian Rockies. "This was the first time they had ever seen a human being of a complexion different from their own."

Thus Alexander Mackenzie, following the Peace River's headwaters westward, won friendship of awe-struck Indians in his historic journey to the Pacific. North West Company partner, one of the dauntless "Pedlars" who dared infringe on the fur-trading monopoly of the Hudson's Bay Company, Mackenzie was opening a way west, the first white man in an unknown maze of river and lake, forest and muskeg—the haunt of wandering, hardy peoples.

Before Mackenzie, explorers, missionaries, trappers, and birchbark-borne *voyageurs* had deeply penetrated the wilderness from the east, traveling freely among many of Canada's scattered Indian tribes. Ships of Russian sealers and British map makers had touched the northwest Pacific coast, meeting Indians of advanced culture. But no one yet had bridged east and west. Mackenzie was first to cross North America north of Mexico just as he was the first, four years earlier, to follow north-flowing water to the Arctic Ocean itself.

These journeys took the Scottish trader into lands of all three major native groups of the far north—Algonquian, Athapascan, and Eskimo (map, page 24).

Many times he followed the Nor'-westers' fur trail from Montreal to his own Fort Chipewyan on Lake Athabaska, in what is now northeast Alberta. By waterway and portage it struck straight through country of Cree and Chippewa (page 44).

The Cree (page 19) were the largest and in many ways most typical of northern Algonquian tribes. They ranged south of Hudson Bay almost to the Great Lakes, east to the base of the Quebec-Labrador peninsula, and west to the northern Great Plains. There one branch, the Plains Cree, took on the typical Plains culture of their neighbors, the northern Blackfoot and the Assiniboin. True nomads, they moved their camps with seasonal migrations of game and fish. Woodland Cree, masters of light, portable, bark canoes, ranged far and wide on lakes and rivers. Their canoes and nets were sewn with vegetable-fiber twine, their conical tepees covered by skins or birch bark.

Cree men wore tight leather leggings to the hip, leather breechclouts, and moccasins. In winter they donned mittens and fur caps often hung with animal tails, and threw a fur robe over the shoulders. Women wore a knee-length skin dress, belted at the waist, adding detachable sleeves in winter.

In former times Cree men tattooed themselves, sometimes over the entire body, while their wives usually contented themselves with two or three simple lines on the face. Men of status usually took more than one wife; if a wife died, the widower married her sister.

Mackenzie said of the Cree: "Their eyes are black, keen and penetrating; their countenance open and agreeable . . .

"Of all the nations which I have seen on this continent, the Cree women are the most comely. Their figure is generally well proportioned, and the regularity of their features would be acknowledged by the most civilized people of Europe. Their complexion has less of that dark tinge which is common to those savages who have less cleanly habits."

A corpulent Cree, went another account, was "a much greater curiosity than a sober one."

Early traders said the Cree from childhood excelled in fraud and cunning in trade, but in all else were scrupulously honest and trustworthy. Amiable, extremely generous, they were of model behavior until liquor was introduced.

Before modern trade goods came in, the Cree used birch-bark or stone containers. They made arrowheads and axes of stone; knives, fishhooks, and awls of bone. The fur trader and his new and desired goods changed Cree life rapidly. Tribesmen diverted more energy to trapping fur animals. White man's disease struck. Smallpox, introduced in 1786, alone cut Cree numbers from 15,000 to about 3,000.

The first of all Canada's Indians to meet white settlers were the Micmac. French colonists who landed in "Acadia" —present-day Nova Scotia—in 1604 found the Micmac fairly densely settled there and in near-by regions. Fierce and warlike, these Algonquians early became good friends of the French and enemies of the British. Like their northern neighbors, the Nascapi, they painted their leather costumes in bright patterns.

More advanced in political organization than northern tribes, they gave their chiefs real authority. During historic times, the Micmac absorbed European ways, including some farming.

The Nascapi, by contrast, remain nomadic. They and the closely related Montagnais sparsely occupy the entire Quebec-Labrador peninsula, save only its north and west coasts. Basically Eastern Woodlands peoples, their customs have been much modified by severe climate and by contact with Labrador coast Eskimos, whom they once fought continually, but now fully associate with.

Early-day Nascapi lived in skin-covered conical tepees winter and summer, but Eskimo influence shows in the crude snowhouse they sometimes made over a frame of spruce boughs. And to the usual Algonquian leather breeches, leggings, moccasins, gloves, and fur cap, Nascapi added the Eskimo's long coat, decorating it with red, blue, yellow, and brown painted designs (page 160).

Their canoes and snowshoes were Eastern Woodlands, their toboggans Athapascan, their sleds Eskimo. Among southern Nascapi bands, men and women provided the pulling power, for neither horse nor dog was used.

Typical of northern tribes, the Nascapi set deadfalls for the flesh-eating bear, lynx, and cougar; snares for the herbivorous moose, caribou, deer, hares, rabbits, and ptarmigan; and shot caribou from ambush, or speared them from canoes while swimming (opposite).

These northern nomads preserve caribou flesh by drying, then pound it, and make it into pemmican, their basic food while roaming the interior in search of game. They live in alternate abundance and want. Sometimes after a long period of hunger followed by a successful caribou hunt, they gorge themselves sick with incredible quantities of meat.

Summer in the northland brings weather almost as warm as winters are cold. Sheets of surface water spawn hordes of mosquitoes; biting flies abound. No white traveler venturing into the Barren Grounds has failed to reserve his best eloquence for describing the insect pests. Flanking Hudson Bay,

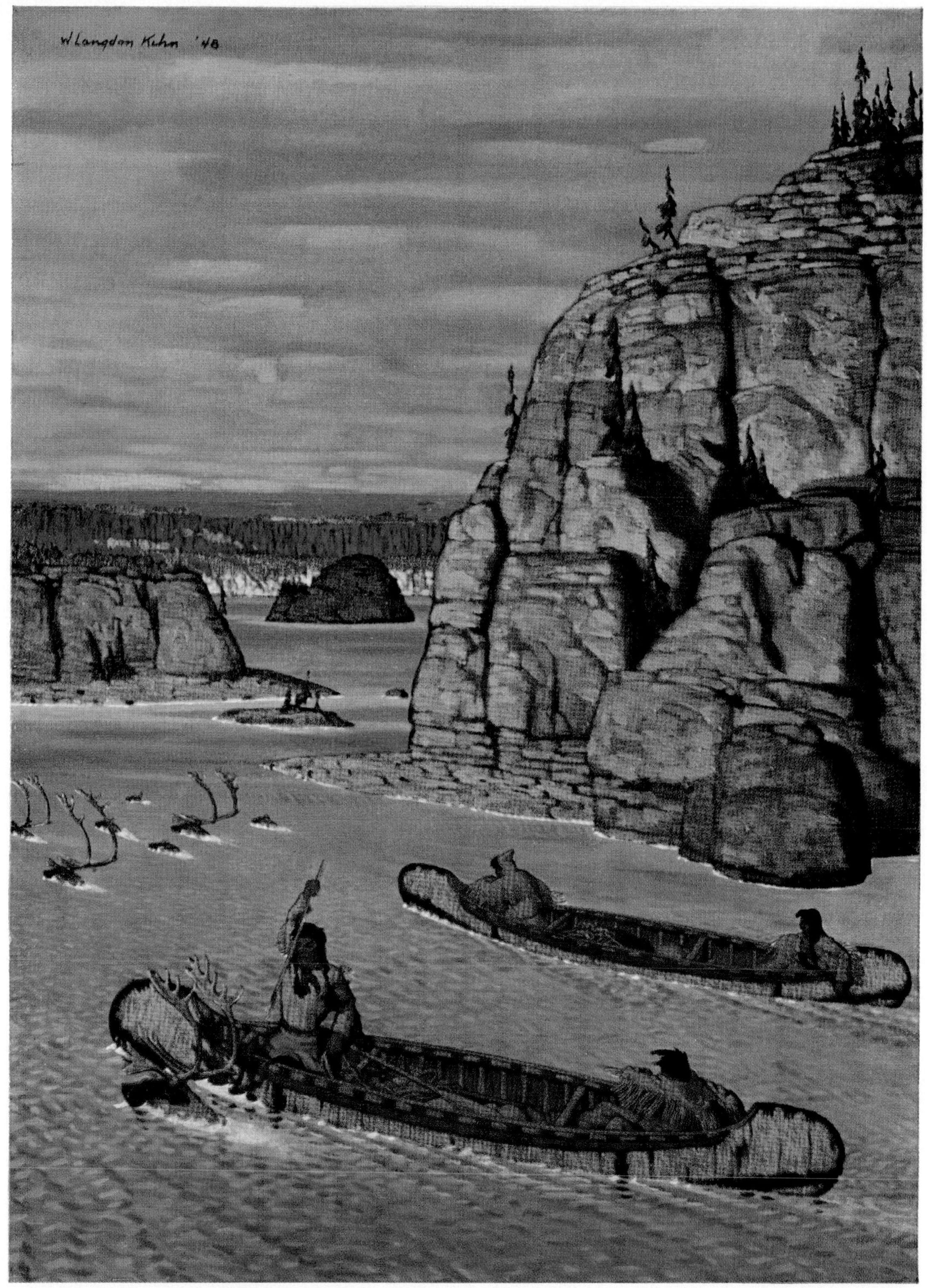


PAINTING BY W. LANGDON KIHN

**Yellowknives Spear Swimming Caribou in Great Slave Lake.** To slow their fleet prey, northland hunters drive reindeer into water, overtake them in swift birchbark canoes. The Yellowknife earlier lived along the Coppermine River, and prospered trading knives they made of yellow copper. White man's steel broke their monopoly, warfare thinned their ranks, and they moved south to better hunting grounds.

**Summer Work** of this provident Montagnais on Quebec's Pointe Bleue Reservation readies snowshoes for winter trapping rounds hundreds of miles north. This tribe and the neighboring Nascapi excel in snowshoe craft. For different uses, they make some almost round, some long and narrow, some with upturned toes. Taut moosehide web inside wooden frame keeps wearer from sinking in soft snow.

HOWELL WALKER, NATIONAL GEOGRAPHIC STAFF

this bleak desert north of the tree line, summer grazing range of caribou and musk ox, extends 2,500 miles from Labrador to the delta of the Mackenzie River.

In summer Eskimo hunters penetrate this no man's land from the north, Indians from the south. These latter include the Chipewyan (page 161), Caribou-eaters, and Beaver, wandering tribes long tapped for fur by the "Company of Adventurers of England Trading into Hudson's Bay."

From Fort Chipewyan, Mackenzie explored his river flowing west out of Great Slave Lake. He had found the second longest stream in North America, from its source in the Rockies to its mouth on the Beaufort Sea.

This wide drainage basin, and that of the Yukon River across the mountains to the west, is homeland to the Athapascan-speaking Tanana, Kutchin, Hare, Yellowknife, Nahani, and Slave—trackers of caribou through scraggly spruce forests.

Geologically, this territory is an extension of the Great Plains to the south. What the buffalo was to Plains tribes the caribou is to Indians of the far north. Stalking, snaring, trapping customs the Athapascans share with Algonquian tribes to south and east. But they originated a massed hunting technique later adopted by buffalo hunters of the Plains.

In this community venture, throngs of Indians howling like wolves drive a caribou herd into a large circular corral with a funnellike entrance having wings, perhaps a mile apart. Trapped inside, the milling animals are shot.

Magical aid was normally sought by the hunter. One method, common also in parts of Asia, was to carve animal images on a caribou shoulder blade, then hold it over a fire until cracked by heat. The cracks pointed toward good hunting.

The Indians hunt mainly during late summer and in the winters, which are long and severe, although snowfall is not heavy. In early summer they fish for salmon in Yukon headwaters, whitefish in the Mackenzie basin. These migrating fish are taken in nets or in basket traps, while natives hook lake trout up to 30 pounds in all seasons.

Of political organization among Athapascan groups one early explorer said: "The authority of the chief is limited, for the Indians are very unruly and not at all disposed to submit to authority.

"The chiefs are chosen either for their wisdom or courage, and not at all on account of birth. They have no insignia of office, and as for privileges they have all that they can take, and none that the others can withhold from them.

"The chiefs and old men are all who are entitled to speak in council, but any young man will not hesitate to get up and give his seniors the benefit of his wisdom."

In contrast to weak chiefs were the shamans, who could stir up winds, drive away a storm, foretell success or failure in hunting or warfare. The shaman could cure, he could kill. Any person harboring a grudge could hire him to send sickness into an enemy.

Punishment for crimes lay entirely in the hands of the offended. For adultery the woman alone was punished—beaten or cast off. For murder, the victim's relatives avenged his death. But if a shaman had been paid to kill him, the shaman was regarded innocent. Revenge was taken against the individual who paid him.

**Brisk Weather, Brisk Business Mix at a Hudson's Bay Post.** North beyond all trees on the inhospitable west coast of Quebec's Ungava Peninsula, the Port Harrison trader fights cold with caribou-skin parka, warm gloves, and fur-lined cap while tending his unheated store. The Eskimo couple offers a fine catch of red, white, and silver fox pelts, worth many aluminum credit tokens, known as "made beavers." Several lie beside the order pad. With these the natives buy coffee, tea, tobacco, matches, traps, ammunition. Guns and steel traps came to Eskimo country with the first Hudson's Bay Company traders. Founded in 1670, the company long held a monopoly in Canada's fur trade.

RICHARD HARRINGTON

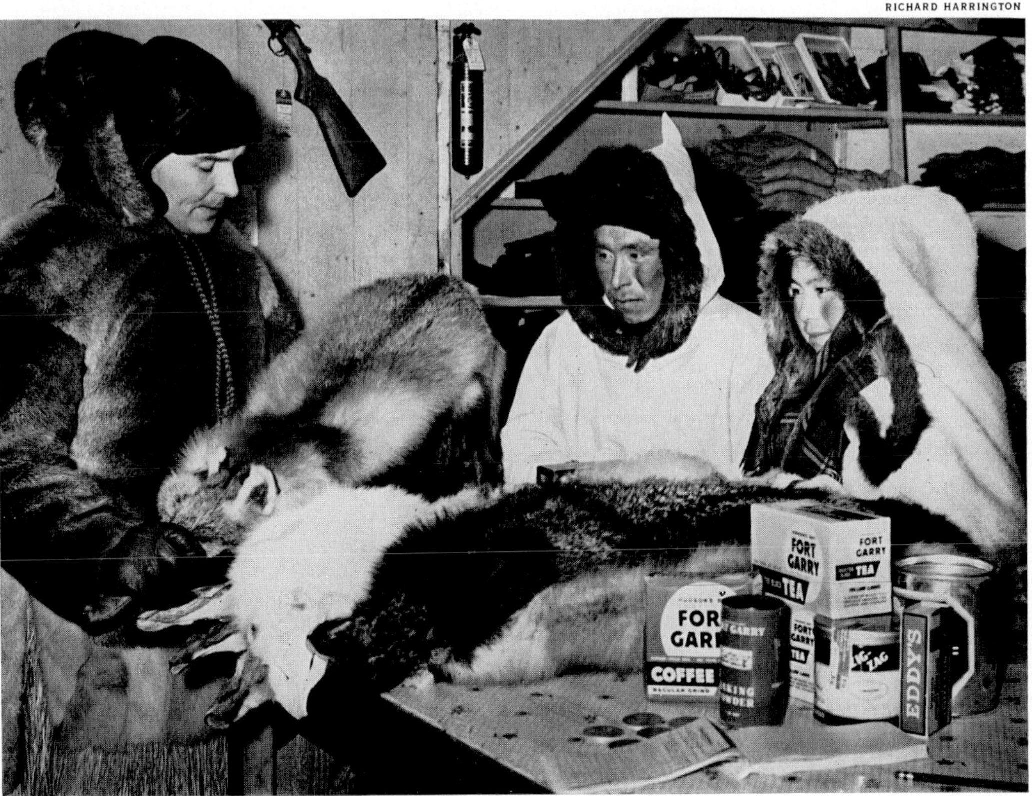

PAINTINGS BY W. LANGDON KIHN

## Hardy North Country Indians Roam Lands Locked in Snow

In winter camp in Quebec's Gulf of St. Lawrence district, early-day Nascapi (above) prepare for the trail. The man ices sled runners, his wife smoke-tans a caribou hide on a tripod over a half-smothered fire. Near-round snowshoes hanging on a dead snag offer wide support in soft snow, yet are easily maneuverable on upland trails. Bright designs band Nascapi skin clothing.

Northern tepees, not so tall and steep as the familiar Plains dwelling, were covered with skins or bark. Even when snow drifts high, fire inside maintains warmth. Amid conical Nascapi tepees, a dome-shaped lodge at center hints kinship with the igloo. Northern Nascapi bands adopted the Eskimo's dog, but this southern group puts human brawn to work pulling sleds.

Dogs and snub-nosed toboggans provide transport for old-time Chipewyan crossing treeless plains (right). Biting Hudson Bay winds whip snow past caribou-skin tepees pitched before the austere battlements of Fort Prince of Wales. Commanding the region's best harbor and a voyageur route to the Peace, Athabasca, and Mackenzie River country, this British outpost thrives on fur trade with Indians and Eskimos. Soon, in 1782, the French will destroy the fort, but some walls will remain in later Churchill, Manitoba, 20th century terminus of the Hudson Bay railway.

Chipewyan nomads ranged from Lake Athabasca to Hudson Bay, and north as far as Caribou Eskimo country. Through the long winter they followed the migrating caribou, whose hides provided shelter and fringed-leather clothing, whose flesh was their daily fare.

Typical of northern and western Athapascan tribes are the Kutchin. Formerly called the Loucheux, they live between the upper Yukon and the lower Mackenzie. Much of their territory lies north of the Arctic Circle, where winters of 50° F. below zero are followed by summers up to 90° F.

As with the Nascapi of Labrador, the dressed caribou-skin costume of the Kutchin somewhat resembles Eskimo dress. Their fringed coat had a pointed tail both in front and behind, the latter convenient for sitting on blocks of ice. Coats were embellished with porcupine quills dyed in different colors, and with rows of Dentalium shells. The finest porcupine-quill embroidery in America was that of the Athapascan tribes, who probably originated the art.

Kutchin trousers sometimes were in one piece with the moccasins. In winter a hood was attached to the coat, and detached mittens were worn, fastened Eskimo-like to a line passed over the neck. Women's clothing usually was more ample to allow room for a suckling baby under it, and there was no tail in front.

Kutchin women placed their infants in bark cradles (page 163). Most other northern tribes substituted the moss bag, a simple sack with a lining of moss which

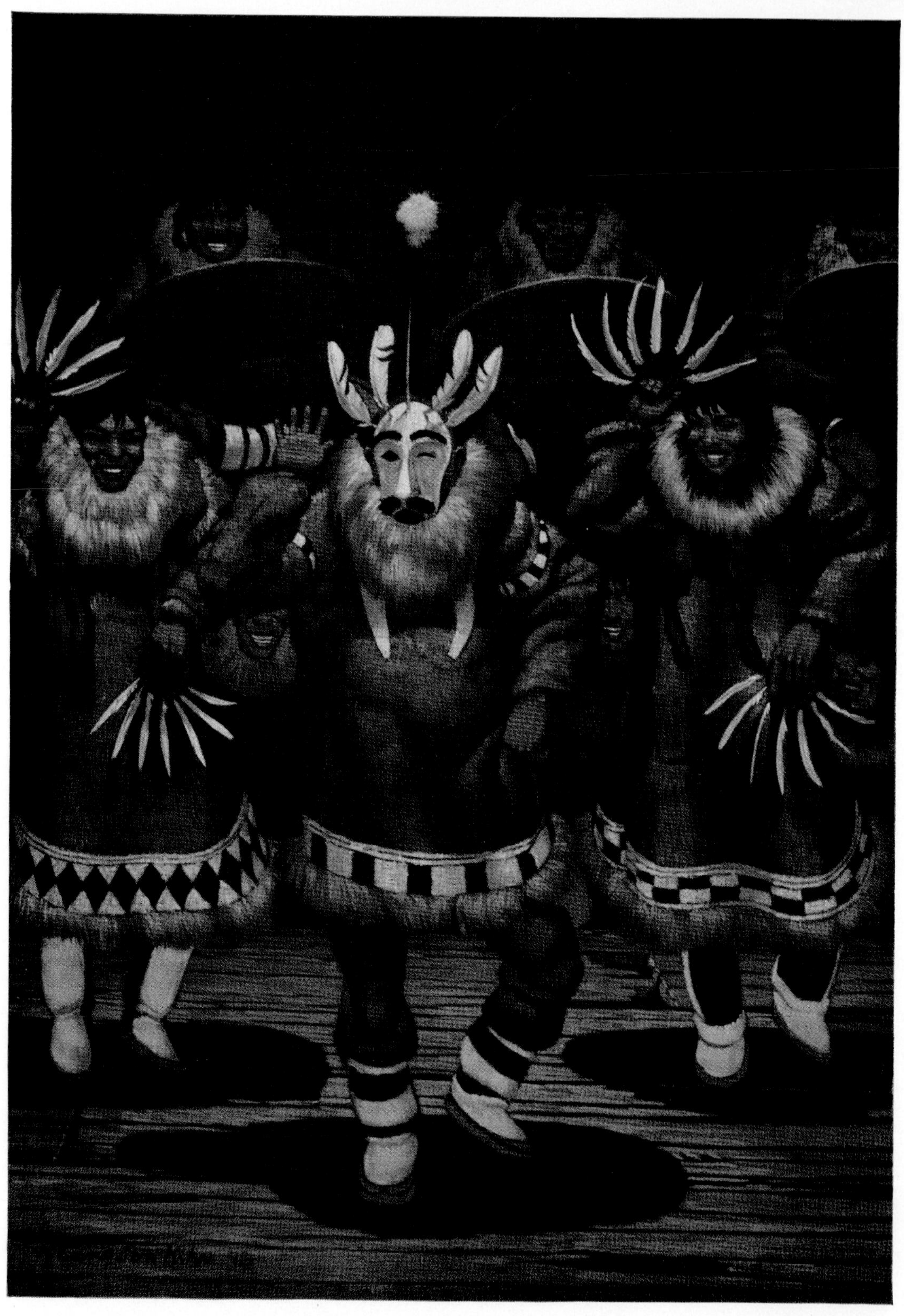

**Eskimo Comedians Mimic a Kutchin Dance.** Laughter splits swarthy Alaskan faces as feather-shaking dancers jig to the beat of one-faced drums. Despite a bleak habitat, Eskimos are cheerful and fun-loving.

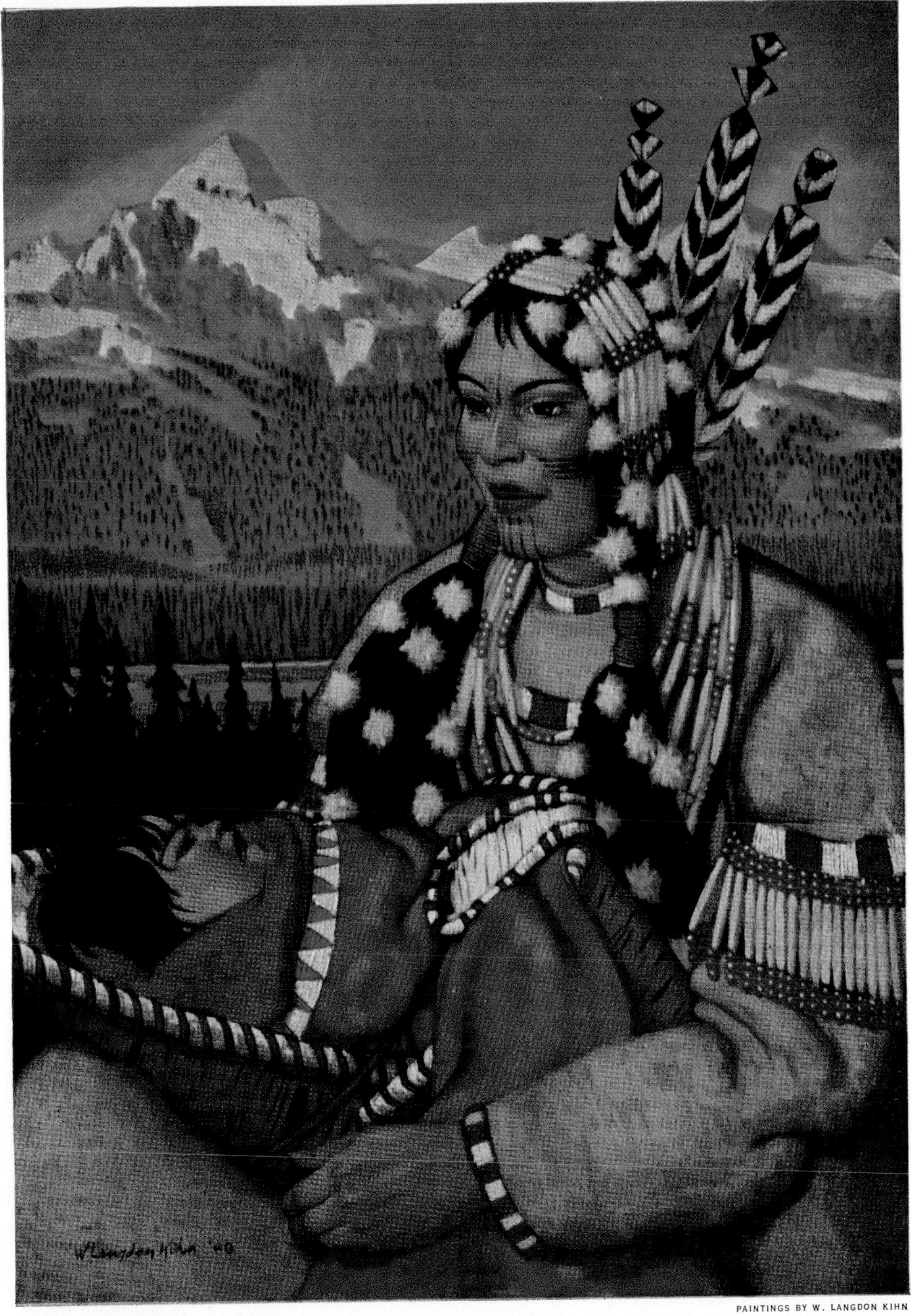


PAINTINGS BY W. LANGDON KIHN

**Artful Headdress, Soot Tattoos Beautify a Kutchin Mother.** She cradles her baby in a chair-shaped bark basket. Bone beads, porcupine-quill embroidery, trimmed feathers adorn her caribou-skin costume.

could be changed frequently. Wives of north-woods traders adopted this practical device.

In winter, the Kutchin and their neighbors live typically in a gable-roofed log house. Logs are set vertically for walls, horizontally for the roof, which is made weatherproof with moss and turf. A hanging skin covers the door opening. When on the move, Kutchin live in dome-shaped structures of skins over poles.

A woman's life was no joy. Women, not dogs, pulled Kutchin sleds. When a new camp was selected, the men, arriving first, awaited the women dragging lodges and other paraphernalia, then lounged around while the women set up camp.

In addition to moving camp, the woman had to retrieve game killed by the male hunters and back-pack it home. She dried the meat in summer, made all clothing, dressed skins, repaired snowshoes, performed the camp drudgery. Her husband could beat her for disobedience. So severe was her lot—far harder than among most Indian tribes—that mothers often killed infant daughters to spare them a woman's life.

Men did the cooking. They always ate first, selecting the choicest items for themselves and throwing what was left on the ground for the women.

Although game was abundant at times, there were often

## By Age-old Ingenuity the Eskimo Masters His Frozen World

In slanting light of the spring sun, Central Eskimos (left) prepare for their long inland migration. Caribou antlers top a heavy-laden sled. Ivory goggles with narrow eyeslits cut down reflected glare, prevent snow blindness. Harpoons jutting from the snow kill and tether wary mammals of icy seas. In bulging sealskins in foreground, oil and blubber are packed for the journey. White Arctic fox pelts hanging from the lance behind the woman will buy needed staples at the trading post.

From Coppermine east across the Canadian Arctic, such igloo villages as this one house Central Eskimos through long, dark, bitter cold winters. Unlike Alaskan and Greenland Eskimos, who use snow only for temporary shelter, these Hudson Bay people, in a region empty of wood or stone, build large snowblock dwellings that are marvels of engineering. Domed construction does away with inner frame. Clear panes of ice admit light. Long entrance tunnels keep out howling wind and marauding polar bear. Though temperature outside plunges far below zero, body heat, oil lamps, and cooking fires keep tight igloos warm—often above 60°F.

Families strip to the waist for indoor comfort (below). Cross-legged on a skin-draped snow platform, a man drills ivory with a bow-and-socket tool. Pipe-smoking woman tailors fur clothing. Another cooks with shallow stone dish over a seal-oil flame. Girl standing on fur-covered floor plays Eskimo version of cat's cradle.

PAINTINGS BY W. LANGDON KIHN

T. H. MANNING

**Igloos, Like Fallen Snowmen, Dot the Arctic Shore.** Tethered dogs will soon form yelping teams as Central Eskimos set out to hunt on the ice. Except for the tent, this sealing camp on an island near Coppermine, Northwest Territories, could have been photographed a century ago. Each domed snow-house is home for about five persons. Early Eskimo invented sleds like the ladder-shaped one at left, and bred large dogs to pull them. The dog travois of Plains Indians probably came from the Eskimo.

periods of want and famine. Old people, sick or no longer able to care for themselves, were frequently abandoned by their families in the wilderness.

The Kutchin once practiced slavery. Slaves were either war captives or tribesmen without protecting friends or relatives. Most warlike of Athapascan tribes, the Kutchin fought with their Indian neighbors, and more often with the Eskimo. Mostly they were the aggressors. Their motive: to gain prestige, booty, and captives.

Indian women usually submitted docilely to their captors, but Eskimo women often bided their time in apparent submission, awaiting revenge.

Before a war party set out, a dance feast stirred up the proper military spirit. On the way to their objective the warriors killed every creature they encountered. But upon meeting their prospective victims, they would act as friends until their hosts were off guard. They then knifed men, women, and children, except such women as they wished for wives. For each victim he had thus killed in "warfare" a man tattooed a line on his arm.

Times of plenty saw many less grim pastimes than war. The Kutchin liked singing, dancing, and long stories; they gambled, using sticks for dice; they wrestled joyfully, or pitted men against women in a tug of war.

At the start of a tribal wrestling match the two smallest boys grapple. The winner then takes on the next larger boy, who rushes in before his opponent can get his breath. Thus the match continues without pause until the strongest men are wrestling. A better wrestler may throw three or four opponents until, exhausted, he in turn is thrown and leaves the field to his conqueror.

When the male champion has been determined, the women have their turn, the contest beginning with two little girls.

In winter the Kutchin play a dangerous game. Four trees, growing in the form of a square and about 30 feet apart, are selected, and two moose-skin thongs stretched diagonally between pairs of trees, forming an X about 20 feet above ground. Where they intersect a small leather platform about a foot square is attached. Participants stand on this tiny platform in turn and jump up and down.

Each time the player lands on the square the cords' elasticity throws him higher, until he is thrown more than 10 feet above the platform. The higher he bounces the more difficult it is to keep balance. The object is to see who can complete the greatest number of jumps before falling to the ground far below.

Of course each participant finally comes a cropper, to the hearty amusement of the spectators.

Cultural signposts among the Kutchin point in several directions. Hunting customs they share with Athapascan neigh-

**Seal Carved in Ivory** shows skill of a culture predating even the Old Bering Sea people of 2,000 years ago. This grotesque figurine comes from Ipiutak, long-buried town of 800 houses north of Bering Strait at Point Hope, Alaska. Log tombs yield human skulls set with carved walrus-ivory eyeballs, nose plugs, and mouthpieces. Coming from Asia, 160 miles away, these mysterious people excelled the practical Eskimo in artistry, but did not have seal-oil lamps, sleds, or slate tools. Later came the Eskimo wave that peopled the Arctic as far east as Greenland.

AMERICAN MUSEUM OF NATURAL HISTORY

bors and Algonquian tribes. From the Eskimo come tailored skin costumes, the use of built-up sleds, wrestling as the favorite sport. Other Kutchin traits recall the Tutchone, Tahltan, and Carrier tribes of the south—in turn swayed by the potlatch, slavery, and prestige-through-wealth concepts of the spectacular Northwest Coast tribes.

Mackenzie opened Athapascan country. He traveled among the Kutchin. It was the Carrier who led him at last to the Pacific. But he reached another world, too, in his journey down the Mackenzie River to its mouth. There, facing sea ice, on a quaking muskeg coast with permafrost not far beneath, he had come to the land of the Eskimo.

Here live in many respects the most remarkable aborigines in the New World. Spread thinly across some 6,000 miles of Arctic coast and great islands from East Cape, Siberia, to eastern Greenland, these people for centuries have had to adapt to a stark, cruel environment, or die. Nowhere else in the world did a primitive people extend themselves so widely. Yet they show surprising uniformity in physical characteristics, language, and customs.

Although the Eskimo are unmistakably of Asiatic origin, many ethnologists refer to them not as "Indians" but as a group apart. Nomenclature is unimportant, since the term "Indian" in any case is arbitrary.

It would be easy to explain their individuality by saying that the Eskimo were late arrivals from northern Asia who spread rapidly along the uninhabited Arctic coast, by-passing established tribes. But archeology proves this is not so. In Alaska extensive remains have been found which date back 2,000 years or more. These remains—not even the earliest known—show that these ancient people were true Eskimo who already had developed an amazing culture.

Similar traits can be found as far west as the Ob River and as far south as Lake Baikal in central Asia. Along Siberia's Arctic coast today several different language and culture groups show descent from separate northward movements of ancient people from inner Asia down the long rivers that flow to the Arctic.

One of these movements reached the shores of Bering Sea in easternmost Siberia. Here walrus, seal, fish, and birds supplied the necessities of life.

Crossing Bering Strait in their skin-covered boats, these people soon settled in permanent villages on the Diomede Islands, St. Lawrence Island to the south, and on the Alaska coast. Sea-nurtured, they felt no need to penetrate the American interior.

These Old Bering Sea people lived in communities of small rectangular houses excavated in the ground. Floors were of stone, walls of driftwood and whale bones laid horizontally between stakes, roofs probably of wooden rafters covered with turf. A long, low entrance tunnel shielded the interior from cold.

They did not construct platforms in their houses as did the later Eskimo. They cooked their food in round-bottomed pottery vessels, they carved plates and spoons of driftwood. Open, shallow pottery lamps gave heat and light.

Their skin-covered boats were the kayak and the umiak, types still used by the Eskimo (page 172).

They traveled overland with small, low, heavy-runnered sledges, as well as whalebone toboggans, both drawn by human power. The only dogs were a small-sized breed apparently raised for food.

Chief weapon, and key possession of these and later Eskimo, was the harpoon. With detachable head of ivory or bone fastened to line and float, this complex spear proved indispensable for hunting sea mammals. Since both form and decoration changed with different periods, a prehistoric Eskimo site can be dated by

PAINTING BY W. LANGDON KIHN

**Hunters and Huskies Battle Pain-maddened Polar Bear.** Daring Eskimo lunges to spear 1,000-pound beast with knife lashed to a stick. His companion draws sinew-backed bow. Eskimos also hunted bear with fist-sized "death pills" temptingly strewn on sea ice. The frozen balls, containing sharpened whalebone pieces wound up like clocksprings inside strips of seal blubber, sprang open in bear's stomach.

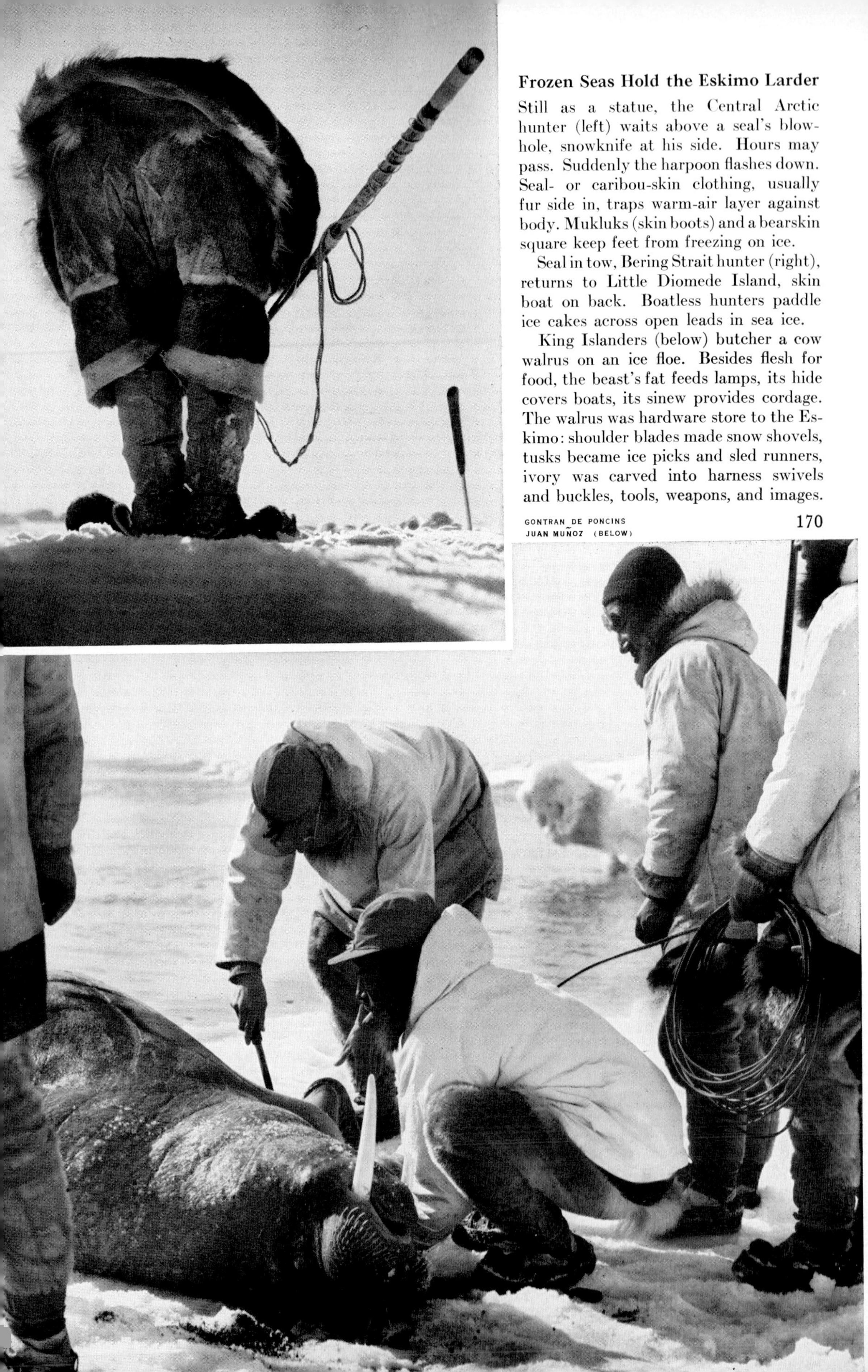

## Frozen Seas Hold the Eskimo Larder

Still as a statue, the Central Arctic hunter (left) waits above a seal's blowhole, snowknife at his side. Hours may pass. Suddenly the harpoon flashes down. Seal- or caribou-skin clothing, usually fur side in, traps warm-air layer against body. Mukluks (skin boots) and a bearskin square keep feet from freezing on ice.

Seal in tow, Bering Strait hunter (right), returns to Little Diomede Island, skin boat on back. Boatless hunters paddle ice cakes across open leads in sea ice.

King Islanders (below) butcher a cow walrus on an ice floe. Besides flesh for food, the beast's fat feeds lamps, its hide covers boats, its sinew provides cordage. The walrus was hardware store to the Eskimo: shoulder blades made snow shovels, tusks became ice picks and sled runners, ivory was carved into harness swivels and buckles, tools, weapons, and images.

GONTRAN DE PONCINS
JUAN MUÑOZ (BELOW)

AUDREY AND FRANK MORGAN

the style of harpoon heads found in it.

These designs were made with sharp flint gravers; holes were drilled with an ingenious bow and socket technique. An ivory or wooden "mask" fitted over the Eskimo's mouth and held the upper end of the drill shaft. The bowstring was looped around the shaft. Moving the bow back and forth spun the drill rapidly.

Prospering for several centuries, the Old Bering Sea people inched south along the Alaskan coast, and north to where a group developed that archeologists call the Birnik people.

About a thousand years ago a sudden change and expansion took place. New traits and ideas from Siberia broke through the old conservatism. With them came the use of iron.

Decorative designs grew bolder, more rigid with iron engraving and carving tools. The art of flaking away stone to make ax, knife, or scraper gave way to ground-stone implements, usually of slate. Larger whaling harpoon heads came into use, and Eskimo ingenuity created bird arrows, bolas, and fishhooks.

The bird bola consisted of a number of ivory balls on strings. The hunter hurled it at birds. When any part of the bola struck a bird, the remainder whirled about, entangling it.

As the complex sinew-backed bow increased in power, archers began to wear wrist guards to protect them from the bowstring's rebound. For warfare, body armor of bone plates came into use.

With more food, population increased. Houses became larger. Population pressure began a strong eastward movement along the Arctic coast, a movement which did not stop until scattered groups fringed the entire coast as far as eastern Greenland in the north, Newfoundland in the south.

Archeologists call these Eskimo the Punuk in their Bering Sea habitat, the Thule in central and eastern Arctic.

The rapidity and vast extent of their population spread came partly because until they reached Hudson Bay they encountered no other humans along their line of migration. From there to Greenland, however, they met a long-settled people. These, the primitive Dorset, were related in some ways to the Eskimo.

The Dorset culture still remains a mystery. Although no trace of them has yet been found in the west, archeologists believe the Dorset stem from the Denbigh people, whose recently discovered remains in western and interior Alaska are the Arctic's earliest yet known.

Traveling eastward, the Dorset people finally settled north and east of Hudson Bay from Labrador to Greenland. They disappeared with the arrival of the Thule, being displaced, or merging with them.

Later, islands along the central Arctic coast were abandoned by the Thule. Within the last thousand years the land there has risen more than 30 feet, closing straits and shoaling the sea. Whales no longer visited the section. The Thule, largely dependent on whales for subsistence, moved to the mainland.

Excavations in western Greenland reveal that the Thule at Inugsuk traded with the Norse in the 13th century. This first archeological evidence of European influence provides a definite point of departure in dating Eskimo culture. Norse sagas and documents tell of much earlier Greenland meetings with Eskimos, the first American aborigines to meet the white man.

PAINTINGS BY W. LANGDON KIHN

## Sled and Kayak Carry Eskimos on the Endless Search for Food

Beneath eerie curtains of the aurora borealis, Central Eskimos (above) trudge toward the coast to winter in snow houses and hunt food out across the ice. Men as well as dogs in fan-shaped harness haul sledges piled high with wood for trail fires, caribou meat, even a rakish kayak. Through dark months ahead, seal and walrus will become staff of life, existence on the sea ice a grim battle for survival.

At spring's end when sunlight floods the north country, Eskimos migrate inland in pursuit of caribou, and to fish in lakes and streams. On the Barren Grounds Eskimo and Indian have met and swapped traits over long centuries. Tailored skin clothing, the sled, other Eskimo inventions thus made their way south. The bark canoe of Eastern Woodlands may stem from the kayak.

The kayak (left) ranks high among Eskimo achievements. These tricky, one-man canoes are literally closed skin tubes. The hunter makes the one opening watertight by lacing his clothing over the manhole rim. Deft use of the double-bladed wooden paddle rights his craft when capsized, sometimes by rolling full circle.

Stalking walrus, the hunter leans forward, conceals himself behind the saillike blind mounted on the bow. He hurls his harpoon with a throw stick. Sinew line snakes out from tray on foredeck. Inflated sealskin buoys up the carcass while towing.

Unlike the kayak, the umiak—"woman's boat"—is a bulky open craft that can carry a sizable load. Ancient Eskimos propelled umiaks both by paddles and oars, the only instance of oars used by American aborigines. Outboard motors now do much of the work.

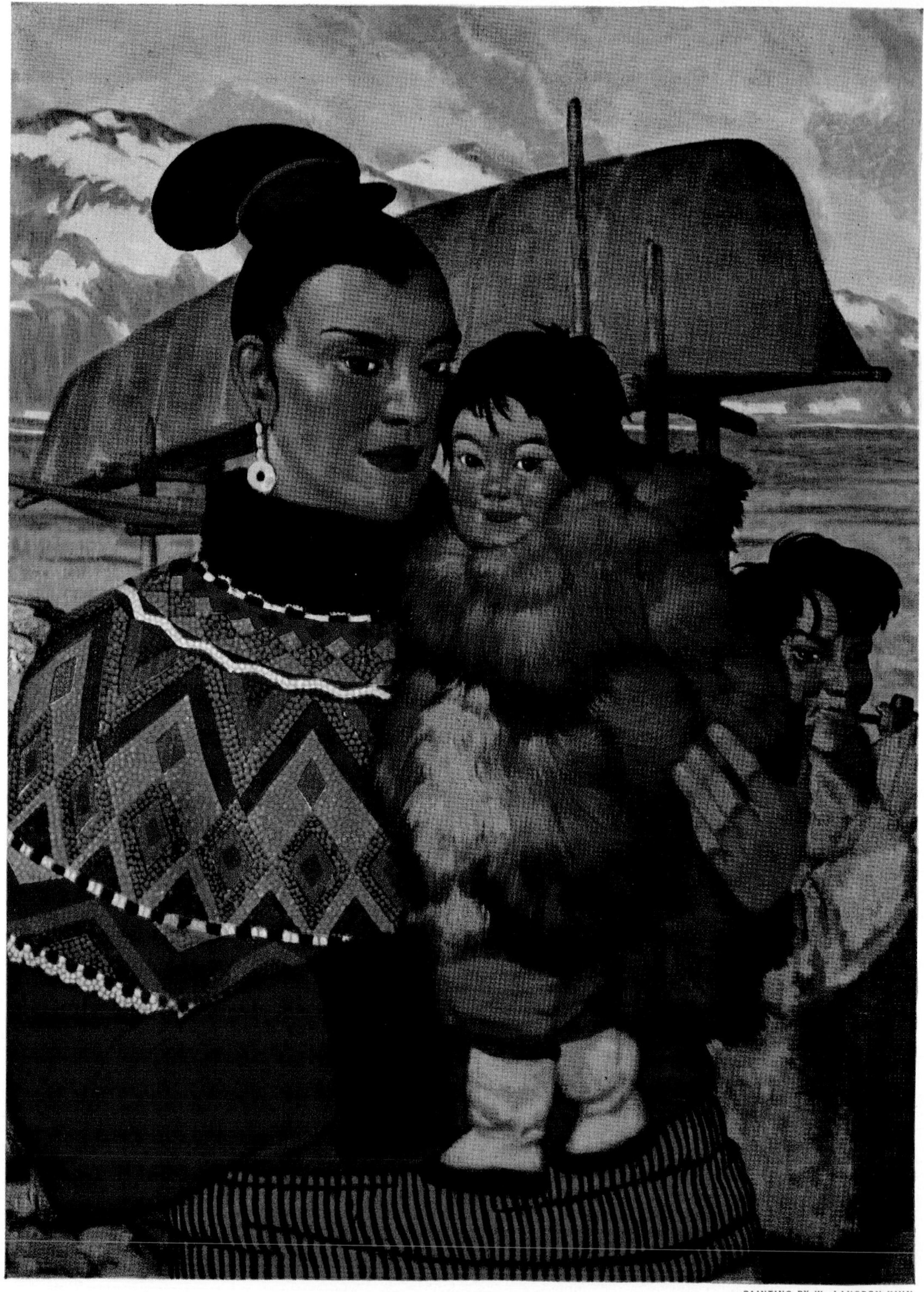

PAINTING BY W. LANGDON KIHN

**Greenland Madonna and Child.** Woman's bead cape and hair bun show white man's influence. Child's furs, skin boat are traditional. Norse from Iceland settled on Greenland about A.D. 900. Of American aborigines, the Eskimo have had longest contact with Europeans, remain among the least affected. Despite vast spread, their culture is strikingly uniform; a Greenlander can converse with an Alaskan Eskimo.

Once the Arctic coast was settled, about A.D. 1000, minor local differences began to appear among the Eskimo. In modern times we classify them as Western, Central, and Eastern Eskimo.

The mind's-eye image most of us have when we say "Eskimo" is that of the Central Eskimo. How well we picture parka-clad men wandering far across the ice in search of breathing holes of seals, there to wait hours on end, spear in hand (page 170). The patience and skill of the Eskimo is proverbial, and his knowledge of the quarry's behavior unsurpassed.

Early in life, boys join their fathers on hunts, sharing their hardships in the severe climate. They learn to set nets of whalebone under the ice. On warm days when seals emerge to bask on the ice, they slither belly down across the hummocks, inching toward their wary prey, leaping up, hurling the harpoon.

Summers, when the family moves inland and lives in skin-covered tents, boys take part in caribou hunts and fish in lakes and rivers.

In the winter communities on the sea ice, they help their fathers build snowhouses, hemispherical in shape, with compact snow blocks locked with a key block at the dome's apex. Snow platforms edge the wall. Covered with furs, these are used for lounging and sleeping (page 165). Heating the newly built house forms a glaze of ice over the interior, making it strong and compact. Light comes in "windows" made of ice.

These igloos, considered so typical of the Eskimo, were used regularly only by the Central Eskimo, not by the early or later-day Alaska Eskimo.

The Eskimo's ingenuity is further illustrated in his stone or pottery lamp. In a woodless region, life on the sea ice would be impossible without it. In a bowl of stone or pottery, seal or whale oil burns from a wick of twisted moss or other absorbent. The lamp furnished light during the long winter night, it heated the almost airtight winter houses, it cooked the Eskimo's food.

In aboriginal times the Eskimo made fire by striking together two pieces of iron pyrites, driving a spark into tinder, or by friction produced with the bow drill.

Eskimo garb was also remarkably adapted to the severe climate. In the Eastern and Central groups the hooded coat was cut away at the sides and had a long tail down the back, looking for all the world like a modern full-dress coat. Knee-length trousers, skin hip boots, and mittens completed the costume.

Clothing was generally of caribou or seal skin. In Alaska garments were also tailored bird skins or skins of small mammals sewed together. Intestines of sea mammals made light rain gear; polar-bear fur, the best ice-free mittens.

Like their Indian neighbors to the south, the Eskimo have little if any political organization. Lacking chiefs, the family is the basic social unit. Again the most influential individuals are the shamans, who influence the leaders, interpret dreams, make or break up marriages, and foretell weather and the movements of game. The shaman is also the doctor.

When the Labrador Eskimo medicine man is called, he is blindfolded. The patient lies on his back on the ground. The shaman, when worked up to a proper state of frenzy, throws himself on his victim and begins to chase the evil from its hiding place. Meanwhile, the patient is on the receiving end of a series of violent blows and jerks.

As the spell develops, the shaman gives vent to hideous sounds, shouting as the evil spirit supposedly flees to another part of the body. After a time the shaman announces that he has ousted the spirit, placed it under his control.

If it escapes and again gets into the victim's body, the shaman continues until the patient either recovers or dies. If the former, the doctor's reputation is enhanced. If the latter, he merely blames his failure on outside interference. In any case he collects a substantial fee.

When a Labrador Eskimo is seriously ill, his relatives move him outside before death if possible. If he dies in the house, a hole must be cut in the side of the house, through which the body is removed. The hole is then closed to prevent the ghost of the departed from returning, as it would had the body been taken through the door.

The dead, wrapped in skins, are left near a rock or on a hilltop, covered with stones. The frozen ground prevents burial. For the same reason the Nascapi neighbors hang their dead from tree limbs when death occurs in winter.

Through the influence of the great fur-trading companies, by the mid-19th century both northland Indian and Eskimo had adopted many of the white man's ways. The Indian, ideal fur hunter, took to guns and steel traps, textile clothing, metal tools, and cooking utensils. Gradually the canvas-covered or aluminum canoe replaced his birchbark craft; trader's canvas covered his tepee.

The Eskimo with his native mechanical genius now propels his boats with gasoline motors. The phonograph has become as important to the igloo as the blubber lamp. Skin clothing, especially in summer, has given way to European-style attire.

Missionaries following the traders did to the native's beliefs and ideas what the trader had done to his material culture. In remote regions, remnants of old ways are still strong; in others they have almost disappeared.

Tribal territories change and shrink as the white man continues his inexorable march. Gold miners, bush pilots, uranium prospectors press into the once lonely realm of the wandering aborigine. The click of the Geiger counter has become the new heartbeat of the north.

Only the old people remember the past, and, like mankind the world over, sigh and pine for "the good old days."

**Sioux Kinsmen Meet**

In eagle-feather war bonnet, bear-claw necklace, and bone-bead breastplate, Chief Crazy Bull views the National Geographic Society's exhibit of Indian paintings by W. Langdon Kihn which lined Explorers Hall at The Society's Washington, D.C. headquarters.

Crazy Bull holds an eagle-feather fan; porcupine quillwork decorates his sleeve. He lingers before the portrait of his grim-featured Sioux relative, One Bull (page 12), witness to Custer's Last Stand.

How the artist came to paint One Bull's portrait, and his vivid account of 14 years in the field in search of the American Indian past is told in the following chapter.

NATIONAL GEOGRAPHIC PHOTOGRAPHER
JOHN E. FLETCHER

CHAPTER 8

# PAINTING THE NORTH AMERICAN INDIAN

## BY W. LANGDON KIHN

FROST SETTLED ON THE DESERT as the Navajo fire dance ended. The first red sliver of the rising sun jutted into view; colorfully costumed Indians sang their haunting Bluebird Parting song, and then quietly drifted away. One small group remained, drinking coffee from a pot sitting on campfire coals.

Cold and lame from standing all night watching the dance (page 101), I took a tin cup from my car and walked over to help myself to the brew. As I stood quietly, sipping my hot drink, a stocky Navajo approached, glittering with turquoise earrings, silver-buttoned buckskin moccasins, sporting a wide-brimmed hat and fine blanket.

"How did you like our dance?" he asked.

"Great," I replied.

"I see you're from Connecticut," he went on, glancing at my license plate. "What part?"

"A little town you probably never heard of—Hadlyme."

"Sure," he replied promptly, "I know Hadlyme. I know the Connecticut River from Hartford to Saybrook."

"How come?" I asked.

"I went to Yale," he grinned.

That incongruous conversation in the middle of a desert wilderness scented by sweet smoke from burning piñon logs is one of many incidents I recall from 14 years during which I completed the 103 paintings on North American Indians in this book.

I began the project in 1935, humbled by its scope and its problems. No series of paintings on such a large scale had ever before been attempted. Except for a few isolated groups of Indians who still resist the white man's era, traces of aboriginal culture have almost vanished from North America.

With exhaustive research I set out to recapture the dress and paraphernalia of each main group of Indians at its historic peak. Obviously, I was slated to visit reservations, to watch ceremonies, and explore beautiful remote Shangri-Las where the American Indian had carved his destiny.

Often, as I traversed deep forests, wide plains, and mighty mountains that formed the backdrop for the American Indian, I turned my mind back through time. In my imagination I pictured strange families of a thousand years ago occupying stone and adobe dwellings carved from the golden rock walls of towering cliffs.

Or, facing the green-blue sea that washed a deserted totem pole village, I visualized a brightly painted war canoe laden with costumed warriors, stealthily skirting a spruce-jungle cove.

My wife and I would leave Connecticut in a car loaded with painting and camping equipment, books, and luggage and head for Indian country. I would choose a general area to study, such as the northern plains or southwest desert. From there on, we never knew exactly what to expect.

We put up where we could, sometimes boarding, sometimes camping. The Indians themselves, among whom I have many personal friends, often played host.

One thing that impressed me from the outset was the amazing tribal differences among American Indians. Just as each nation of the world has its own traits, so does each Indian tribe possess its unique personality. But common to all tribes is an ancient, deep-rooted, well-justified mistrust of the white man. Sometimes it was a difficult barrier to overcome.

On the Blackfeet Reservation in Montana I met a striking type of this colorful Algonquian tribe. Grabbing my interpreter, I told him to ask the prospect to pose. Ten dollars for posing was the immediate demand.

One dollar, I told my interpreter, was all I could pay.

The Indian spoke scornfully. "I know you white fella, smart fella. You make picture and take him back to New York town. Then you hang him up in big brick tepee. Pretty soon another white man come along and you sell him picture for ten dollar. I want ten dollar for posing."

I told him he was crazy; that if I made a dollar on my pictures I would be lucky.

"A dollar?" queried the Indian, a disconcerting glint in his eyes.

"That's right."

"All right," he said, "I'll buy picture for one dollar."

Generally, the Blackfeet seemed a happy, even-tempered people. My old friend Eagle Calf (page 72) kept me laughing with yarns like his story about Fish Wolf Robe.

Fish Wolf Robe returned from a sun dance in Canada in a secondhand Model T. When the tires blew out, he stuffed them with hay. He clattered up to Eagle Calf's tepee at midnight. That worthy went out in his long-sleeved, ankle-length union suit to see what the rumpus was about. When Fish saw Eagle Calf in the moonlight in his white undies, he thought he was a ghost. He yelled, and the last Eagle Calf saw of him that night was when he disappeared over the nearest hill.

A different type of people are the totem pole dwellers of the Northwest. These Indians are a suspicious lot, constantly involved in intrigue.

Many years ago I was painting on the Northwest Coast in the Indian village of Nootka, Vancouver Island. The picturesque cluster of frail wooden shacks, clinging precariously to rocky cliffs, housed Indian families that worked in the large pilchard cannery.

One morning I met an incredibly old man with a wizened face and one penetrating squint eye. He looked like a Chinese pirate. Calling the cannery owner's son, I requested him to ask the Indian if he would pose for me.

At first the old fellow would have none of it. But my friend insisted. A long parley ensued, in Chinook (a gibberish tongue, part Indian, part Spanish, English, French, and what not). Finally, the old Indian grinned and came along with me.

Afterwards the white boy described how he'd told the Indian I was a "Boston man" (American) who had come from "way back east in New York and Washington where all the big white chiefs live to paint famous Indian chiefs like you.

"This man hang his pictures in a big potlatch house," the boy continued. "He invite all big white chiefs to come see all big Indian chiefs. When they come

NATIONAL GEOGRAPHIC PHOTOGRAPHER ROBERT F. SISSON

**The Indian's Heroic Age Lives Again.** W. Langdon Kihn puts final touches to his painting of a Columbia River Indian netting salmon (page 128), one of his 103 paintings in this book. New York-born Mr. Kihn began art studies at 15. Today more than 50 museums and galleries here and abroad have exhibited his work. Commissioned by The National Geographic Society to capture on canvas major North American Indian groups at high points in their history, he roamed from Florida to Alaska, from California to Labrador. By car, train, boat, canoe, horseback, and plane he probed some of the continent's most remote wildernesses. He visited chiefs and tribesmen, sketched costumes, jotted notes on ceremonies. His artistry and painstaking research have produced the most complete, authentic, and dramatic picture record of the North American Indian ever achieved.

and look around, they say 'Where's Sam?' And if you don't pose for this man there'll be no Sam."

Sam could not bear the thought of not having his picture hung in the white man's potlatch house.

I finished most pictures in my Connecticut studio using sketches and notes made in the field. Geronimo (page 115) and Chief Joseph (page 124) are composite pictures done from existing photographs. The features of Pocahontas (page 61) were taken from a portrait made of her in England in 1616.

Some canvases, mostly portraits, I painted on the spot. Sometimes these were of Indians who had supplied information. Occasionally subjects belonged to notable families.

For the better part of a day I went over the Little Big Horn battleground in Montana with One Bull (page 12).

The old warrior, a nephew of Sitting Bull, actually took part in the fight that wiped out General George A. Custer and his cavalry detachment in June, 1876. One Bull's firsthand recollections of the battle will not be heard again. In his nineties when I talked with him, he died a few years later.

I was also fortunate to meet and paint Chief Shaiks (page 147) at Wrangell, Alaska. He was the last descendant of a line of hereditary chiefs dating from the time of Russian occupation in the mid-18th century. Until his death, a year after he posed for me, Chief Shaiks remained an influential figure among the Tlingit.

One particular portrait, that of the Hopi girl with the "squash blossom" hairdo (frontispiece), proved to my satisfaction that most of the more primitive tribes are adjusting rapidly to what we call civilization. The Hopi are a tribe of the Pueblo, mild, soft-spoken Indians of the Southwest who live, dress, and conduct their ceremonies much as they did when Cabeza de Vaca and his Negro lieutenant Estevan found them more than 400 years ago.

Before the Hopi girl's last sitting as my model, she gave birth to a stillborn child. In earlier days, her people would have believed that I had somehow drawn the life out of the unborn child. Probably they would have killed me. I was thankful that their views on the matter were modified.

Indians that have been in close contact with us for generations now live much as we do. They have houses, autos, radios, jobs in all walks of life. Eskimos often power their primitive skin umiaks with outboard motors, many Navajos drive to fire dances in pickup trucks, and I once watched the christening of a plane which Indians at Oregon's Klamath Reservation had bought to patrol their forest reserve.

My last field trip traced the oldest migration routes in northwestern America, from Alaska's coast to the interior. In 18 hours' flying from Nome to the Mackenzie delta, we accomplished a trip that would have taken those early migrants from Asia years to complete.

We soared over high mountains and fertile valleys spotted with game. Landing at Fort Yukon on the Arctic Circle, we were met by a temperature of 93 degrees and myriads of mosquitoes. Soon after take-off, we plunged into the boiling smoke of a forest fire which blotted out the sun and forced us to skim low over the twisting Porcupine River.

After what seemed an anxious eternity, the smoke thinned, the mountains dwindled, and we slipped in to land at Old Crow, northernmost Indian outpost of Yukon Territory.

The isolated village contains a score of log cabins, a log trading post, a mission, and the log residence of the Royal Canadian Mounted Police. A jungle of spruce, poplar, alder, and willow hems in the community, adding to its remote atmosphere. The population of about 125 Kutchin Indians, formerly called the Loucheux, lives exclusively by hunting and trapping.

In such a setting I expected to find a people uninfluenced by the distant outside world. I anticipated ancient rituals from the pagan past. I looked for unique costumes, tuned my ears for Indian songs.

After a day or so, invited to a village dance, I accepted gladly, preparing myself for a flood of fascinating material. The rigors of the trip to Old Crow would now seem worthwhile—I thought.

A surprise was in store. The dance turned out to be a Hudson's Bay jig, a good deal like a New England square dance. The music consisted—not of chants, savage and insistent—but of English and Scottish tunes played on a fiddle and guitar by two Kutchin braves!

# PART II

# ANCIENT LIFE IN THE NEW WORLD

PAINTING BY H. M. HERGET

**Yum Kax, God of Harvest, Sows Corn on the Earth Mother,** adorned with serpent headdress. His bright knitted bag holds grains of the Maya staff of life; his hat, resembling a bishop's miter, is a conventionalized ear of corn. Man's face fastened to the god's back may be a severed human head or a mask of stone or wood. More than 1,000 years ago a Maya sculptor fashioned the original of this scene on a 16-foot stela found in 1921 at Piedras Negras, Guatemala.

CHAPTER 9

# THE MAYA OF YUCATAN

## BY SYLVANUS GRISWOLD MORLEY

DURING THE EARLY YEARS of the Christian Era there developed in what is now northern Guatemala a civilization called the Maya.

This civilization, destined to become the most brilliant cultural expression of ancient America, was based upon agriculture, chiefly the raising of corn.

Because the early Maya were primarily farmers, they became interested in the phenomena of time, the passing of the seasons, the several stages of the farmer's year—when the forest should be felled, the dried wood and leaves burned, the corn planted and harvested. All these were of vital concern, so their priests during the millennium before Christ turned to the study of time measurement and astronomy.

Although the Maya in their knowledge of the apparent movements of heavenly bodies—the sun, moon, Venus, and probably other planets—excelled the ancient Egyptians and Babylonians, their greatest intellectual achievement was the invention of a chronology, exact to the day within a period of 374,400 years.

For the first time in human history, a system of chronology used numbers involving the concept of the abstract mathematical quantity of zero, one of man's outstanding achievements. All the essential elements of modern arithmetic were used by the Maya 2000 years ago, at least five centuries before the Hindus developed the fundamentals of Arabic notation in India (page 198).

By their accurate system, Maya priests were able to predict eclipses and the heliacal rising and setting of Venus. Of even greater importance to the Maya farmer, they had determined the length of the tropical year with as high a degree of accuracy as Pope Gregory XIII did a good thousand years later.

The excellent weather calculations of these astronomer-priests were largely responsible for the accumulation of food reserves. This growing wealth meant more time off from the routine of keeping body and soul together, so that people were able to turn to other pursuits. Architecture, sculpture, painting, ceramics, jade engraving, weaving, and featherworking became highly esteemed.

Thus, during the fourth to eighth centuries of the Christian Era, there rose numbers of cities, with public buildings made of stone, decorated with stucco, and brilliantly painted.

There were lofty pyramids, surmounted by towering temples, progenitors of our modern skyscrapers; great monasteries for the numerous priesthood; probably palaces for the ruling caste; astronomical observatories; ball courts where a game like modern basketball was played; vapor baths, and other specialized masonry constructions. These buildings were arranged around large squares

PAINTINGS BY H. M. HERGET

**Kneeling Penitent Makes Blood Offering to the Gods.** Dressed in gorgeous raiment, he pulls a thick cord studded with thorns through a slit in his tongue. Maya priest with ceremonial staff supervises. Reddened cord and drops of blood fall into carved stone vase. Bloodletting from pierced ear lobes was also a common form of self-mutilation to express religious devotion. This scene was carved on the underside of a door lintel in a Yaxchilán temple. Some of the finest Classic Maya sculpture was created at this ceremonial center in the Usumacinta River Valley. Even today Lacandone Indian descendants of the Maya come to Yaxchilán to burn copal incense on ancient altars.

or plazas, or on top of artificially raised terraces sometimes of enormous extent.

In the plazas and on the terraces stood beautifully sculptured monuments, ranging from 5 to 25 feet in height. These were erected at five- or ten-year intervals to commemorate the principal astronomic events of the passing years, to set forth corresponding calendar corrections for the period, like our own leap-year corrections, and for other ceremonial and religious purposes.

This first florescence of Maya culture I have called the Old Empire.* It was the highest civilization, judged by its intellectual and esthetic achievements, ever produced by the American Indian.

The Old Empire was probably not so much a political entity as a cultural unit, like the city-states of ancient Greece: Athens, Sparta, and Corinth; or the city-states of Renaissance Italy: Venice, Genoa, and Florence. The Maya constituted a loosely associated group of powerful communities enjoying a common and exceedingly homogeneous culture.

The Old Empire stretched from what now is western Honduras to the highlands of central Chiapas, Mexico, always keeping to the Atlantic side of the Continental Divide. Thence it extended

*Instead of Morley's "Old Empire" and "New Empire" concepts, archeologists today refer to Formative, Classic, and Mexican periods.

north across the heavily forested lowlands of northern Guatemala (the Department of Petén) and adjacent parts of the States of Chiapas and Tabasco, Mexico, on the west and British Honduras on the east, and still farther north into the Yucatán Peninsula (map, page 189).

Uaxactún, deeply buried in the jungle of northern Guatemala, is representative of Old Empire cities. Its peculiar importance lies in that it is one of the oldest centers of Maya civilization.

The writer will never forget the day he discovered the oldest Maya monument, standing in its lonely court on the Acropolis of Uaxactún. As he came through the thick bush he caught sight of the tall shaft of stone leaning far to one side, with two columns of hieroglyphics engraved upon its back, so covered with dried moss and living lichens as to be all but indistinguishable.

Climbing up the shaft, he fell to work cleaning off the dried moss which obscured the details of the inscription. Suddenly there flashed from the stone the number 8—three dots and one bar, as the ancient Maya wrote it—and beside it the sign for the baktun. Baktun 8.

Most older Maya monuments were erected in Baktun 9, a period extending from A.D. 176 to A.D. 571. Just as we start our calendar from the birth of Christ, the Maya began theirs from a date some 5,000 years ago which must have marked a great event in their myth-

**Religion Filled Youths' Lives in Maya Days.** Noble maiden contemplates Yum Kax (page 182), one of many deities in the Maya pantheon. Her elaborate headdress, heavy bracelets, and rich-embroidered kirtle fringed with jade beads reveal her as a chieftain's daughter. To her, each day had its astrological significance, each event its patron god. Right: A young craftsman deftly depicts religious scenes on a graceful jar. No pre-Columbian Indians produced more artistically decorated ceremonial ware than the Maya. The potter's finest work went into the tombs of nobles.

**From His Stately Throne, the Chief Bids Courtiers Be Silent.** The artist re-creates a drama in stone from a Piedras Negras lintel, finest known specimen of Maya skill. While Europe languished in the Dark Ages, Indian pyramid builders carved such masterpieces as this, dating from A.D. 761.

PAINTING BY H. M. HERGET

Chief's extended arm, heads of squatting nobles were carved in the round. Natural poses, perfectly proportioned figures suggest Greek art; rich garments, fans, tassels show amazing realistic detail. Some 158 hieroglyphs form a border on the original, now in Museum of Archeology, Guatemala City.

PAINTING BY H. M. HERGET

**Priests Sacrifice a Parrot.** Copal resin burns on stone altar carved with sun god's face and serpent heads like gargoyles. Snakes dominate headdresses. The Maya did not seek charity from their gods. They willingly paid in human, animal, fruit and vegetable offerings for all favors granted.

ological history. Instead of our millennium, century, decade, year, month, and day, they figured time in baktuns (144,000 days), katuns (7,200 days), tuns (360 days), uinals (20 days), and kins (one day).

The date of this earliest monument—8.14.10.13.15 (8 baktuns, 14 katuns, 10 tuns, 13 uinals, 15 kins)—falls A.D. 68!

Because this monument records a date in the Maya Baktun 8, the name Uaxactún was given to the city, the word meaning in Maya *uaxac,* "eight," and *tun,* "stone"—stone eight.

Several years later the Carnegie Institution chose Uaxactún for extensive study. Frans Blom, of the Seventh Central American Expedition, in 1924 discovered that the arrangement of temples and pyramids on the east and west sides of the plaza in probably the oldest parts of Uaxactún formed a giant sundial for determining the equinoxes and solstices.

The priests of Uaxactún gave this information to the farmers, enabling them to regulate the different activities of their year; the felling and burning of the bush, planting and harvesting, with ceremonies appropriate to each occasion.

Later excavations at Uaxactún revealed what is unquestionably one of the most magnificent examples of aboriginal American architecture extant—a silvery white, stucco-covered pyramid of exquisite proportions and perfect outline.

The northern half of the Yucatán Peninsula, which I have called the New Maya Empire, was only a provincial region in Old Empire times. It did not reach its cultural zenith until after the 11th century.

One by one the cities of the Old Empire ceased to build new temples and palaces, ceased to erect sculptured stone monuments and hieroglyphic inscriptions setting forth their respective dates in the Maya era; ceased, in fact, to function as governmental and religious centers. Meanwhile the cities of Yucatán increased in prosperity and were becoming new fountainheads of Maya culture.

Finally the former centers of the Old Empire were abandoned. The forest returned, and again the jaguar, tapir, peccary, and deer stalked the courts where kings had ruled and priests performed their rites of human sacrifice.

Earthquakes, foreign conquest, civil war, recurrent epidemics of yellow fever and malaria, climatic changes bringing an increased rainfall so abundant that the land was no longer tillable by the Maya system of agriculture; intellectual and esthetic exhaustion following a long period of forced productivity; social disorganization, political decay, and governmental disintegration—all these have been assigned at one time or another by different writers as causes for the collapse of the Old Empire.

While some of these factors undoubtedly played their part in the Maya decline, I believe the chief cause was the

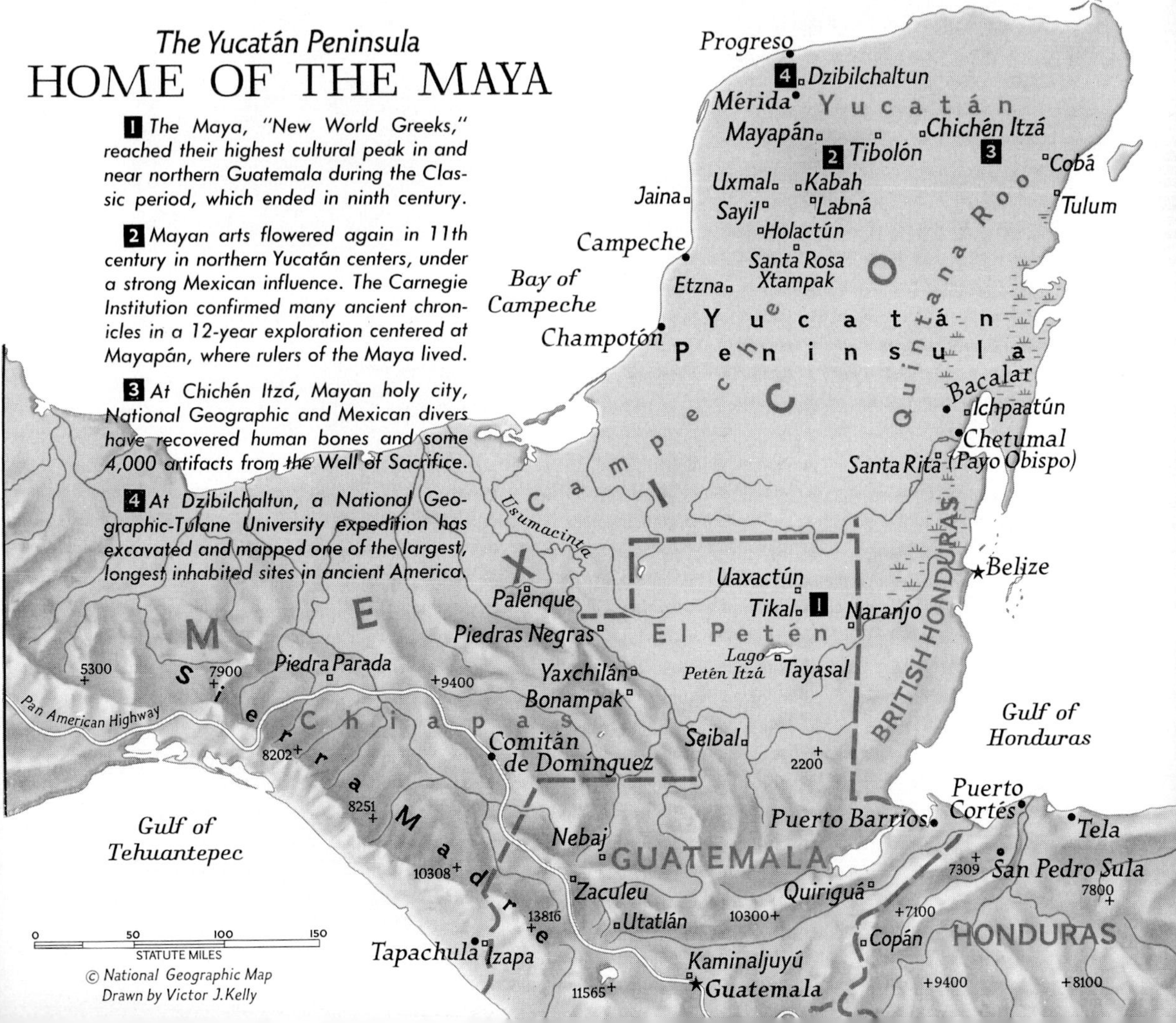

The Yucatán Peninsula
HOME OF THE MAYA
1 The Maya, "New World Greeks," reached their highest cultural peak in and near northern Guatemala during the Classic period, which ended in ninth century.
2 Mayan arts flowered again in 11th century in northern Yucatán centers, under a strong Mexican influence. The Carnegie Institution confirmed many ancient chronicles in a 12-year exploration centered at Mayapán, where rulers of the Maya lived.
3 At Chichén Itzá, Mayan holy city, National Geographic and Mexican divers have recovered human bones and some 4,000 artifacts from the Well of Sacrifice.
4 At Dzibilchaltun, a National Geographic-Tulane University expedition has excavated and mapped one of the largest, longest inhabited sites in ancient America.
Progreso
Dzibilchaltun
Mérida
Yucatán
Mayapán
Chichén Itzá
Tibolón
Cobá
Uxmal
Kabah
Jaina
Sayil
Labná
Tulum
Holactún
Campeche
Santa Rosa Xtampak
Bay of Campeche
Etzna
Quintana Roo
Yucatán Peninsula
Champotón
Campeche
Bacalar
Ichpaatún
Chetumal
Santa Rita
(Payo Obispo)
Usumacinta
MEXICO
Uaxactún
Belize
Tikal
Naranjo
Palenque
Piedras Negras
El Petén
Lago Petén Itzá
Tayasal
BRITISH HONDURAS
5300
7900
Piedra Parada
+9400
Yaxchilán
Bonampak
Sierra Madre
Chiapas
Pan American Highway
Gulf of Honduras
Comitán de Domínguez
Seibal
8202
2200
Puerto Cortés
Puerto Barrios
Tela
Gulf of Tehuantepec
8251
Nebaj
GUATEMALA
7309
San Pedro Sula
10308
Zaculeu
Quiriguá
7800
+7100
13816
Utatlán
10300
Copán
HONDURAS
0 50 100 150
STATUTE MILES
Tapachula
Izapa
Kaminaljuyú
© National Geographic Map
Drawn by Victor J. Kelly
11565
Guatemala
+9400
+8100

law of diminishing returns. Maya agriculture consisted in felling a patch of forest at the end of the rainy season in December or January, in burning it toward the end of the dry season in March or April, and in planting it at the beginning of the rains in May. This system had two serious drawbacks.

First, the corn harvested the second year from any field was only about two-thirds the first year's yield, while the third year's crop shrank still another third, due to the intense growth of weeds.

In practice the Maya find it easier, now as then, to clear forest and make a new cornfield than to fight the weeds a third year in the same

PAINTINGS BY H. M. HERGET

**Noble and Priest** went clothed in resplendent attire. Standing before a stucco-covered temple, a portly noble (above) displays contrasting skirt and tunic of heavy cloth. Olivella shells from oceans east and west cloak his upper arms. Hard palm wood forms his staff.

Ornate ceremonial bar identifies priest (right), whose flaming headdress has a carved wood frame. Grotesque head decorating his jaguar-fur skirt represents a Maya god. Small face mask peers from tasseled belt. Even the sandals are topped with jaguar skin. The painting interprets a figure carved on a mid-ninth century monument at Seibal, in northern Guatemala.

**Masters of Calendar Lore Were the Maya Priests.** Their massive pyramid temples dominated the ancient cities; their jaguar skins, jade, and quetzal plumes set them apart from the common people, whose lives they greatly influenced. Priests alone could fathom the Maya calendar, foretell the good or evil portents of each coming day, and determine the propitious time for sacred rites.

field. Thus most available land must have lain fallow in the populous ancient times awaiting reforestation so it could be cleared again. Today, depending upon the fertility of the region, reforestation takes from three to ten years.

The second drawback was even more serious. If the burnings are continued long enough, reforestation is retarded and the abandoned cornfields become overgrown with grass. When this stage was reached, Maya agriculture ended.

Even today the Maya find it hard to turn the stony soil, everywhere interspersed with outcroppings of limestone. They have few hoes, picks, harrows, plows or spades. Many know only the ax or the machete, with which they fell the forest, and the wooden planting stick, with which they make holes in the ground and plant corn. Their ancestors had only the stone ax and planting stick (page 201).

In ancient times the trees were killed by cutting a ring around the bark with a stone ax. When they had dried out they were burned standing.

**Worshipers Throng Chichén Itzá, Holy City of the Maya.** Priest and warrior, noble and commoner assemble for rites vital to their existence. Rising gleaming white from green Yucatán jungle, Maya cities were not abodes of the people, who lived in scattered villages, but great ceremonial centers, mostly open and undefended, and skirted by thatched homes of priesthood and nobility.

PAINTING BY H. M. HERGET

From their round, gargoyled observatory Chichén Itzá's astronomers scanned the sky. Narrow openings pierced thick walls, formed lines of sight on stars, sun, moon, and planets. In background: El Castillo (left), largest structure and chief sanctuary to Kukulcan, city's patron deity; Temple of the Warriors (right), named for sculptures of fighting men on the myriad pillars of its colonnade.

I believe that by the eighth century the Old Empire region had been transformed from forest to vast man-made savannas. The ancient Maya priests surely must have foreseen what was impending and made many appeals to the gods to send more abundant crops. The Maya deities did not hearken to these prayers.

Long before affairs had reached this crisis in the south, the centers in Yucatán were increasing in size and power. Archeologic evidence has traced the Maya movement into Yucatán through chains of dated cities. One extends from northeastern Petén up the east coast of the peninsula and thence inland (Ichpaatún, Tulum, Cobá, and Chichén Itzá). Another runs up the west side (Santa Rosa Xtampak, Etzna, Holactún, and Jaina). The eastern cities generally predate the western ones, confirming a tradition that the Maya entered Yucatán from the east.

There is strong evidence that the first Maya in Yucatán found people already settled there who may have spoken Mayan, but who certainly did not have Maya culture. They had no stone architecture, no calendar, no hieroglyphic writing, and no typical Old Empire pottery. And herein lies the archeological catch.

If the Maya had found no previous occupants of the region, the pottery they made after reaching Yucatán would have

**War Prisoners Learn Their Fate.** Bound with rope, necklaces removed, faces scarred, ear ornaments torn out in degradation, they have played the game and lost. Now they face sacrifice. Those with hope gaze up as their unfettered leader supplicates the victorious war chief. Two haughty subchiefs hover by. A large sculpture found in four pieces at Piedras Negras depicts this rare early Maya martial scene. Carved with hard stone tools, it stands 10 feet 4 inches high, weighs 4 tons as restored in the Museum of Archeology, Guatemala City.

PAINTINGS BY H. M. HERGET

**Maya on the Warpath,** like later-day Indians, donned awesome regalia to frighten foes. Club-sword mounted with sharp obsidian, small round shield, served in hand-to-hand fighting. Bow and arrow came later to Yucatán.

Not bent on land conquest, the early Maya fought to gain captives for sacrifice. The sun, after its nightly descent into underworld, required blood to recover from ordeal. Thus needs of a theocratic society bred a warrior class.

**Into the Sacred Well** hurtles a maiden. The rain gods are angry; drought parches the cornfields, famine threatens the Maya. A human sacrifice must be offered. Amid the chanting of a dirge to muted drums, blue vapor swirls upward from incense burners. Priests seize the terrified girl and hurl her into the depths 80 feet below. As they perform the barbaric rite at dawn, thousands throng holy Chichén Itzá and shower jeweled offerings into the abyss. Early in the 20th century, dredging recovered the bones of numerous men, women, and children.

National Geographic in 1960–61 joined Mexican divers in a new descent into the sacred cenote. Like a giant vacuum cleaner, the expedition's air lift sucked at the silt-thick bottom (right), spewing out copal incense, gold beads, polished jades, and potsherds, as well as mud, rocks, and water. Divers retrieved more human and animal bones, found a grotesque four-inch rubber effigy that had survived five hundred years' immersion.

The expedition sketched the first map of the cenote's underwater contours, tested new techniques of archeology. The Mexican government collected more than 4,000 artifacts. Experts believe that pumping the well dry would yield more treasures.

KODACHROME BY BATES LITTLEHALES, NATIONAL GEOGRAPHIC STAFF

PAINTING BY H. M. HERGET

been much the same as they had made in their former homes in the south. But such is not the case. H. B. Roberts, Carnegie Institution expert on Maya ceramics, found the pottery used throughout Yucatán in New Empire times entirely different from that used in the Old Empire region whence they came. This pottery is related to the earlier wares on the Veracruz coast.

It is evident that a distinctive indigenous ceramic art had already been developed by inhabitants of Yucatán. The bearers of the Maya tradition simply took over native styles of pottery, but imposed architectural and other elements of their own culture.

Yucatán must have held not a few disappointments for these early adventuring Americans. It is at best but a parched land, limestone in formation, with no rivers or streams and only one or two lakes. Here and there a few natural wells—great holes in the ground, sometimes several hundred feet in diameter—have formed where the limestone crust has fallen through, exposing subterranean water. These the Maya called *cenotes,* and wherever they existed important population centers were established.

The site of Chichén Itzá was peculiarly favored, for here the Yucatán plain is pierced by two great natural wells within half a mile of each other. Destined to become holy city of the New Empire, Chichén Itzá seems to have been founded toward the end of the seventh century; Mayapán and other important cities of

# MAYA CALENDAR AND NUMERAL SYSTEM

FASCINATED BY MYSTERIES of time and astronomy, the Maya perfected a calendar and numeral system that rank as outstanding intellectual achievements.

No narratives of personal glories or national calamities fill their written records. Not even the homely record of weighing baskets of corn. Instead, strange and complex figures tell of the beginning and end of time cycles, predict the movement of heavenly bodies, correlate moon-month and sun-year, and chart dates for rituals honoring the gods.

Maya priest-scholars set forth an imaginative concept of time as a series of burdens carried on the backs of divine bearers. Each day brought by the sacred bearers held its own promise of happiness or misery, success or failure.

The thought was mystic but the chronology was as accurate as our own Gregorian calendar, and so precisely organized that no two days could be confused. One monument at Quiriguá calculates in stone a theoretical date 400,000,000 years ago!

As we do today, the Maya wrote figures in two distinct ways, comparable to Roman and Arabic numerals. Maya "Roman" numerals were dots and bars, as shown below. A dot stood for one; a bar, five. Combined, they reached 19—maximum number of days before the next time unit, the Maya 20-day month. Starting off the numeral system is the shell sign for zero.

For their "Arabic" system, from zero through 19, the Maya designed fantastic heads (right). These were of two kinds. Zero through 13 were represen-

= 0
= 1
= 2
= 3
= 4
= 5
= 6
= 7
= 8
= 9
= 10
= 11
= 12
= 13
= 14
= 15
= 16
= 17
= 18
= 19

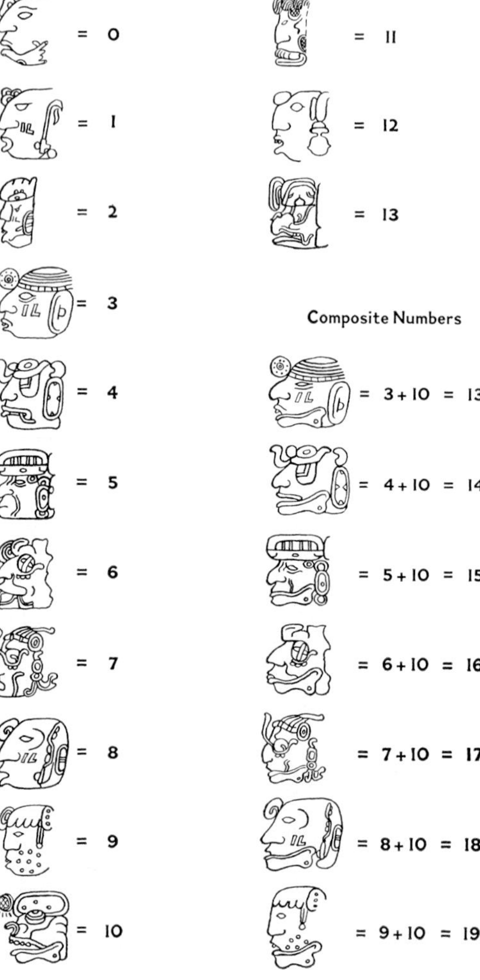


ted by patron deities such as Death, Sun, and Rain. From the second number 13 on, the heads were composites. Each combined the skeleton jaw from number 10 with one of the other number signs, 3 through 9.

Thus the compound sign 13 consists of the jaw plus 3, the godhead whose band and disk oddly resemble the mirror worn by a modern physician.

In writing large numbers, the Maya multiplied by means of position, involving use of the zero. So accustomed are we to the zero that we hardly realize what an amazing concept it is. Try, for example, to multiply MCMLXXXIV times MCMLXXXIV!

Without their system, the Maya and their cultural forebears would have had to write impossibly complex combinations of higher figures. To calculate long time periods would have taken stone calendars the size of the Washington Monument!

With the zero, they were able to use a limited number of recurring symbols, giving them value accord-

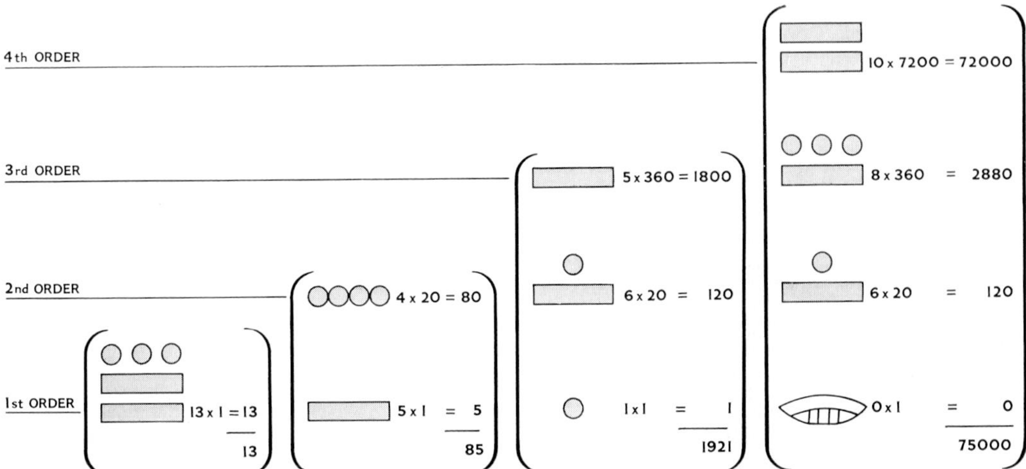


ing to their position in an overall figure. This is similar to the way we indicate 1,255,378 by the decimal system of units, tens, hundreds, thousands, and so forth from right to left. But where our system progresses by tens, theirs mounted by twenties. Too, instead of writing numbers horizontally as we do, the Maya placed theirs one over the other.

The above chart gives examples of Maya dot-and-bar numbers through the first four orders of the time count. The figures represent days, beginning at the first order with 13 units (13 x 1).

At the second order, four dots are multiplied by 20 (the number of days in a Maya month) and added to five units, producing 85.

The third order brings an exception, the only one to break the even rise of Maya figures. At this point the multiple becomes 360 (that is, 1 x 20 x 18) instead of 400 (1 x 20 x 20). This deviation probably arose from the Maya wish to bring this count as near as possible to the length of the solar year.

With the fourth order, progression by twenties returns, providing a Maya 20-year period of 7,200 days. In the last column's grand total of 75,000 the final, all-important unit zero is obtained by the simple step, 0 x 1 equals 0.

The Maya calendar comprised two cycles: a sacred round of 260 days endlessly repeated, and the conventional 365-day solar year. The cycles were interlocking, like teeth of two unequal cogwheels. As the wheels revolved and cogs meshed, each day took on a double identity.

From the religious count came 260 "day god" symbols, formed by combining numbers 1 through 13 with 20 names. The solar year provided a "month god" position for every day (such as our May 30). There were 18 full months of 20 days in the Maya year, plus an ill-omened fragment of five days.

The sequence of both sets of names and numbers was so staggered that it took 18,980 days or 52 years for the dual identities to duplicate. Hence the Maya 52-year cycle was a complete time unit in their calendar, as the century is in ours.

Pictured below are eight dates from the Maya solar-year cycle that correspond to some of our holidays or celebrations. In each hieroglyph, the number in bars and dots indicates position in the month, the sign at right the name of the Maya month.

These parallels are based on the Maya calendar of the 1560's described by Bishop Diego de Landa.

Two examples, 11 Zac and 12 Mol, show how the sculptors filled unused numeral spaces with decorative detail. Thereby the Maya reveal not only their artistry but the infinite care with which they fashioned in stone a monument to their philosophy of time.

19 Mol
January 1

11 Zac
February 22

3 Cumbu
July 4

18 Zotz
October 12

14 Ceh
March 17

8 Pax
May 30

8 Xul
November 11

12 Mol
December 25

the north, perhaps 300 years later. Early in the 11th century a number of these Yucatán city-states established a confederacy called the League of Mayapán, dividing the country into spheres of influence.

With the peaceful conditions that followed, the country prospered under wise leaders, and a true Maya Renaissance flowered.

The façades of the New Empire buildings, instead of being decorated with stucco, were elaborately sculptured with geometric designs, mask panels of the rain god and other decorative elements, and brilliantly painted. Sculpture languished as an independent art, became chiefly an adjunct to architecture.

A strong Mexican influence, associated with the Toltec culture centered at Tula, north of the Valley of Mexico, appeared at Chichén Itzá. Clearly

**Grinding Corn and Weaving** was women's work then as now. Child on back, a Maya woman patiently bends over stone muller and metate. She soaks dried kernels overnight to loosen hulls, then grinds grain to pasty dough for tortillas, toasts them on a hot griddle, keeps them warm in a gourd until served.

Nor has looming cloth (right) changed much since Maya days. Spanish conquerors mistook fine Indian garments for silk. Homes past and present were walled with saplings, roofed with thatch. Ancient Maya domesticated turkeys, bees, dogs, but had no beasts of burden. Sculptors ignored women in carvings, but pottery figurines reveal their daily life.

PAINTINGS BY H. M. HERGET

reflected in the city's new architecture and customs, this foreign influence even gave Chichén Itzá a new religion—the worship of the golden-haired god, Quetzalcoatl, the "Feathered Serpent," whom the Maya called Kukulcan.

Because it represents a blending of two important cultures, the Maya and the Toltec, Chichén Itzá was chosen by the Carnegie Institution for intensive explorations begun in 1924. Many imposing structures were revealed and a flood of light thrown on the life of these ancient people.

Chichén Itzá's two cenotes, or wells, are each about 200 feet in diameter, with their water level

**Maya Seed Their Fields,** armed with planting stick, bag, and gourd. Milpa (clearing) agriculture still survives, begins with dry-season felling and burning of forest trees. Stick planting follows. Ripened ears are bent over and left to dry on stalk. Gourd water bottle still refreshes Maya planter or hunter, corn comprises four-fifths of his family's diet. A sick Indian reveals his state by saying: "I ate only two tortillas this morning." Average Yucateco consumes 20 per meal. Maya also cultivate beans, squash, tubers, cacao, papaya, and avocado pear.

PAINTINGS BY H. M. HERGET

**Bronzed Warriors Behold the Holy Shrines of Chichén Itzá**

Pre-Aztec Toltecs came from the central Mexican highlands to establish a new stronghold at Chichén Itzá. They made it flourish anew as the holy city of Kukulcan, Mayan version of the Mexican deity Quetzalcoatl, the Feathered Serpent. They built the city's principal structures, including the temple (El Castillo) looming in distance, where Kukulcan was worshiped. Their dramatic Sacred Well rite drew pilgrims from all parts of the Mayan world. Their weapons and militaristic spirit changed Yucatán's once-serene ways.

The feathered serpent columns which guard the portals of many Chichén Itzá temples show Toltec influence. The Chac Mool statues of reclining human figures (page 215), the stone fretwork roof ornaments, the jaguar and eagle sculptures, the turquoise-crowned figures in the reliefs, the exquisite turquoise mosaic plaques, some hieroglyphics—all these are Mexican importations.

The Toltecs, remaking religion and architecture over the centuries, put a strong Mexican stamp even on *tlachtli* (right), Maya game combining features of basketball and soccer. Using elbows, knees, and hips, but not hands, players sought to drive a solid rubber ball through a stone ring high on the opponents' wall. Shouts ricocheted in the enclosure. Tradition says spectators vanished when a player scored; the feat made him winner of their clothes and jewelry. One of Chichén Itzá's courts is larger than a modern football field.

80 feet below ground. The city takes its name from them, Chichén Itzá meaning in Maya "The mouths of the wells of the Itzá." The Xtoloc Cenote, or Lizard Well, in the center of the city, was used as water supply. The Well of Sacrifice, at the northern end, served a more sinister purpose. Tradition holds that in times of national necessity such as drought, maidens were hurled into its gloomy depths at dawn as living sacrificial victims (page 196).

The Spanish chronicles naïvely observe that if the girls managed to survive until midday, ropes were lowered to them and they were pulled out. Then they were questioned as to what the gods had told them was in store for the Itzá, whether an abundant year or famine. If the deities indicated the former, there was great rejoicing. If the latter, stones were hurled into the well and the people fled with loud cries.

The spectacular nature of this cruel rite—maidens at the brink of the dark pool, the incensing of priests, the sides lined with waiting thousands, a push, perchance a startled cry, a splash below, and silence—all combined to arouse such interest in the ceremony that Chichén Itzá became Mecca of the Mayan World.

Pilgrims came from far and near to hurl treasures into the depths: jade earplugs, noseplugs, beads, plaques, and pendants, copper bells and rings, carved bones, shells, wooden weapons,

KODACHROMES BY JUSTIN LOCKE

**Massive Stone Rings** carved with feathered snakes were goals for Maya youth. Players made offerings in temples at court's open ends to help put ball through 18-inch hole 24 feet above court floor. Courts also served as auditoriums. Less athletic descendants hold oranges for sale.

**Jade-studded Jaguar Throne,** found in 1936 in a secret chamber of Chichén Itzá's pyramid of Kukulcan, is a prized relic of ancient America. Carved from a single block, painted bright red, it has fangs of white stone. Flat back cradles large turquoise mosaic honoring the sun god.

KODACHROMES BY JUSTIN LOCKE

**Henequen, or Sisal, Is Green Gold of Yucatán.** Ancient Maya wove fiber into cloth, rope, nets. With steel scraper, modern villager strips tough strands from 50 long, thick leaves a day. Wife separates fibers. Dried strands hang white from hammock behind her. Henequen, related to century plant, took its commercial name from Sisal, coast village near Mérida. A secondary industry, hunting chicle to make chewing gum, led to discovery of several jungle-buried Maya cities.

masses of sacred copal incense, goldwork from Costa Rica and beyond, cloisonné-like pottery from northwestern Mexico.

Judging from the objects recovered from the well in the 20th century, practically the entire cult of the Well of Sacrifice was of Mexican rather than Mayan origin. Studies of the bones brought up reveal—venerable traditions to the contrary—that not only girls, but infants and adult men and women were sacrificed.

The Mexican impetus set off a building boom all over the northern part of Chichén Itzá. Temples and sanctuaries rose to the new god, all adorned with highly realistic representations of the Feathered Serpent—in columns, balustrades, cornices, and bas-reliefs.

The so-called Castillo, which is not a castle at all but the principal temple of Kukulcan at Chichén Itzá, dates from this period. It covers an acre of ground and towers more than 100 feet above the broad plaza at its base (page 192). Four balustraded stairways ascend its terraced sides, and the sanctuary on the summit is entered through a doorway flanked by feathered-serpent columns.

Other buildings of the Mexican period are the Tlachtli-ground or Ball Court (pages 203–05) and the Temple of the Jaguars, the Temple of the Tables, the High Priest's Grave, and the Caracol or Astronomical Observatory.

This observatory was a building of primary importance. The scientific life of the community centered here, and it is thought by some to be the most beautiful structure in the city (page 192). The round tower, 37 feet in diameter, is composed of two concentric circular passages which surround a solid core of masonry. A spiral stairway ascends inside the latter, emerging in a small chamber near the top, from which observations of important astronomic phenomena were made through small tunnellike passages.

Another enormous construction is the Group of the Thousand Columns. This vast architectural complex of pyramid-temples, colonnaded halls, sunken courts, terraces and platforms includes a central plaza more than five acres in extent.

The most imposing structure excavated at Chichén Itzá is the Temple of the Warriors, standing at the northwest corner of this Group of the Thousand Columns (page 193).

This magnificent building stands on a pyramid's broad summit. Approximately 70 feet square, it was originally 22 feet in height. A pair of feathered-serpent columns, 15 feet high, divides the entrance into three doorways. The exterior walls are sculptured with alternating panels of grotesque human masks; conventionalized representations of Kukulcan; and of the serpent-bird, a fearsome mythological conception with the body, feet, and wings of a bird, the head of a serpent with forked tongue, and a human head issuing from its mouth.

The front chamber is a long colonnaded hall; behind it is the sanctuary. The painted columns still preserve their colors in practically their original brilliancy—red, blue, green, yellow, brown, black, and white. Enormous plumed serpents weave around the sides of both chambers. Imagine the barbaric splendor of this building in its heyday, broad summit thronged with priests gorgeously robed in jaguar skins, feather cloaks, and embroidered cottons, half seen in clouds of swirling incense!

The buried temple proved a treasure house. Found in a far corner of the outer hall, buried beneath rubble, was the Chac Mool—the reclining human figure which had originally stood before the temple portals. Its carving is almost perfectly preserved, except for the nose and part of the headdress, apparently battered off intentionally (page 215).

But the greatest discovery of all, the finest specimen recovered from the Maya area, was found under the sanctuary floor where the Atlantean altar had originally stood. As an electric torch was flashed into the interior of a limestone jar,

**School Days in Maya Land** find young Yucatecos learning Mayan as well as Spanish. No hieroglyphs perplex them in the dimly lit classroom, for they write their ancient American tongue phonetically in A B C's. Girls are garbed in same spotless, embroidered Mother Hubbards their elders wear.

**The Glory That Was Tulum Shines in Its Majestic Ruins.** Back to the Caribbean, Tulum stands on a 40-foot cliff on Yucatán's east coast. A half-mile stone wall, thicker than its 15-foot height, protected three land sides. The five gateways were narrow, low, and dark to thwart invaders.

KODACHROME BY JUSTIN LOCKE

Archeologists find thrilling parallels to Greek architecture in Tulum's little Temple of Frescoes, foreground, with its carved figures of a plunging god. Behind the ceremonial square rises the lofty Palace. The Maya city flourished a dozen centuries ago, and again in the Mexican period.

a beautiful ball of jade reflected the light. This proved to be an almost perfect sphere, two inches in diameter, highly polished. The Indian laborers at once identified it as a *sastun,* or conjuring stone, such as old Maya medicine men far back in the bush still use in their incantations and magic.

A carved jade pendant, pierced for hanging on a cord, some jade and shell beads, and some bones of a tiny bird, possibly a hummingbird, successively came to light. Still the jar guarded its most precious secret. In the bottom there flashed the blue of turquoise, the first ever found in a Maya city. Brushing disclosed the scalloped edge of a mosaic, in perilously fragile condition.

Slowly and with infinite pains the sifted earth was removed until there lay revealed a mosaic plaque 8¾ inches in diameter. The wooden back to which the pieces of turquoise had been fastened had long since crumbled to dust. Indeed upon this dust rested the mosaic, so that any blow would have shattered the arrangement of the more than 3,000 cut and highly polished pieces. It took a skilled preparator, summoned from New York, three weeks to reset the mosaic on a new base. The com-

**Quiriguá Stela Wears Bird-nest Beard**

Eleven centuries have marked little change on the god's Buddha-like face. For each hotun, 1,800-day period in Maya reckoning, Quiriguáns erected such a sandstone shaft. Carved figures of gods front and back wear tall feather headdresses; near-naked bodies are heavily ornamented at waist, wrists, ankles. Hieroglyphs on sides record the period's astronomical events, calculate mythical dates of ages past.

Quiriguá lies in eastern Guatemala's fertile Motagua valley, now banana land. Ancients probably rafted stones to city when river was at flood. They carved boulders into tortoises, jaguars, sky monsters.

pleted plaque was later put on exhibit in the National Museum of Mexico.

After some two centuries the League of Mayapán dissolved in a fierce quarrel between the leaders of Chichén Itzá and Mayapán. The "True Man" of Mayapán, as the ancient Maya called their ruler, Hunnac Ceel, brought in foreign allies from the interior of Mexico. Possibly it was they who introduced the bow and arrow into Yucatán. With the aid of these allies, Hunnac Ceel defeated Chac Xib Chac, ruler of Chichén Itzá. Thus the Cocoms, ruling house of Mayapán, became leaders in northern Yucatán.

By the clever expedient of compelling all the other Maya chieftains to reside at Mayapán, the Cocom capital, the Cocom rulers in effect held these chieftains hostage while they pursued their tyrannical ways.

But increasing oppression finally goaded the Maya to revolt. Banded under the leadership of Tutul Xiu, they sacked Mayapán. The Cocoms moved on to Tibolón, east of Mayapán. The victors founded a new capital at a place called Mani, meaning, "It is finished." The Chichén Itzáns abandoned their city and settled at Tayasal on Lake Petén Itzá in northern Guatemala. And there in 1525 their ruler, Canek, was visited by Hernán Cortés.

This last independent branch of the Maya managed to survive because of their extreme isolation for another century and a half until 1687 when they were finally conquered by the Spanish Captain General and Governor of Yucatán, Martín de Ursua y Arizmendi.

The modern Maya, who still comprise probably half the population of the peninsula, are friendly folk, endowed, in my opinion, with more likable qualities than any other Indian people.

They are short in stature, the men averaging about 5 feet 1 inch and the

**Sacred Plume-giver to the Maya**

Carvings, pottery from Maya and Aztec centers alike link the quetzal with worship, prove male fondness for the sweeping iridescent green tail feathers. Supplying the demand enriched highland Maya in the bird's limited habitat.

Crest and upper parts are green, belly is crimson, as on mounted specimens held by a Guatemalan woman. Quetzal is her country's symbol of liberty, appears on national coat of arms, stamps, and coins; gives its name to the Republic's equivalent of the dollar.

KODACHROMES BY LUIS MARDEN, NATIONAL GEOGRAPHIC STAFF

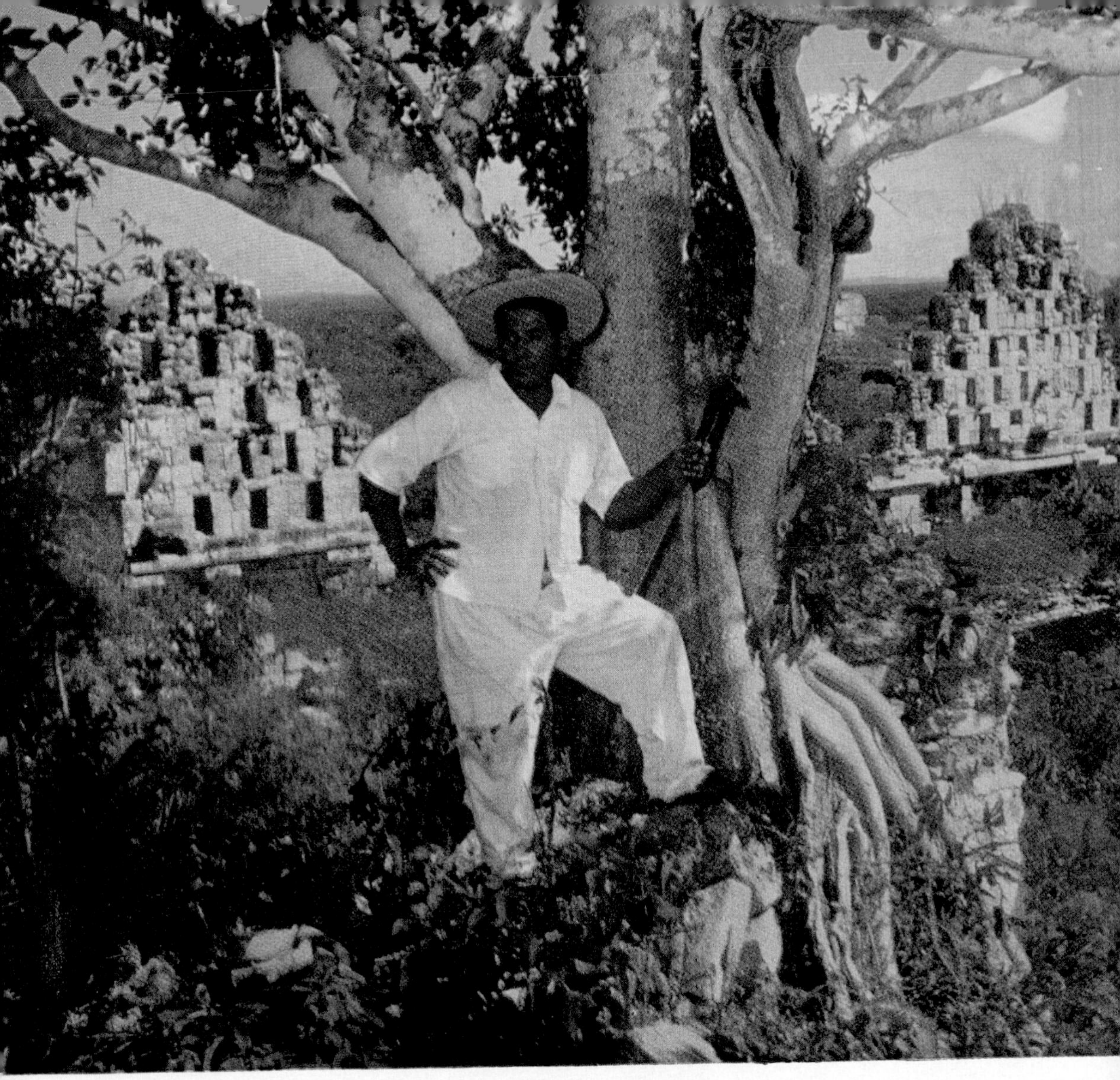

women only 4 feet 8 inches. All Maya have exceedingly broad heads, which is probably their most marked physical characteristic; their hands and feet are small and beautifully formed.

Add to this eyes nearer black than brown, a strong, well-formed, expressive mouth, and a skin of dark, golden brown with warm high lights, and you have one of America's handsomest native races.

The Maya home consists of a palm- or grass-thatched hut with sides of saplings, often daubed with mud. It is rectangular, with rounded ends, usually about 25 feet long, 10 to 12 feet wide, and 15 feet high to the ridgepole of the steeply sloping roof. In typical houses there are no windows and only two doorways, in the middle of the long sides (page 206). Everybody sleeps in this combination living room, bedroom, dining room, and chapel, frequently two to a hammock, with dogs lying beneath and occasionally a setting hen in a corner. The men and boys eat in the main house, women and girls in the kitchen.

The Maya Indian is devout. He was in ancient times when, under the direction of his priests, he reared tremendous stone pyramids and temples to his gods. He was equally devout during the Spanish colonial period when, under the su-

**Ancient Builders in Stone** left their mark on Yucatán. Ruin at Uxmal (left), struggling to escape Nature's cloak, is House of the Pigeons; the many openings in this nine-gabled façade resemble a vast dovecot. White buildings of so-called Nunnery in background enclose a spacious court. Towering Temple of the Magician is all but hidden behind gable ruin to right of tree. Governor's Palace stands at far right.

Skill in cut-stone veneer shows in famous arch at Labná (below). Arcade sides converge at top, are surmounted by flat capstone in place of keystone unknown to Maya builders. Such corbeled arches served not as doorways but as ceremonial gateways to quadrangles walled by buildings.

KODACHROMES BY JUSTIN LOCKE

**Long-lost Maya Center** rises from rubble. Dzibilchaltun, in northern Yucatán, covers 20 square miles, may be the largest and longest inhabited site in ancient America. A National Geographic-Tulane University expedition has surveyed the vanished metropolis, explored its sloping well to a depth of 144 feet, restored the Temple of the Seven Dolls (above). Seven clay figurines found under the sanctuary floor all had some deformity; they may have embodied a formula for curing disease.

pervision of the Franciscan fathers, he built the enormous churches and spacious monasteries, and exchanged his pagan deities for the white man's God.

Even today much of his own former religious beliefs colors his comprehension of the Church's teachings.

The Maya dances of today are not those of old pagan times. The latter were thought by early Franciscan fathers to be immoral, pertaining to the Devil, and they were speedily replaced by Spanish dances such as the *jarana* and *zapateo*.

But the chief business of the Maya man today, as it has been of his forefathers for century after century, is to raise corn for his family. And the chief occupation of his womenfolk today, just as it was a thousand years ago, is to prepare that corn into tortillas for the family's daily meals.

The way each goes about his or her task has remained practically unchanged throughout the centuries. The man now has a steel ax and machete to fell the forest, instead of ringing the trees with his stone ax. His wife, when she lives in a village, takes her corn to the local mill.

In remoter villages a few women have hand-turned grinders somewhat like a small coffee grinder, but the majority still use a stone slab with a stone grinder held in the hand (page 200). From 75 to 85 percent of everything the average Maya eats is corn in one form or another. The rest consists of *frijoles* (beans), chili, chocolate, honey, squashes, native tubers, and fruits.

A study of Maya agriculture has established two interesting facts. First, the simple system of raising corn practiced today in much of the Yucatán Peninsula

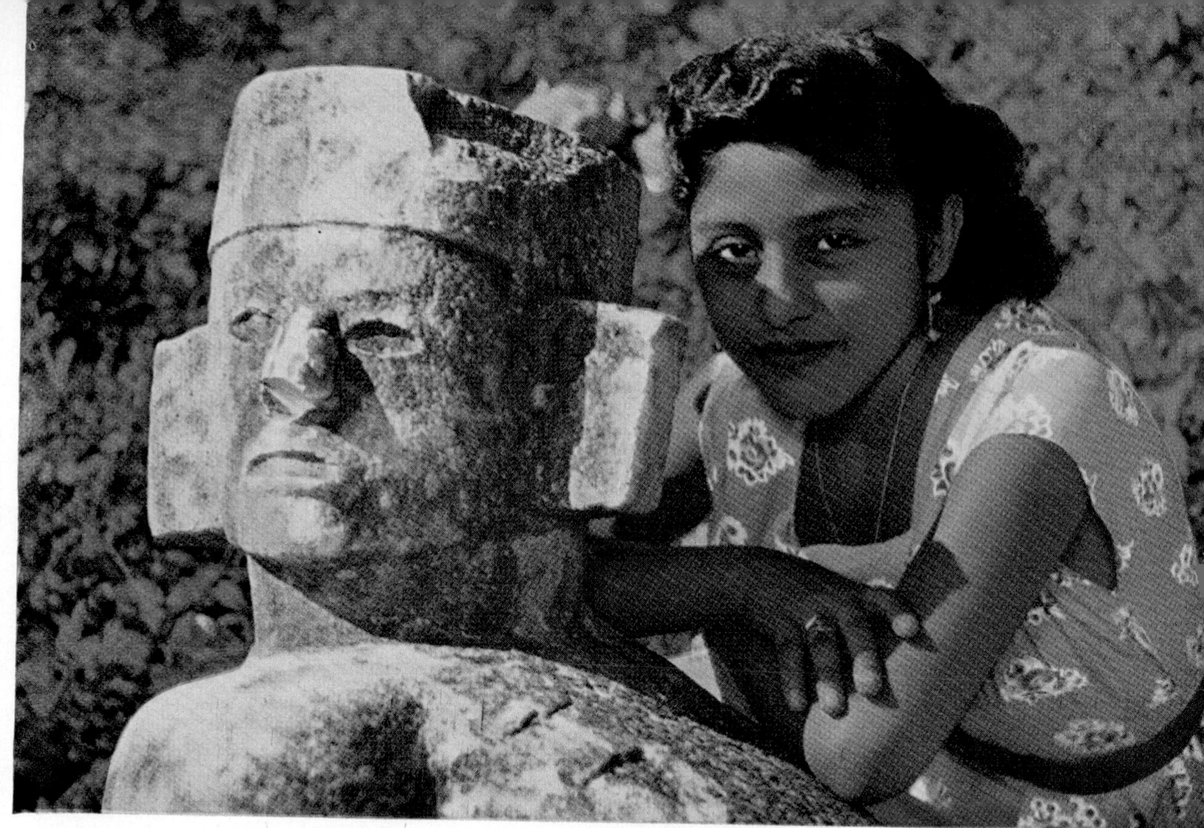

KODACHROMES BY JUSTIN LOCKE AND (LEFT) WILLIAM W. CAMPBELL III

**Chac Mool Keeps a Secret.** Giving ear to a modern Chichén Itzá lass, he is one of 12 of his stone-silent kind found in the Maya city. These heroic-size, half-reclining figures with knees drawn up, body resting partly on elbows, hands touching flat bowl on abdomen, lounged before temples or daises within to hold incense or offerings to the gods. Found also in several highland sites, they apparently originated with the Toltec invaders, possibly with a Bacchic cult of drunkenness.

would support a much larger population than the million or so people who live there. Second, to support a family of five, a Maya Indian has to work in his cornfield only about sixty days a year.

These facts explain the larger population of pre-Columbian times, and how the ancient Maya found time to build their many cities of cut stone.

An environment admirably suited to raising corn, which made the food quest relatively simple; a superabundance of excellent and easily quarried building limestone, which when burned gave them lime for mortar and also furnished a coarse marl gravel that served as sand; wise leaders, who developed a highly efficient governmental organization under which large public works were planned and successfully carried out; and finally, the Maya themselves, elevated and sustained by a lofty religious philosophy—these are the principal factors that made the Maya civilization the most brilliant cultural achievement of ancient America.

Today, silent are the temples, courts, and colonnades; gone the rulers, priests, and sacrificial victims; gone the artisans and builders; gone those humbler folk whose unremitting toil alone made all this pomp and pageantry possible—back to Mother Earth, enshrouded by the living green of tree and bush and flower.

But of a moonlit night, standing on the lofty terrace before the palace of the kings, the silent city of Chichén Itzá at your feet, temples and pyramids rising white and spectral above the dark forest, you will sense that breezes whispering through the trees bring stirring tales of other days, other men, and other deeds. He who would may listen then and hear.

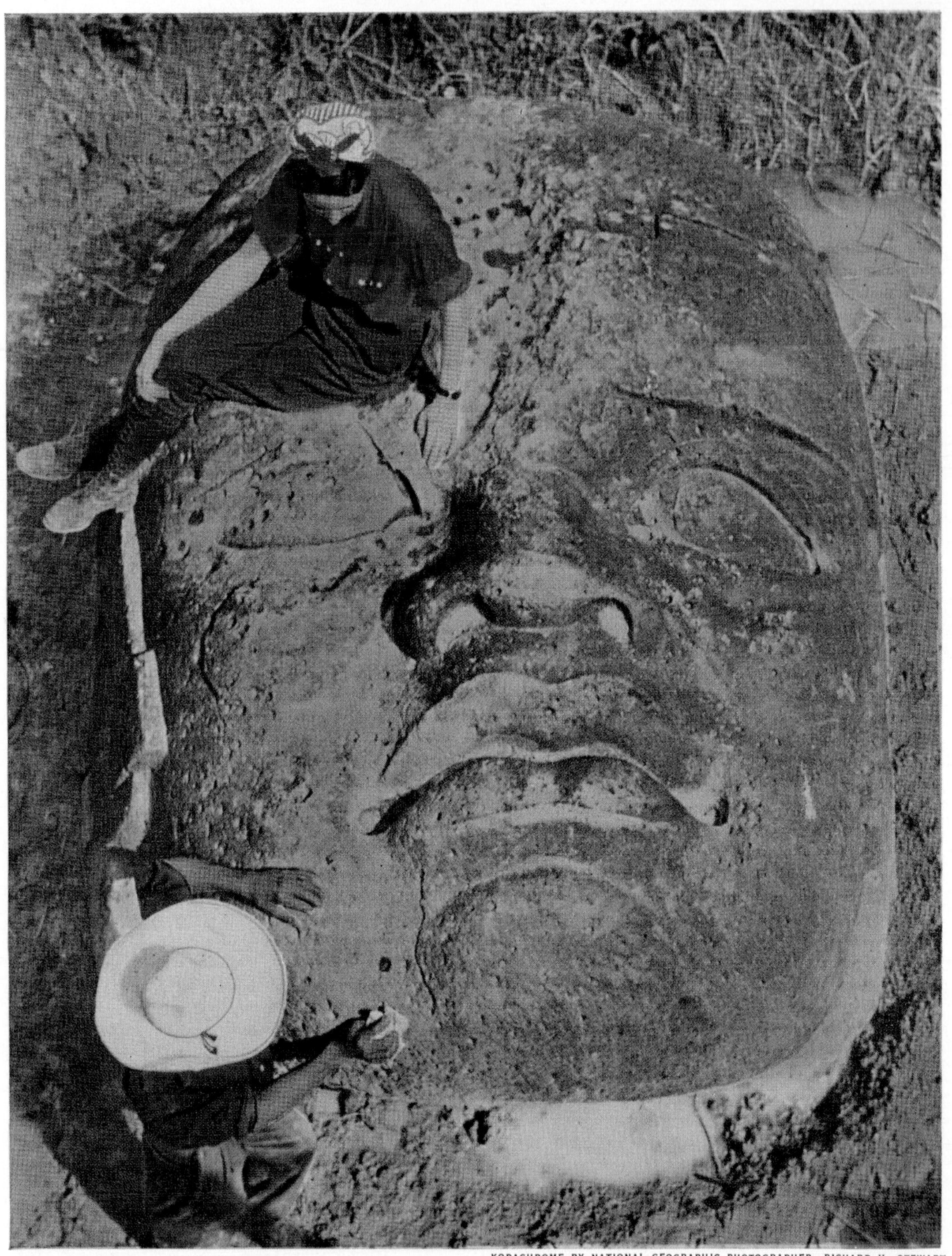

KODACHROME BY NATIONAL GEOGRAPHIC PHOTOGRAPHER RICHARD H. STEWART

**El Rey, 30 Tons of Carved Lava, Gets His Colossal Face Scrubbed.** Workmen called him el Rey because he was the King of 11 enormous heads found at three sites near the Bay of Campeche by Dr. Stirling, leader of the southern Mexico expeditions. All, like a football eleven, wear helmets. Flattened on back, the sculptures presumably stood against a high wall and are believed to be portraits in stone of leaders of the vanished La Venta culture. A marauding tribe, conquering the flat-nosed sculptors centuries ago, tried to destroy the heads but could only mar and topple them. This well-preserved 1945-season find at San Lorenzo needed only to have fragments restored to section above right eye.

## CHAPTER 10

# LA VENTA MAN

## BY MATTHEW W. STIRLING

DEEP IN STEAMING SWAMPS near the coast of southern Mexico, a family of colossal stone heads stares inscrutably across abandoned plazas where the mysterious La Venta, or Olmec, people once performed barbaric rites.

I saw the first of these heads in 1938. Its existence had been known locally since 1858. Natives with visions of buried treasure had excavated it, then had dropped their spades in disappointment when only an immense carved face appeared. Over the years erosion reburied the head (page 224).

One day at the turn of the 20th century, a Mexican trudging in a tobacco field 15 miles from the almost forgotten head saw a piece of pale-green stone gleam in the dark moist earth. He picked up a small jadeite figurine about eight inches tall, and could not resist a smile.

The carving depicted a bald-headed Indian priest whose wide-open eyes radiate infectious good humor (page 218). This object was destined to become one of the most famous archeological finds in the New World. Curious-looking incised figures on the godlet's stomach eventually were deciphered as a date corresponding to 98 B.C.

The beautifully carved relic baffled archeologists. They called it the Tuxtla Statuette for its discovery site near San Andrés Tuxtla. Its carved glyphs were quite different from those on dated Maya monuments found far to the east in the Peninsula of Yucatán (Chapter 9).

Assuming the date was contemporary with the figurine, was it placed there by early Maya, or did some other group in the Veracruz region invent the calendar and later pass it on to the Maya?

These questions turned tantalizingly in my mind in 1938 as I set out on a long trail leading to the second answer and to the discovery of La Venta Man.

First, I sought the great stone head that had disappointed jungle treasure seekers so long ago. I swung onto a horse and jogged for eight jolting hours along a small tributary of the Papaloapan River. Within a mile of the village of Tres Zapotes I found the object of my quest. The weather-blackened head was buried to its forehead in a plaza formed by four mounds. Brushing stubborn earth from its face, I saw for the first time its grim, sullen expression.

When I returned to Washington, D. C., staff members of the National Geographic Society examined my photographs of the colossal head and realized the potential importance of the Tres Zapotes site. We organized the first of nine expeditions into La Venta country cosponsored by the Society and the Smithsonian Institution. The field staff—besides my wife Marion and me—included Dr. and Mrs. C. W. Weiant and National Geographic Photographer

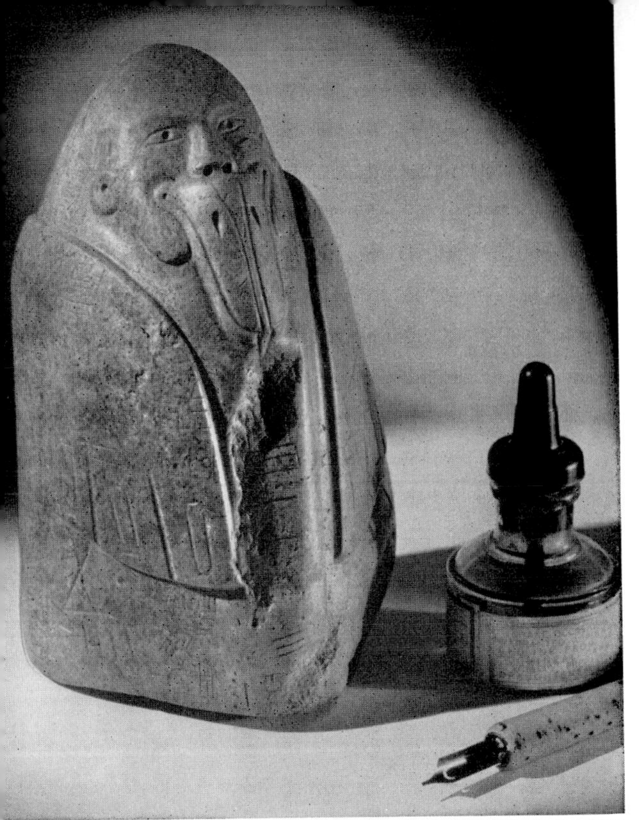

NATIONAL GEOGRAPHIC PHOTOGRAPHER WILLARD R. CULVER

**Cheerful Duck-billed Godlet,** the Tuxtla Statuette, was plowed up in southern Mexico in 1902. It created an immediate stir. Bars and dots on the jolly figurine's stomach indicate a Maya calendar date for 98 B.C.—but the find was outside Maya territory, and earlier than any known Maya date. This enigma led to the discovery of La Venta culture. La Venta lapidaries usually depicted pudgy men with long heads, flattened noses, fleshy jowls and necks. This specimen of pale-green jadeite, in Smithsonian Institution, wears duck-bill mask on lower face; robe draped over shoulder represents folded wings of a bird.

Richard H. Stewart. With us in later seasons were Dr. Philip Drucker and Dr. Alexander Wetmore of the Smithsonian Institution and artist-naturalist Walter A. Weber.

On January 1, 1939, we single-filed into the heart of one of Mexico's most isolated backwashes. Long ago, a numerous and prosperous people pushed back the jungle to live in prosperity on the level plains and high ground at the foot of the Tuxtla Mountains. It was a friendly place: the earthen barrier sheltered them from lashing, Gulf-born hurricanes; abundant crops sprouted from rain-soaked tropical soil.

We set up camp near Tres Zapotes, a thriving farm village. At once we noted an interesting analogy. Its inhabitants were again wresting the rich soil from the jungle and planting the same crops grown by ancients—maize, beans, and squash. We found the Tres Zapoteans cheerful, honest, and hard-working, eager to wield our shovels.

We immediately began excavating the colossal head. Finally it stood fully exposed. We gazed at ten tons of perfectly proportioned workmanship, six feet high and 18 feet around.

Square, pug-nosed, and heavy featured, the face wears an expression of

**Oldest Dated Work of Man** so far known in the Western Hemisphere, this broken stone slab was discovered by the first Stirling-led National Geographic Society-Smithsonian Institution expedition into La Venta territory. Earlier Tuxtla Statuette find was only 15 miles away.

Delicate dot-dash symbols, interpreted by the Spinden correlation, read November 4, 291 B.C. The stone's reverse is carved with a weeping rain god. Weathering indicates this shattered stela lay on its back for centuries before being set up and re-used by a later people. If three more inches had broken off top or bottom, date could never have been determined!

NATIONAL GEOGRAPHIC PHOTOGRAPHER
RICHARD H. STEWART

NATIONAL GEOGRAPHIC PHOTOGRAPHER RICHARD H. STEWART

**American Prehistory in Cross Section.** Workers slice through a temple mound at San Lorenzo, revealing the structure's stages of growth. Pottery, figurines, artifacts from the different time levels show evolution of style. La Venta mounds were forerunners of Maya and Aztec pyramids.

profound ill humor. It is incredibly lifelike, strikingly dissimilar to any other American Indian sculpture that I had seen. Topped by an incongruous helmet, the sturdy face might easily have depicted a 20th century football player.

"How do you suppose it got here?" someone asked.

We knew that the nearest source for this massive basalt block was the base of Mount Tuxtla, 10 miles away. But none of us could imagine how ancient engineers, working without wheels or draft animals, could have performed the feat—and crossed the gorge between Tres Zapotes and mountain. The quarrying alone would be a prodigious task.

Our admiration for these artistic, ingenious people grew as workmen's spades uncovered other large carved stones, including a great open-mouthed jaguar deity representing the Earth Monster (page 228).

Grim suggestions of pagan bloodletting turned up in the heavy clay soil: a stone chest and a barrel-shaped piece of basalt with a shallow basin on top. We could envision high priests spilling human blood into the basin, transferring it to the stone storage chest as mankind's most precious offering to the gods. Indians of southern Mexico were practicing sacrifice of this nature when the Spaniards splashed ashore in Veracruz.

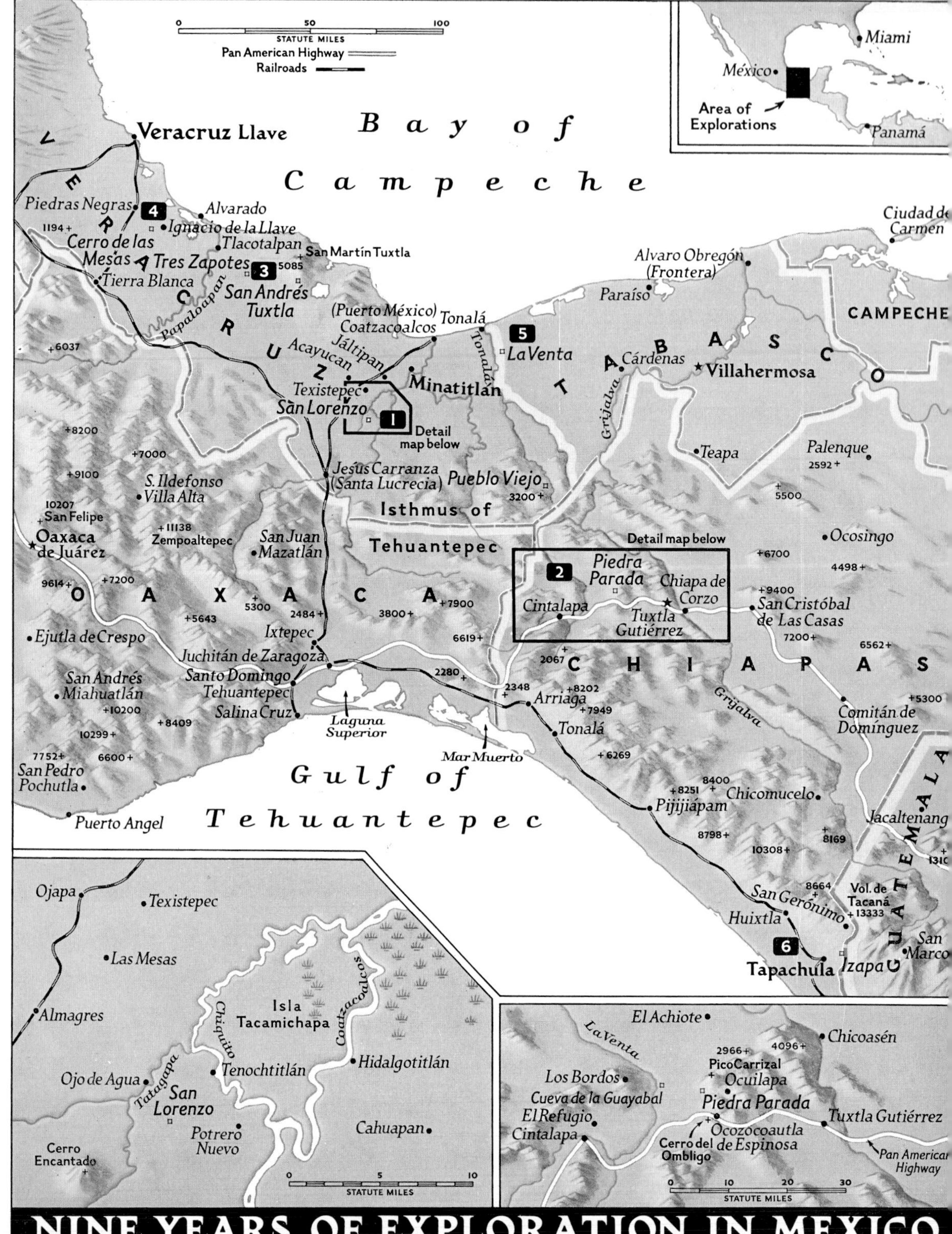


# NINE YEARS OF EXPLORATION IN MEXICO

**1** *Here La Venta (Olmec) culture reached its height. Discovered were five colossal stone heads, two 9 feet high, and the remains of an aqueduct.*

**2** *Piedra Parada, heretofore unexplored archeologically, is in an area of stone structures, ball courts, and caves containing much pottery.*

**3** *Here were found the New World's oldest dated work, 291 B.C. (Spinden correlation), and ceramic styles from 1000 B.C. to A.D. 1000.*

**4** *A cache of carved jade, numbering 782 pieces was found at Cerro de las Mesas. Ceramics found at this site link a history chain extending from 300 B.C. to A.D. 1400.*

**5** *Ceremonial center of La Venta culture. Here were colossal heads, carved jade, and mosaic floors of jaguar motif. Tombs of priests held rich gifts of semi-precious stones.*

**6** *Exploration at Izapa revealed over thirty stone monuments and altars curiously carved with man-beast figures. These indicate a pre-La Venta period, as yet unstudied.*

Our explorations soon convinced us that our spades were cutting into the site of a great aboriginal city. Although tall tough grass and dense jungle camouflaged much of the land, we counted 50 ceremonial mounds in a stretch of two miles. The growing awareness that this was a hitherto unknown culture heightened our sense of expectancy.

On January 16, 1939, under broiling hot sun, I tramped to a distant section of our workings to examine a flat stone a workman had pointed out. Digging bared traces of a weathered design. The back appeared to be plain. The workmen were on their knees in the muddy excavation pit, carefully cleaning soil from the stone with their hands. Suddenly, one called out in Spanish.

"Chief! Here are numbers!"

Peering close, I saw that a beautifully carved row of bars and dots ran across the stone in low relief (page 218). These immediately suggested a Maya calendar date, something we all had hoped for but had not dared to expect.

The stone obviously was a fragment broken from a large stela, a slab bearing inscriptions. By good fortune, almost all the date was preserved on the section we found.

I copied the characters and hurried back to camp. Excited, we started to decipher the bars and dots. Checked and rechecked, the date was 6 Eznab 1 Uo.

November 4, 291 B.C.—oldest recorded date ever found in the New World!

Predating the Tuxtla Statuette by 193 years, carved a generation before Rome and Carthage launched the Punic Wars, it ranks as the Rosetta Stone of Middle American archeology.

For four months thatched huts by the colossal head were our not entirely com-

**Tomb of Three Ancients** at La Venta at first defied penetration because of its skillful stone fitting. Nine basaltic columns on each side, five at rear, supported roof. Sloping columns at front formed a ramp; when removed they revealed interior packed to roof with clay. Workers finally uncovered flagstone platform at rear of tomb. On it a layer of brilliant cinnabar held mere traces of human bones amid masterpieces of jade carving.

Under a 10-inch "clamshell" was an exquisite polished jade female figure with pleasant features and long hair. Near by were an ornate headdress, a frog, heart, flower, beads, and figurines—all in vivid green and translucent blue jade.

NATIONAL GEOGRAPHIC PHOTOGRAPHER RICHARD H. STEWART

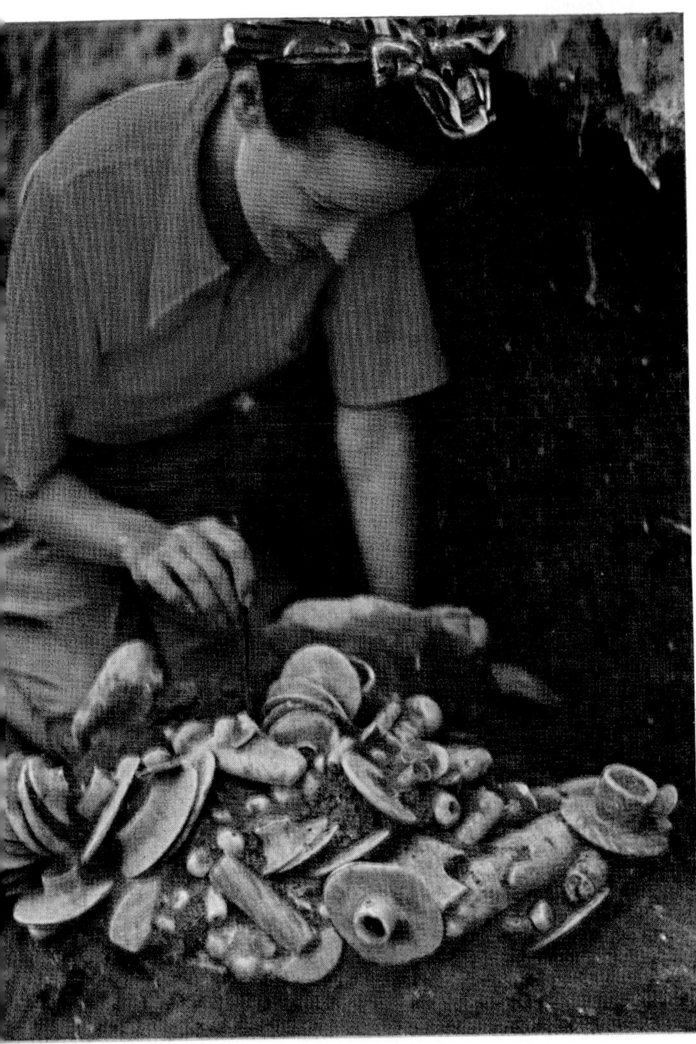

**Largest Jade Find in the New World** comes to light as Mrs. Stirling brushes away concealing earth. This thrilling moment reveals varied workmanship and colors, styles early and late, indicating pieces came from far and wide (page 230).

fortable home. We shared them with ants, ticks, mosquitoes, biting flies, and plump worms. At times northers lashed camp, halting work and filling excavations with muddy water.

We found evidence that two distinct peoples had occupied the site in remote times. Near the surface rested charred bones in covered pottery vessels, an obvious sign of cremated burials. Deep beneath were direct interments in an entirely different type of pottery.

Still unanswered, however, was the riddle of the ancient Indians who lived and died on the place where we dug and walked.

We returned to Mexico early in 1940 to dig deeper into the secrets of Tres Zapotes. At a depth of 20 feet, sealed beneath a layer of volcanic ash, spaders penetrated a deposit of dark-colored earth filled with pottery fragments and figurines. The artifacts left little doubt that Tres Zapotes was one of the longest-inhabited sites in Veracruz State. Ceramic styles covered a span of 2,000 years, from ten centuries before Christ's birth until five centuries before the Spanish occupation.

A small mound yielded the second season's most exciting discovery: a group of pottery vessels covering figurines, among them wheeled toys (page 226). Previously it had been doubted that the principle of the wheel was known in the New World.

Now we started a new phase of exploration: side trips in southern Veracruz and neighboring territory, a rich archeological storehouse with a definite bearing on the interpretation of such classical high culture zones as the Maya of Central America, the Zapotecan of Oaxaca, and the Toltec and Aztec of the Valley of Mexico.

We recalled that a Tulane University expedition, headed by Frans Blom and Oliver La Farge, had pressed in 1925 to La Venta, a village east of Tabasco State's Tonalá River. They photographed the top of a stone head, but lacked time to excavate. The stone might be a twin to our colossal head at Tres Zapotes.

Thus we set forth for La Venta, a remote pinpoint of a place destined to give its name to a rich prehistoric culture.

We boated up the wide river and into a small coffee-colored tributary mirroring immense webs of mangrove trees. Unseen monkeys chattered and quarreled in the upmost branches.

A pleasant surprise awaited us. An oil-prospecting team had pitched camp two days before at the derelict village of Blasillo. The hospitable Mexicans cleared a space for our cots in their storage tents and their Chinese cook placed a superb dinner before us.

Next morning, camp guides and carriers led us through foot-sucking thickets toward a dry, sandy rise in the heart of an expansive mangrove swamp. Patches of corn and bananas appeared. A half-hour of easier walking brought us to La Venta itself, a large clearing containing the homes of elderly Sebastián Torres and his two sons-in-law and their families.

The La Ventans generously vacated one of their houses for us. They speak Aztec among themselves, but they also know Spanish so we had no difficulty communicating with them.

A colossal stone head? No, they knew nothing about it. Yes, there were several carved stones, perhaps a great many covered by jungle growth. But take care. Ghosts of Aztec emperor Montezuma and his court come out to dance and sing among the ruins on moonlit nights.

We soon stood on the jungle-tangled top of a huge

**Red-painted Ear Plugs, Pointed Beard, and Satanic Leer** of this life-size clay head found at Cerro de las Mesas reminded the Stirlings of a similar figure, page 227, unearthed a year earlier 50 miles southeast at Tres Zapotes. Below: Broken before burial, arms and legs of a fire god were found piled on a cross-decorated brazier, worn atop the hollow idol's head to hold hot coals. Prize jade cache lay near by.

KODACHROMES BY NATIONAL GEOGRAPHIC PHOTOGRAPHER RICHARD H. STEWART

mound 105 feet high. The pyramid sloped down to a rectangular base 100 yards square. North stood a sweeping enclosure walled by stone columns ten feet high. Windblown earth now filled the corral, but the formidable close-set pillars indicated that it once served as a sanctum. Three symmetrically placed smaller knolls loomed south of the main mound.

We were standing on the crest of a major ceremonial shrine.

Next day we began excavating two intricately carved stone altars. Before one, a workman uncovered 99 large jade beads arranged in the position of necklaces and armlets. The other altar was artistically the finest object we discovered. Five babies, carved with amusing realism, rest in the arms of adults. We dubbed them the "Quintuplets."

Stone after stone appeared from La Venta's sandy soil, but no sign of a giant head. We began to fear that the jungle had camouflaged it forever.

Excavating a jutting stone pillar occupied us for a week. To our surprise, the stela emerged 14 feet high, almost seven feet wide, and 34 inches thick. The delicate low-relief composition depicts two seven-foot adults apparently talking to each other. One is a handsome individual with aquiline nose and long, flowing beard. Both figures wear tall head-

**"Kettle" Inspired Expeditions.** What was trash to fortune-seeking Mexicans a century ago became treasure to modern archeologists. Excavation of colossal heads and other La Venta objects raised the curtain on a new culture and shed light on early American intellectual and artistic achievements formerly attributed to the Maya. All this stemmed from a seeming inverted kettle (above) once partially unearthed by Veracruzanos who hoped it held buried loot. Intrigued by accounts of giant heads bedded in clay to the eyebrows and cloaked by Mexican jungle, the National Geographic Society and the Smithsonian Institution in 1939 launched the first of nine expeditions that found the "missing link" of Middle American antiquity. A replica of one of the heads rests in National Geographic headquarters.

Right: Although the party worked only through the four-month dry season, unscheduled rains occurred. The excavation could not be drained. Bailing it by hand took two tedious days, had to be repeated three times one week.

NATIONAL GEOGRAPHIC PHOTOGRAPHER RICHARD H. STEWART

**Helmeted La Venta Enigma.** Dr. Stirling kneels beside largest of five gigantic basalt heads found at La Venta. Time-worn and battle-scarred, the inscrutable face has lost lower jaw and most of its flat nose—probably the work of pre-Columbian vandals. But finely carved teeth remain intact. Engineers as well as sculptors, the mysterious La Ventans somehow transported 30-ton stones across rugged terrain from distant basalt sources. "Helmets" are believed a practical decorative touch serving in place of elaborate feathered headdresses fragile and difficult to carve.

NATIONAL GEOGRAPHIC PHOTOGRAPHER WILLARD R. CULVER

**Wheels for Toys, but not for Labor-saving.** Earliest known New World use of wheels dates back 12 centuries to this smiling dog and laughing jaguar. Mounted on hollow tubes, they were found beside round disks at Tres Zapotes, suggesting that La Ventans inserted wooden axles and used the disks as wheels. Sole similar discovery prior to Dr. Stirling's was tiny coyotelike figures dating from about A.D. 1400 uncovered 13,000 feet high on Popocatepetl. Recent finds confirm pattern: all are in Mexico, all animal effigies in clay, all toys. Opposite: Like a character from Faust, this lifelike clay head with pointed beard and crafty grin ranks with best of ancient ceramic art.

dresses. Like other headdresses on La Venta statuary, none bears the ornamental bird plumes so widely used by related Indian cultures.

Another crew shoveling earth from a flat-topped stone north of La Venta's dominant mound disclosed an unusual base in the form of a head. Archaic style and aged appearance suggest it to be one of La Venta's oldest treasures.

A hole runs through this gaunt old altar, starting at the left ear and emerging at the mouth. It was not difficult to imagine a high priest speaking into the stone ear, his stentorian tones emerging awesomely as if by magic from the mouth itself!

A workman mentioned faintly recalling two other stones in the forest near by. He hacked through matted undergrowth. Suddenly we stumbled upon a large hemispherical pate almost smothered in vines. I looked at it closely and grinned. The eyes were covered and there was little else to judge by. But I knew this must be Blom's colossal head.

Excavated, the stone proved to be a good two feet taller than the colossal head at Tres Zapotes. But the two looked like brothers; both had the same broad nose, thick lips, helmetlike headdress, and dyspeptic expression.

A small boy approached. "Señor," he said, "I have seen some stones near the new *milpa* (maize field) where my papa is working."

In the forest a half mile away he pointed out three round stones bulging from the earth about 30 yards apart. Here were three more immense heads. Two bore a new sculptural feature, finely carved teeth (page 225). The fifth and last stone head unburied at La Venta showed its appreciation by displaying a foolishly happy, befuddled smile.

Among the 20 sculptured monuments excavated during our second season in Mexico were the finest specimens of stone carving ever brought to light in ancient America.

The National Geographic-Smithsonian expedition returned to La Venta several more seasons, firm in its conviction that this art represented in a pure form an ancient fountainhead of Middle American culture. Scattered examples of the art style previously had been called Olmec, after the legendary "rubber people" dwelling along the Veracruz coast.

While neither stone temples nor palaces stood at La Venta, the people who raised the huge stelas and statues were skilled engineers as well as artists. No igneous rock of the type from which the monoliths were carved exists closer than 50 miles from the swamp-enfolded island.

Geometry-minded La Ventans oriented their constructions to an imaginary line bisecting the summit of the central mound. To explore this line, we dug a deep wide trench. Alongside, workmen uncovered a vividly colored jaguar-mask mosaic 23 feet below topsoil. The ancient builders had laid green paving blocks in a yellow clay border. They tamped blue clay into the sacred beast's eyes, nose, and mouth (page 228).

The profusion of jade and serpentine axheads showed that the ax was a sacred symbol, and meant as much to La Ven-

**Earth Monster Yawns** as a native work crew strains to pry his massive monument from deep jungle mud at Tres Zapotes. Turn page sideways to see three stocky figures carved in low relief inside wide-stretched mouth of grotesque animal believed to symbolize the Earth Monster. Scene may represent a wedding, as central figure appears to be a woman facing kneeling figure to her right.

tans as the cross to Christians. Rich burial gifts of semiprecious stones pinpointed La Venta as a ground set apart for the interment of priests and notables.

As yet we had found virtually no human skeletal material, invaluable to the archeologist. Our expedition to Cerro de las Mesas, a village in southern Veracruz, bared the first well-preserved human remains in quantity.

Cutting through an upper mound that enclosed another like onion skin, we came upon five pottery vessels. Each contained the neatly sawed-off face of a human skull.

The lower or primary mound apparently was built to protect the remains of a single individual. The body had been tightly flexed and laid on its side in the exact center of the mound, the head cut off and placed face down in a large, orange-colored marine shell filled with red paint. Buried in the paint were two jade beads and a carved monkey's head.

The skull itself was large and thin; the forehead had been flattened. The

**Green Tiger in Tile** glares out of deep La Venta pit. Polished stone mosaic, here viewed upside down, represents eyes, nose, and fangs of a jaguar. Tilers set blocks into an asphalt base over a stone platform, bordered them with yellow clay. Four diamond-shaped elements provide decorative fringe.

La Venta art, like Egyptian, eventually became stylized. Natives today fear jaguar, *el tigre*, as did ancient forebears to whom it was sacred.

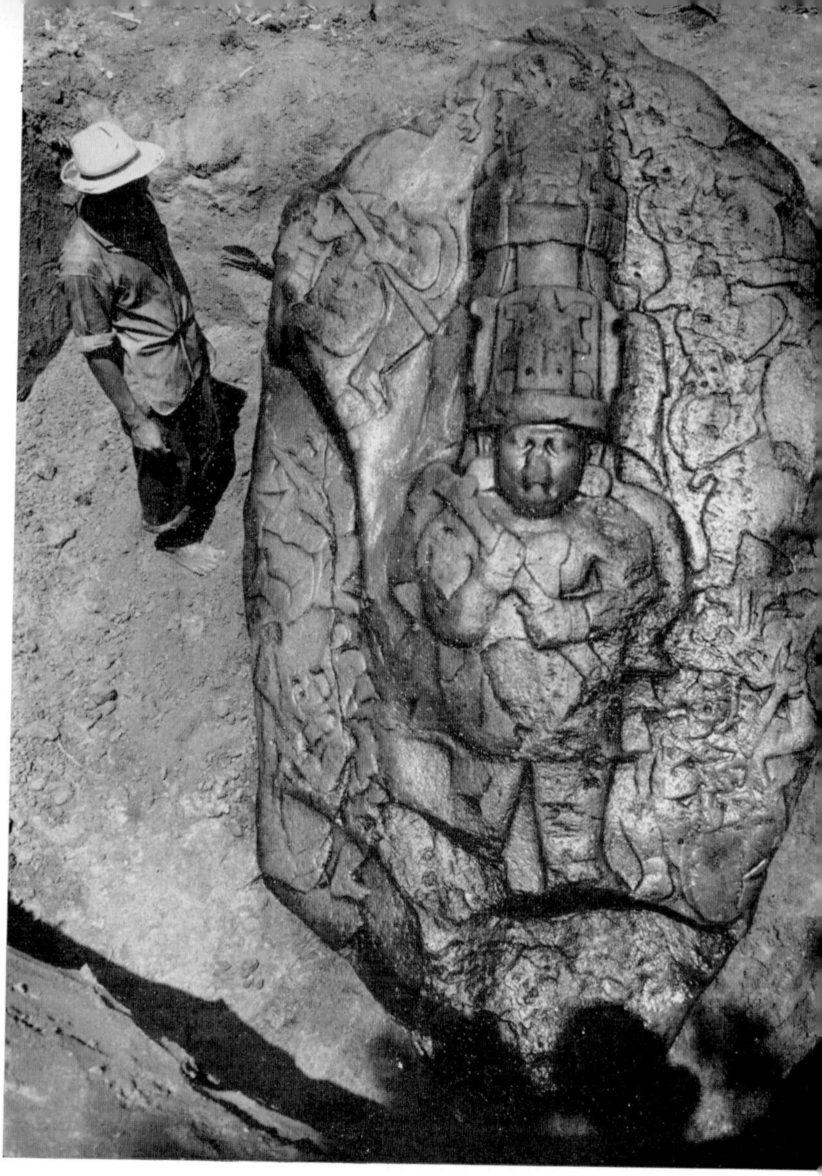

**Polished Stone Priest** holds court in La Venta jungle, his elaborate headdress doubling his height. Around him in bas-relief whirl six grotesque figures probably representing gods. To set him erect as his sculptor intended, workmen dug a hole at his feet, tipped his ten tons of basalt into it.

Near by, two large altars with projecting tablelike tops were unearthed. One, the "Quintuplet" altar, grimly suggests infant sacrifice. At either end two costumed figures each hold an adult-faced infant. In front a seated figure holds a fifth baby, infant-faced. The second altar features a life-size man with jaguar-head headdress, wide bead collar, seated cross-legged in an arched niche. Altar's relaxed figures provide contrast to the stiff conventionality of most Middle American art.

NATIONAL GEOGRAPHIC PHOTOGRAPHER RICHARD H. STEWART

effect, grotesque to our eyes, probably was greatly admired by the man's contemporaries. The teeth were carefully and neatly inlaid with circular pieces of gold-colored pyrite.

Buried with the body were massive shell beads, a turtle shell containing lustrous Panama seashell rattles and engraved with a plumed serpent. Just north of the skull lay a highly polished stone yoke, one of those mystifying carved works often found in Veracruz.

A curious sandwich arrangement of buried cement floors at the Cerro de las Mesas site yielded 52 pottery vessels of hard red ware. Each cradled the skull of a young adult with two or three vertebrae attached, an indication that the heads had been severed. The 52 skulls had been artificially flattened during the owners' lifetime. In many the front teeth bore chipped notches. The heads probably represented a mass sacrifice performed on a grimly memorable occasion.

Near by we discovered a deep trench filled with an orderless jumble of human bones. This find conjured up a picture of less important victims being shoved over the ceremonial mound's rear edge from a blood-stained altar.

Skeletal remains at Cerro de las Mesas mutely witnessed that the custom of ap-

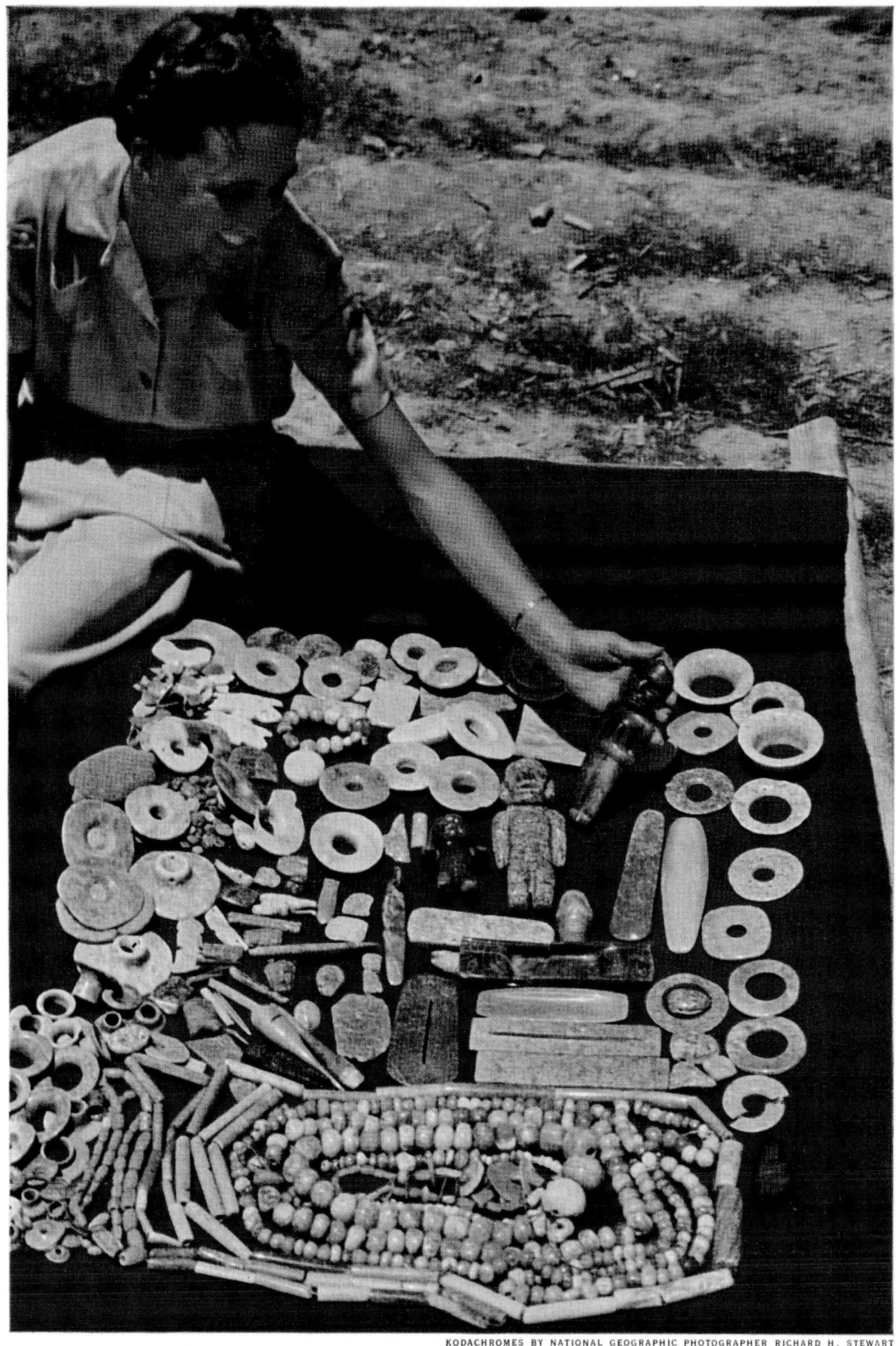

KODACHROMES BY NATIONAL GEOGRAPHIC PHOTOGRAPHER RICHARD H. STEWART

**Treasure-trove at Cerro de las Mesas—782 Pieces of Fine Jade.** Held upright is priest wit' knife in hand. Most prized find is realistic infant at center. Long, dark canoe below figurine: has typical La Venta faces carved on flat prow and stern. Beads, found loose, are in many shapes.

plying skull pads to deform the head in infancy was practiced by the site's later occupants, not its first inhabitants.

The season was running out. One more day, and our work would be through. For reasons known best to himself, Miguel, a Mexican assistant supervising the digging crew, ordered workmen to remove a wedge of earth that had been left as a wheelbarrow ramp in one corner of the trench. They struck a big chunk of cement and fragments of an incense vessel.

Sensing that something important might lie below, Miguel took over with his trowel and eased earth from the top of the pile. He uncovered a red-painted stone monkey, a similar turtle, a thin circular piece of polished jade, then another, and another.

At this point Miguel sent for me.

It was evident he had stumbled onto a discovery of exceptional importance. Apparently the large potsherds, the chunk of cement, and stone figures formed a protective cover.

Carefully we worked around the entire deposit until we had exposed a huge

**Stone Figurines and Jade Jewelry** from child's tomb at La Venta include small, hollow ear plugs. Pendants below were attached to them. Statuette at left has lost one of its black obsidian eyes. Other two have eyes of fool's gold (iron pyrites). Below: Clay image released from long vigil at Cerro de las Mesas was one of many burial offerings indicating the tomb occupant's prominence. Man's teeth were inlaid with pyrite ornaments.

pile of jade. Here and there under the mass of large ear ornaments, beads, and jade tubes we got teasing glimpses of pointed implements, sections of human images, and carved plaques.

Painstaking work the rest of the morning cleared the earth completely from around the pile (page 222). Another half hour was spent taking out all the jade—782 magnificent specimens. This fortune in stones, ranging in color from porcelain white to shades of green and deep blue, was the largest find yet made of the most precious substance known to Mexico's ancient civilizations (page 230). It certainly did not accompany a burial; doubtless it constituted tribal property rather than individual wealth.

The jade may have been an offering at a temple's dedication or the enlargement of a mound. Or perhaps the owners buried the treasure on the approach of an invader, possibly the Aztecs.

We scarcely expected to match that windfall on a subsequent trip to La Venta. But in rich tombs at that sandy, swamp-girt treasure island we did discover emerald-green masterpieces of Oriental quality. In all, we counted 340 handsomely carved specimens, 300 of them imperial green jade, first of their kind uncovered in the New World.

Rumors of other huge carved stones lured us inland to the San Lorenzo highlands in the 1946 season. There we found a great carved altar almost exactly like the larger one unearthed at La Venta. Still another depicted two chubby figures with arms upraised as if to hold the altar's heavy table top.

A surprising new feature of the ancient culture was the mass of hollowed trough-shaped stones and flat rocks we found in a gully. These stones were apparently part of an aqueduct.

The wide variety of pottery, clay figures, and other artifacts we recovered at San Lorenzo demonstrated changes in style and form with the passage of time.

An old Mexican, serving as a guide, led us across a group of typical La Venta mounds to a steep ravine. He pointed to *el Rey*. Lying on the slope, face up, top of the head down, was the colossus of all the colossal heads. The moment we saw it, we knew we were gazing at a La Venta masterwork (page 216). Four other finely preserved heads also came to light at San Lorenzo.

Over the years La Venta Man's trail had taken us beyond Veracruz and Tabasco to the Mexican States of Campeche, Oaxaca, and Chiapas. We traveled on foot, in dugout canoes, on jogging mules and horses. Further exploration, including Dr. Drucker's 1955 work at La Venta, has continued to shed light upon a civilization that our investigations made known for the first time.

From the great stone monuments and exquisite little artifacts, long buried and ignored, we learned that these interesting people were one of the first to emerge from the simple early agricultural level of Middle America and achieve civilizational stature. Carbon-14 dating shows that Olmec culture began before 1000 B.C. and reached its peak between 800 and 500 B.C. In the jungles of Veracruz and Tabasco they erected big ceremonial centers that flourished before the rise of Maya, Zapotec, Toltec, and Totonac cultures. The great earth mounds that loomed from hot leafy jungles were precursors to the soaring stone pyramids of the Aztecs and Maya.

The early dates we found on La Venta monuments suggest that these Olmec people originated the marvelous calendar that subsequently gave the Maya their supreme claim to intellectual fame.

La Venta, or Olmec, people were America's first great artists. Their pure delicate work in stone contrasts strikingly with gaudy embellishments that characterize most later sculptural art in Middle America. They were apparently the first New World artists to use jade,

NATIONAL GEOGRAPHIC PHOTOGRAPHER RICHARD H. STEWART

**Zotzil Indians Wear Sandals Straight from Mayan Monument Art.** A stiff leather projection fits around heel and protects ankle. Short pants have no pockets, so these central Chiapas highlanders carry money, packages, lunch, and oddments in net bags with shoulder straps. Pink-tasseled black-and-white scarfs cover noses and mouths on dusty roads. Serapes vary in Zotzil villages from white with pin stripes to pure black. Flat-crowned hats are heavy, double-weave straw.

that beautiful and difficult medium so highly prized in pre-Columbian America.

They even possessed books. In a trench at Cerro de las Mesas we found what was apparently an ancient illustrated volume. Its pages had entirely disappeared, but still remaining were green, red, blue, and purple designs, welded together so tightly that it would be virtually impossible to separate them.

About A.D. 200 these cultural pioneers disappeared, submerged by a people of different physical type and culture who sought to destroy the monumental works of art they found.

La Ventans were not a race of conquerors; they did not even extend their boundaries widely beyond their southern Veracruz and northern Tabasco homeland. But they gave to ancient Mexico its first great cultural impetus. Their effect did not cease until Cortés and his men brought to a sudden end 2,500 years of New World development.

# MONTE ALBÁN AND MITLA

WILLIAM G. PRESTON; ROBERTO A. TURNBULL (RIGHT)

**The Richest Archeological Find in the Americas** came to light on the heights of Monte Albán, near Oaxaca in southern Mexico. There the theocratic Zapotecs reached their height, A.D. 500–1000, then abandoned the metropolis to long-time enemies, the Mixtecs, in turn conquered by the Spaniards. Zapotec and Mixtec cultures long posed tantalizing mysteries. Some 35 years ago shapeless grass-covered mounds (right) still shrouded the impressive plazas, courts, pyramids, and platforms above.

In 1931 Dr. Alfonso Caso of Mexico's National Museum made archeological history when he discovered sensational tomb treasure in gold, silver, jade, and turquoise; ornaments and utensils in onyx, marble, rock crystal; rare jet and amber; carved jaguar bones; priceless ropes of pearls. Famed Tomb 7, first used by its Zapotec builders, was taken over by Mixtecs who buried the treasure with nine nobles and priests and one woman. More than 150 Monte Albán tombs have now revealed secrets indicating the important Zapotec-Mixtec role in the cultural give and take among the La Venta, Maya, Teotihuacán, Toltec, Aztec, and other civilizations.

WILLIAM G. PRESTON; ALFONSO CASO (TOP RIGHT)

**Mitla's Hewers of Stone** spared no effort in beautifying the city that enshrined the tombs of Zapotec kings and priests, and served as home of their Great Prophet, a high priest so sacred that any commoner who looked upon him was believed to die. Mitla became leading Zapotec city after the abandonment of near-by Monte Albán to the Mixtecs. "Abode of the Dead," Aztec conquerors called it. A city "prouder and more magnificent" than any they had seen in New Spain, said early Spaniards.

The upper chambers of Mitla's massive rectangular palaces stand on low platforms rising around square central courts. The Hall of Monoliths (above) with its 14-foot columns contrasts in massive simplicity with structures (right) which catch the eye with intricate mosaics that sweep both inner and outer walls—a geometry in stone made up of countless individually carved segments held in place by pressure. Below ground stretch enormous cruciform corridors, the tombs from which souls of the departed wandered into the earth's interior in search of the kingdom of the dead.

In one upper chamber the Great Prophet "sat and slept . . . his throne like a high cushion . . . all of tiger skin, stuffed entirely with delicate feathers or with fine grass," wrote Oaxaca-born Spanish friar Francisco Burgoa (1600–1681). In a special underground sanctuary the prophet consulted images of the gods "with hideous grimaces and writhings . . . which filled all present with fear and terror." Into another "dark and grewsome room" Zapotec priests threw bodies of sacrificial victims and those slain in battle. It led, Burgoa claimed, to a 30-league passageway penetrating the earth's depths. No such tunnel has ever been found.

**Food-bearer to the Dead.** This funerary urn from a Monte Albán tomb, with serpent's split tongue protruding from its mouth, represents the serpent god Quetzalcoatl. Behind its bold-carved front is a container for food or drink to nourish the tomb's occupant during his journey into the next world.

Such urns were sometimes in human form. Others pictured animal gods, combinations of gods such as the serpent and the jaguar, or people wearing the masks of deities. Quetzalcoatl was a popular symbol. In various guises as creator of the world, god of wind and rain, and patron and bestower of all culture, this snake divinity roams through the mythology of advanced Indian civilizations of Middle America.

On this urn of the classic Zapotec period III (A.D. 500–1000), the god wears a long-eared cap decorated with shells of the same type sculptured beside the undulating feathered snakes of Teotihuacán's Temple of Quetzalcoatl. The similarity forges another link in the long chain of evidence that points to the close relationship among Indian deities, from the Maya long-nosed god Itzamna to the many-featured snake divinities of the La Ventans, Toltecs, Aztecs, and other related cultures.

WILLIAM G. PRESTON; ALFONSO CASO (LEFT)

**Riddles in Stone** stand at the entrance to this Monte Albán pyramid. Dots and bars that show clearly on the largest slab recall the Maya numeral system (page 198). But no other glyphs have been deciphered to link the dates with any specific events. Human figures carved on other slabs are nicknamed "dancers" because of their strange shapes and extravagant gestures. Their unknown creators gave them twisted feet, heads flat or grotesquely elongated. Were they meant to caricature defeated and despised enemies? Or did they portray deformed pilgrims seeking miraculous cures at Monte Albán temples? Archeologists find no answers.

The toothy grin of a skeleton-jaw mask dominates the "jaguar knight" breastpiece (left) found in Monte Albán's fabulously rich Tomb 7. Made of gold parts soldered together, it represents a man wearing a jaguar-head helmet. Serpents decorate the ear plugs; a small bird hangs at the throat. The A-O monogram on the lower right plate identifies the piece as Mixtecan, for this year symbol was used by the Mixtecs, never by Zapotecs.

**Reminiscent of La Venta Sculpture,** these curiously deformed "dancers" decorate many Monte Albán stones. Heavy, infantile features, thick snarling lips, and head coverings like football helmets are distinguishing traits of both art forms—another evidence of the exchange of ideas and techniques that must have taken place among the early coexistent civilizations in this part of the Americas.

Some of the bas-reliefs were imbedded in the walls of Monte Albán's Great Platform, one of whose stairways is being restored by workmen below. The carvings are not characteristic of Zapotec sculpture; and since they were used as construction material apparently taken from an earlier building, scholars assume they were carved by pre-Zapotec people. Among the workmen are descendants of the Zapotec and Mixtec Indians who originally used this massive structure.

WILLIAM G. PRESTON (RIGHT)
ROBERTO A. TURNBULL

PAINTING BY H. M. HERGET

**Feather-decked Aztec Fighter Prays for Victory** at altar of his war god, Huitzilopochtli. Lavish ornaments of gold, silver, pearls, and turquoise accent the scowling, teeth-bared visage of Tenochtitlán's chief deity. Deer symbol at center of forehead shows Huitzilopochtli also to be god of hunting. Two humming birds rest on his cuffs. Smoke curls up from incense burner at his side. War club, decorated shield lie at feet of the warrior, whose torso is sheathed in cotton-quilt armor. Feather headdress and bustle, turquoise ear and lip ornaments indicate military order.

# CHAPTER II

# THE AZTECS OF MEXICO

## BY FRANK H. H. ROBERTS, JR.

HIGH ON THE TEMPLE PLATFORM atop Tenochtitlán's great pyramid, an Aztec youth awaits his fate.

Within the temple broods the war god Huitzilopochtli, a monstrous idol, "with broad face and terrible eyes," weighted down by gold and jewels. Near by stands his brother, Tezcatlipoca, "God of Hell . . . girt with figures like little devils with snakes' tails."

Their victim lies stretched on his back across the low sacrificial stone, centered stagelike on the open platform. Two black-robed and painted priests hold his feet; three others grip his arms and head. A sixth, dressed in red, bends over the prostrate youth.

Suddenly the red-garbed priest raises his hand. Sunlight glints on the polished stone of the sacrificial knife.

With practiced skill the priest plunges the dagger into the youth's naked breast. From the gaping hole he tears out the still warm and bleeding heart. He offers it to the sun, then places it in the copal-burning censer before the war god.

Such typical rituals of the Aztecs were described by eye-witness soldiers and priests of the Spanish conquest of the 1520's. The barbarous color and brutal drama of human sacrifice characterized life among these fierce, war-making Indians of Mexico's high central valley.

Victims of the heart offerings were captives, criminals, children, or young men and women especially chosen and prepared for the occasion by a series of rites extending over a considerable period of time.

The ceremony was held at the end of every year, and a more elaborate one at the end of every thirteenth year. Other sacrifices were made whenever the gods needed to be propitiated. The longer the period between, the greater the number of victims.

Religion dominated Aztec life. The people spent much time and energy placating a complex group of deities. They believed that failure to honor their divinities with sufficient offerings would bring about the end of the world at the close of the 52-year calendar round, a period that corresponds to our own century.

Besides the ever-demanding war god (opposite) and Tlaloc, god of rain, there were deities associated with flowers, maize, the earth, the sky, drunkenness, the lower regions, birth, and death. Each day, night, week, month, and year had its own particular god or goddess.

Magic and shamanism were widespread, sorcerers and witch doctors on every hand. People consulted fortune-tellers to determine whether the fates were propitious for a journey, a business transaction, or any ordinary feature of their daily life. Certain days were regarded as unlucky and no new undertaking would be started then. A child born on one of these days was doomed to misfortune throughout life.

Prophecy played a major role in the priests' busy routine. Half their duties were nocturnal. Incense of copal and rubber had to be burned before images of the gods four times each day, three times each night. On altars the priests placed such offerings as food, clothing, and flowers.

Blood, however, was the most important offering. Earlier peoples of Middle America, the Maya of Yucatán for example, had such sacrificial rites. But it is with the Aztecs that they are most often associated.

Pigeons or quail were common offerings. Priests poked thorns through their own tongues, cheeks, and ears to obtain blood. Torn and ragged ears characterized a priest (opposite).

Besides the all-important ritual of tearing out the heart, other human victims were drowned, in rites similar to those at the Sacred Cenote at Chichén Itzá by the Maya (page 197), or shot with arrows. Occasionally priests clubbed a victim to death, or sealed him in a cave to starve to death. Some victims died in sacrificial combat.

From the writings of Bernardino de Sahagún—a Franciscan monk who went to live among the Aztecs about 1530—we have a graphic description of the sacrificial fight at the *temalacatl*. This was a stone set on a platform in the center of the great temple enclosure where all could see. Similar to a large millstone, it had a hole in the center to which the victim was tethered by a rope around his waist. The captive could walk around the stone but could move only so far before the rope checked him.

The rite began when a number of priests emerged, each in costume representing a god, from the thatch-roofed temple atop the pyramid. They descended the stone steps in a long line, followed by four warriors: two "Jaguars" and two "Eagles." Armed with swords and shields, these men advanced in fighting attitude, making motions like fencers.

When the procession reached the foot of the stairway, it advanced to the stone and formed a wide circle around it. The priests seated themselves and began at once to play on their flutes, trumpets, and shell horns, to whistle or to sing.

The victim was dragged forward and given a native liquor, pulque. He raised the bowl to the east, the west, the north, and the south, as if offering it to the cardinal points of the world, then drank the liquid through a hollow cane.

A priest approached with a quail, tore its head off before the captive, took the captive's shield, raised it high above his head, and threw the beheaded quail behind him. The victim was made to take his place on the stone, then tied with the rope by a priest dressed to represent a bear (page 246).

The captive was now handed small clubs and a sword edged not with obsidian blades, but with feathers. The skirmish began. One after another the warriors, armed with real weapons, fought the victim. Sometimes a brave captive wore down the four who sought to kill him. In such cases a fifth, who was left-handed, was sent against him and usually conquered him.

The victim's breast was then torn open and his heart offered to the sun. The body was thrown down the steps, bumping along till it reached bottom. There it was skinned and cut up, and the flesh distributed for cannibalistic ceremonies. A warrior paraded the skin about the streets; everyone who met him presented him with a gift. These gifts were taken to the man who had captured the victim and he distributed them as he saw fit.

The insatiable Aztec gods demanded ever more victims for sacrifice. This provided a ready excuse for war, as did the

PAINTING BY H. M. HERGET

**Faces and Bodies Painted, Two Priests Plan a Rite.** Ragged ears tell of self-inflicted cuts that gushed forth blood offerings to the gods. Bedraggled hair, recalling Medusa's writhing snakes, is matted with sacrificial gore. Yet Aztec ceremonies could be less somber when honoring light-hearted deities. The Flower Prince was god of pleasure, feasting, and frivolity. Priests here dress for the occasion in appropriate bright hues, wearing fringed cotton robes, and head-dress and back ornaments of light basketry, decorated with carvings and topped by quetzal plumes.

**Visiting Aztec Diplomat Swings Badge of Office—a Fan.** Temple guards snap to attention as the ambassador approaches a Tenochtitlán shrine. Boatmen paddle produce-laden canoes along the Venice-like canal. Beyond, a rich chieftain goes in fancy litter, preceded by army of retainers.

PAINTING BY H. M. HERGET

Aztec towns occasionally formed military alliances. The Mexican valley's "Big Three"—Tenochtitlán, Texcoco, and Tacuba—once took to the field together. But normally ties were loose. Even tribute-paying tribes kept political independence. This Aztec lack of unity aided the Spanish conquest.

desire for spoils and tribute. Attacks on Aztec traders traveling to other cities also caused conflict. War was chief occupation and consuming passion of the Aztecs. They felt idle without one.

An Aztec declaration of war was a formal proceeding, decided on in council. Highest in military command was the Chief of Men, assisted by war officers in charge of the city's subdivisions.

These officers, elected on merit, could not be deposed. They were distinguished by the cut of their hair, by lip and nose plugs, by their wide and flowing mantles, and by towering plumes of green feathers. Designs indicating war honors, number of captives taken, or exploits of extreme bravery ornamented their shields.

Below the officers came three classes of meritorious braves: the Jaguars or Beasts of Prey, the Eagles, and the Wandering Arrows. They won their titles by capturing one or more prisoners. They served as scouts and skirmishers in the army's van, led small bodies of men, and on occasion commanded larger subdivisions.

Meritorious braves cropped their hair close over the ears. Their masks or helmets imitated wild-animal heads. Sometimes they wore skins of those animals.

Warriors generally donned armor of quilted cotton,

**Armed with Feathers, Near-naked Captive Fights for Life.** His opponents, protected by shields and armor, wield weapons edged with sharp obsidian blades. He parries their deadly blows with feather-fringed sword. Spectators watch tensely as priest in black-bear costume referees this unequal ceremonial combat. The victim, a war prisoner, can win freedom by outfighting two "Eagle" warriors, two "Jaguars," and finally the left-handed warrior behind carved, drum-shaped stone. Failure means death in the heart-sacrifice ritual. Rope tethering him to the stone limits his movements. Yet occasionally an exceptional fighter did win against such odds. One winner, offered a high post in Tenochtitlán's army, preferred sacrificial death with its promise of a place in the warrior's special heaven.

**Moment of Death Follows Year of Pleasure.** To appease their gods, Aztecs sacrificed thousands of men, women, and children each year, their own as well as outsiders. Most died ingloriously. But one special category of victims was feted and worshiped a year before death. The handsomest and most intelligent of youths was chosen. He feasted on delicacies, was taught to play the flute, to walk and talk with royal air. Late in the year he was married to four maidens, reared as goddesses for the honor. In the final ritual, the young man broke his flutes, one after another, as he mounted steps to the sacrificial temple. At the top, priests seized him, tore open his chest, offered the still throbbing heart to the god Tezcatlipoca. The youth's soul then ascended to the highest of all Aztec heavens.



PAINTINGS BY H. M. HERGET

three-fourths to an inch and a half thick. (page 240). The Spaniards were quick to adopt this apparel, so effective was its protection against arrows and javelins.

Sometimes the legs were similarly encased and the entire suit covered with feathers and plates of gold or silver. Besides their cushioning effect, feathers also identified military groups. Some uniforms had white and red feathers, some green, some blue and yellow. Others simulated actual birds.

Aztec warriors fought principally with javelins tipped with obsidian or copper. They also used slings and stones, bows and arrows, swords and clubs.

The sword, called *maccuahuitl* or sometimes *macana,* was of wood, about four feet long, four to five inches wide, an inch or so thick. Pieces of obsidian were fastened in grooves along the edges with cement made from the roots of a tree pounded with earth and mixed with the blood of birds and bats.

Warriors defended themselves with small round shields of the parrying type. Made of netted canes interwoven with cotton and covered with painted boards and feathers, they were so strong that only a crossbow shot at close range would penetrate them.

Aztec combat tactics showed good knowledge of military technique. But their expeditions were short and, like American Indians in general, they usually stopped fighting at nightfall. During the conquest, only two engagements took place at night. *Noche triste,* "Sad Night," the Spaniards called one, when Cortés and his men were driven from Montezuma's capital after a furious battle (opposite).

The Aztecs were warlike, and in the thrall of bloodthirsty gods. But they were also a many-sided people, with a complex and advanced culture. Theirs was the last of Mexico's great Indian civilizations. Their featherwork, gold, and wood crafts were unparalleled for their time. Their designs and symbols live on in the architectural ornament of new and old buildings in Mexico City.

Mexico's modern capital rises above the ruins of the Aztec capital, Tenochtitlán, that Cortés conquered. The present-day National Palace stands on the palace site of the Aztec king, Montezuma. The massive Cathedral is rooted in the rubble of the Aztecs' great sacrificial temple.

Practically every excavation for new construction in the city adds its quota of Aztec relics to the extensive collections in Mexico's National Museum. One such lucky find was an awesome statue of Coatlicue, Earth Goddess, wearing a skirt of writhing snakes.

The story of the Aztecs is better

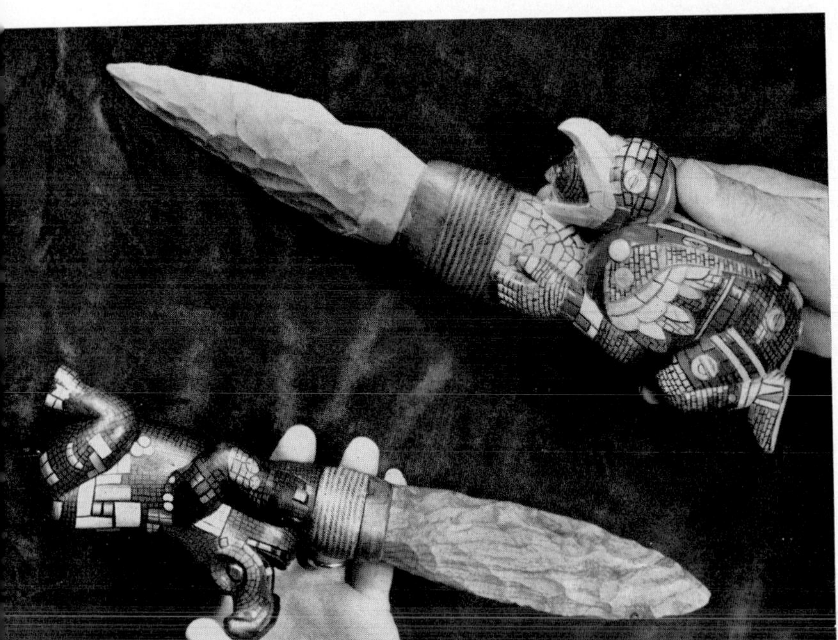

**Jagged Blades** and carved handles tell grim story of sacrifice. With these knives priests cut out victims' hearts and offered them to insatiable gods. As many as 50,000 persons, mostly war captives, died each year in Aztec rites. Blades were of flintlike stone or obsidian, handles often adorned with delicate turquoise mosaic. Handle of upper knife represents man in eagle costume.

LUIS MARDEN, NATIONAL GEOGRAPHIC STAFF

LIBRARY OF CONGRESS

known than that of many New World peoples, thanks to archeological relics, pictograph manuscripts, and other native and Spanish records. But where the early wandering tribes came from, and when and where they stopped before founding Tenochtitlán are still mysteries that tantalize scholars.

The Aztecs entered the Valley of Mexico early in the 14th century, when Europe was deep in the Middle Ages. Then a crude hunting people, they came into contact with communities of high culture bordering a great lake.

According to some accounts, the newcomers settled near Chapultepec, where they acquired certain cultural traits of

**Aztecs Launch Furious Assault on Spaniards**

Tenochtitlán, 1519: Bearded Cortés and Marina, his Indian mistress and interpreter, with mounted aide and four Tlaxcalan allies, stand off attack behind smoking cannon in palace courtyard. Aztec warrior (upper right) fires the chapel, indicated by Virgin and crucifix. Montezuma (upper left), hostage of the Spaniards, begs his people to let the dons leave in peace. In answer they hurl stone (shown in motion) that fatally wounds him. Earlier the invaders had entered the Aztec capital unopposed. Then during Cortés's absence, a lieutenant massacred unarmed citizens dancing at a religious festival, and war was on. Cortés rejoined his beleaguered garrison. But all were driven from the city with heavy losses during the Noche Triste, "Sad Night." Eventually the Spaniards, reinforced by Indian allies, returned to conquer. Pictograph was made by a Tlaxcalan Indian artist of that time.

the Acolhuacans. Between about 1367 and 1376, the Acolhuacans drove them out, forcing them to take refuge on two small reed-covered mud banks or islands in the center of the lake.

Aztec tradition explains the choice of their future permanent homesite in more picturesque and flattering terms. It had been predicted that they would stop and found their dynasty when they saw an eagle on a cactus eating a serpent.

Upon reaching the borders of a large lake they saw a beautiful island, and the priest who led them beheld a huge eagle with a snake struggling in its talons. The bird came to rest on a cactus plant, killed and devoured the reptile. The Aztecs, overjoyed at the prophecy's fulfillment, at once established their city.

The legend is symbolized today by the eagle, serpent, and cactus in the Mexican coat of arms and flag.

However founded, the island settlements grew into two towns, Tenochtitlán and Tlaltelolco. Though the space between them was little more than a broad canal, they progressed as independent units for more than a hundred years. In the 15th century the sixth ruler of Tenochtitlán conquered Tlaltelolco and united the two.

Meantime the Aztecs were growing to real power in the Valley. Maxtli, skilled general of their fourth ruler, Itzcoatl (1427–1440), conquered many neighboring cities and tribes, exacting rich tribute from them. Tenochtitlán prospered and expanded, until by the time of the

**Scepter, Crown, and Cloak** of this high priest are lavishly decorated with insignia of gods he serves. Behind him rise Tenochtitlán's great pyramid temples, tier on tier of stone. His power is great in both religious and temporal matters, for he and his subordinate priests direct the elaborate rituals on which all tribal life is based.

They make intricate astronomic calculations that harmonize sacred and solar calendars. They teach youths to read and keep pictograph records. They follow lives of demanding ritual to win success in war and bountiful crops from capricious gods.

PAINTINGS BY H. M. HERGET

**Wood Carver Whittles Temple Decoration Amid Busy Market**

Around him macaws scream, children chatter, women gossip, merchant and customer bargain. Bernal Díaz del Castillo chronicles: "When we arrived at the great market place, called Tlaltelolco, we were astounded at the number of people and the quantity of merchandise that it contained, and at the good order and control that was maintained. . . . Let us begin with the dealers in gold, silver, and precious stones, feathers, mantles, and embroidered goods. . . . Indian slaves both men and women . . . tied to long poles, with collars round their necks. . . . In another part there were skins of tigers and lions, of otters and jackals, deer and other animals. . . . Let us also mention the fruiterers, and the women who sold cooked food, dough and tripe in their own part of the market; then every sort of pottery made in a thousand different forms from great water jars to little jugs . . . then those who sold honey . . . and yellow ointment and cochineal. . . .

"There are also buildings where three magistrates sit in judgment, and there are executive officers . . . who inspect the merchandise [which was] so numerous . . . and the great market place with its surrounding arcades was so crowded with people, that one would not have been able to see and inquire about it all in two days."

conquest tribute was pouring into the coffers of Montezuma II from all southern Mexico, the Veracruz coastal plain, even from Guatemala.

By all accounts Tenochtitlán in its heyday was a beautiful city. Governmental buildings and houses of the rich were made of cut stone, middle-class homes of adobe blocks. Only dwellings of farmers and the poorer classes were wattle and daub with thatched roofs.

Most larger buildings enclosed cool courtyards and patios. Walls were plastered a gleaming white or colored dull red. Trees dappled the city green, lake and canals sparkled blue. Fruit-and-vegetable-laden canoes, gay splashes of color from gardens and rooftop flower beds, and the bright-hued garments of the populace made an enchanting scene.

Aztec wives busied themselves sweeping rooms and courtyards. They ground maize, or corn, to make meal for the tortillas, even as it is ground today in many parts of Mexico (page 261). There were rich sauces and other foods to prepare, such as *guacamole,* a dish of tomato, alligator pear, and chile. And there were babies to tend.

Older men taught young boys. Teenage boys were schooled for priesthood or military service, or apprenticed to merchants or artisans. Education for girls was not so rigorous. Unless they took vows of chastity and went into a religious order, girls married between the ages of 11 and 18, arrangements being made by parents or priests.

Tenochtitlán's markets (page 250) were as pulsingly alive as those of to-

**Daily Life in Aztec Times** found man as burden bearer, woman as weaver. Turkeys, parrots, squash, and green vegetables ride to market on farmer's back (left). Then, as now, barefoot men jogged miles, carrying heavy loads by tumpline round the head. American Indians domesticated the turkey long before Columbus sailed. Maize or Indian corn, sweet potatoes, beans, peppers, tomatoes, and cacao or chocolate also swelled the Aztec larder.

Below, mother teaches her daughter the art of basket weaving, using reeds from swamps that once surrounded Tenochtitlán. Her blue basket design is attractively simple, like the red pattern of her dress. Corn grows high between weaver and thatched homes traced against the sky.

PAINTINGS BY H. M. HERGET



**Stone-and-adobe Igloo** in modern-day village descends from the Aztec steam bath. Children (left) watch a resident of Huexoculco, in the Valley of Mexico, fan furnace flames in one of the community's 70-odd sweat baths. Resembling Finnish steam baths, the huts are called *temascales* (from Aztec *tema,* to bathe, and *calli,* house).

Bather enters on hands and knees, plugs the door, pours water on hot stones to produce steam, and swelters in darkness, sometimes for hours, like lobster boiled alive in a pot. Sweat baths, in wide use among North American tribes, were prescribed by Aztec medicine men for many ills. Aztecs bathed often—too often for health, Spanish chroniclers felt. Bernal Díaz del Castillo wrote that Montezuma bathed every afternoon.

JUSTIN LOCKE

day's Mexico City. Merchants and artisans bartered their wares. Feather quills filled with gold dust occasionally served as currency.

Gold and silver workers displayed their art. Wood carvers, workers in stone, creators of intricate turquoise or shell mosaics, feather workers, pottery makers, bodyguards, and burden-bearers thronged the market place. Spinners and weavers produced cotton cloth; tailors fashioned it into garments. Others made ornate headdresses for officials and warriors. Sandal and weapon makers, tanners and basketweavers plied their trades. Vendors of honey, herbs, and pitch pine for torches thronged the arcades.

The artisan looking up from his work, the merchant at his stall could tell at a glance the rank of the person approaching. Everyday dress for the Aztec man was breechcloth, hipcloth, mantle or cape, and sandals. The mantle and ends of the breechcloth were short and plain for the lower classes, long and embroidered for those of higher station. The elaborateness of a woman's short skirt and sleeveless blouse served to reveal

**Pagan celebrants** climbed broad stone steps to a now-vanished temple atop the mighty Pyramid of the Sun. Rising 216 feet above the valley, it dwarfs all other structures along Teotihuacán's "Highway of the Dead," which leads from the Pyramid of the Moon to the serpent-decorated Temple of Quetzalcoatl. Aztecs, arriving long after the city was built, ascribed divine origin to the abandoned remains.

Sungod glowers from the center of an Aztec calendar stone (left), on exhibit in Mexico's National Museum of Anthropology. Four rectangles around the face stand for earth, air, fire, and water. In the encircling band march 20 symbols, one for each day of the Aztec month. Beyond, mythology and astronomy symbols in the 24-ton basalt monolith denote time, gods, man, and nature.

Eighteen 20-day months made up the Aztec solar year, leaving a five-day period into which the whole year's bad luck was crowded. Major time cycle was 52 years. As its closing night neared, panic deepened, fed by the prediction that the world's end would coincide with the end of one of these cycles. With the new dawn, the people celebrated their escape by lighting fires, feasting, making human sacrifice.

KODACHROME BY THOMAS R. SMITH, NATIONAL GEOGRAPHIC STAFF; EKTACHROME BY OMAR MARCUS (LEFT).

the wearer's position in the social scale.

Village chiefs wore a white mantle, ambassadors carried a fan (page 244). Priests usually dressed in black; even their bodies were stained black. But the robe of the sacrificial priest was red.

Scantily clad farmers (page 253) trudged in from outlying districts carrying fruit, sweet potatoes, tomatoes, squash, beans, peppers, and cacao or chocolate. The maize they brought was a variety developed by the Aztecs; this matured rapidly, an essential quality for the high, arid plateau country. Tobacco, cotton, hemp, rubber, copal resin for religious ceremonies were also on display in the market place. And turkeys, fish, and birds.

Some vegetables came by canoe from floating gardens, or *chinampas,* such as today may be seen at Xochimilco, not far from Mexico City. These chinampas go back to Tenochtitlán's early days when the Aztecs, weak and hemmed in by their foes, subsisted on fish, birds, aquatic plants, and such vegetables as they were able to grow on rafts of reeds and wattlework heaped with mud from the lake.

Through the years the floating islands increased in size and numbers. Plant roots interlaced, eventually anchored at the bottom of the lake, and the islands became a series of rectangular plots separated by canals just wide enough for the passage of canoes.

"New World Venice" Cortés called the Aztec capital. One of the conqueror's soldiers described it as a place of wide and handsome streets, formed half of hard earth like a brick pavement and half of canal, side by side, so that the people traversed them by land or water.

Many boulevards of modern Mexico City follow the course of these main

**Toluca Valley Family** sorts carrots in wooden canoe. Beyond, ripening grain turns fields to gold. Pre-Aztec farmers cultivated this fertile valley watered by the Lerma River. Near-8,800-foot altitude makes winters brisk, but in summer cool nights follow warm days.

At Calixtlahuaca (Aztec for "Plain Dominated by Buildings"), near the valley metropolis of Toluca, the archeologist's shovel has revealed evidences of several Indian cultures. One was the Matlatzinca, linked with ancient Toltecs of the near-by Valley of Mexico. Modern Toluca crafts produced woven skirt and handbag of woman in picture.

KODACHROMES BY JUSTIN LOCKE

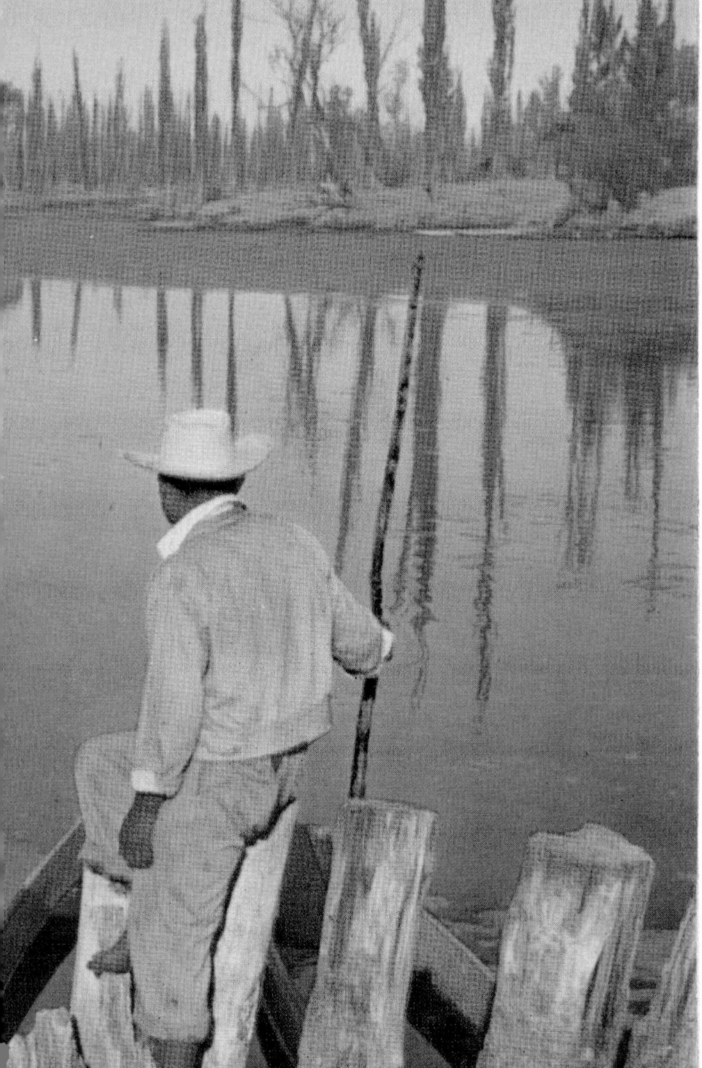

**Floating Gardens at Tlahuac** grew food for Tenochtitlán. Tree-bordered fields on opposite shore were once Aztec *chinampas*, plots made by piling lake-floor mud on reed-and-wattle rafts. Gardeners built huts on them, could row their "farms" from place to place. As at Xochimilco, Tlahuac's better-known neighbor, the gardens grew, interlaced, finally took root.

Lakes, ponds, and swamps dotted the high Valley of Mexico in olden days. With hungry tribes competing for farmland, the handy island gardens provided a vital source of strength to the Aztecs. Now this blue and green vale of Tlahuac—10 miles southeast of Mexico City—is a watery oasis in country where dust storms often swirl across dry beds of former lakes. Drainage projects channeled and dried up most of the water that made enchanting scenes of fertility recorded with amazement by 16th century Spaniards. Modern problems are to grow crops and trees to hold down soil; to obtain drinking water to supply huge, industrial Mexico City, and at the same time leave sufficient for near-by farming requirements.

canals. People walk today on pavement where the Aztec went in his canoe.

Meeting the problems of their soggy site made the Aztecs exceptional engineers for their time. They erected buildings on piles and constructed great causeways leading from the city to various towns bordering the lakes. The Pan American Highway now runs into the city along one of the ancient causeways.

Aztec skill erected a great dike during the years 1440–1450 to prevent the Lake of Texcoco flooding the city. The work, extending some ten miles from Atzacoalco on the north to the hill called La Estrella on the south, was constructed with a core of clay and stone, crowned with a wall of rubble masonry.

On either side a strong stockade broke the force of the waves. Openings for canoes pierced the dike. Sluice gates controlling the water level opened in summer to let fresh water into the lake depleted by evaporation.

For governing purposes, the Aztecs separated their island home into four quarters, each containing a phratry, or clan, of kindred peoples or those of common descent. Twenty *kins* made up a phratry. Each kin elected and deposed its own officers, consisting of a governor and a group of "Elder Brothers," or council. There was also a group of councilors known as "Grandfathers," who qualified by prowess in war, wisdom in council, shrewdness in trade, or courage. Courage alone could not secure it, but was essential, since the honor came only to candidates who underwent cruel ceremonial rites.

At the head of each phratry was a war captain. These four captains served on the great tribal council in company with representatives from each kin, Elder Brothers, and certain temple priests. The great council met every 80 days, sepa-

## AZTEC PICTURE WRITING

THE DATE is 10 Rabbit. That year, says the pictograph at left, Chief Ahuitzotl died and Montezuma II succeeded.

The Aztec time symbol (10 dots surrounding the rabbit head) corresponds to our A.D. 1502. The bound mummy represents death, its crown royalty. The attached animal, Aztec symbol for a small water creature, gives deceased chief's name. Crown, throne, and speech scroll at Montezuma's mouth symbolize a monarch: "He who speaks."

Earlier in the year 10 Rabbit—square at left above—Ahuitzotl took Tehuantepec (cat head on hill at right). The shield denotes war, the flaming temple conquest.

Thus, by fanciful designs and prancing and posing humans and animals, the Aztecs recorded their war-filled history. Interpreters divide pictographs into three groups: those for persons and places, those for dates, and those for events, including natural phenomena and objects like gold, jade, and feathers. Often all three types combine to tell a story.

A place-name example is the cat's head topping a hill in the above picture. In Aztec language "tecuani" meant man-eating cat, possibly a jaguar. "Tepec" stood for hill or town. Hence Tehuantepec for the town that Ahuitzotl conquered.

This uses the rebus principle—a phonetic method of expressing words or syllables by objects whose names sound like the words but whose meaning is different. "I can bear pain" is shown by four pictures—an eye, a can, a bear, a window pane.

Some scholars say that the central Mexican highlanders, no innovators despite their many accomplishments, adopted ideas of picture writing from the older and more complex technique of the Maya. Other authorities trace sources to Toltec or related cultures.

Aztec date symbols were taken from their calendar, similar to that of the Maya (page 198), but far less exact. Each of the 20 days of the 18 months in the Aztec solar year bore its own name and number. Each successive year was known by the signs of the day on which it began. But only four names could start the year, because of the chronological order of days and the "lost" five-day period at year's end. Symbols for these were Reed, Flint, House, and Rabbit.

In the picture above, the year 5 Flint or Flint Knife, corresponds to 1484. Linked with it a highly adorned priest brandishes a weapon as he executes a victim, shown weltering in blood.

This gruesome scene depicts the dedication at Tenochtitlán of the great temple of the Aztec war god Huitzilopochtli, traditionally the beginning of human sacrifice by the Aztecs. Gore stains temple stairway. Surmounting pyramid is the hieroglyph for Tenochtitlán—ancient name of Mexico City. It pictures a cactus growing out of a stone.

The sun's disk with a segment cut from it (figure *a* at top of next column) tells of an eclipse of the sun. This occurred in 5 Rabbit (1510).

In 10 House, three years before Columbus's first voyage of discovery, a comet swept over the Valley of Mexico (figure *b*). The Aztecs pictured the fiery

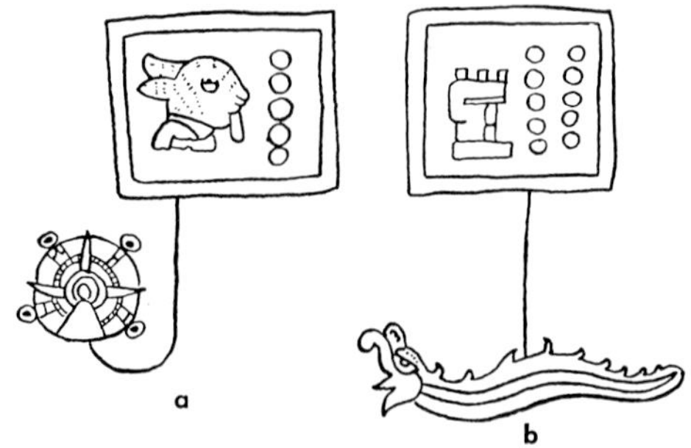


trailing body as a serpent writhing across the heavens. Montezuma regarded it as an evil portent of the fall of his empire. When the fair-skinned Spaniards landed in Mexico in 1519, he felt the end had come. His attitude helped make the conquest possible.

In figure c below, earthquake and volcanic eruption take curiously static forms. Reading the picture from bottom to top, the speckled rectangle is the earth. The Aztec word for movement, a sort of winged eye, indicates the quake. Joined to it are a star and smoke curls, hieroglyph for the eruption's "smoke ascending to the stars." The date was 2 House (1533).

It snowed heavily in Tlachquiahco Province in year 11 Reed (1503), says figure *d*. Great cloud bank represents snow. H-shaped object pelted with rain signs is combination hieroglyph for province's name.

By such simple symbols, easily understood once the key is learned, Aztecs recorded migrations, famines, defeats, victories, tribute paid by other tribes. Their picture accounts, painted in books of fiber paper or deerskin, lack the detail and flow of written narrative. But skeleton outlines tell the world in spritely fashion much about how this people lived and the degree of civilization they achieved.

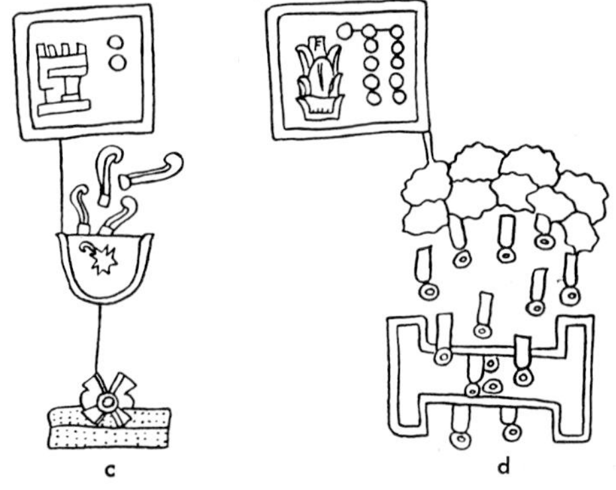


rating into two judicial bodies which sat simultaneously and passed on all important affairs. A smaller council, composed of one speaker from each kin, met every 20 days in a directing and judicial capacity. Final power was vested in the Chief of Men and the Snake Woman, actually a man. The Chief of Men was both legislator and executive. Eventually he became king, or emperor.

The Snake Woman was a second emperor. He functioned as secretary of state in charge of intertribal affairs. He kept tally of tribute paid by Aztec-conquered cities, towns, and villages, using pictograph records such as those shown above.

**Woman Grinds Corn Beneath Adobe Bins**

Thatch-topped bins near Atlatlahuca, in hot country southwest of Mexico City, keep grain safe from rodents. Aztecs used similar granaries—huge clay urns covered with thatch to shed rain; kept hulled corn in house in pottery jars. One early codex shows farmer and wife pouring grain into a tall vessel. Aztecs worshiped corn gods and goddesses. Xilonen, "Young Maize Mother," was linked with still older cults. Stealing maize was punishable by death or slavery.

The woman's grinding stones shown here have remained unchanged in form for thousands of years. Their grist will make tortillas such as the Aztecs ate, except that early cakes—from size of clay griddles found—were much larger than present ones. Discoursing on Indian diet, chronicler Bernal Díaz wrote, "The Indian fig is an agreeable, nutritious fruit; and the tortilla, made of maize flour with a slight infusion of lime—might pass for a very tolerable camp fare."

**Cholula Boy Draws Sap from Maguey Plant to Make Pulque**

Time-honored way to prepare this favorite Indian drink is to suck "honey water" through gourd, then transport liquid in goatskin bags for fermentation in bull-hide vats. Tradition says Toltecs popularized pulque. Aztecs esteemed the drink, believed it enabled them to commune with the gods, gave it to victims at sacrificial rites. One conquistador called the maguey "something between a tree and an artichoke," told how Indians made clothing, rope, roofs, needles of its leaves, fibers, and thorns. In Mexico today maguey-fiber basketry catches the tourist's eye.

Beyond Cholula's buildings distant Popocatepetl, the Aztecs' "Smoking Mountain," lifts its snowy head. In past centuries Popo erupted violently. Today it only fumes. Cortés's soldiers scaled the 17,887-foot peak and descended into its jagged half-mile-wide crater to get sulphur from the pit to replenish their gunpowder.

KODACHROMES BY JUSTIN LOCKE

At one time the tribe owned all land in common and chiefs were chosen by the people. Undesirable chiefs were deposed. Then gradually a tendency toward inheritance of office developed. As more tribes and territories were conquered during the rule of the powerful Itzcoatl, social classes based on captured wealth began to appear. For the first time there was distribution of spoils.

The new land went to the warriors, creating a group of rich landowners. Artisans in certain crafts gained special privileges. The priesthood grew stronger, with members in civic as well as religious posts.

Whether the system was a monarchy or a democracy is largely a matter of definition. Even after inheritance of office became common, an Aztec man was nominally elected to his position and when not satisfactory was ousted. Although there was a definite lineal descent of the post of Chief of Men toward the end of Aztec dominance in the Valley, he was voted on in council. The Snake Woman was elected for life, but could be removed for cause.

True, there were slaves, but not in the usual sense. Their labor belonged to another, but their persons did not, and it was possible for a slave to have slaves of his own. His children were born free. The owner of a slave's labor could not sell it without the slave's consent.

Parents sometimes sold a child; an impoverished family would offer one of its members as security on a loan. Lawbreakers, occasionally a war captive spared from sacrifice, became slaves. But many others voluntarily accepted bond-

**Magnificent Gardeners,** the Aztecs contributed many flowers to the world. Their descendants, still speaking the old Nahuatl tongue, grew these gladiolas, tuberoses, and carnations in Xochimilco's "floating gardens." Vendor's stall sits in Mexico City suburbs before the Shrine of the Virgin of Guadalupe.

Indians in dark shawls and white cottons visit the Guadalupe shrine (opposite). Here in pagan times stood a temple to the Aztecs' "Little Mother," Tonantzin. In the transition to Christianity, the Virgin, protector of the Indians, succeeded the Aztec deity naturally. In 1531 Her vision appeared to a simple Indian. A church was built, and ever since Guadalupe has been Mexico's leading shrine, drawing December pilgrims to the Festival to the Virgin.

KODACHROMES BY JUSTIN LOCKE

age, especially when crops failed. To obtain food, a luckless farmer might become a slave to share the bounty of his more fortunate neighbor, or place himself under the protection of a wealthy merchant or landowner.

The lowliest laborer and the richest noble were accorded equal justice under the laws laid down by the Aztec monarch and the penalties stipulated for violation of his edicts. The accused was heard by the magistrate of his phratry, an official elected for personal ability and integrity.

There were two major divisions of crime among the Aztecs—a crime against one's own group, and an offense against another group. The group to which an offender belonged was obligated to see that he was brought to justice.

Murder was punishable by death. Intemperance, except for those aged 70 or over, or during festivities, was dealt with severely: the young were put to death; middle-aged men had their heads shaved—a shattering disgrace. A priest who broke the laws was put to death. In certain cases the offender paid for his crimes on the stone of ceremonial combat.

Slanderers had their lips cut off. Theft was punished according to the amount or nature of the stolen goods and the number of offenses charged against the individual. Stealing gold or silver was a major crime; offenders were flayed. Lesser crimes brought imprisonment.

**Great Stone Faces** reflect ancient Toltec glory. Ruined Tollan, capital of the Toltecs, stands near modern Tula, about fifty miles north of Mexico City. Its giant figures were sculptured not in one piece but several, put together with mortise and tenon. Feet buried in earth, the colossi once supported a temple roof with their flat heads. In the 12th century a nomadic tribe took over from the civilized Toltecs, burned their temple, tossed the statues into the rubble.

Below: Teotihuacán's sculptured reptiles project from the Temple of Quetzalcoatl, the Plumed Serpent. Tláloc, the spectacled rain god, shares the frieze. The grotesque but magnificently carved stone serpent heads once were painted, and had eyes fashioned of glittering volcanic glass.

Ruins of the mysterious ceremonial city northeast of Tenochtitlán so impressed the Aztecs that they, too, made it a religious site, named it Teotihuacán, "Place of the Gods."



KODACHROMES BY JUSTIN LOCKE

**Near This Old Aqueduct Tower at San Bartolo Naucalpan** a converted Aztec chief found the lost image of the Virgin of Los Remedios. Enshrined there, it is honored by a colorful September fiesta.

A whole class of outcasts was made up of those driven from their own groups for violating laws, exiles from other tribes, and those who failed to cultivate their gardens or to pay their taxes. The Aztec citizen gave about one-third his wealth in taxes. Each section of the city had great storehouses for food, clothing, animal skins, pottery, gold, silver, feathers, tools, and similar objects paid into the treasury.

To be shorn of one's civil rights and cast out was serious indeed. It cut a man off from the protection and subsistence of his group. He became a solitary, hungry wanderer, to be killed by foes unavenged, to fall prey to wild beasts.

Besides the blood-drenched rites for which they are most remembered, the Aztecs danced and sang in ceremonies where the main offerings were flowers and fruit. Love of flowers and music is one of the traits handed down to present-day descendants (page 262). Aztec music was produced by wooden and pottery flutes, conch shells, rattles, drums, and rasping instruments made from notched bones.

The Aztecs enjoyed all kinds of games, the best known being *tlachtli.* This was played as the Maya played it at Chichén Itzá (page 203).

Tumbling and juggling were popular. Montezuma II, emperor at the time of the conquest, was especially fond of acrobatic performances. Favorite dancers occupied a house near his palace. Dwarfs and midgets also entertained him.

Montezuma's zoo and aviary impressed the Spaniards. They saw animals new to them and were amazed at the variety of species. They were fascinated by the serpents, particularly those "with bells on their tails," the rattlesnakes.

All birds known in Mexico, and some from other areas as well, comprised the aviary collection. Besides eagles, macaws, and quetzals, there were tiny parakeets and many long-legged water birds. They were kept for their feathers, which were plucked from time to time for use in fans, headdresses, and cloaks.

From their world of color and variety, the Aztecs looked forward to a future life provided with many heavens.

Those slain in battle, victims of sacrifice, and women who died in childbirth were promised the highest heaven. Death from storm or lightning sent the soul to a hilltop heaven of plenty. A person prosaically dying in bed from natural causes went below to a place called Mictlan. Death from corruptive diseases sent the spirit even lower.

Funerals of the wealthy were elaborate, with jade, gold, and other offerings placed in the tomb. A poor man was fortunate if an ordinary clay vessel went to the grave with him.

But rich or poor, chief or peasant, each Aztec played his part in shaping an early New World culture that offers one of the most fascinating of studies.

The heart of that civilization, the Tecpan or temple enclosure of Tenochtitlán, has now become Mexico City's Zócalo, the *Plaza de la Constitución.* Could its original scenes be recaptured by some magical picture playback, today's plaza strollers would be enchanted, as were the Spaniards, to see the Aztecs' royal palace rising in splendor, to hear the roars and chatter of Aztec zoo and aviary.

In the open park would loom the massive circular stone of ceremonial combat. Near by would be etched the sinister outlines of the great sacrificial temple and the skull rack on which its victims' heads were impaled.

The ancient buildings are long vanished, their stone fragments tossed into the canals or buried in the foundations of the modern city. But here and there among the Indians thronging the streets the stamp of Aztec lineage still stands out. And in the charm and gaiety of life in the Mexican capital the Aztec love of flowers, dancing, and art lives on.

CHAPTER 12

# HUNTING PREHISTORY IN PANAMA JUNGLES

## BY MATTHEW W. STIRLING

BREAKERS BOOMED on the desolate northern Panama shore. We steadied our canoe, waiting a chance to ride one in to the beach. Our craft soared high, then sagged deep into the foam-flecked trough of a curling Caribbean roller.

I saw my wife Marion and National Geographic Photographer Dick Stewart shoot shoreward with their canoe-load of baggage. My assistant Bob Rands and I followed right behind. Just as we crossed the bar, the frail vessel veered sideways. Heavy surf smashed aboard. Our crew paddled desperately. We beached just in time.

Soaked to the skin, we stood 130 miles west of the Panama Canal on one of this hemisphere's loneliest and wildest coastal stretches. Inland rose a steep, jungle-clad wall of rain-soaked mountains, dipping their toes in the crashing surf.

Near by, Columbus set up the first Spanish colony on America's mainland. But food dwindled, Indians raided, and the "Admiral of the Ocean Sea" abandoned the site. Later explorers shunned this forbidding land.

Now we were seeking pottery, arrowheads, stone axes, ancient graves, other relics of Indians who lived here during and before the time of Columbus. On this third Panama expedition sponsored jointly by the National Geographic Society and the Smithsonian Institution, we aimed to study links between Indian civilizations in South and Central America. Cultural ideas flowing between Inca and Maya empires must have had impact on the isthmus through which they passed. Our job: find evidences of that ancient Indian "golden age."

We hired a guide and headed up Rio Coclé del Norte, poling and towing our canoes through rushing current. Wild fig trees fringed the riverbanks. Monstrous tarpon churned the water.

That afternoon we reached Canoa, the lonely thatched home of an aged woman who promptly led us on a wild goose chase after a mythical burying ground. Near by we found ruins of Spanish gold mines—collapsed tunnels dug by Indian slaves, millstones sheathed in vines.

So began our life in jungle camps. Rain often drenched us, though this was the "dry" season. While we probed sodden diggings, our guide shot game for the pot. "Painted rabbit," or paca, a 20-pound rodent with porklike flavor, was our favorite dish. Fried tapir steaks, dosed liberally with tenderizer, formed another staple.

Sometimes we shot deer, sometimes curassow, kin to wild turkey. Natives sold us rice, bananas, even eggs and chickens. Palm nuts, and our own dehydrated soups, canned fruit, and cheese filled out menus. At night we curled up in mosquito-proof army jungle hammocks, slung between trees. Howler monkeys, insects, frogs sang us to sleep.

We pushed up tributaries of the Coclé del Norte, first Rio Coclecito, then the Cascajal. To buck Cascajal rapids we lightened canoes, hiring extra craft to carry overflow equipment. The Indian crewmen had pointed teeth, chipped with stones, a mark of beauty and health.

Waterfalls, rapids, fallen trees slowed our passage. One poleman kept the big canoe from falling away downstream, another threw weight on his pole to drive ahead a few feet against the sucking current. Over the side, we manhandled boats past rough stretches.

When the river opened into a deep, calm lake, we thankfully made camp. From our hilltop, dry for once, we could see peaks along the Continental Divide. On two previous expeditions we had ranged along its Pacific slope.

From our riverside camp we set to work collecting pottery fragments and stonework. But rain came on the fourth afternoon. It poured all night and at 5 a.m. we broke camp in darkness and shoved off downstream.

First stop was at a native settlement where we had cached our outboard motor and extra equipment to lighten upstream loads. We retrieved these, hired a small leaky canoe, and two Indian boys to man it. We stowed it with archeological treasures, picks, shovels, and food, until only an inch of freeboard remained. But the boys had a fine time guiding it downstream, fishing as they went. They hooked one 10-pounder.

Seemingly past our worst obstacles, we relaxed, enjoyed the downstream run, and thought back on four years of archeological work in Panama.

I remembered a December afternoon when, shivering in light overcoats, we paced the steamer deck, watching New York's snow-draped skyscrapers fall astern. Two days later we basked in tropical sunshine, the overcoats a nuisance.

That was the start of our first Panama expedition. We probed tombs and burial urns in the hilly Peninsula of Azuero.

**Marion Stirling Views Grim Ornament.** More than 200 slain enemies furnished the 800 human teeth in this Panama warrior's necklace. Dr. Stirling unearthed it with the skeleton of its owner from a burial urn near Parita. Pre-Columbian Indians took their choicest possessions with them to the grave, leaving clues to their culture for scientists who patiently dig up the past.

NATIONAL GEOGRAPHIC PHOTOGRAPHER
RICHARD H. STEWART

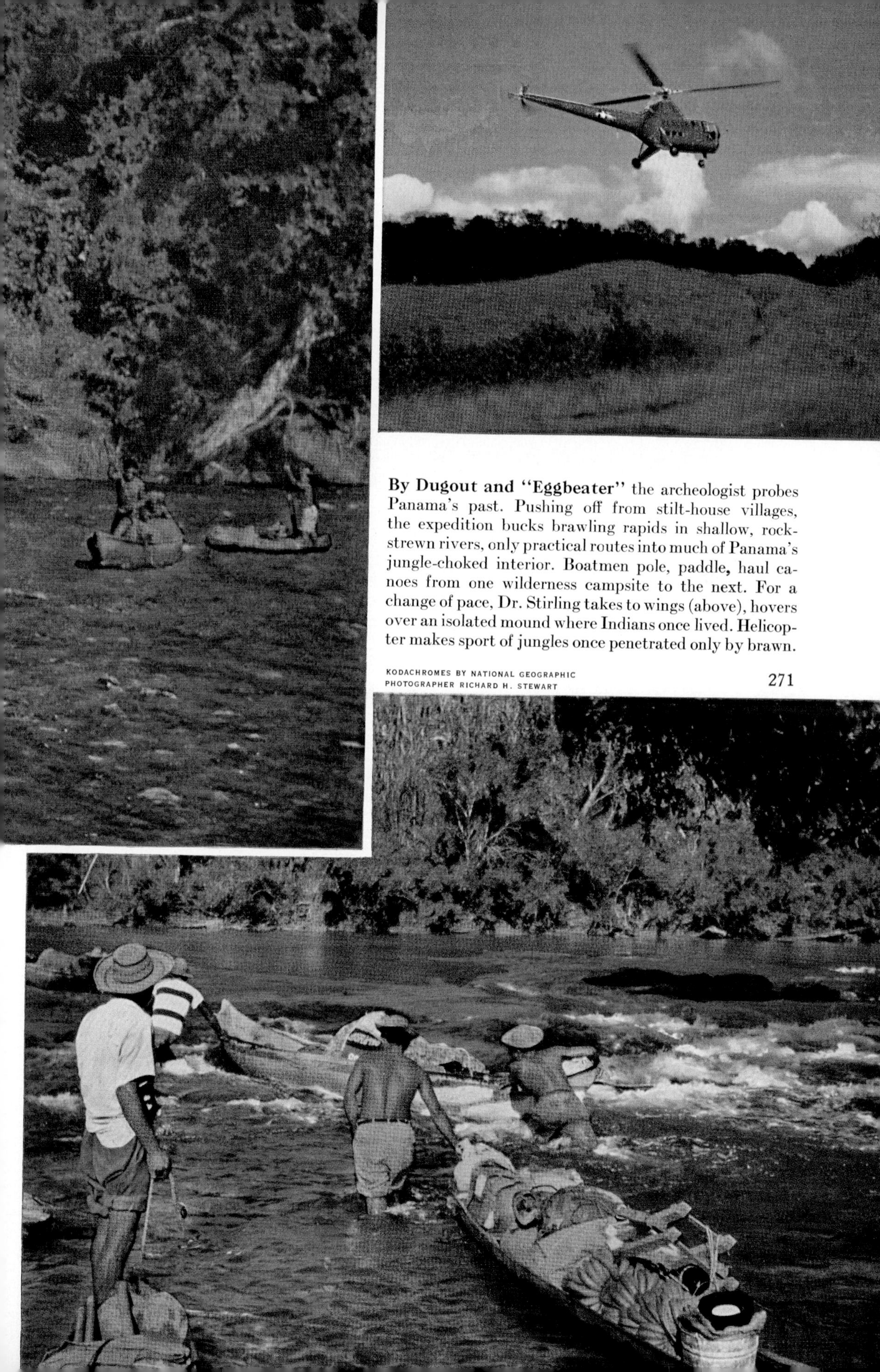

**By Dugout and "Eggbeater"** the archeologist probes Panama's past. Pushing off from stilt-house villages, the expedition bucks brawling rapids in shallow, rock-strewn rivers, only practical routes into much of Panama's jungle-choked interior. Boatmen pole, paddle, haul canoes from one wilderness campsite to the next. For a change of pace, Dr. Stirling takes to wings (above), hovers over an isolated mound where Indians once lived. Helicopter makes sport of jungles once penetrated only by brawn.

KODACHROMES BY NATIONAL GEOGRAPHIC PHOTOGRAPHER RICHARD H. STEWART

**Care for a Fight, Anyone?**
Eyes bloodshot from drinking chicha, cheek scarred by flying fists, a Guaymi tribesman hefts his balsa log, seeks a new target during a riotous balsería. He sports feathered hat, bead lapels, jaguar-tooth necklace. Blood runs freely as village teams compete.

NATIONAL GEOGRAPHIC PHOTOGRAPHER RICHARD H. STEWART

But more vivid are memories of much-alive Southern Guaymi Indians and their spring festival, the *balsería*.

Modern survivors of gold-rich tribesmen who resisted Spain's conquistadores, Guaymi still distrust white men. They often set mantraps along their jungle trails—bows and arrows or loaded guns with trip lines attached.

Few outsiders have watched their strange ceremony. The Guaymi try to conceal both its date and site, informing their own scattered tribes by knots tied in reeds along trails. When we got word of a scheduled three-day balsería we bumped toward the mountains in our truck. At Tolé, north of the Pan American Highway, we spread blankets in the schoolhouse and slept.

Next day, after five hours on horseback, we came to the rim of a natural bowl in the hills. Below us the festival was in full swing. Floating up came the shouting of 2,000 Indians, the blare of primitive instruments.

"Like Times Square on New Year's Eve," said Marion.

The revelry dinned all night as we tried to sleep half a mile away. Early next morning we moved among dancing, chanting Indians, faces striped red and black. Tall, broad-shouldered men wore long trousers, white or blue shirts, some even neckties. Many sported feather headdresses and draped stuffed animal skins over their backs. Women in Mother Hubbard dresses sat with children in corral-like enclosures of slashed undergrowth, guarding gourds of chicha.

This fermented liquor, made from corn, manioc, fruit, or other plants, didn't strike us as strong—although Spaniards described one ancient variety that tasted like turpentine and did double duty as embalming fluid. But the Guaymi, keyed up for their annual festival, got wondrously drunk by mid-morning. While conch-shell or cattle-horn trumpets

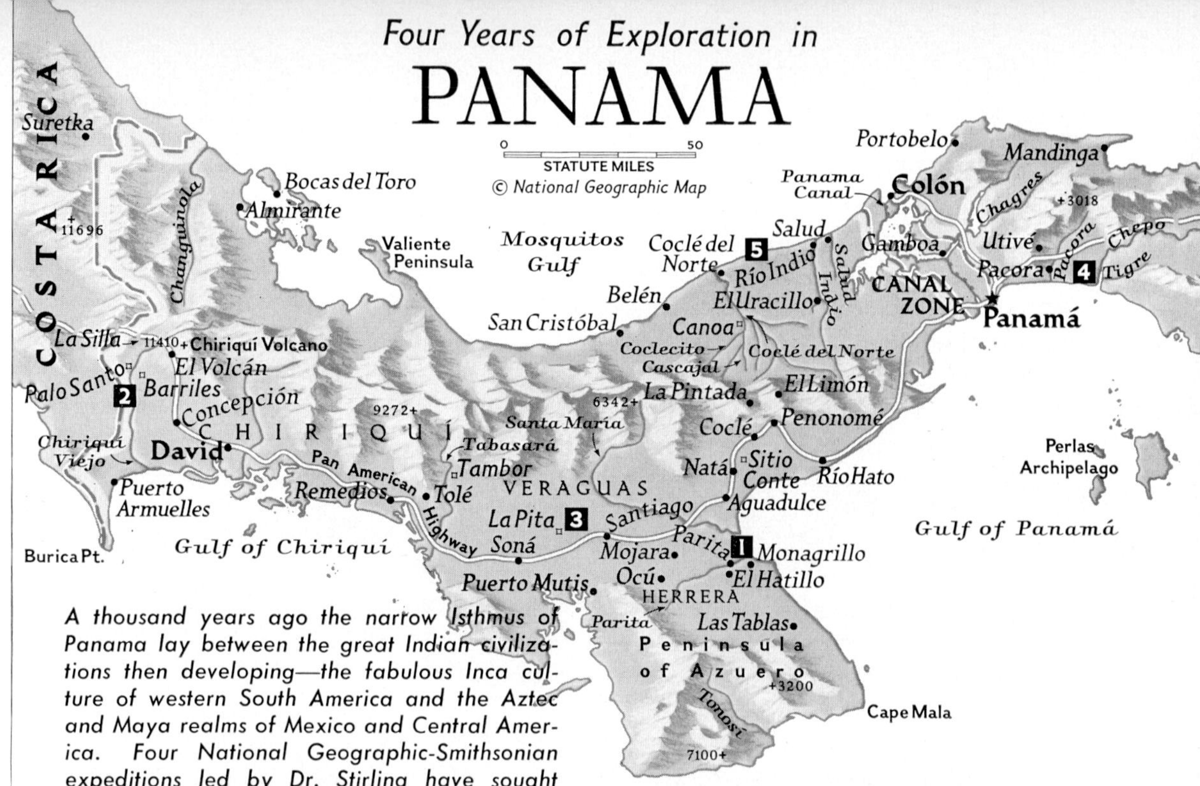


*A thousand years ago the narrow Isthmus of Panama lay between the great Indian civilizations then developing—the fabulous Inca culture of western South America and the Aztec and Maya realms of Mexico and Central America. Four National Geographic-Smithsonian expeditions led by Dr. Stirling have sought clues proving relationships between the two.*

*1 Shell mounds at Monagrillo yielded primitive pottery making this the oldest Panama site so far reported. The designs suggest early pottery types from both Peru and Mexico. Near Parita, man-made mounds revealed urn burials. Sitio Conte to the north proved one of the New World's richest archeological sites.*

*2 Excavations at foot of Chiriquí volcano disclosed a culture indicating a link between those of Chiriquí-Veraguas and Costa Rica.*

*3 La Pita tombs yielded pottery, stone, metal relics typical of the rich Veraguas culture.*

*4 Helicopters, used for the first time in archeological research by the 1949 expedition, helped locate shell mounds along coast and saved weeks in transporting equipment over rugged, trailless country east of Canal Zone.*

*5 Visiting the wild northwest coast virtually unexplored since Columbus, the 1951 expedition traced ancient Indian cultures up the Coclé del Norte, Salud, and Indio Rivers.*

blared, and bells and rattles clamored, reeling men seized six-foot balsa logs and began the strange competition for which the balsería is named.

Holding his light log like a billiard cue, a Guaymi would heave it hard, end first, at his opponent's shins. The other man would weave and shuffle enticingly, waiting for the thrust. When it came he would dance nimbly aside or sprawl in the hot dust, feet knocked out from under him. A friend would grab the log, drive it back at someone on the other team. Crowds roared encouragement.

Vicious fist fights erupted every few minutes. Stakes were high—usually the other fellow's wife. Each battle raged until one man was beaten helpless. At the ringside the woman in question awaited the battered victor.

The effect of chicha advanced with the day. The men (they outnumbered us several hundred to one) swarmed around us—not with hostile intent—but with crushing friendliness. It was not trip lines and mantraps we had to fear. It was being killed with affection. At the first chance we rounded up our horses and quietly rode away.

Now, gliding down the Cascajal, I wondered if the Guaymi across the mountains were working out secret plans for this year's balsería.

Rounding a bend, we came to rapids

**Deep Trenches Unlock Secrets of the Past.** Dr. Stirling records each pottery fragment and depth at which found. This Parita site yielded Indian tombs 23 feet down. One held 32 skeletons.

**Kitchen, Office, and Workshop Combine in a Jungle Home.** Above, Mrs. Stirling cooks while her husband notes archeological finds along Rio Coclé del Norte. Torrential rains, even during Panama's three-month "dry" season, meant pitching camp on high ground to prevent flooding. Archeology is great work for jigsaw-puzzle addicts. At her camp table below, Marion Stirling spent long hours cementing ceramics broken 500 years ago. Figurine with hollow head was worshiped as the jaguar god. Natives often thought the expedition had come to seek gold—as the conquistadores had.

KODACHROMES BY NATIONAL GEOGRAPHIC PHOTOGRAPHER RICHARD H. STEWART

LUIS MARDEN, NATIONAL GEOGRAPHIC STAFF

**Chocó Men Take Pains with Their Looks.** Bangs are carefully brushed. Red and black paint comes from seeds, fruits. Besides aiding beauty, Indians think some designs ward off illness. Chocó wore gold ornaments until Spaniards looted, now weight themselves down with silver or linked coins.

where the river forks to bypass an island. One branch is shallow, one deep and fast with a right-angle turn. Our guide elected to take the larger canoe—"Queen Mary"—through the deep channel.

Hurtling down the flume, we knew we had misjudged the current's force. A great tree loomed in midstream. A sudden eddy caught the vessel broadside, like the crack of a whip swung it against the tree. Dick Stewart and one native were torn from their seats by a limb. They clung to it as the torrent dragged the stern under. The craft capsized.

I clawed at the canoe's bottom, felt my grip weakening, finally let go—to find the water only waist deep. The maelstrom had swept the "Queen Mary" and me to a sand bar. Marion found footing beside me, clutching suitcase and typewriter.

Boxes, bags, cartons bobbed off downstream. Dick's two movie cameras, still cameras, and extra lenses had gone to the bottom. One of our men dived and salvaged them, along with sacks of archeological material. Everything was soaked, much food useless, some film ruined.

We finally reloaded the canoes, ate wet cheese and crackers, and drifted down the Coclé del Norte, reaching its mouth at midnight, drenched as usual.

Next morning we dried equipment, then stared astonished as a U. S. Air Force helicopter whirred down on the beach. Its pilot had come to investigate bones thought to be those of a lost flyer. Dick Stewart hopped a ride to the Canal Zone for new cameras.

The beat of the blades was familiar. On our second Panama expedition we had explored mounds near the Rio Tigre by helicopter. Our two whirlybirds hoisted us over mangrove swamp which would have made tortuous going on foot. We spotted the mounds rising from patches of savanna. Hovering above them, the pilots checked the ground, flattening the seven-foot-high grass with a down-blast from the rotors. We landed, collected bits of pottery, took off to explore more jungle, hung in mid-air to take pictures, returned to base. Five hours did the work of weeks by foot and canoe.

With Dick on his way to civilization and a launch coming for us next day, our troubles seemed over. But when the boat arrived, surf threatened again. Our big canoe twice went through the breakers, carrying bananas out to the bobbing launch. Our own baggage would take two more trips. But the crew had bucked enough combers for one day. They would make only one more trip to the launch.

We stowed everything into the canoe, plus a native passenger, a crate of live chickens, Marion, and myself. At the last minute, Mendoza, owner of the little store at the mouth of the Coclé del Norte, decided to come along. Lucky he did.

Three crew members were aft, two forward, each with a long pole to shove us across the bar, and a paddle for deep water. We cleared the river mouth and hit breakers, smacking through for about 400 yards. But the craft was riding deep, answering sluggishly.

Spotting calmer water, we turned parallel to the surf and drove for it. Immediately a breaker pounded over us. Frothing water flooded aboard.

At that instant Mendoza took command, bellowed orders to the exhausted crew. A second comber swept us, tumbled me from my perch on piled cargo; Marion went half overboard. In the nick of time we hauled her back.

Grabbing plastic army helmet liners, we bailed the foundering dugout. Mendoza kept the crew straining in unison at the paddles. At last the water level inboard dropped, the half-sunk craft inched painfully ahead through the last line of breakers and out to open sea where the launch waited. We were safe.

All the chickens had drowned.

We repaired water-soaked equipment in the Canal Zone, then pushed off for La Pintada, south of the Continental Divide. There in the uplands we traced ancient cultural connections between the Caribbean lowlands and those of the Pacific coast. We scaled cliffs to locate tombs. We found spectacular petroglyphs—rock carvings—and, moving on to the Peninsula of Azuero, struck a rich site which yielded fine polychrome pottery. Our finds indicated that Panama's pre-Columbian Indian cultures mainly stemmed from South America.

As this third Panama season ended, I felt like a cat which has lost eight of nine lives. Yet, two years later we were back. This most recent trip brought us among the Chocó Indians of Darién.

Since 16th century days when Spaniards plundered and slaughtered the Chocó, few white men have laid eyes on them. But a new, booming trade in bananas has cracked their wall of isolation. Indian banana growers venture downriver from their little-known country. Trader's rum is making inroads. In a few years, we felt, "civilization" would spoil them. Now was the time for a visit.

We hitched a ride on an Army cargo carrier, then transferred to an "African Queen" type vessel, the *Lila,* for the journey up the Sambú River. On board we saw our first Chocó Indians, a pretty 18-year-old girl and her younger brother.

She looked ill at ease in baggy blue cotton dress. But as the *Lila* chugged out of mangrove swamps to nose between high jungle-clad river banks, the girl celebrated homecoming by stripping down to the brief wraparound typical of her people. Self-confidence restored, she and her brother dove neatly from the gunwale and swam ashore as the vessel neared the trading post of Sábelo.

Sleepy Sábelo had boomed with the influx of Colombian Negroes, middlemen of the banana trade. We also saw many Chocó in Sábelo—small, well-built banana planters who had canoed to town with their families. Men zealously guarded their wives, and no wonder. With gleaming black hair and skin as fair as a European's, many women were strikingly handsome.

To guide us into real Chocó country, Ailipio, a shy, wiry five-footer with a smattering of Spanish, offered his services and those of his 24-foot piragua, carved from an espavé log. Finely balanced, the craft never ducked us once.

Ailipio nonchalantly spun the flywheel of his outboard motor and off we went. Somehow we never got used to seeing a near-naked, painted Chocó expertly steering a sputtering outboard.

We stopped at one of the large thatched houses, raised on stilts, which line the riverbank at about half-mile intervals. There we picked up Nicaño, Ailipio's muscular nephew, valuable bow man when we went over the side to nurse the dugout through white water.

Flatlands gave way to mountains. The river's crystal water reflected virgin jungle or arching banana fronds near Chocó houses. Chattering monkeys chased through the canopy of trees. Flocks of parrots rose screaming.

We swung toward shore, landed on a flat rock between two Indian houses—Ailipio's and his mother-in-law's. Why would our guide live so far upstream when his work took him so often to Sábelo? He had a second house downriver, he said, complete with second wife.

We swam in the whirpool at Ailipio's door and watched our host and his two sons spearing fish from small canoes. They would dive under for uneasy minutes, then reappear yards from where we expected, triumphantly waving a fish.

Pushing upstream next morning, we battled increasing current. Once we landed to explore a Chocó burying place. Dishes, spoons, clothing, carved wooden toys covered each grave. One with a concrete slab on it seemed out of keeping. It belonged to a rich Chocó, Ailipio explained, first to buy an outboard motor. The family had debated whether to bury the motor with him, according to custom. They decided it would serve better on the river.

Indian houses grew less frequent. As we passed each one, Ailipio exchanged shouted gossip with its owner until out of earshot. We investigated a fish trap of cane stalks and watched an Indian skillfully finishing his dugout canoe with razor-sharp machete.

Further on, in a new jungle clearing, two men carved decorations on a huge canoe high on the bank. They greeted us and posed with rich silver ornaments and heavy earrings.

Reaching the last house at the head of canoe navigation on this "Main Street" of the Chocó, we had the thrill of knowing that we had probably traveled farther into the fascinating Chocó country than any white man before us.

We would spread our air mattresses on the sleeping platform in a Chocó house and rise at dawn with our hosts to swim before breakfast. Womenfolk folded away sleeping mats and swept with twig brooms until the airy room was spotless. They dropped garbage through wide

**Bright Pottery Designs Reveal High Culture**

Humanized reptile faces peer from 500-year-old earthenware found in Panama. Crocodile-design cups at top are red, black, and purple on white. To right of turtle plate is a conventionalized king vulture. Such fanciful ware bore food and drink for pre-Columbian Indians, proving they had an eye for beauty as well as utility.

Though breakable, pottery doesn't perish. Color, shape, and style tell the expert when and where each vessel was fashioned, thus helping fill gaps in our knowledge of ancient Indian life.

NATIONAL GEOGRAPHIC PHOTOGRAPHER RICHARD H. STEWART

spaced palm flooring to hogs waiting under the house. Long-haired Chocó men primp at their facial make-up while women finish house chores.

Then the workday starts, women tilling seasonal crops, men harvesting or loading bananas, hunting, fishing, or clearing land. Men take their make-up kits with them to freshen up the bold black, red, or purple designs on their faces. They are not so concerned about their black body stain, which starts to wear off after a week of swimming half a dozen times a day.

A typical Chocó house is a self-sufficient family community: perhaps an elderly couple, their married daughters, sons-in-law, grandchildren, and of course dogs. While elders work, little girls tend fires and babies at home. Small boys help their fathers. A Chocó five-year-old can pole a canoe expertly.

Work ends at mid-afternoon when women serve the second meal. We tried such Chocó food as roasted green bananas, but preferred our rations. The Indians dabbed at our spaghetti and pretzels, but shied from onions, bacon, ham.

Chocó home life appealed to us. Women weave baskets. Men make or repair spears, blowguns, bows and arrows. We entertained well-mannered, frisky Chocó youngsters with magic tricks until bedtime. Parents raise them with large doses of affection and an unrestraining hand.

When finally it was time to leave Chocó country and get back to archeology, we realized the simple, self-reliant life we had shared with these Indians would make us homesick for them. Ailipio came to see us off.

"When will you return?" he asked.

"Some day, God willing."

"If I am alive, I will come to be with you again. You are my friends."

We felt the same way.

PAINTING BY H. M. HERGET

**Noblemen Meet on Road, Swap Yarns of the Inca's Court.** "A tribute of lice!" laughingly relates the highland official in vicuña-wool tapestry tunic (center). This humiliating tax was imposed by the late 15th century Inca Tupac Yupanqui on a newly conquered province unable to pay a more substantial levy. The amused listeners are a coastal gentleman in striped cotton robe with gold earplugs and gold-headed staff of office, and a befeathered dweller of eastern Andes slopes.

CHAPTER 13

# THE INCAS
# EMPIRE BUILDERS OF THE ANDES

## BY PHILIP AINSWORTH MEANS

HALF AN HOUR after I descended from the airplane which brought me to Cusco, Peru, its implacable, modernistic roar still sounded in my ears. Consequently, when I strolled into the huge plaza where the Indian market is held every day, I felt chronologically confused. In my ears the 20th century whirred, but before my eyes was a scene that belonged to the 16th century at the latest.

Hundreds of Indians, mostly women, were carrying on a leisurely trade. I saw a few people of Spanish blood in modern dress walking in the arcades along the margins of the plaza, but everyone else in the scene was Indian.

Perhaps the most striking indigenes of all were the llamas, those haughty and beautiful cousins of the camel. With their tall, pointed ears gaily decked with streamers of colored wool, and sometimes even with little bells of copper or of silver, they seemed to tread the earth with scornful pride.

Little by little the airplane roar yielded to the staccato, purring-clicking sibilance of a strange language rising into the thin, cold air around me. Presently I realized that it was Quechua, the ancient general tongue of western South America.

Drawing nearer, I observed the trade going on in the booths. The first I saw was partly modern in aspect. A woman was selling Woolworthian trifles for small coinage. Between customers she busied herself with an up-to-date portable sewing machine.

A few steps farther on, however, I came upon another booth altogether antique in appearance. A sturdy Indian woman was offering a haunch of llama meat, another reluctantly adding a potato at a time to a pile on the ground.

Both women were unhurried, all their emotions concentrated in their faces. The expression of the seller was one of determined avarice; that of the buyer one of increasing hesitancy (page 299).

I could see that very soon the buyer would reach her limit and take her potatoes to some other booth whose mistress had less lordly ideas about the potato value of a haunch of llama.

I was, indeed, witnessing an authentic barter trade such as was universal under the Inca Empire. My mind turned back to olden times when, between about 1100 (the Crusades were then stirring Europe to holy zeal) and the middle of the 15th century (when Gutenberg and his printing press were helping to inaugurate our modern age), the Incas built up a solidly organized realm of amazing size.

I reflected that, in a period equal to that between Columbus's arrival in the

Antilles and our own Mexican War, a family of American Indians had created an empire worthy to be compared with the realms of Alexander, Caesar, Charlemagne, Napoleon; an empire which outshone others because its benevolent and sagacious ruling caste, the Incas, strove successfully to make all their subjects prosperous and happy within the framework of their separate cultures (map, page 287).

The Incas and their subjects were not a whole people as were the Maya. About A.D. 1100, the Incas were a small tribe of Quechua-speaking llama herders dwelling on a lofty plain some leagues southwest of Cusco. Their homeland had the stark, grandiose beauty of the Andes, but it was unfit for agriculture and for shaping an improved mode of life.

Although nothing outwardly distinguished the Incas from hundreds of other little tribes, an inborn genius for growth and organization stirred within them about this time, filling them with a conviction that a "manifest destiny" awaited them.

Their first step toward dynastic grandeur was a tribal migration from their bleak homeland down into the fair and fertile valley of Cusco, rimmed with sublimely soaring, snow-crowned mountains and watered by the headlong torrent of the Huatanay River.

Ancient legends of how it was done are numerous and quaint, but contradictory. The version preserved among the Inca caste itself, and transmitted to us by reliable Spanish chroniclers, is that the Inca tribe, led by Manco Capac and his sister-wife Mama Ocllo, marched upon Cusco.

There they gained dominion over the folk already in the valley by a picturesque and wily appeal to their credulity and superstition.

A beautiful lad named Roca was clad in a garment covered with spangles of burnished gold. Thus arrayed, he appeared at the mouth of a cavern above Cusco where the rays of the sun fell dazzlingly upon him.

Pointing aloft to that radiant figure, which seemed to be a part of the sun fallen to earth, the strategists persuaded the wonder-struck multitude that the shining boy was the Son of the Sun, to whom their entire allegiance was due.

Thus between the years 1100 and 1140, Sinchi Roca (War Chief Roca), the first really historic ruler of the Inca dynasty, was accepted by the dwellers in Cusco as a divine monarch sent to govern and protect them. By gaining their reverence and loyalty, Sinchi Roca formed the nucleus of what was to become a mighty empire.

Of the legends concerning Inca origins, this version seems most nearly authentic. A curious aspect is the incestuous marriage between Manco Capac and his sister, Mama Ocllo. It may have been a custom of the primitive Incas, as this legend implies; or it may be an element inserted into the legend much later when, the Empire having grown great and its rulers proud of their sacred blood, sister-marriage became obligatory.

At any rate, the Incas, from Sinchi Roca down to Pachacutec, the eighth Inca, seem not to have married their sisters; rather, they allied themselves with daughters of powerful chiefs whose friendship they needed. Not until their might became such that this support could no longer enhance it did the historic Incas, beginning with Tupac Yupanqui, revive or initiate the practice of wedding their sisters to preserve the holy purity of their blood.

Only from an airplane high above the majestic mountain panorama can one clearly understand the magnitude of the empire-building accomplished by the Inca dynasty. From this lofty viewpoint one sees endless, tumbled Andean ranges, flanked on the west by a long strip of coastal desert crossed by occasional

PAINTING BY H. M. HERGET

**Wildly Swaying Throng Snake-dances Through Cusco's Holy Square,** bearing a great woolen rope of many colors. Its pumalike head reaches the imperial carpet before the Inca, who sits on his brilliant throne flanked by high priests and the flexed mummies of his ancestors. These bundled Incas of past glory have been brought out in state from the Temple of the Sun, whose trapezoid-shaped windows overlook the square. During the great January rite, begun with the full moon, llamas and guinea pigs were sacrificed to the creator-god Viracocha in the hope of bountiful crops.

©AERIAL EXPLORATIONS, INC.

green bands of westward-flowing streams, and on the east by a vast jungle world stretching away toward the Atlantic.

The huge area wherein the Incas shaped their empire was one of infinite diversity, severed by all but impassable barriers: deep chasms carved by rushing rivers, leaping ranges of peaks crossed only by difficult passes where the air is thin and piercingly cold, deserts where all things shrivel under the onslaught of the sun.

Left to themselves, the innumerable peoples of highlands and coast would never have coalesced into an empire. Each tribe, ensconced in its compact valley home, would have gone on living on the produce of its fields and llama herds with no thought for the world beyond the mountains. True, sundry chiefs here and there, especially on the coast, formed confederacies and kingdoms of some extent, but none knew how to build an empire on the scale that the Incas achieved.

The Incas began their career in a modest way. At the end of the reign of Sinchi Roca their realm included only Cusco and the country around it. The southern

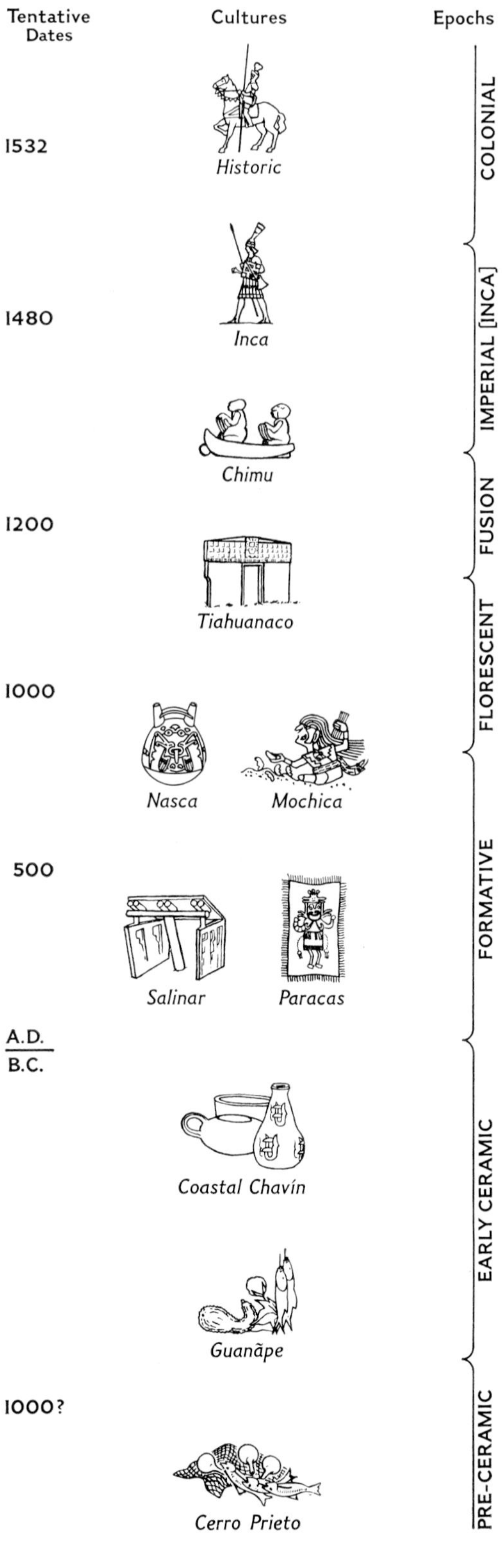

**Great Wall of Peru** knifes inland across sharp Andean spurs, plumbs deep valleys, straddles the Santa River north of Chimbote. Fourteen fortresses command hilltop vantage points flanking this Western Hemisphere counterpart of China's ancient wall. One large military post studied from the air appeared to have 15-foot rock breastworks enclosing a 200-by-300-foot area.

The northward course of Inca empire surged past this 40-mile wall built by the Chimus (page 296), who flourished in the centuries immediately preceding the rapid Inca rise to power. Some 25 principal rivers like the Santa tumble from the Andes to Pacific across Peru's barren coast. Before Inca roadbuilding, each isolated river valley tended to develop a culture of its own. Northern valleys outpaced the southern. Beyond the coastal cordillera evolved the highland Tiahuanaco of Lake Titicaca and the Inca, centered along headwaters of Amazon tributaries.

Chart at right shows when notable cultures reached their zenith, often after centuries of development and influence by coexistent groups.

## NOTABLE CULTURES IN PERU

| Tentative Dates | Cultures | Epochs |
|---|---|---|
| | | COLONIAL |
| 1532 | *Historic* | |
| | | IMPERIAL [INCA] |
| 1480 | *Inca* | |
| | *Chimu* | FUSION |
| 1200 | *Tiahuanaco* | FLORESCENT |
| 1000 | *Nasca*, *Mochica* | |
| 500 | *Salinar*, *Paracas* | FORMATIVE |
| A.D. / B.C. | | |
| | *Coastal Chavín* | EARLY CERAMIC |
| | *Guanãpe* | |
| 1000? | *Cerro Prieto* | PRE-CERAMIC |

PAINTING BY H. M. HERGET

**High Priest of the Sun,** the Villac Umu, holds aloft a golden bowl shaped to focus sun's rays on tinder contents and set it smoldering. With it he will light a ceremonial fire on the altar behind. The cult of sun worship is far older in Peru than in Mexico; this suggests Andean origin. Cusco alone had some 3,000 Virgins of the Sun.

frontier was La Raya Pass, at the headwaters of the Urubamba River, into which, after rushing through Cusco, the Huatanay River flows.

Across this pass in the Vilcanota Range an east-west defensive wall of uncut stones laid in clay was found. Likely it had marked the boundary in pre-Inca times between Quechua-speaking people to the north and Colla-speaking folk of the Titicaca Basin to the south. The wall and rough-stone houses for its defenders may still be seen.

Small though it was, the realm Sinchi Roca left at his death must have been perfectly organized internally. Even then the ruler's chief care was to ensure the well-being of his subjects and thus make them his zealous supporters. To do less would have belied the sacred character to which he pretended.

The second Inca, Lloque Yupanqui (Left-handed One Who Will Be Renowned for Pious Actions), ruled about 1140 to 1195.

Having begun his reign by inspecting all his realm and visiting his vassal *curacas* (chieftains), he passed beyond the Vilcanota wall and came to grips with the Collas (also called Aymarás), a sturdy folk who were creating a state not dissimilar to the Inca's own.

Skillfully combining diplomatic blandishments with martial force, Inca Lloque Yupanqui brought into his realm the northern half of the Titicaca region, then organized it in accordance with Inca policies of merciful rule and justice for all. At his death Incadom was equal in extent to Massachusetts, Connecticut, and Rhode Island.

Mayta Capac (Diligent Great One), who ruled from about 1195 to 1230, continued his father's policies and conquests. On reaching the ruins of Tiahuanaco, near the southern end of Lake Titicaca, Mayta Capac beheld the vestiges of an architectural style far superior to rough stone laid in clay, hitherto the only construction known to the Incas. He saw, as we may see today, superbly cut and carved stones held together when necessary by copper clamps set in sockets (page 292).

The practical lessons to be derived from this superior technology—practiced some centuries before by people of the Tiahuanaco Empire (A.D. 600–900)—were not thrown away upon Inca Mayta Capac, who seems to have had a genius for engineering and architecture. From building methods he studied at the abandoned capital of these mysterious people arose a vastly improved Inca architecture.

Likewise this great engineer was the first Inca to build a suspension bridge of stout aloe cables swung from massive piers of masonry. The fame of this bridge spread far and wide, increasing his already high prestige among the tribes (page 294).

Mayta Capac also was the first Inca to lead his army across the coast range and down to the Pacific. There he had to contend not only with men but with the hot, dry, dense air of the lowlands.

To the large-lunged mountain folk the coast is very trying, so Mayta Capac began to use a system later brought to high perfection by his successors. He divided his large army into sections; each served only a short time on the coast and afterward went back to the mountains to recuperate.

By a characteristic combination of military and diplomatic tactics, Mayta Capac brought part of the southern coast's civilized population into the Empire. Typical was his treatment of wizards in that region. Instead of trying to suppress them and thereby driving them underground, he recognized them as a professional class whom the people might consult freely. Doubtless he argued that their spells might do a little good while not strong enough to do much harm.

In a relatively short reign, from about 1230 to 1250, the fourth Inca, Capac Yupanqui, continued his father's conquests on the coast and so increased the realm that at his death it was equal to New England, New York, and New Jersey combined. He improved the internal organization and in general ruled wisely.

Inca Roca, about 1250 to 1315, wishing to expand his empire north through the highlands, found the way barred by the most formidable foe the Incas had yet encountered.

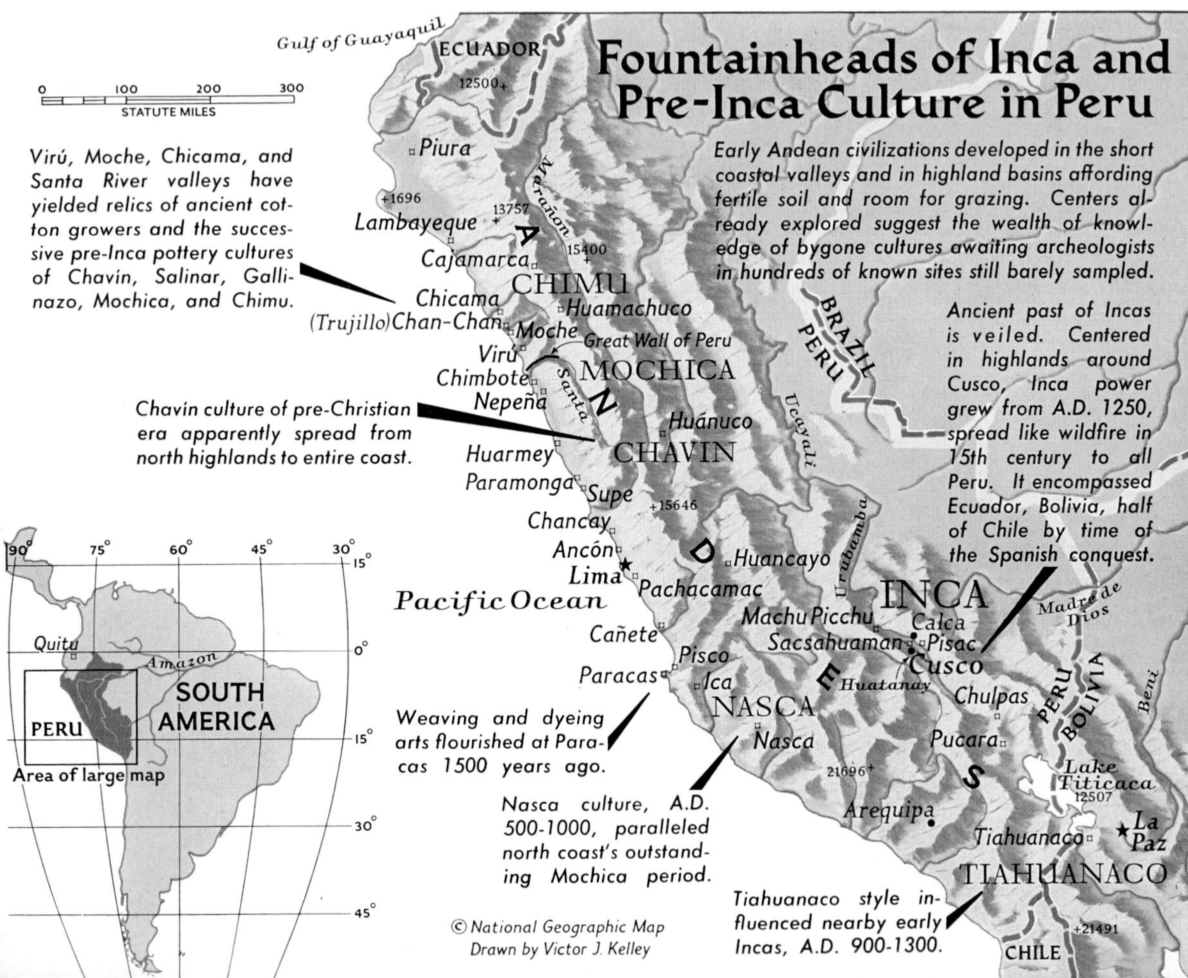
Fountainheads of Inca and Pre-Inca Culture in Peru
Early Andean civilizations developed in the short coastal valleys and in highland basins affording fertile soil and room for grazing. Centers already explored suggest the wealth of knowledge of bygone cultures awaiting archeologists in hundreds of known sites still barely sampled.
Virú, Moche, Chicama, and Santa River valleys have yielded relics of ancient cotton growers and the successive pre-Inca pottery cultures of Chavín, Salinar, Gallinazo, Mochica, and Chimu.
Chavín culture of pre-Christian era apparently spread from north highlands to entire coast.
Ancient past of Incas is veiled. Centered in highlands around Cusco, Inca power grew from A.D. 1250, spread like wildfire in 15th century to all Peru. It encompassed Ecuador, Bolivia, half of Chile by time of the Spanish conquest.
Weaving and dyeing arts flourished at Paracas 1500 years ago.
Nasca culture, A.D. 500-1000, paralleled north coast's outstanding Mochica period.
Tiahuanaco style influenced nearby early Incas, A.D. 900-1300.
0 100 200 300
STATUTE MILES
Gulf of Guayaquil
ECUADOR
12500
Piura
+1696
13757
Lambayeque
Marañon
15400
Cajamarca
CHIMU
Chicama
Huamachuco
(Trujillo)Chan-Chan
Moche
Great Wall of Peru
Virú
MOCHICA
Chimbote
Santa
Nepeña
Huánuco
Huarmey
CHAVIN
Paramonga
Supe
+15646
Chancay
Ancón
Lima
Huancayo
Pachacamac
Pacific Ocean
Machu Picchu
INCA
Calca
Sacsahuaman
Pisac
Cusco
Cañete
Pisco
Paracas
Ica
Huatanay
NASCA
Nasca
Chulpas
Pucara
21696+
Arequipa
Tiahuanaco
La Paz
TIAHUANACO
Lake Titicaca
12507
+21491
CHILE
A N D E S
BRAZIL
PERU
Ucayali
Urubamba
Madre de Dios
PERU
BOLIVIA
Beni
Quito
Amazon
SOUTH AMERICA
PERU
Area of large map
90° 75° 60° 45° 30°
15° 0° 15° 30° 45°
© National Geographic Map
Drawn by Victor J. Kelley

**Up Temple Steps at Pachacamac a High Priest Bears the Sun's Golden Image.** Another priest carries two gold cups. Chosen Women of the Sun, soldiers, courtiers, minor priests follow.

PAINTING BY H. M. HERGET

Beyond in the courtyard, low-walled at Pacific's edge, the inhabitants lie flat on their faces. The Inca's armies have just taken the holy city. The victors will combine its religion with their own.

These were the Chancas, a people of forest-country origin who had come up into the highlands north of Cusco from eastern jungles. They were fierce, ambitious, courageous. Inca Roca was far from successful in his encounters with these implacable foes. Thus the Chancas became a black and menacing cloud on the northern horizon of Incadom.

Nor was his son, Yahuar Huaccac (He Who Weeps Blood), a man fit to confront the grave peril of the Chancas. This, the sixth Inca, who ruled about 1315–1347, seems to have been cursed from his childhood by some malady or evil influence. Modern psychologists would explain him in terms of an inferiority complex because of unfortunate events in his youth. However that may have been, we know that he was the only Inca who was feckless and cowardly, and the Chanca menace increased mightily in his time.

Finally something drastic had to be done. The Chancas were on the march. With hideous yells and frantic brandishing of weapons they moved furiously southward, intent on capturing Cusco. Had they succeeded—and they very nearly did—Incadom would have been utterly crushed and all its hard work undone.

Prince Hatun Tupac, son of the inefficient Inca, was the man sorely needed to oppose so redoubtable an enemy. First receiving in a dream mysterious counsel from a deity who announced himself to be the creator-god Viracocha, the prince assembled the bravest of Inca manhood, adding half-reluctant allies from other parts of the realm. At the head of these forces he marched to the broad plain of Anta and there awaited the enemy.

Presently the Chanca horde came swooping down the pass into the plain, shrieking warlike cries, trumpets and

drums resounding defiantly. Battle was joined. For many hours the lines of struggling warriors swayed back and forth, plying star-headed clubs, javelins, slings, knives of flint or bronze.

Prince Hatun Tupac was in the forefront of combat, exhorting his men, himself slaying many a foeman. At last the tide turned in the Incas' favor. The Chancas began to retreat. Only then did the prince's hesitant allies, who had been waiting to see whom fortune would approve, join in with the Inca troops.

As these new contingents came up, the prince and his men in triumph shouted to the enemy, "Behold! The very bushes and rocks of the plain are becoming soldiers to defend our Father the Sun!"

To the Chancas it seemed truth itself. Their retreat became flight, then headlong rout. Prince Hatun Tupac had saved the day and so assured his dynasty's fu-

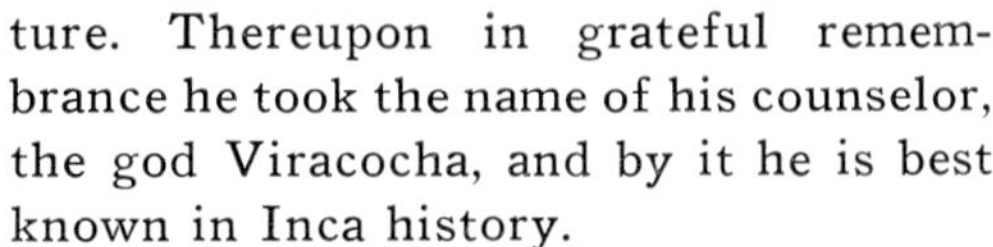

ture. Thereupon in grateful remembrance he took the name of his counselor, the god Viracocha, and by it he is best known in Inca history.

Viracocha's conquest of the Chancas was solemnly celebrated in Cusco. A superb triumphal pageant was held in Coricancha, the Temple of the Sun. Captains of the victorious army, soldiers, and citizenry all took part. In their midst were countless Chanca prisoners and their womenfolk.

Lances bedecked with gay plumes, multicolored shields, massive war clubs with gleaming bronze heads shaped like stars, served as panoplies for the scene. Jubilant music, joyful dancing, and piercing shouts of thanksgiving combined into a paean of praise to the god Viracocha and to his imperial namesake.

Borne in a golden litter, the Inca entered the temple last of all. At his coming the prisoners were forced to throw themselves flat on the ground. Over the pathway formed by their prostrate bodies the Inca and his greatest nobles marched to the altar chanting a verse whose refrain was "My enemies I tread upon."

Here we have a very different aspect of Inca statesmanship from the merciful and generous one to which we are accustomed. There was, however, good reason for it. The Inca Viracocha had just overwhelmed the most formidable enemy his house had ever known. Puma-eyed and proudly vengeful, he thus signalized, for all the Andean world to see, the invincible character of the Inca dynasty.

This was all the more necessary because of the fatal weakness his father had displayed. By this terrible warning the Inca Viracocha foretold the fate that awaited all who opposed the Inca family.

The reign of Viracocha, about 1347–1400, marks the beginning of the great period of Incadom. Conquests were made in the southern highlands down to and including Tucumán (in northwestern Argentina) as well as beyond the Chanca

**Inca Prince Rides to Cusco**

Lordly as the surrounding snow-capped Andean peaks, a member of the imperial family approaches the capital in splendor, his litter cushioned on the shoulders of sturdy retainers. Favored nobles bear his feather-adorned canopy. Golden fox heads tip the poles supporting his ornate throne.

Priests follow with their *quipus*, or knotted-cord records; then warriors clad in polished bronze plate armor with javelins, war clubs, painted shields, and handleless battle-axes. Ax motif appears in the prince's headdress. Tapping copper and tin wealth of the Andes, Inca smiths alloyed them to make bronzes to suit varied needs. Weapons and tools were cast in bronze of low tin content and cold-hammered. More tin went into bronze ornaments. Iron and steel were unknown.

PAINTING BY H. M. HERGET

## Moderns Marvel at Sacsahuaman Walls

Superb example of cyclopean masonry, the zigzag ramparts of the great fortress of Sacsahuaman stand imperishable on heights north of Cusco.

Ancient builders, without steel tools, blasting powder, or machinery, quarried enormous blocks, transported them miles across ridges and ravines without draft animals or the wheel, dressed and raised them into position without cranes. Largest stones exceed 25 feet in height, weigh hundreds of tons. Irregular in shape, they fit tight without mortar.

Sheep, first brought in by the Spaniards, graze beside the massive gateway of Tiahuanaco (left) at southern end of Lake Titicaca. In the frieze, 48 man-bird figures face toward the central god or ruler, whose cheeks run with tears. The monolith was carved more than 1,000 years ago by Indians whose culture had impact in the central Andes. Incas found Tiahuanaco in ruins and abandoned.

WALTER HENRICKS HODGE (TOP LEFT); ROBERT GERSTMANN, BLACK STAR (LEFT)

MARTIN CHAMBI J.

region in the north. Social institutions, also the material aspects of Inca civilization were being improved throughout the realm which, at Viracocha's death, was equal to the sum of New England, New York, New Jersey, Delaware, Maryland, and eastern Virginia.

The Inca Pachacutec (All-Teacher), son of Viracocha, ruled about 1400–1448. He it was who brought the empire to its finest flowering.

Taking to heart the lesson of the Chanca war, he resolved to prevent further incursions into his realm by savage folk dwelling in woodlands east of the Andes. Accordingly, he built a long line of fortresses along the eastern frontier. The most noteworthy is the great citadel of Machu Picchu, excavated and cleared by the National Geographic Society-Yale University expeditions led by Hiram Bingham in 1912–1915 (Chapter 14).

Neither Pachacutec nor any other Inca was merely a brutal conqueror. He fought valiantly when he had to, but preferred pacific methods. Once the submission of a hostile chief was won, the Inca proceeded also to win his devotion. The vanquished was given a high administrative post and his dependent officials were tendered positions equal to those they had previously held.

Whenever possible, each tribe or state was taken into the Inca realm as a going concern, without loss of prestige to anyone who upheld the overlordship of the Sapa Inca, Sole Emperor; and the defeated people were thenceforward protected and encouraged exactly as were all his other subjects.

Characteristic of Inca sagacity was the amazing knowledge of geographic factors applied to colonizing. Either a tribe long accustomed to Inca rule was moved to some newly conquered region, where they taught the inhabitants the ways of the Inca house, or a newly vanquished people was moved en masse to a district whose denizens would be their teachers.

In either case the place to which colonists were to be sent was always as similar as possible to their homeland. To determine this the Incas used relief maps, executed in colored clay, whereon the natural features of each part of the realm were clearly indicated.

As a further means of inwardly strengthening the empire, sons and kinsmen of the great vassals were brought to Cusco. There, in company with youths of the imperial caste, they were educated in both military science and the peaceful arts at the House of Teaching.

The supreme authority of the Inca flowed down through many grades of administrative officials, the humblest of whom had supervision over ten families, in a spirit of fatherly guidance. It reached into every household in the land, and saw that all wants were filled, that life, though laborious in just degree, was happy and free from care.

The household was the unit of society. Its head, called *puric,* or full-grown man, performed the heavy labor, aided by his wife and older children. Neither the very young nor the old were called upon for manual toil.

The puric alone paid tribute to the state. Justly apportioned, it took such forms as a part of the family's produce from the fields or as a reasonable stint of work by each puric on roads, irrigation channels, terraces for agriculture, or other public works. Or, if a man were skilled in some handicraft, his output during a certain time was paid into the government's storehouses which

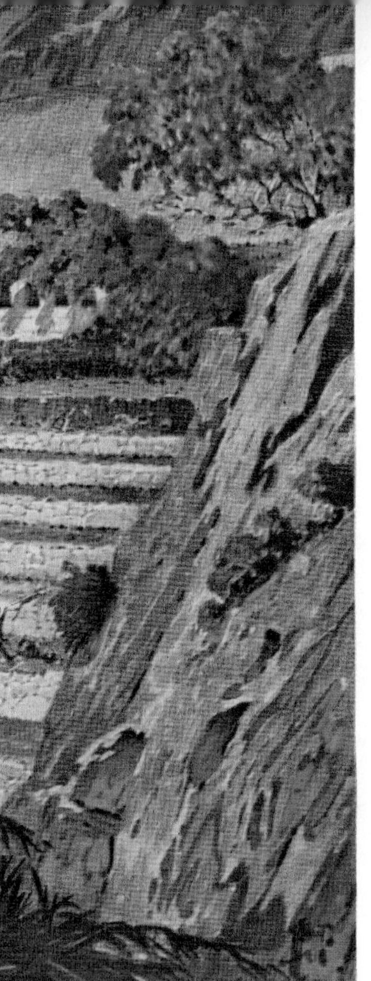

## Bridges, Paved Highways Linked the Far-flung Andes Empire

Across a deep ravine from their thatch-roofed home, dark-eyed daughters of an Inca official go down to a mountain spring. In bright cotton dresses embroidered in vicuña wool, they tread wide stairs. Fitted stone also walls cottage and garden terraces below. Massive stone piers anchor stout aloe or liana cables of the suspension bridge on which the girls crossed the gorge.

Llamas bearing tribute of textiles, pottery, and provisions destined for the ruling Inca approach a road supervisor's house and traveler's rest (below). One temperamental beast protests overload in typical llama fashion by ejecting toward the herder "a wounderful stinking water." Also intended for the royal "Son of the Sun" is the jug of chicha on the herder's back.

The remarkable engineering talent of the Incas conquered formidable natural barriers that kept pre-Inca cultures apart despite beeline proximity. Their gift stands convincingly revealed by recent archeological mapping of route remnants over the entire 3,100-mile north-south range of 15th century Inca power. Some 10,000 miles of paved roads ran south from Quito deep into Chile and Argentina. They climbed from seacoast to 15,000 feet, crossed western-slope desert, traversed cliff faces on masonry shelves, descended to fringe the Amazon jungle. Not built for the wheel, roads ascended in steps, slipped through tunnels just wide enough to admit a loaded llama.

The famed Inca bridge spanning the Apurimac River (novelist Thornton Wilder's "Bridge of San Luis Rey") on the Cusco-Lima route linked precipice walls 150 feet apart. Suspension cables 16 inches thick swung high out of range of flash floods. Built around 1350, it finally plunged into the roaring gorge in the 1880's.



PAINTINGS BY H. M. HERGET

©AERIAL EXPLORATIONS, INC.

**Chan-Chan, Ancient Chimu Capital, Has Crumbled Into Dust.** Chief Peruvian coastal ruin and one of the world's most extensive archeological sites, Chan-Chan spreads over some 11 square miles adjacent to modern Trujillo. The city may have housed as many as 250,000 at its height. Aerial view shows the remains of one of the central palaces, together with the sunken gardens, homes, shops, avenues, plazas, and temple pyramids that surrounded it. Dark rectangle at center was probably a reservoir. Chan-Chan comprised at least ten major sections like this, each flanked by adobe walls up to 30 feet high. These have disintegrated with passing centuries. From Chan-Chan, Chimu culture spread 600 miles along Peru's coast, then fell to Inca Pachacutec; the great fortress at Paramonga was last to surrender. Conquistadores took rich booty from the abandoned capital.

provided for all the needs of society.

The land flourished. Hundreds of villages held periodic fairs where goods were exchanged. The people knew neither the complications nor benefits of money.

Adjacent to every village were its fields, some on the flat valley floor, others on masonry terraces along the hillsides. Their walls still exist, making beautiful and intricate patterns in the landscape (page 324). Water burbled through carefully made irrigation channels fed by streams or springs, and flowering plants grew along their banks. Hedges of fantastic cactus or of blooming shrubs marked the limits of each tribe's lands.

Here and there a white granite temple gleamed, an altar or a sundial carved from one mighty block of stone upon its summit (page 286). At appropriate places rose the mansions of local officials, bowered in feathery trees and adorned by radiantly colored blossoms (page 294).

The plowing season was solemnly inaugurated every year by the Inca in person, using a golden plow on certain fields of the Sun above Cusco. In the garden of the Temple of the Sun, now the Monastery of Santo Domingo in Cusco (page

301), all food crops, flowers, and shrubs, even insects and butterflies were imitated in delicately wrought gold, as if to encourage Nature herself.

Ordinary farmers used plows of heavy wood, with footrests and handles (page 298). Preparing the furrows was done by human strength alone, for the haughty and intractable llama, though he will carry up to 100 pounds on his back, has never permitted himself to be harnessed as a draft animal. If his load is even a trifle too great to please him, he will, in the words of an old chronicler, "turne round his head and ejecte from his mouthe a wounderful stinking water."

Like their modern descendants, husbandmen of Inca days knew the value of fish heads as fertilizer. Those of the coast also made use of guano brought from the bird islands off the shore. For weeding and tending crops a variety of simple but effective tools was used. Their like may still be seen on many an Indian farm.

This mighty and diversified realm had been created by a development of the relayed-army technique begun by Mayta Capac. It was lashed to the supreme authority of the Sapa Inca by a splendid system of roads, paved, and provided with steps where necessary (page 295).

**Conquering Incas Built a Terraced Temple to Outshine Pachacamac's Shrine.** South of Lima stand ruins of the pre-Inca temple of Pachacamac (foreground) and the Inca Temple of the Sun. With dramatic effect, the Incas erected their radiant temple overlooking the vast Pacific to divert worship in this ancient pilgrimage center from the creator-god Pachacamac, region's supreme deity, to the Inca creator-god Viracocha (page 288). Viracocha was not bloodthirsty like Aztec deities, but burials of strangled women at Pachacamac show the Incas did make human sacrifices.

DEVER, BLACK STAR

**Incaland: Home of Potato**

Amid terraced farm slopes of the Andes an Indian digs with foot plow; his sister wields a hoe, his wife carries home a bag of potatoes. Many wild species grow in cool highlands of Peru, Bolivia, Ecuador, and Chile. Hundreds, perhaps thousands of years before the Incas, Indians found plants with pea-sized edible tubers. Adept farmers, they cultivated them, improved taste and size through centuries, developed varieties suited to elevations from sea level to 14,000 feet.

Spanish conquerors, bent on finding precious stones and metals, recorded nothing of the potato's origin. Some took plants home to Spain, where the exotic vegetable languished for decades before spreading elsewhere. Ireland became its stronghold; from there it moved to the New England colonies as the "Irish potato." The Orient still slights the white potato, but in the world as a whole it has come to rate as the single most important vegetable.

Over these highways sped *chasquis,* or post-runners. Each ran a distance nicely calculated to permit him to go at top speed from his posthouse to the next, bearing a *quipu* (knotted-string record), an oral message, or even a watertight basket in which fish from the sea swam in salt water until they reached the imperial kitchen.

Over these roads huge armies could be marched quickly. Even the deepest chasm ceased to be a barrier, for marvelous suspension bridges of thick aloe ropes fixed by massive masonry piers on either bank leaped across them.

The Sapa Inca was borne along the roads in his magnificent litter which rested on the shoulders of specially trained bearers, while noblemen proudly carried the poles which upheld the gorgeous canopy (page 290). Whenever the imperial litter halted, the multitude cried aloud: "Most high Lord, child of the Sun, thou art the sole and beloved Lord. The whole earth truly obeys thee."

Naturally enough, the privilege of traveling by litter was reserved to the very highest persons: to the Sapa Inca and his empress, to governors or viceroys of the four grand provinces which made up the Realm of the Four United Parts, as the Empire was officially styled, and to specially favored conquered kings or conspicuously successful generals whom the Inca wished to honor. Everyone else, no matter how high his rank, walked.

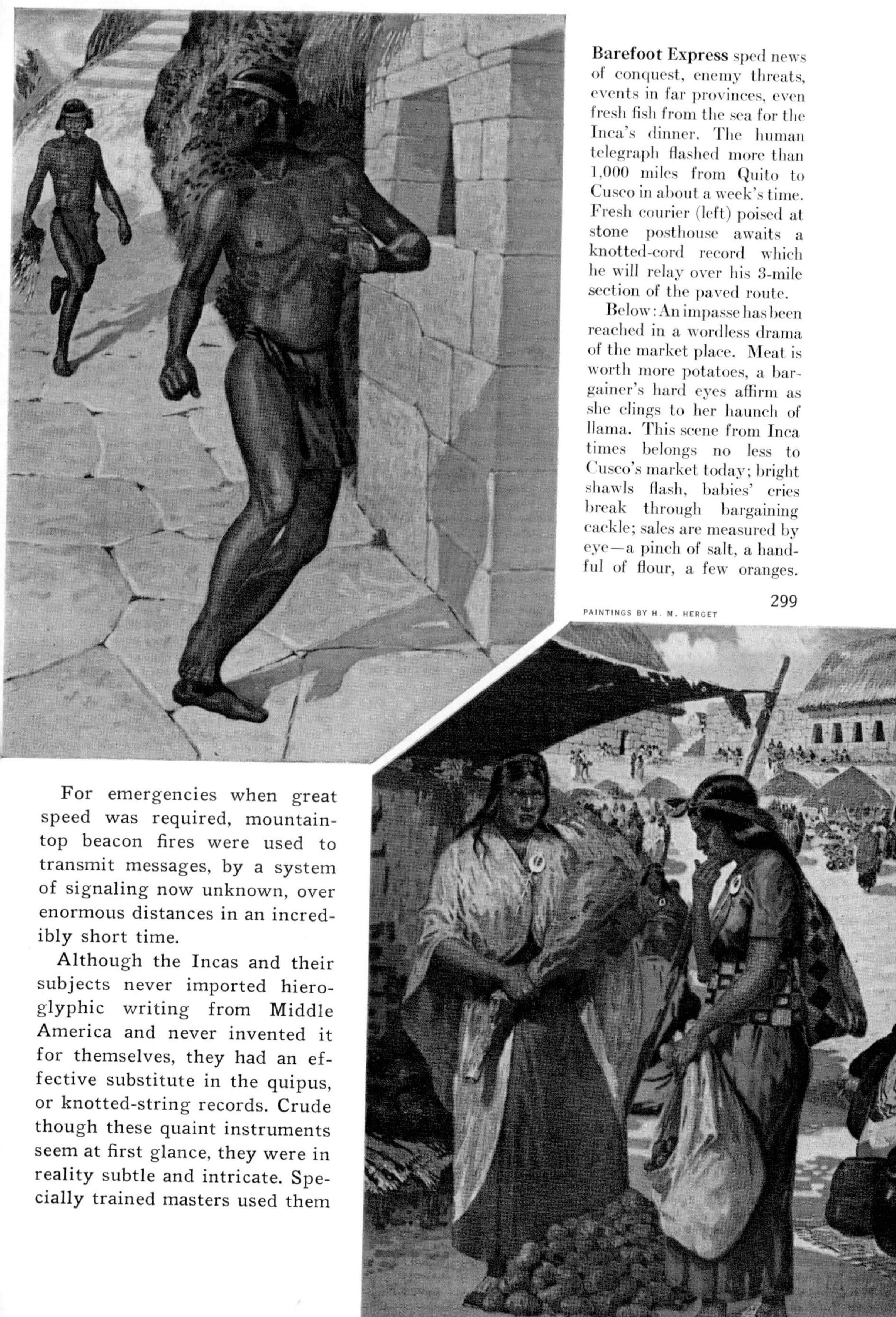

**Barefoot Express** sped news of conquest, enemy threats, events in far provinces, even fresh fish from the sea for the Inca's dinner. The human telegraph flashed more than 1,000 miles from Quito to Cusco in about a week's time. Fresh courier (left) poised at stone posthouse awaits a knotted-cord record which he will relay over his 3-mile section of the paved route.

Below: An impasse has been reached in a wordless drama of the market place. Meat is worth more potatoes, a bargainer's hard eyes affirm as she clings to her haunch of llama. This scene from Inca times belongs no less to Cusco's market today; bright shawls flash, babies' cries break through bargaining cackle; sales are measured by eye—a pinch of salt, a handful of flour, a few oranges.



PAINTINGS BY H. M. HERGET

For emergencies when great speed was required, mountain-top beacon fires were used to transmit messages, by a system of signaling now unknown, over enormous distances in an incredibly short time.

Although the Incas and their subjects never imported hieroglyphic writing from Middle America and never invented it for themselves, they had an effective substitute in the quipus, or knotted-string records. Crude though these quaint instruments seem at first glance, they were in reality subtle and intricate. Specially trained masters used them for arithmetical calculations, and possibly for simple narratives.

Quipu-ology, the study of these knot-records, was a third-year subject in the four-year course at the Teaching House, where ruling caste youths were educated. Even today one sees llama herders counting flocks by means of a simplified survival of the ancient system.

For studying the movements of sun, moon, and stars, and for determining the seasons of the year, the Incas used several methods. One was the sundial, to be found in every temple (page 322). Carved, as a rule, from a large boulder, its upper surface was flat save for a stout column of the same stone, carefully shaped when the dial was made. The shadow cast by this gnomon, besides marking the hours and seasons, was the object of much esoteric learning now lost to us.

Again, groups of towers were used whose shadows told learned men about the equinoxes and solstices and so aided them in appointing days for festivals held throughout the year. Seemingly simple compared with modern calendars and astronomical observatories, the ancient Peruvian techniques enabled the Incas to measure time nearly as accurately as we do.

It is in their architecture, however, that the applied science of the ancient Peruvians may best be seen today. Whether it be in the stupendous megalithic masonry of Fort Sacsahuaman (page 292), above Cusco, or in the beautifully regular courses of the best walls at Machu Picchu and other sites, we see the result of endless patience and of astonishing structural skill.

All building was done, we must remember, with no machines beyond the inclined plane, the crowbar, and perhaps a rudimentary pulley. For the rest, Incaic masons depended on stone or bronze knives, infinite polishing and grinding with sand and water, and concerted pulling of materials along the ground by large numbers of men. It is doubtful that even the crudest form of rollers was used or known.

Yet how impressive the best architecture of ancient Peru! In the early days of rough stones laid in clay, a style which continued to be used in common structures, it was crude enough. But the superior methods of construction Mayta Capac learned at Tiahuanaco formed the basis of continued progress by his successors. Under Pachacutec the present glorious curved walls at Coricancha (the Temple of the Sun in Cusco), at Pisac, at Machu Picchu, and at many other places, marked the final stage of architectural development.

Lacking the carved ornateness of Mexican and Maya buildings, the structures made in the Inca period depend for their effect on balance and proportion. Tapering doorways with monolithic lintels, similar windows and niches, serve to break up surfaces otherwise too plain to be sightly (page 283).

On the coast, where sun-baked clay was the chief building material, stepped pyramids with gaily painted terraces supported the temples and mansions of the great chiefs (page 288). Humbler folk lived in gabled houses of many colors. In both coast and highlands roofs were of thatch; but to judge by a few surviving examples, so exquisitely made as almost to rival the masonry.

Wise men preserved from father to son

**Inca Walls Defy Time and Quake,** Spanish frosting topples. To erase Inca memory, Spaniards built their Monastery of Santo Domingo on the foundation of the Inca holy of holies, Cusco's Temple of the Sun. What must today's Indians think as they compare their ancestors' mortarless stones with the conqueror's cemented works, here crumpled by 1950's severe earthquake? Although ancient Peruvians never attained the true arch, they showed amazing architectural skill. They ground granite blocks to a mathematically determined arc to build the curving outer walls.

KIP ROSS, NATIONAL GEOGRAPHIC STAFF

PAINTING BY ROJAS PONCE, COURTESY OF COLUMBIA UNIVERSITY

**Beneath a Jaguar Headdress Glares the Mochica God of Fertility.** This hardwood image with red eyes and long white tusks of shell was unearthed in Peru's Virú Valley in the 1,000-year-old tomb of a warrior-priest regarded as the god in human form. Buried with him was a boy, like the lad here sowing turquoise "seeds" in furrows formed by Ai apaec's digging stick. At lower right is a serpent.

the oral traditions and the knowledge of nature accumulated through many generations. Bards, singers, and dancers graced by their special skills the ceremonial life of the court and festivals of the people.

There were, naturally, contrasts in way of life between the great and the ordinary folk. This becomes apparent when we study the marriage customs. The Inca and all his caste were polygamous. Multiplicity of wives and concubines was regarded as a privilege suitable only to the great.

A part of Yahuar Huaccac's inferiority complex is made manifest by his special addiction to carnal delights: in his enormous harem he could display prowess in this respect if in no other. All the Incas, to be sure, had hundreds of mates, and the Chosen Women (Virgins of the Sun) were accustomed to yield themselves to the Sapa Inca, Son of the Sun, whenever he willed it. The First Wife, however, was *Coya,* or Empress, all her days.

Among the lowly, marriage was not only monogamous but universal. Spinsters and bachelors were practically unknown. Marriage was a civil rather than a religious rite. At stated intervals each village chief assembled before him all youths and maidens who wished to be married. Arranging men in one row and girls in another, he married each couple in turn as they came up to him.

This arbitrary method was not so cold-blooded and mechanical as it may seem at first, for in Incaland as elsewhere love had its way. We may safely assume there was jockeying for position in both masculine and feminine lines of the about-to-be-wed, so that the right couple in each case finally stood before the marrying chief.

Having acquired his wife, the young puric, aged 25 or so, led her to his little stone or adobe house where appropriate ceremonies were held by the kinsfolk of both. Afterward the young wife aided her husband in growing potatoes, maize, and other crops (page 298).

Chicha, a maize beer singularly unpleasant to our refined notions, was, and still is, brewed by being chewed by old women who spat the masticated kernels into a jar of brackish water, where they fermented for eight days. Strained and otherwise treated by the wife, this undainty liquid became a drink of considerable potency and charm, such as even finicky modern folk can swallow, if need be (pages 306, 309).

When children began to be born to the puric and his wife, the always benevolent government allotted additional land for the support of each child. Then as now, the Indian mother merely retired behind a hedge or into her house, there to give birth alone without aid from midwife or physician. Under these conditions infant mortality must have been high; but at least the survivors were uncommonly tough.

Pachacutec's days were passed in the austere majesty of massive masonry palaces at Cusco and other places. Huge courts were thronged with colorfully clad retainers, whose sole ambition was to lay down their lives for him. Flowers, brilliant featherwork, superb tapestries of vicuña wool in lustrous hues, vessels and ornaments of gold, and all that was fairest of his subjects' handicrafts adorned the stately niche-lined apartments where he dwelt when not campaigning at the head of his armies.

Fortunately, many of these things have survived from his day to ours and may be seen in museums in Peru, Ecuador, Bolivia, the United States, and many another country of which Pachacutec never heard.

Aside from all his surrounding splendor, the Emperor Pachacutec was a great soul, a noble philosopher whose heart held charity for his fellow men. Many of his sayings have been preserved for us

## Modern Quechua Work, Pray, and Play at the Heart of the Ancient Empire

Near Cusco a somber Inca descendant (above) herds his llamas to safety to let a truck pass on the winding Pisac-Calca road. The beasts seem annoyed. Prized source of hides, meat, wool, and labor, the "camels of the Andes" recognize their master's voice, obey his sharply hissed commands. Right: Staff bearers meet after Sunday Mass to form an escort of honor for the Pisac priest. Ritual was intoned part in Latin, part Spanish, part Quechua. Below: Indian dancer's mask (center) pokes fun at Spanish mustaches. Costumed drummers and dancers at the gayest fiestas frequently wear mournful expressions. Grin (right) is rare.



KODACHROMES BY KIP ROSS, NATIONAL GEOGRAPHIC STAFF

by Indian and Spanish chroniclers. Among them are these:

*Envy is a worm that gnaws and consumes the entrails of the envious.*

*It is very just that he who is a thief should be put to death. Adulterers, who destroy the peace and happiness of others, ought to be declared thieves, and condemned to death without mercy.*

*Judges who secretly receive gifts from litigants ought to be looked upon as thieves, and punished with death as such.*

*The noble and generous man is known by the patience he shows in adversity.*

*The physician herbalist who is ignorant of the virtues of herbs, or who, knowing the uses of some, has not attained to a knowledge of all, understands little or nothing. He ought to work until he knows all, as well the useful as the injurious plants, in order to deserve the name to which he pretends.*

*Drunkenness, anger, and madness go together: but the first two are voluntary and to be removed, whereas the last is perpetual.*

Such words as these, reveal that the Incaic mind was not wont to compromise with wrongdoing.

If vagabonds and other mischievous persons were flogged with a sling for a minor offense and hanged by the feet until dead for a grave one, there was also a strong humanitarian note in the

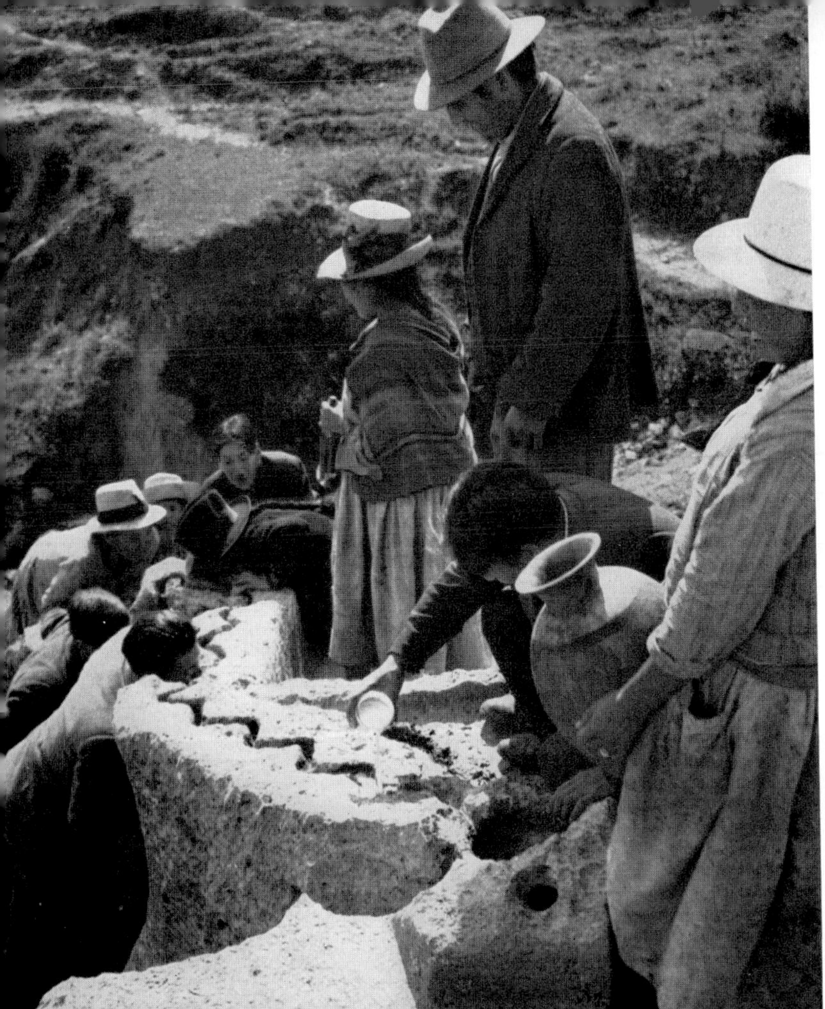

**Chicha on the Rocks**

Ancients carved the snake-like channel in this sloping stone near the fortress of Sacsahuaman (page 292). Descendants still use it with gusto on weddings and other festive occasions.

Chicha, maize beer of past and present, is poured into a hollow near the top. As it twists downhill, celebrators lap it directly from stations along the sparkling flow. Their earnest efforts to waste none frequently result in inebriation.

Serpent symbol suggested by the writhing groove is common not only to Andean cultures but to those of Central and North America (pages 66, 116, 237). Incas interpreted good or bad omens from movements of snakes and spiders. To prophesy the fortunes of war, priests paraded stones around a ceremonial fire in Cusco's holy square, bearing painted images of snakes, toads, pumas, and jaguars.



law's differentiation between robbery from malice aforethought, for which the perpetrator was duly punished, and robbery committed to obtain badly needed food. For this, chastisement was inflicted, not on the thief, but upon the official whose duty it was to forestall need so grievous!

The prisons maintained by the Incas for punishing criminals of all classes, especially traitors and nobles who shirked their high duties, were terrible places filled with poisonous snakes and other horrors. But, so the old chroniclers tell us, they were almost always empty of human inmates.

Pachacutec also was a daring original thinker. Before the assembled priests of Inti (the sun) he once reasoned out the existence of a god still higher than the sun. He pointed out how that luminary always follows a set path, performs definite tasks, and keeps certain hours as does a laborer. He showed that the solar radiance can be dimmed by any passing cloud. The sun must, Pachacutec argued, have a master who is master also of all created things.

He ended by proclaiming to the priests the omnipotence of his father's counselor, the Supreme Deity, the creator-god Viracocha. He ordained, however, that the worship of Viracocha be confined to the ruling caste, as being too subtle and sublime for ordinary folk. He commanded the people be taught that Inti was greatest of the gods.

Thenceforward, when addressing the sun, the Incas always spoke to him as to a kinsman. To Viracocha they prayed with the deepest awe and humility.

Beyond question the reign of Pachacutec was the zenith of the Inca Empire. At his death, about 1448, it was equal in extent to the Atlantic States from Maine to South Carolina, inclusive.

From northern Peru down into Bolivia and northwestern Argentina its diversified territory of highlands and coastlands spread, a work of empire-building which can be grasped only if we visualize a Roman Empire consisting of a series of Switzerlands bordered on one side by a long coastal Sahara and on the other by a Congo-like wilderness of tropical forest.

Pachacutec and his generals had conquered all the great coastal kingdoms up to the Gulf of Guayaquil, as well as the wilder and more backward folk, wor-

AMERICAN MUSEUM OF NATURAL HISTORY

**Andean Artistry** models the alpaca (top) and the llama. Lake Titicaca region yielded these hollow silver examples of Inca skill in working the abundant native silver, gold, copper, and lead.

Mochica art on vessel (left) from a young woman's grave in the coastal Virú Valley portrays tippling warriors. Man at right drinks from goblet, holding chicha jar on right arm. Swashbuckling companion waves empty goblet to punctuate his tale. Fired at too great heat, jug warped and broke in the making.

COLUMBIA UNIVERSITY

KODACHROMES BY KIP ROSS, NATIONAL GEOGRAPHIC STAFF

**Peruvian Styles Change Slowly.** Pisac musician (left) plays the flute of his Inca ancestors but departs from their loose robes and wrap-around skirts. Early Spaniards put the Indians in short trousers. The poncho, sleeveless, hand-dyed, and home-spun, came later. Above: Calca townswomen quaffing chicha, the native beer, wear their pie-pan hats "sunny side up"; when it rains they reverse the brims. Age-old formula for chicha: Let corn chewed to a pulp ferment in crock of brackish water.

shipers of the puma, of the dog, and other strange or repellent deities, in the highlands behind the coast.

Nevertheless, when he came to die, he seems to have been filled with melancholy forebodings, and his death chant has a note of sadness in it:

*I was born as a flower of the field;*
*As a flower I was cherished in my youth.*
*I came to my full age; I grew old.*
*Now I am withered, and I die.*

In the time of the Inca Tupac Yupanqui, about 1448–1482, Incadom was further enlarged by the conquest of most of what is now Ecuador. This Inca, son of the great Pachacutec, began his career in the east, however, rather than in the north. His father had stopped forever invasions from that direction by his series of frontier citadels; now the son determined to invade the eastern wilderness.

During long preparation he assembled a fleet of more than 250 war canoes, gaily adorned with carvings, canopies, and banners. In them he and a great following journeyed down the Amaru Mayo (Serpent River, now the Madre de Dios) as far as its junction with the Beni.

The sylvan savages were poor folk from the Inca's point of view. The only tribute he could wring from them after much desperate fighting was macaws, monkeys, honey, and beeswax. Besides, the climate of their land was noxious in its dampness and heat to men accustomed to the free, thin, cold air of the mountains. Consequently, the Inca contented himself with a merely theoretical conquest in that region.

Later, having conquered and Inca-ized the best parts of the Kingdom of Quitu

**Living Sky-high on the Bolivian Altiplano**

Festive occasion for Aymará Indians is their annual livestock fair on the wind-swept Andean plateau (left). Many have tramped vast distances to trade highland cows, leather, cheese, frozen potatoes for lowland coca, fruit, bamboo, and factory clothes, dyes, and gadgets. Such fairs have come down from Inca times.

Below: Market-bound Indians enter La Paz by an old llama trail. Saucered amid frosty peaks, this world's highest capital (11,900 feet) tops Lhasa, Tibet, by 80 feet. Most Bolivians live two miles above sea level. A large-lunged few dwell as high as three miles.

Below left: Indian women barter before the church at Laja. Here La Paz was founded in 1548. But the altiplano proved so cold and barren that the city was soon transferred to its sheltered valley. Today, some 2,000,000 Indians wrest a living from the bleak altiplano, which extends through western Bolivia north into Peru.

KODACHROMES BY T. IFOR REES

(Ecuador), and having humorously exacted a tribute of lice from a certain province which seemed to produce nothing else (page 280), the Inca Tupac Yupanqui again took to boats.

He built a great flotilla of rafts of buoyant balsa wood. These pointed craft each had a hut with a hearth in it amidships, and a mast with a square cotton sail near the bow. They could carry a surprising number of fighting men and a considerable cargo of weapons and supplies. Their like may still be seen on the Guayaquil estuary.

The naval expedition of Tupac Yupanqui sailed from Tumbes, in northernmost Peru, and was gone for nearly a year. There is good reason to think it visited the Galapagos Islands.

This maritime excursion is unique in Inca annals. As a rule, neither the Incas nor other folk of ancient Peru were expert on the sea. Coastwise trading ventures on rafts and fishing voyages off the coast in boats of other quaint but cumbersome types were the nearest they ever came to mastering the Pacific Ocean.

The heir of Tupac Yupanqui was the Prince Titu Cusi Hualpa. Better known as Inca Huayna Capac (Young Chief Rich in Virtues), he ruled from 1482 to 1528 or 1529. His reign was largely taken up with struggles to extend his realm south in Chile and north in Ecuador.

The Empire had grown too large to be administered as well as Pachacutec had done. When we consider that it was equal in size to all the Atlantic States combined, and that its territory was far more diverse than is that of those States, we can readily understand the disruptive forces which were beginning to crack the mighty fabric.

That the Inca Huayna Capac himself fearfully realized the overgrowth of his realm is made evident by his last will. He inscribed it in some incipient form of writing upon wooden rods or tablets.

In that document he gave the southern four-fifths of the realm to Prince Inti Cusi Hualpa, better known as Huascar. Huascar, his legitimate heir, was the son of his sister-wife. To his favorite but bastard son, Atahualpa, he gave Quitu. Atahualpa's mother was almost certainly a daughter of the last independent King of Quitu, so there was a certain measure of justice in bequeathing that kingdom to her son.

Filled with dread of the future, partly caused by the first faint rumors of white-faced and bearded strangers who rode on fierce and huge llamas and who commanded the lightning, the Inca Huayna Capac sought what solace he could find in his harem of several thousand women.

At last, sick and affrighted, he died in his palace at Quitu (present-day Quito). His body was taken in state to be buried at Cusco, but his weary heart was laid to rest in his beloved Quitu. This rending of the Inca's corpse is strangely prophetic of what was soon to befall the Empire itself.

As might have been expected, Huascar and Atahualpa speedily went to war with one another to gain supremacy. When, a few years later, Francisco Pizarro led his tiny band of Spanish adventurers into the land, Huascar was prisoner of his half-brother, who was enjoying a usurped and transitory grandeur as Sole Inca.

The story of how Pizarro captured Atahualpa by a trick, wrung from him the promise of a roomful of gold (worth well over $3,000,000) in ransom, and finally condemned him to death after it had been honorably paid, has been graphically told by Prescott and many others.

At length, in 1533, Atahualpa, whom all eye-witnesses describe as a grave and majestic monarch, handsome in person and very proud, was garroted amid the wailing of his women and vassals.

With him died not only the Inca Empire but also an entire and unique po-

KODACHROME BY CARL S. BELL

litico-social philosophy and a civilization based upon the happiness of all. Money lust and gold hunger entered Peru along with Christianity, and the long struggle began between the just and fair intentions of both the church and the king of Castile and the determination of all too many individuals to wring as much wealth as possible from the Indians in the shortest possible time.

Inca civilization was not, as many suppose, utterly obliterated. Rather, because of the liberal attitude of the Ro-

**Graceful Bulrush Boats Ply Lake Titicaca**
Early Spaniards, recalling the coast's balsa-wood rafts, misnamed these cork-light Indian craft *balsas.* The name has endured. Unsinkable hull and sail are made of pithy rushes from marshes that conceal millions of waterfowl. Larger balsas carry a dozen people; some transport llamas. When waterlogged they are pulled ashore to dry. Indians cut the rushes, dry them in cornstalklike shocks, then bind them with grass twine into bundles that form keel, hull, and gunwales to turn back waves.

The versatile rush (*totora*) thatches houses, makes rain capes; its young roots provide tender food. Lake Titicaca, 12,507 feet high, some 50 miles wide, is world's loftiest great lake. Its basin cradled advanced Indian civilizations.

man Catholic Church, of the kings of Castile, and of the best men among the conquerors, it was blended with Spanish colonial civilization. The same thing happened wherever Spain ruled—in Central America, in Mexico, in our own Southwest.

Today, in what was Incaland, the descendants of the Incas' subjects still constitute some two-fifths of the total population. Thus in many a remote Andean village, while the soft, opalescent evening is closing in, we may become aware that an Indian concert is in progress in the square.

Drawing near, we see instruments that are pure Inca: flutes, Panpipes, clay trumpets, drums, and rattles. They combine to build a pulsating music at once exciting and contagious, filling the mind with thoughts of bygone times.

Moment by moment knots of Indians come to the dance, until the whole adult population of the village is treading an antique and stately measure under the silverbright radiance of Mama Quilla, the moon. The insidious lilt of the orchestra commands their every motion.

The fervor mounts and mounts until the square is filled with whirling skirts of women and swaying forms of mantle-draped men. The frenzy lasts until the dancers drop exhausted and the wailing, throbbing melody dies away like a sigh on the cold night wind.

Departing, we realize that we have witnessed something Pachacutec must often have seen in the Golden Age of the Incas, long ago. We can almost convince ourselves that his spirit, brooding and wistful, has been among us.

**Dancers and Distaffs Whirl in Aymará Land**

Celebrators feast, drink, and dance themselves dizzy at a Bolivian fiesta. Men in Sunday best appear somber next to their barefoot women, who spin like tops, skirts billowing, colors flashing. The more skirts, each a different solid color, the greater a dancer's prestige. If oranges, purples, and reds clash, so much the better.

A squatting mother (opposite) spins yarn, guides it onto her spindle. Highland Indian women spin whenever their hands are free—whether sitting, walking, or dancing. They love bright shawls, voluminous skirts, high-crowned hats. Ignoring the splendor of their rugged mountain scenery, they make colorful dyed cloth compensate for drab homes and Spartan conditions. Since ancient times llama, alpaca, and vicuña have supplied their wool. The vicuña's, finest and rarest, was for rulers and nobles only in Inca days.

Derbied vendor (right) offers a plaster doll representing Ekeko, Aymará god of abundance. His dwarfish figure is commonly adorned with miniature boats, houses, even automobiles, symbols of prosperity. La Paz publishes tiny newspapers in his honor at its January *Alasitas* ("buy") fair.

KODACHROMES BY CARL S. BELL

KIP ROSS, NATIONAL GEOGRAPHIC STAFF

**Swirling Mists Shroud Machu Picchu,** lost city of the Incas. High Andean peaks guarded this sanctuary of Virgins of the Sun, last stronghold of a dying empire. The forgotten, jungle-claimed citadel was rediscovered by Hiram Bingham, leader of three National Geographic-Yale expeditions.

## CHAPTER 14

# DISCOVERING MACHU PICCHU

## BY HIRAM BINGHAM

CROSSING THE BRIDGE made me wonder if this jaunt to find an alleged "Inca ruin" wasn't more quixotic than practical. There I was on hands and knees, inching across a half-dozen slender, vine-lashed poles that just cleared the foaming, icy Urubamba River.

Days of rugged travel through magnificent Andes gorges in Peru's southern highlands had brought me with two Yale colleagues to the base of a 10,000-foot mountain called Machu Picchu. The trip had been hard enough without this added excursion on the strength of local rumor. Still, if there really were ruins it was my job to visit them.

I crawled across the bridge and with Arteaga, my guide, and a Peruvian sergeant attacked the precipitous slope. On all fours, we pulled ourselves up through slippery grass. Arteaga moaned that this was just the place to find a fer-de-lance, that vicious snake reputed to spring after its prey.

Drenched with sweat and gasping for breath, we struggled up jungle-shaded cliffs, digging with fingernails to keep from falling. Directly under us, far below now, the frothing rapids of the Urubamba roared angrily.

Calling on every reserve of strength we clambered through the thinning tangle of jungle. Gradually the ground leveled. At last, we straightened to see a grass hut. Friendly Indians approached with dripping gourds of cold spring water. We drank first, then looked around. We stood in a high clearing on a steep saddle of the mountain.

In the distance, massive summits, some snow-clad, reared wild crests. From far below came the snarl of the rapids, echoing through the dark, misty gorge. I drank in the view between gulps of water and lungfuls of air, and wondered just what I was doing on such a remote spot, nearly a mile and a half above sea level, on this blazing July day in 1911.

The answer was involved. With my Yale companions, who had decided to spend the day in camp (very wisely, I thought), I had come to Peru to collect geologic and geographic data, above all to find the last capital of the Incas.

Spanish accounts tell of the Inca prince whom Pizzaro appointed ruler after Atahualpa's death. Manco II, delighted at the honor, accepted without realizing he was slated to be a puppet. He rebelled and fled from Cusco down the Urubamba Valley with his loyal followers. In a region sealed off from the rest of the world Manco set up a mountaintop community: Vilcapampa.

There, he and his three sons ruled free of Spanish domination. Surrounded by nobles and Chosen Women, virgins dedicated to serving the sun god, these last four Incas held out for 39 years after Cusco had fallen to Spain and the power

Lofty Temples and Gabled Palaces Gleam as the Sun Deity Blesses Them with Lowering Rays

KODACHROME BY EDWARDS PARK, NATIONAL GEOGRAPHIC STAFF

**Built on a Complex of Terraces, the Mountain Retreat Probably Sheltered Some 800 People**

of the Andes empire had been shattered. Spanish troops finally captured and beheaded the last Inca, but his age-old sanctuary, the sacred capital, never knew the tramp of a conquistador's boot. Vilcapampa vanished from the world's memory.

On the trail of this lost city, my colleagues and I had followed clues which led us to the foot of Machu Picchu. We had explored a number of Inca ruins, none of which seemed to fill the bill. We had chased down many a rumor of lost cities and been disappointed. This mad expedition up an almost unclimbable mountain would be, I felt, yet another disappointment.

Our Indian hosts said there were old structures "a little farther on." Possibly some huts, I thought. I gathered strength, stilled quaking legs, and with two companions set out along the soaring ridge.

It was easy going at first. The thinner air of 8,000 feet refreshed me. New summits slid into view on the far horizon. I felt utterly alone except for low, scudding clouds. Then I rounded a knoll and this was the sight I faced: Tier upon tier of Inca terraces rose like giant stairs along the steep slope of the saddle. Each terrace, hundreds of feet long, was banked with massive stone walls up to ten feet high. Our Indian friends had cleared many of them, tilling the rich soil as their Inca ancestors had done.

But what group of Incas had needed a hundred such terraces in this lofty wilderness? Enough food could be grown on this mountaintop to feed a city.

In sudden excitement I forgot my fatigue and hurried the length of a wide terrace toward the tangle of jungle forest beyond it. I plunged once more into damp undergrowth matting the ridge's hump, and fought my way forward through vines and foliage.

Then I stopped, heart thumping wildly. A mossy wall loomed before me, half hidden in trees. Huge stone blocks seemed glued together, but without mor-

**Up These Stairways Paraded Inca Priests and Chosen Women.** Windows piercing massive walls overlook the Grand Canyon of the Urubamba. The hidden refuge had more windows than busy Inca Cusco, 50 miles away, for weather was milder at Machu Picchu's 8,000 feet than at Cusco, two miles high. Masons hewed lintels from single blocks weighing up to three tons. Semicircular Temple of the Sun, center, resembles that at Cusco (page 301). Sacred sundial (page 322) stands on eminence at right.

FRANKLIN L. FISHER

**The Discoverer Returns.** Hiram Bingham dedicates a new highway leading to the lost city's doorstep, a far cry from the hazardous cliff-climb which first brought him to Machu Picchu in 1911. Inca terraces, such as those spilling down slope in background, gave him his first surprise glimpse of the forgotten refuge.

Until the opening of the new *Carretera Hiram Bingham,* visitors zigzagged up to the ruins from the Urubamba Valley on mule back. Once a network of narrow Inca roads linked the citadel with the outside world. Dr. Bingham's three National Geographic Society-Yale University expeditions, which freed the ruins from the jungle's green grip, traced the moss-grown paving of these trails through forest and landslide rubble.

World War I called him away from his archeological labors; later he became Governor of Connecticut and United States Senator. The 1948 road opening marked his first return to Peru in years.

A. OGDEN PIERROT

tar—the finest Inca construction. Awed, I traced the wall through the shadowy underbrush. It was part of a ruined house. Beyond it stood another, and beyond that I could make out more houses almost encased in twining growth.

Eagerly I searched farther, seeing everywhere the gleam of white granite masonry. Under an overhanging ledge appeared a small cave, its walls lined with niches of the finest cut stone—a royal mausoleum. Above the same ledge rose a semicircular building with gracefully sloping outer wall, like that of Cusco's Temple of the Sun. Its straight courses of curved masonry diminished in size toward the top, the work of master craftsmen. No pin could penetrate between tightly fitted blocks.

Stone steps led to a clearing where two white granite temples stood against the sky. Each had three walls. One temple had never been roofed. I stared at a huge rectangular block along its rear wall and decided I was looking at the throne on which mummies of dead Incas had been placed to receive homage from priests and worshipers.

The clearing was a sacred plaza. Across it was a temple with three great windows looking out over the canyon. Here high priests in gold trappings had worshiped the sun. One gabled compound of beautifully built houses must have sheltered the ruler himself. I could picture its palaces floored with vicuña rugs and soft textiles woven by the Chosen Women.

Down the forest-mantled slope I found houses crowded together in a bewildering array of terraced levels linked by stairways. Here had lived those who worked the fields. Here women filled narrow-necked water jugs at stone basins.

Exploring this vast ruin, I was struck by its defenses. The Urubamba River, far below, tumbles around three sides of this soaring mountain shoulder. On the fourth stands the pinnacle of Machu Picchu, fortified, as we learned later, by a watch tower where a handful of men could

KODACHROME BY KIP ROSS, NATIONAL GEOGRAPHIC STAFF

**To This Massive Sundial Inca Priests "Tied the Sun."** They sighted past the upright to mark the sun's course. Winter's lengthening shadows alarmed the populace; their sun god was slipping away. But at the solstice, calendar-wise priests tied their deity so he could go no farther, and must return bringing summer. In one piece weighing many tons, Machu Picchu's granite *intihuatana* was carved from the city hilltop on which it stands. Spaniards took pains to destroy these pagan symbols, but this stone remains intact—further sign no conquistador ever found the hidden city.

withstand the onslaught of thousands. As I well knew, invaders who managed to cross the river would face sheer cliffs. Those who got past observation posts and scaled the height of the ridge would meet an outer wall built along the ends of the farm terraces. Next came a dry moat and inner wall.

I gradually understood, surveying this sacred citadel perched like an eagle's nest on a cliff-ringed mountain saddle, that here indeed was a lost city come to light. Could it be the same Vilcapampa I sought? I now believe it was. In these royal buildings had lived the last of the Incas. This was their sanctuary, their towering fortress which defied all invasion, then lay forgotten for 300 years.

Bursting with news of my discovery, I returned home. Machu Picchu cried for complete archeological exploration. I was greatly pleased when the National Geographic Society joined with Yale University for this purpose.

First tasks facing the new expedition were to bridge the Urubamba and build an improved trail up the saddle. Kenneth C. Heald, our topographer, solved these problems despite snakes, reluctant Indian labor, and a grass fire that chased him over a cliff. As soon as the trail was finished a long line of porters moved up it like ants, each laden with supplies. In the ghost city work hummed.

We felled trees that had sprouted on ancient walls, hacked away bushes, burned debris, scrubbed moss from stones. Gradually axes and machetes chewed away the jungle to reveal the breath-taking details of Machu Picchu. At least 100 stairways coursed through the many-leveled city. One, with some 200 steps, formed "Main Street," splitting the city in two. Along its length, a series of catch basins trapped water from the one slender stone aqueduct. Water must have flowed freely to supply the city's needs. But we found the spring-fed flow only a trickle. Perhaps water failure explains the end of Machu Picchu.

The finest stairway led to a little hilltop commanding the city. Here we discovered a carved *intihuatana,* a stone column where Inca priests worshiped their solar deity (opposite). On festival days, nobles, priests, and Chosen Women ascended these steps in a colorful, solemn parade. Beside their sacred stone, they blew kisses to the sun.

Dwellings vary. Some have carefully matched masonry, others were built quickly with small stones. Many have steep-pitched gables with carved stone rings to which thatched roofing was lashed. Groups of houses have their own characteristics—perhaps a private garden plot of terraces like the court of a modern apartment, a carved granite shrine, or interior niches which might have held mummies. One large house boasted the equivalent of a streamlined kitchen. Built into its floor are concave grinding stones on which the Inca housewife ground maize or crushed frozen potatoes.

Inca stone masons may have used bronze chisels to carve rings and cylinders in granite. But no iron tools or derricks helped them fashion and move massive units that wall their buildings. Some walls at Machu Picchu have keyed blocks, cut to prevent lateral slipping. One choice house near the temples shows what masons could do with a single hewn stone. It forms half the wall, at left of the door. Part of the interior niches and a lower corner of the room were carved from its mass. Spanish writers marveled at a stone with 14 angles in a Cusco palace. This one has 32 angles!

The semicircular temple I had admired when I first saw Machu Picchu seemed to grow in beauty as we cleared away underbrush and moss. Its wall leading to what may have been a priest's house is a masterpiece of masonry. I rate it the finest wall in America. Where it joins the priest's house, stones are keyed, hooking into one another so earthquakes, settling foundations, torrential mountain rains could not spread them.

While Machu Picchu was being freed of smothering jungle, we dug for archeological treasures. Outside the principal buildings we found fragments of pottery, perhaps broken during religious festivals and drunken orgies that followed. Seeking bronze ornaments and utensils, we offered a Peruvian dollar to any workman finding a burial cave.

The bonus offer paid off. Before season's end, we had opened about 100 caves, unearthing the bones of 173 humans. Close to 150 were women, strengthening my belief that Machu Picchu was a sanctuary for the Chosen Women. With some skeletons lay buried objects—jars, dishes, bronze and silver jewelry, stone disks perhaps used as counters.

One day we found the remains of a *mamacuna,* or high priestess, the superior of a convent. Beside her was a concave bronze mirror, used to ignite tinder by focusing the sun's rays—a piece of "magic" which the common worshipers watched with awe from the plaza.

Our excavations yielded only three post-Columbian objects, revealing how completely Machu Picchu had remained sealed off from the world.

Today a narrow gauge railroad carries tourists from Cusco to the base of the mountain. A fine, new highway sweeps up to the old stronghold that withstood the world for so long. Now the world has come to this mountain domain. The humblest traveler can stand on the ramparts and stroll silent stairways of this last citadel of a great empire.

THREE LIONS

**Staircase of the Gods at Pisac.** Peru's Indians tilling ancient gardens that march with giant strides up Andes slopes little realize that forgotten ancestors toted on their backs every bit of this soil. These "works of enchantment," at U.S. labor rates, would cost as high as $60,000 an acre!

## CHAPTER 15

# AMERICA'S FIRST FARMERS FOOD GIVERS TO THE WORLD

### BY O. F. COOK

AMONG ITS ANCIENT WONDERS the world includes the hanging gardens of Babylon. These have been a tradition for 3,000 years—yet they were little more than a transient toy. Larger, higher, all but imperishable are the hanging gardens of Peru, climbing steep Andes slopes like giant staircases.

No plaything, they once supported multitudes of ancient people. Today's Peruvian Indians, still using these monumental terrace farms, consider them the work of the gods.

Long before Columbus, natives of the Andes grappled with the vast reclamation project of transforming barren desolation into fertile fields. Centuries of toil, engineering skill almost beyond compare turned rocky valley floors and steep canyon walls into rich acres. Tier upon tier of terraces scaled sterile slopes, massive stone retaining walls contrasting with the fragile green of growing crops. Spouting jets and gleaming trickles of water laced downward from step to step. High on the mountainside, small figures bent to their toil.

The hanging gardens of the Andes marked the high point of ancient America's agricultural development.

In its most primitive form, New World farming had been a slash-and-burn affair. The native selected a patch of jungle, felled trees, burned them along with undergrowth, and planted his crops with a sharp stick (page 201). After harvest he moved away, letting the jealous jungle reclaim its own. Some tropical Indians still follow this method, using land, then abandoning it (page 350).

Tillage was the next stage, practiced by farmers who settled on land to use it year after year. Perhaps with a digging stick, the tiller scratched at his top soil, destroying weeds and loosening humus for seeding.

But soil tilled year in and year out must be nourished to continue growing crops. Indians found the answer by spreading manure, dead fish, seaweed, decayed vegetable matter on their land. This practice of fertilization was their next step in learning agriculture's art. Irrigation followed, probably first in regions where streams could easily be diverted to soak into thirsty soil.

All these stages of agriculture must have flourished in ancient Peru. They continue there today. But they pale before that final stage—staircase farms of "made" or transported soil—evolved by settlers in tortuous gorges centuries before the rise of the Incas.

The first terrace builders are a forgotten race without written record or even tradition. They must have achieved their

W. G. ERVING

**Stolid Oxen, Gift of the Spaniards,** tug a wooden plow through the loam of a central Andean cornfield. Plows, often fashioned from tree limbs, are now tipped with steel but otherwise resemble those that ancient farmers used on wide bottomland terraces. Plowing then was by manpower, since the haughty llama detests harness, spits in the face of anyone foolhardy enough to try to hitch him. On steep hillside fields, today's Quechua farmers till by hand, turning soil with wooden spades to the rhythm of a chant, while women break clods with clubs. Digging sticks, wooden rakes have changed little since Inca days. Steel sickles, machetes, hoes, axes now make Indian's work lighter.

skill gradually, perhaps through millenniums. In their soaring Andean homeland they faced seemingly impossible difficulties. Level land lies only along coastal deserts or on high plateaus where bitter climate forbids crops. Lower, warmer mountainsides are rock-strewn and water-coursed. A rubble of stones, washed down by torrential rains, chokes valley bottoms.

This soilless land offered its pre-Inca settlers poor prospects for farming, but mouths had to be fed. Clearing away stones, the first farmers found that building them into walls took less space than simply tossing them into mounds. Surplus stones went behind each wall, forming a level bed on which soil could be spread. From this beginning the terrace idea grew, the technique of building them became an art. We still cannot imagine the work that went into moving huge rocks, fitting them together with joints so fine that the naked eye has difficulty distinguishing them. Hundreds of people must have strained at some boulders. Patient weeks of grinding made the perfect fit.

Behind each retaining wall, the builders tamped down two distinct layers of earth. First they dumped subsoil—small coarse stones and clay packed to within two or three feet of the wall's top. To fill the remaining space, Indians transported topsoil, often from distant sources. Llamas may have helped carry stones and loam. But since most terraces occur below the high altitudes where these beasts of burden work best, it is likely that farmers themselves toted soil on their backs in baskets or mats. Legend says earth for Cusco's Inca Garden came from near Quito, more than a thousand miles away!

Reclaiming the gullied wasteland of valley bottoms, ancient engineers banked fresh, rich soil behind walls sometimes 15 or 20 feet high, forming broad fields. They even narrowed and straightened rivers, hemming them in with successive walls of rock.

Swift mountain streams usually loop back and forth between their valley walls. Peru's rivers, by contrast, often flow arrow straight in channels of constant width. Below Ollantaytambo, the Urubamba River rushes along a canal-like course for nearly five miles. Though little remains of the ancient walls built to confine it, the channel's artificial nature is obvious. Straightening such streams added a few feet of growing space, a few rows of crops—but labor was abundant, land scarce, and food vital to survival.

Rising from these artificial bottomlands, narrow mountainside terraces climb skyward, sometimes in banks of 50 or more. Most are eight to 15 feet wide, up to several hundred feet long. On the steepest pitches, high walls built with backbreaking labor provide fertile strips as little as a yard wide.

Farmers did not confine cultivation to walled terraces, which usually keep to lower slopes below 11,000 feet, but carried it all the way up. In higher regions there was no need to dispose of rocks in terraces; stones simply rolled down precipitous mountain walls. Wherever soil accumulated, crops were grown. Just below Urcos short ridges climb a narrow

**Harvesting the Precious Potato,** a Peruvian couple grubs with crude hoes on their Andean plot. Fuel-short highland Indians make one dung-fed fire cook food for two days, usually eat cold boiled potato with parched corn, wheat, barley, or beans. Quinoa cooked in a thick porridgelike mass offers variety. Meat is a rare treat. Natives preserve potatoes by an Inca dehydrating method. They expose tubers to mountain air, letting them alternately freeze and thaw, trampling them barefoot at intervals to drive out juices. Resulting chuño keeps indefinitely. Llama herders carry it in wool sacks, may eat it in soup for breakfast, or mixed with stew for the day's only other meal.

HARRY TSCHOPIK, JR.

path of precious loam squeezed between a break in a cliff wall.

Even today's Quechua Indians till slopes so steep that squashes have to be staked to keep them from tumbling down the mountain, and where potatoes, after being dug, must be picked instead of shaken from the vines. Cool and cloudy, these high shoulders need less irrigation than the valleys far below.

Ancients fashioned narrow transverse ridges of earth along these heights, a few large ridges at intervals with many smaller ridges between. The large ridges, not cultivated but left in grass, trapped the run-off rain water and allowed it to seep down rather than gouge out gulleys and wash away precious soil. This "contour plowing" technique is today hailed as a modern, scientific method of preventing erosion on hillside fields!

The areas once farmed in this way are much more extensive than the lands still cultivated in the valleys below. Traveling through valleys whose every upper slope shows signs of former cultivation gives one a feeling that a great age has vanished from these mountains. Its mementos are so widespread the eye can scarcely avoid them even when it glances up to the glaciers and eternal snows. Ancients tilling the misty heights stood against the same icy background.

From these glaciers came water to nourish crops. Aqueducts linked terrace farms with high mountain freshets. A Spanish writer tells of one aqueduct extending 120 leagues, with a depth of 12 feet. Wherever possible, these channels were carved along the very crests of sharp mountain ridges, and today have worn deep grooves. Water crossed cliffs in ditches carved out of the rock face, sometimes tunneled through obstructions, sometimes rode on built-up masonry. From the topmost terrace of a series, water filtered "downstairs." At Machu Picchu it apparently jetted picturesquely from one terrace to another, perhaps affording welcome shower baths for field workers.

Gaps or passageways can still be seen cutting across a flight of ruined terraces. Probably these were designed both as paths and as drainage channels to keep heavy rains from cutting away topsoil or undermining walls. Soils hereabouts are tenacious, keeping shape and resisting erosion, a condition that helped the terrace builders.

Many terrace and irrigation works must have been laid out the way modern engineers plan a reclamation project. Had wandering settlers taken what plots they liked, level bottomlands would show signs of having been occupied first. Stones spread fanwise around field boundaries would indicate clearings. Instead, the regular terrace patterns and carefully planned aqueducts show that "blueprints" were drawn and scanned before a stone slid into place.

Ancient Egyptians lavished skilled labor on building pyramid tombs for their sovereigns. Peruvians, concerned with life rather than death, spent their efforts on agricultural structures. They built tombs, too, but modest ones in caves or on high rocky cliffs where farming was impossible.

Peru's staircase farms grew and developed more species of plant foods than any other region in the New World. Some of these food gifts have been of inestimable value. Conquering Spaniards stormed through Peru seeking gold. But the samples of the humble potato they shipped back to Spain proved in the long run to be the Inca's real treasure.

The instinctive prejudice against new food plants kept the potato in the background of European diet for two centuries. People forgot the land of its origin and called it the Irish potato. It didn't begin to be grown as a crop until the French Revolution. Even then it had to be forced on the public by the persistent efforts of the French philanthropist, Parmentier, who demonstrated its food possibilities by establishing a large number of soup kitchens for the poor of Paris. Potato soup still bears the name Parmentier—a homely memorial to the philanthropist.

Today the value of the world's annual potato crop probably far exceeds that of all the gold the Spaniards took from the Incas.

Many other crops that explorers came upon elsewhere in the Americas were cultivated in the Andes: the sweet potato, maize, cassava, pineapple, bottle-gourd, cotton, tomato. The lima bean, the peanut, and quinine are of undisputable Andean orgin. Maize is another story. Controversy still smolders over its country of origin—Mexico or Peru.

In Peru, agriculture is a matter of altitude. Geographically you are in the tropics. Agriculturally you may be anywhere between the Equator and the Arctic Circle. From among plantations of sugar, coca, and cacao at Santa Ana you can see at the other end of the valley some peaks of the cordillera covered with glaciers and perpetual snow. It is like looking from Jamaica to Alaska. Even on foot you can climb in a few hours through the full range of farming possibilities.

The cultivation of cassava, or manioc, characterizes the lowest farm belt, extending in the Urubamba Valley to an altitude of about 6,000 feet. From here to 11,000 feet the potato is the chief crop. Higher still, the land is mostly used for grazing. On some slopes above the Pass of La Raya, between Cusco and Lake Titicaca, potatoes thrive at altitudes above 14,000 feet.

Peru is still a fountainhead for new varieties of this food staple. It boasts many kinds of potatoes of better quality than those we cultivate in the United States. Many have awkward shapes and deep eyes, making them hard to peel, but it should be possible to interbreed and combine their best features.

**Market Day at Pisac** offers Andes Indians a chance to gossip and display a wide range of crops. These vegetables call to mind that ancient Peruvians domesticated more food and medicinal plants than any other early people. Potatoes, lima beans, peanuts, quinine are four of many contributions.

KODACHROME BY KIP ROSS, NATIONAL GEOGRAPHIC STAFF

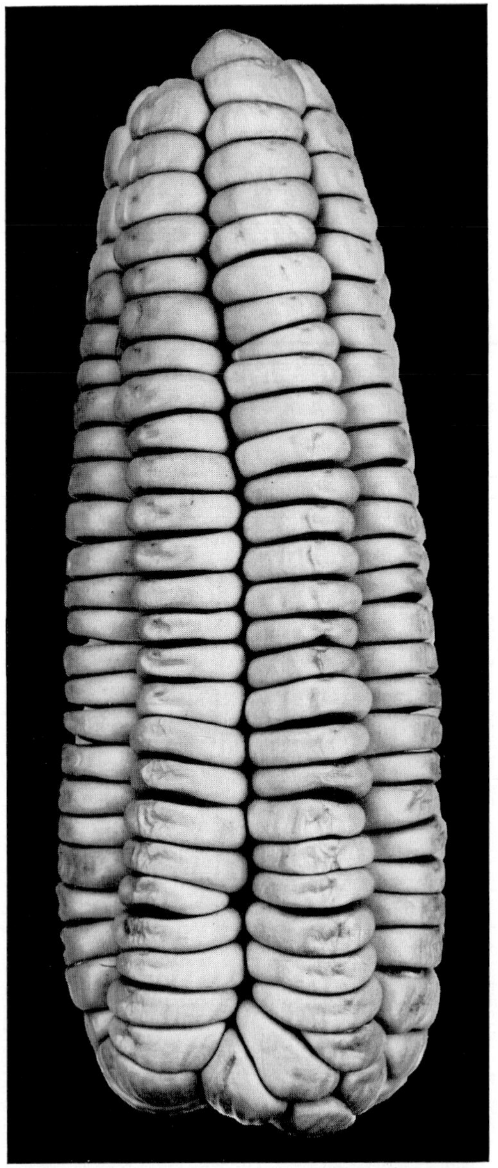

O. F. COOK AND G. B. GILBERT

**Indians Eat Cusco Corn Kernels Like Grapes**

They squeeze the meat from the thick skin of boiled inch-wide kernels of this unique Peruvian corn of 9,000- to 11,000-foot heights. Pygmy corn grows near Lake Titicaca at nearly 13,000 feet, while in the tropical lowland belt thrives a large-eared variety with normal kernels. Perhaps this latter spread to Central America. Many experts claim Mexican origin for corn. Mexico's teosinte grass crosses readily with maize and was formerly thought to be its ancestral form. Also, maize was more vital to Mexico than Peru because it competed with fewer food crops. But Peru has more kinds of corn than anywhere else.

In the high altitude belt, among their potatoes Indians plant other root crops: the oca, a relative of our sheep sorrel; anu, kin to the flowering nasturtium; and allucu, of the Madeira vine family. Another root crop, the yacon, like the Jerusalem artichoke, grows in the lower altitude of the potato belt. Below 6,000 feet a series of sweet potatolike crops flourishes.

Maize, the chief seed crop, sprang abundantly from the terraces. The Andean variety, Cusco corn, has inch-wide kernels, almost the size of chestnuts, which natives eat a kernel at a time. Above 12,000 feet maize is raised in only a few places, not as a regular food, but as a luxury for making native beer, or chicha. To take the place of maize, the natives of elevated districts use plants closely related to one of our common weeds, called "pigweed" or "lamb's-quarters."

Near the Pass of La Raya, two varieties of pigweed thrive. One, quinoa, growing three or four feet tall, is used for chicha making as well as providing a breakfast cereal somewhat like oatmeal. Cañihua, smaller, has gray seeds which Indians grind into flour—a ration for shepherds on the high plateaus.

Peru's Indians today, looking in awe upon the terraced wonders their far-distant ancestors built, no longer know the secret of their construction. The art has passed from this hemisphere.

It reached its highest point with the early Incas. Theirs are the finest walls with the tightest fit between masonry blocks. Later Inca terraces appear to have been hastier jobs—stones merely bedded in dirt and faced with clay to give a smooth appearance.

But if late Incas lowered construction standards, they also organized agriculture to a high level, assuring bountiful crops to support a great population free from want. Rulers controlled the land and its uses, keeping an eye on every farm activity from planting to harvesting. Public storehouses were maintained, not only in towns and cities, but along highways and in lofty passes between the valleys, to ensure that the surplus from one area speedily made good for crop failure in another.

When the country was devastated by the Spaniards, "the chiefs assembled, the *quipus* [knotted-cord records] were examined and checked, and if one province had lost more than another, that which had suffered less made up the difference; so that the burden was shared equally by all," says the account of Cieza de Leon, written about 1550. "To this day these accounts are kept in each valley, and there are always as many accountants as there are lords, and every four months the accounts are made up and balanced."

Inca religion aimed largely at improving crops. Feeling that prosperity of all depended on the wealth of the Inca, every farmer made sure the royal larder was filled, the regal acres fertile. Even today Peru's rural Indians buy medicinal and aromatic plants at market so they can make burnt offerings—"paying the Incas"—and be assured of good crops and healthy flocks. They bury small images of clay or metal in the ground—models of fields and farmsteads with rows of sheep and cattle.

At the time of the conquest, Peru's farm system had given its people a way to live and let others live. Converted to agriculture as an ideal of existence, they were freer from predatory instincts than Europeans. Looting Spaniards suffered by comparison.

A few realized they were destroying something that could not be replaced. One old conquistador, last of Pizarro's band, wrote a deathbed "confession" to his king, describing the Inca realm, with "neither a thief, nor a vicious man, nor a bad, dishonest woman. . . .

"Crimes were once so little known among them," he continued, "that an Indian with one hundred thousand pieces of gold and silver in his house, left it open, only placing a little stick across the door, as the sign that the master was out, and nobody went in. But when they saw that we placed locks and keys on our doors, they understood that it was from fear of thieves, and when they saw that we had thieves amongst us, they despised us."

**Ancient Maya Carved a God Sowing Maize**

This Guatemalan stone figure with maize headdress (page 182) symbolizes the importance of corn to ancient civilizations in the New World. Indian corn fed hungry Pilgrim settlers on New England shores; it remains an important American food contribution to the world.

SYLVANUS GRISWOLD MORLEY, CARNEGIE INSTITUTION

# SOLVING SECRETS O

PUEBLO BONITO, "*Beautiful Village,*" *rises in magnificent relief beneath sandstone walls of New Mexico's Chaco Canyon. Called the foremost prehistoric ruin in the United States, it stands 100 miles south of Mesa Verde's cliff dwellings, 100 miles north of Zuni towns, 100 miles east of Hopi pueblos. Ancient crossroads, high point of early Pueblo culture, Pueblo Bonito was at last unearthed and fully described by seven National Geographic Society expeditions, 1921–27.*

*Smithsonian archeologist* NEIL M. JUDD, *who led the work, relates how he reconstructed the life of the forgotten builders of the apartment city. To date the ruin, three other National Geographic expeditions, 1923, 1928, 1929, collected beams from some 40 Indian ruins to extend a "tree ring calendar" back to Pueblo Bonito's time. Astronomer* ANDREW ELLICOTT DOUGLASS *describes finding the key beam that closed the gap in a thousand-year chronology.*

*But mysteries still remain in the Southwest. Giant figures, visible only from the air, sprawl on high mesa tops on the California-Arizona border. National Geographic Society Trustee* GENERAL GEORGE C. MARSHALL *tells of seeing the gravel effigies. At his suggestion the Society sent an expedition to study them, resulting in a fascinating theory of their origin and purpose.*

## CHAPTER 16

# HE SOUTHWEST

## EXPLORING PUEBLO BONITO

BY NEIL M. JUDD

THERE IS IMMEASURABLE JOY in starting work on a gigantic rock pile, the accumulation of fallen walls and centuries of wind-blown sand, and finding a series of ancient dwellings unfolding.

Pueblo Bonito again stands clearly outlined on Chaco Canyon's floor. A hundred thousand tons of earth and stone and sand have been carted away. Summer after summer, from 1921 to 1927, we dug deeper into a maze of empty rooms, repaired broken walls, pieced together the life of an unknown people.

This ruined desert apartment house—a city within itself—is one of the most remarkable Indian achievements in the United States. No other apartment building of comparable size existed in Amer-

**Walls Rise Again** as Pueblo Bonito emerges from the ruin of centuries. Excavation often found several building eras layered on the same spot. Kiva "Q," by its circular shape, must have been built by the Late Bonitians. Indian belief required it to be at a lower level than dwellings it replaced, for its floor roofed the earlier world from which men ascended to the earth. This kiva is one of more than 30 uncovered at the three-acre site.

National Geographic Society expeditions unearthing Pueblo Bonito devoted much time to repairing or rebuilding walls to protect excavated rooms from weather damage. Mud plaster still clings to some original walls. So skillfully did foreman Jack Lavery imitate the ancient masons' work that Zuni laborers nicknamed him *Enote Nahme*, "Prehistoric Grandfather."

O. C. HAVENS

ica until the Spanish Flats were erected in 1882 at 59th Street and Seventh Avenue in New York City. Its foundations cover as much ground as the United States Capitol. In its heyday it housed perhaps 1,200 people and contained fully 800 rooms, terracing back from two inner courts like giant steps to outer walls four stories high.

Toward the last these walls had neither doors nor windows. A fortress, beleaguered, desperate, Pueblo Bonito could be entered or left only by ladder.

Outside, low earth ridges trapped water flooding down from the mesas after midsummer thunderstorms, irrigating fields of corn, beans, squash. Rainfall ruled the city's prosperity, just as a thousand years later it governed our excavations. When the rain god smiled, 35 or more Indians, ten white men, and eight or nine horses kept busy in the ruins. But when hot July winds chased clouds beyond the horizon, our labor force shrank and we measured our well twice a day.

Our Navajo neighbors came in with lard buckets, canvas bags, even barrels to complain that their water holes were dry. We shared our meager supply and agreed that the whole country had been drying up ever since the white men arrived. When they returned with all their goats and horses, we clamped on the lid and told them to dig their own wells deeper.

Then there was the mother-in-law problem. I'm sure no previous National Geographic Society expedition was ever thus bedeviled. The Navajo believe that a man goes blind if he looks upon his wife's mother. Whenever the mother-in-law of one of our Navajo workmen passed by, he would abruptly turn his back, drop his shovel, and pull his shirt over his head until she disappeared.

Day by day—from potsherd, fragment of worked stone, charred beam—we filled in the life of this ancient people who left no written records save some unintelligible cliff markings.

Just as Pueblo women still grind a daily ration of Indian corn between two milling stones, so Pueblo Bonito housewives crunched the precious yellow maize kernels, mixed primitive corn meal dough and cooked it over rooftop fires.

They tanned skins and wove blankets, cotton cloth, and fiber sandals. They shaped and polished the most beautiful prehistoric pottery found anywhere in the United States, decorating it with thin black lines against a white surface. Mothers early taught their young, for we found miniature ladles and pitchers imprinted by baby fingers just learning the art of working long ropes of clay into useful and decorative vessels.

Men tilled the fields and hunted game atop the mesas. Whether at work or play, Pueblo Bonito's men and women brightened cheeks with brick-red rouge dug from compacted clay beneath sandstone cliffs.

While men controlled the ceremonial and religious life of the community in their deep, circular kivas, it was the women who headed household life and brooked no interference in domestic matters. Not only did they own their homes, they also built them—a custom that survives in pueblos to this day.

Of course men helped. They cut and carried stone, felled timber, and seated huge roof beams on the walls. Also, male societies apparently built their own kivas. This might explain why kiva masonry is frequently inferior to that of the dwellings: Pueblo Bonito women were better masons than their husbands.

We found Pueblo Bonito's history in its walls. The crudest were more mud than stones. Then builders began rubbing sandstone blocks smooth on the outer face and chinking cracks between with rock chips. Finally, thin stone blocks were fitted tight and true into walls that needed almost no mortar.

Pueblo Bonito shows two distinct eras in building. The first inhabitants, whom we call the Old Bonitians, began a cluster of crudely built houses in the ninth or early tenth century. Then came some near-strangers, the Late Bonitians. Ap-

**Master Masonry** characterized Pueblo Bonito's golden age, A.D. 1050–1130. Ancient wall builders gave smooth facings to inner cores of stone and adobe rubble, laying shaped stones horizontally, so perfectly fitted they needed no mortar. Many such walls still stand, 800 years later.

NATIONAL GEOGRAPHIC PHOTOGRAPHER J. BAYLOR ROBERTS

parently welcomed in, they at once began rebuilding the pueblo. To these progressive people the great terraced structure owes its final form. Master masons and potters, hewers of wood and stone, they changed, enlarged, strengthened, tore down, and rebuilt with utter disregard for the work involved. What they willed, they did.

These men even had the self-confidence to brace up with puny logs and stones a gigantic cliff, tons of solid rock, that threatened to topple upon their homes. This colossally naïve feat of ancient American engineering gave Pueblo Bonito its Navajo name: *Tse-biya hani ahi,* "Place-of-the-braced-up-cliff."

Such tireless energy made Pueblo Bonito famous. Vendors of brilliant macaws came from Mexico's tropical forests, and native dealers in sea shells from the Pacific coast. They took back with them *chalchihuitl,* turquoise. Then as now Indians of the Southwest prized this stone above all else. Turquoise, symbol of the blue desert sky, spirit of mystic oceans and vaulted heavens!

We felt something of that when we came upon a turquoise treasure (frontispiece). The day my trowel cut away earth to reveal a breathtaking necklace, every Indian on the site, as if by telepathy, dropped his shovel and draped himself over the wall to watch what was going on deep in the room below. They talked in whispers as our tiny brushes swept away the sand. At last the blue-green stones shone out in all their ancient splendor. Reverent murmurs and exclamations rose from the spectators.

Who knows what cost of life and labor went into obtaining the rough, unworked stones; how many hours it took to shape 2,500 beads by rubbing them back and forth across sandstone tablets, to pierce them by drilling each with sharpened flint or other tool!

With such jewels, with corn ripening in the fields or drying on the housetops, Pueblo Bonito was attacked again and again by covetous nomadic tribes. Lone garden workers were slain seeking shelter, boys and young women taken captive and dragged away as slaves. Even the

**Tell-tale Beams** form a precise Chaco Canyon calendar. A thousand years ago weather left its permanent record in trees that gave Indians these ceiling poles. Their inner rings date this house in Pueblo del Arroyo, unearthed a few hundred feet from Pueblo Bonito, as exactly as if it boasted an engraved cornerstone. The oldest such beam from Pueblo Bonito sprouted as a pine sapling in the year 700. It was 219 years old when it felt the bite of a Bonitian's stone ax.

To Zuni and Navajo workmen, reading tree rings seems as mysterious as foretelling an eclipse of the sun. The ancient builders of canyon towns the workmen unearthed had no written language and left no man-made calendars.

O. C. HAVENS

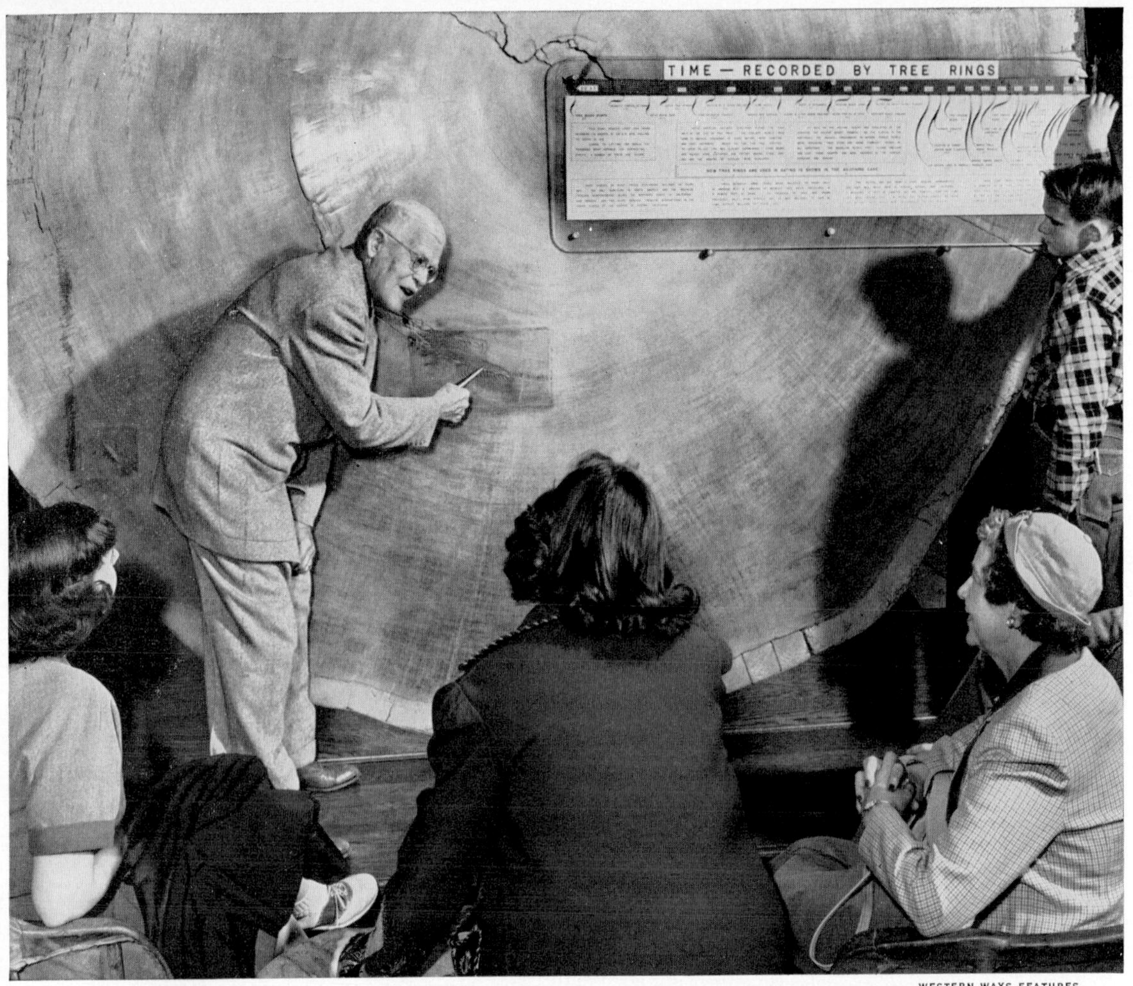


WESTERN WAYS FEATURES

**One Tree Records 1,700 Years of History.** Dr. A. E. Douglass, who first dated Southwest ruins by tree rings, points to a mark left in a sequoia by a fire, A.D. 634. Trees add a new layer of wood each year just under the bark. Climate varies the ring width, leaving indelible testimony of rain or drought. Dendrochronology, this astronomer's gift to archeology, now can trace climate back to A.D. 11 in ancient pine and fir beams from Indian ruins. Another calendar runs through California's "Big Trees" back to before 1,000 B.C. This 10-foot tree, born A.D. 211, fell in 1915.

solid outer wall did not always shield these urban farmers. Hand-to-hand struggles must have been waged in the inner plazas; hafted stone axes and wooden war clubs crushed brown bodies; flint-tipped arrows sought out crouching defenders of the terraced city.

Famine thinned the defenders' ranks as long dry years parched the fields. The soil itself became permeated with alkali, making agriculture impossible. Sealed in their canyon by marauders, they could neither cultivate distant farms nor support themselves through barter.

We found burial rooms that tell a mute story of pillage. Skulls tossed aside, arms and legs torn from bodies crushed on their burial mats, burial offerings overturned and trampled. All this happened shortly before, or just after, the city was finally deserted by its builders.

Invariably I am asked, How old is Pueblo Bonito? When was it built? When abandoned? Answers to these questions came with astonishing exactness when Dr. Douglass turned tree rings into a calendar that dated not only Pueblo Bonito but scores of ruins in the Southwest.

# TREE RING CALENDARS

**BY ANDREW ELLICOTT DOUGLASS**

ANCIENT ORAIBI, crumbling into ruin, baked under an Arizona noon sun. Like Hopi tribesmen of long ago, we entered an abandoned three-story house on its second floor, over a terrace of old rooms now filled with rubbish.

A flat stone lay in the middle of the floor. Lifted away, it revealed a hole into the room below. The sweepings of years from the room above had filled the lower space until there remained only three feet of headroom. I swung down and with a flashlight looked around.

In the center stood an upright post, not more than six inches thick. It held up the floor above, and thus could not be cut. But it seemed stout enough to be bored, so with excitement I watched the tubular core drill bite through at the point of greatest diameter.

That same evening the bit of wood told its story. The post had been cut as early as A.D. 1370; it had supported its ceiling generation after generation for well over 500 years. Before that, its annual growth rings traced clearly the years the tree grew in some long-forgotten pine forest, across unmistakable signs of the Great Drought in the last decades of the preceding century to an earliest recognizable ring from the year 1260.

Our tree ring timetable of the past had reached a new and significant point. We were coming close to the elusive era when Pueblo Bonito was built under the cliffs of Chaco Canyon. But even this new find was not old enough, not as old as we needed.

In the year-by-year growth of ancient trees we had found a key to open the past. Because climate is indelibly recorded in tree rings—scant or abundant rainfall means lean or fat growth rings—certain ring sequences become recognizable, tree to tree, forest to forest, even beyond the range of living trees to the ancient firs and pines felled for beams by the stone axes of prehistoric housebuilders.

In 1922, when the National Geographic Society's great work was just beginning in Pueblo Bonito under Neil M. Judd, tree ring dating was also in its earliest stages. Pueblo Bonito was found to be some 40 years older than Aztec Ruin, 65 miles to the north. But this was only relative age; no meaningful dates could be assigned to either.

Mr. Judd felt that enough old timbers could be found to establish a continuous calendar reaching back from living forests to beams in the oldest pueblos. Thus with the single goal of dating Pueblo Bonito, three National Geographic Society expeditions set out over the next seven years to find the needed timbers.

We took hundreds of borings and sec-

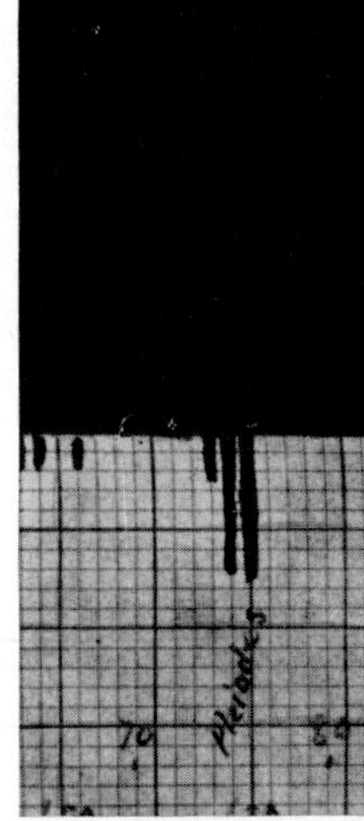

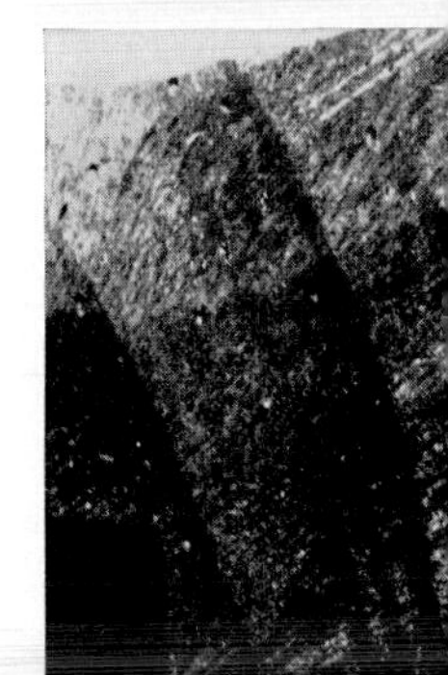

**Charred Rings of HH39,** key to Pueblo Bonito's past. This historic beam section found at Showlow, Arizona, completed the tree ring calendar that solved dating secrets of the Southwest. The ring beneath the arrow grew A.D. 1247; the star (right) shows 1275, beginning of the Great Drought.

How this missing link tied together two separate chronologies is shown in the field charts above. Longer lines represent years of extreme drought, shorter lines less severe years. The upper, "modern" chronology, was anchored in time. Lower chart shows latter part of the "floating" chronology, a record of ancient beams interrelated in time but not specifically tied to a calendar date. The Showlow sequence, reproduced at its right end, matched the oldest part of the modern chronology, groove by groove, year by year!

ANDREW ELLICOTT DOUGLASS

tions from giant tree stumps in old forests, from carved beams Pueblo Indians had salvaged from Spanish missions they destroyed in 1680, from stone-hewn timbers in pueblos still occupied, studied and fitted them into a calendar which, by the end of our 1928 season, reached back to the year 1260.

Meanwhile, from even more ancient Indian sites—Mummy Cave, Wupatki and Citadel, from Mesa Verde, and Chaco Canyon itself—we pieced together a second chronology, one continuous prehistoric sequence 585 years in length.

Nowhere did this earlier calendar appear to overlap with our modern sequence. Reluctantly, we called the new calendar a "floating" chronology. The search began for a link between the two, the bridge from present to past.

We tried very old living pines, even offering a reward for any tree 600 years of age, but without success. We tried to match our floating sequence with the long-lived California sequoia, but no clear correlation could be made.

At Oraibi, oldest continuously inhabited Hopi pueblo, we found some ancient-looking floor planks in a kiva still used for tribal ceremonies. The boards could neither be removed nor cut without offending the gods. With a gasoline lantern I spent seven hours one night lying flat on my stomach with a lens in my eye, nose almost touching the boards, counting and measuring their rings. No avail—they were far too young.

Even to gain access to many beams required high diplomacy. To the Oraibi Chief, Tawa-Guap-Tiwa, I took a present of purple chiffon velvet, so lovely that I was afraid to show it to Mrs. Douglass for fear it would never get to the Indian reservation. Many times we had to appease Indian spirits by placing a piece of turquoise in the hole from which a core was taken, to keep the "spirit of decay" out of the timber.

But it gradually became clear that none of the occupied Hopi pueblos was old enough to link our two chronologies. It was necessary to find the locality

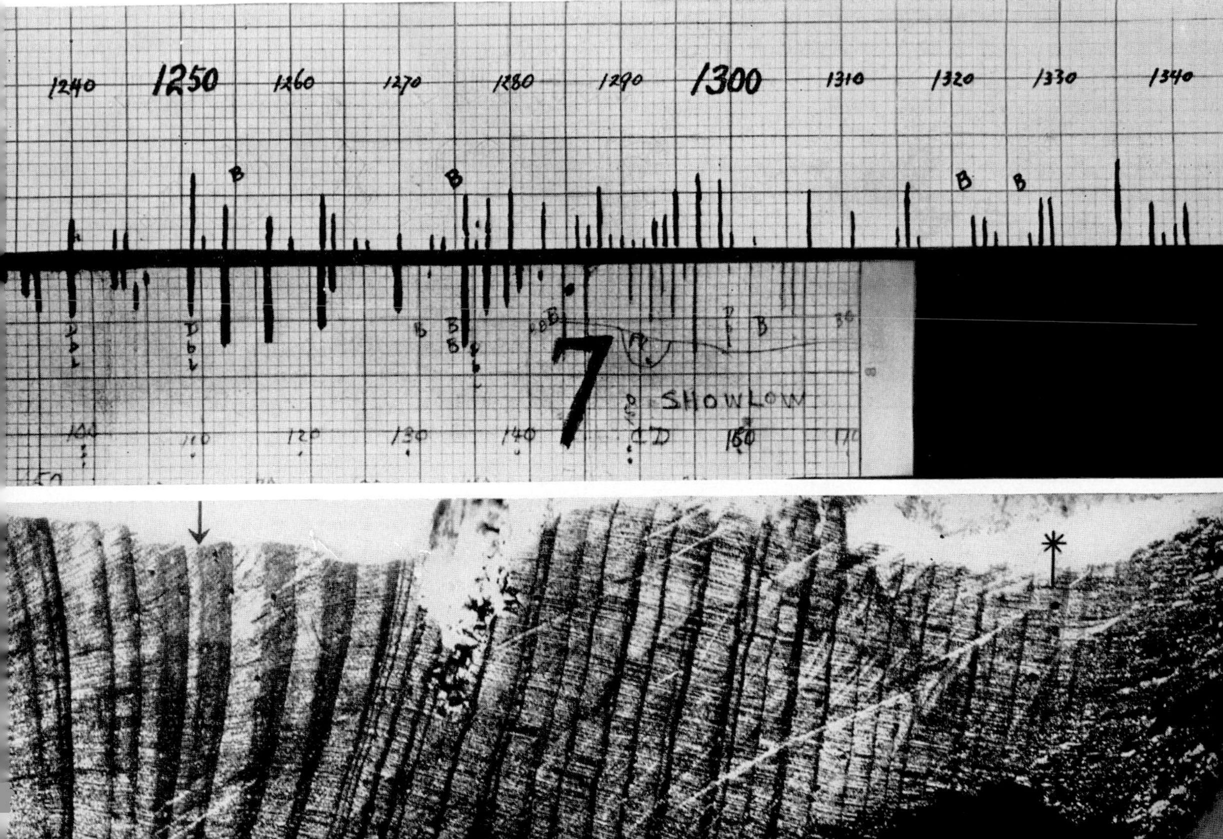

from which the Hopi had last migrated.

Early in 1929 we selected four ruins—Kokopnyama in the Jadito Valley, Kintyel to the southeast, Showlow and Pinedale 100 miles south. Shards of an early orange-colored Hopi pottery had come from each, pointing to the period we wanted.

Showlow, now a thriving Mormon town, takes its name from an early-day cowboy bet. From its buried Indian ruin, pieces of charred wood had been reported—ancient wood!

Charred or half-burned beams were readable to us by that time. We dipped such pieces in paraffin and gasoline, and by delicate handling could study their blackened rings. Even the first charcoal fragments from Showlow seemed, on preliminary examination, to hold tree rings in both the historic and prehistoric sequences.

The day Mr. Judd and I arrived on the site, yet another log was unearthed. We bound it carefully with cotton twine, but even so the timber crumbled almost at touch. Our "solid" log was a mere cone of charcoal with most of the unburned wood decayed away. We numbered it HH39.

Its outermost rings clearly dated to the 1300's, from our fixed chronology. Following the rings inward, we found the unmistakable record—very small rings—that told of hardships the tree had endured in 1299, 1295, the drought years of the 1280's and the 1270's.

Then came the years of the seventh decade of that century. Their rings agreed in every detail with those of the Oraibi beam. But whereas that beam could tell us nothing back of 1260, Showlow's HH39 did not stop there. Here was 1258, a hard year, and 1254, even harder. Likewise, 1251 and 1247 were dry.

Finally, the very core! This charred old stick began life A.D. 1237, just ten years after the Sixth Crusade sailed to battle the Saracens for Jerusalem.

The history within that carbonized bit of ancient beam held us spellbound. We tried to joke about it, but failed miserably. Later that evening we gathered under the spluttering gasoline lamp in the village hotel to determine whether this was really the tie between our new and old chronologies.

From the rings the answer soon came. Year 551 in our "floating" sequence matched perfectly with year 1251 in Beam HH39. And then the surprise! We had no gap to bridge; it had already been closed. Our two chronologies overlapped. But the last rings of the old series were taken from such small fragments that I had never accepted the evidence. HH39 cleared all doubts.

By the time I finally slept, I knew that our calendar reached back now to A.D. 700; that the earliest beam found in Pueblo Bonito was cut from a tree felled in 919; that the Late Bonitians had come probably between 1025 and 1050. I knew that the "Beautiful Village" reached its golden age of construction by 1066, the year William the Conqueror faced Harold the Saxon at Hastings, and that it was still occupied in 1127. By the end of the Great Drought in 1299, Pueblo Bonito almost certainly was empty, sands piling high around its silent walls.

To the American Southwest, Beam HH39 matches Egypt's famous Rosetta Stone. It unlocked the hieroglyphics of the past—in this case the rings of trees.

From it we have been able to date Pueblo Bonito and, more recently, beams reaching back to A.D. 11. Tree rings have given us an accurate chronology of ancient Pueblo culture, a key to the mysterious migrations of these prehistoric peoples. Attacking nomads, drought, and the heavy hand of starvation pushed them on. The pine forests that once grew on the borders of Chaco Canyon died or were cut away; but beams long preserved in dead cities of the Southwest tied together climate and human history.

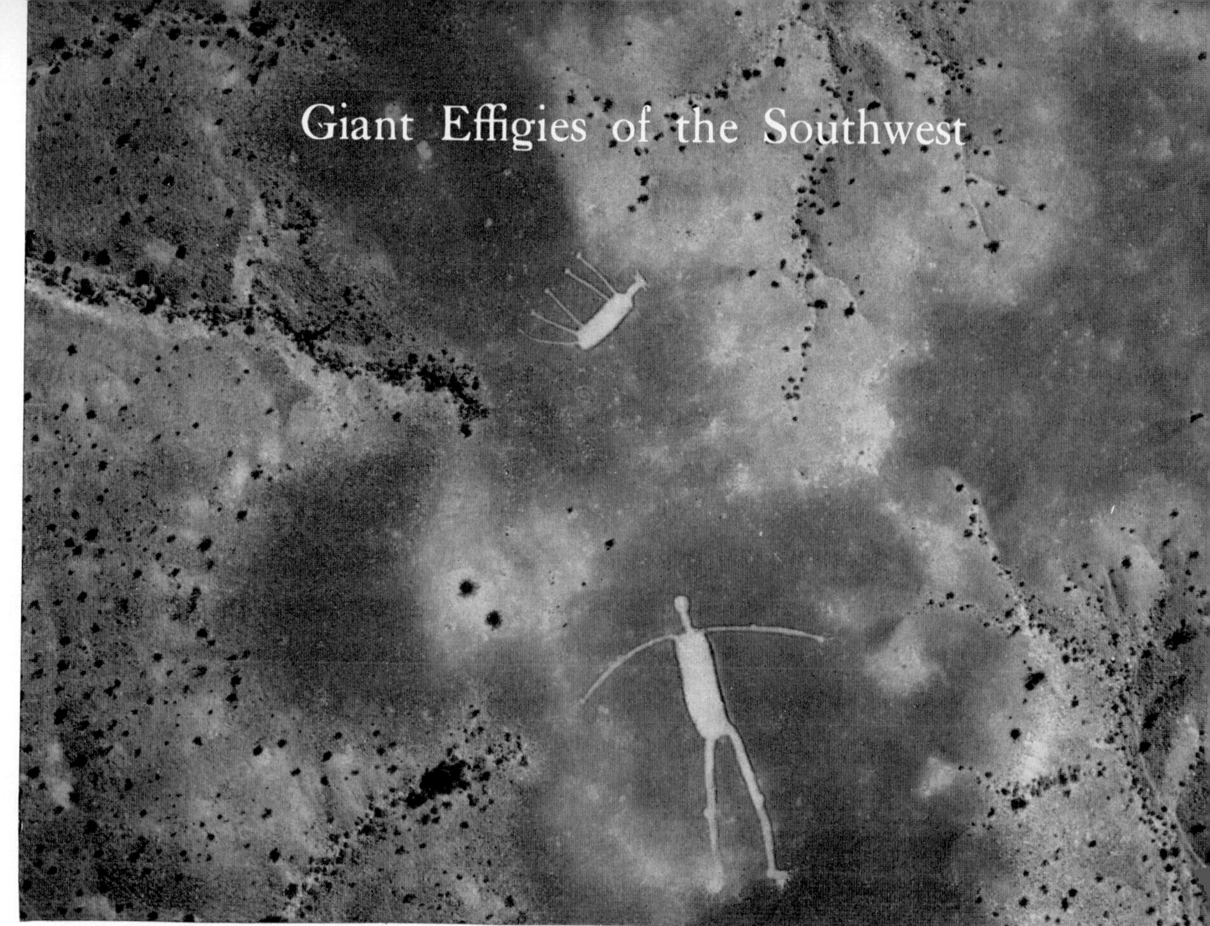

# Giant Effigies of the Southwest

BY GENERAL OF THE ARMY GEORGE C. MARSHALL

OUR PLANE DRONED across the southern California desert in 1943. Gen. Henry H. Arnold, then Commanding General of our Army Air Forces, glanced down at the rumpled mesas and turned.

"Have you ever seen the great effigies near Blythe?" he inquired.

I had not even heard of them. He told me then that on a bluff above the small California town of Blythe, a local pilot, George Palmer, had discovered several great figures outlined in the rocky soil. One appeared to represent a man; others depicted animals.

The curious thing about them was this: So huge were they in outline and so shallow in indentation that they were virtually invisible to anyone standing only a few yards away. Nor were there any hills near enough for a full view. In short, not even their creators could ever have glimpsed their handiwork's total design. This would have been plain only to the gods of the mesa, a passing bird—or people in airplanes, surely an unforeseen invention.

"One of our young pilots brought back a startling photograph [above]," General Arnold said. "Would you like to see what that picture showed?"

We changed course, and soon we were scanning the ridges sloping back from the lower Colorado River above Blythe. Then we saw them: gravel sculptures such as few men had ever laid eyes on—simple in outline, childish in form, yet so gigantic as to take one's breath away.

The sight left me a lasting impression. Who made the effigies? What was their purpose? Here lay a riddle for the National Geographic Society and the Smithsonian Institution to solve!

A GIGANTIC FIGURE SPRAWLS ON THE BROAD, BARE MESA above the Colorado River in southern California, its arms and legs outflung as if for some interminable sun bath. Not far away a misshapen four-legged creature, an odd circle, and a scraggly ellipse mark the desert. In 1932 a civilian flyer first saw these strange figures; later, airline pilots reported others. Who made them, and for what forgotten gods of the sky, no one knew.

In 1951 a National Geographic Society-Smithsonian Institution expedition led by Frank M. Setzler, Head Curator of the Smithsonian's Department of Anthropology, went into desert country to find and study these mysterious, lonely figures. The U.S. Air Force lent a patrol plane, helicopter, and radio truck. In some places the shallow desert sculptures proved to be furrows of dark-brown gravel scraped away from the lighter underlying mesa. In others, paths were stamped in the gravel by moccasined feet. Automobile tracks criss-crossed a few figures, but many seemed unchanged since the time they had been shaped.

Could the four-legged figure be the late Pleistocene horse of 10,000 years ago? Probably not. The great Blythe "horses" have no patina, or "desert varnish." This black-brown coating, baked by the desert sun, comes from the action of certain lichens. It takes less than 10,000 years to form. Thus, since the Pleistocene horse was already extinct, and the European horse unknown to the Indians until after the Spanish came in 1540, the figures must have been made since the 16th century.

The huge effigies—one stretches 170 feet—must have been created by a populous, settled society. Nomads would scarcely take such pains on desert images, then wander on. After 1540, the leading sedentary Indians along the lower Colorado River were Yuman-speaking tribes. The "missing link" was found when Yuman mythology was traced backward from a Pima desert effigy known as Hâ-âk, southeast of Phoenix, Arizona. Legend recounts that Hâ-âk, a ferocious child-eating female monster, was slain by the all-powerful "Elder Brother" summoned by panic-stricken Indians. Mr. Setzler's conclusion: Yuma artists shaped the grotesque California figures—a shrine to Hâ-âk and her destroyer, Elder Brother—between 1540 and the mid-1800's.

NATIONAL GEOGRAPHIC PHOTOGRAPHER RICHARD H. STEWART

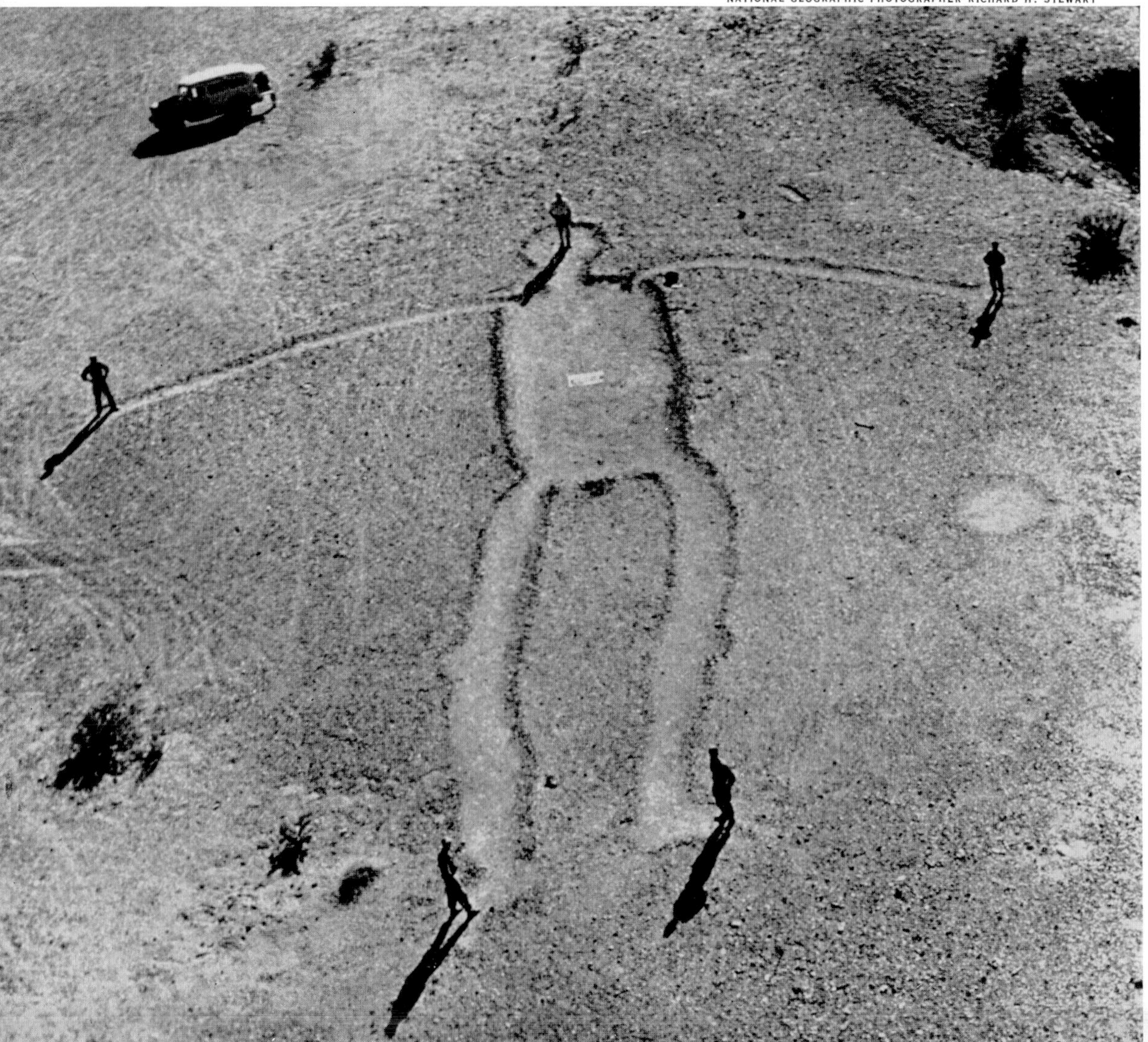

# PART III

# INDIANS TODAY FROM AMAZON TO ARCTIC

KODACHROME BY CLIFFORD EVANS AND BETTY J. MEGGERS

*SYMBOL OF A WAY OF LIFE, Yukuma stalks fish from a dugout on the Essequibo in British Guiana. Legs decorated with plant juice, torso touched with red to ward off harmful forest spirits, this Wai Wai bowman weaves his own loincloth, lives in harmony with his surroundings. Civilization calls him "uncivilized," but who knows better the ways of fish, bird, and jungle animal than Yukuma? The white man's beads and knives are welcome—even the white man's God. But Yukuma will keep his own too: the god who created the Wai Wai, and the other god responsible for white men and everything else, including the airplane Yukuma occasionally hears overhead.*

*Like most tropical forest Indians, Yukuma's hunting-and-fishing people live in small isolated groups, follow a simple, rugged pattern of communal agriculture. Land must be torn from the forest by brute force. Even then the jungle never quite lets go. In two or three years the soil wears out; the natives must move on, hack new clearings, build another settlement. Through the vast Amazon and Orinoco basins, through Panama's narrow waist, and the humid coastal plains of Central America, the rain forest puts a common stamp on Indian life. Highland ways are different. The dweller in arid western Andes is worlds apart from the head-hunting Jivaro of rain-drenched eastern slopes. How strange life among the Chocós of steaming Darién would seem to a Mexican highlander! Yet differences are often of degree rather than kind.*

*Both Guiana lowlander and Guatemalan highlander farm. Cassava cakes correspond to tortillas. But intensive maize cultivation supports large upland populations. Permanent villages, individual homes, elected officials contrast with scattered extended-family groups living in communal jungle huts. Wai Wai abandon fields and change wives frequently; Guatemala Indians almost never. Primitive cosmology contrasts with organized ritual. Sedentary Guatemalans seem ever treading hairpin roads that rise to 10,000 feet; seminomadic rain forest dwellers seldom journey far, seldom trade. While rudimentary agriculture and pottery making have only reached Essequibo country since the 16th century, the Guatemala Indian draws on 2,000-year-old Maya skills. Handicraft specialization brings trade and the weekly market, leading highland social event.*

## CHAPTER 17

# INDIANS OF SOUTH AND CENTRAL AMERICA

*IN SEARCH OF "LIVE" ARCHEOLOGY, a husband and wife team of Smithsonian archeologists pushed into southernmost British Guiana, vast, empty homeland of some 60 Wai Wai, the colony's most primitive tribe.* CLIFFORD EVANS *and* BETTY J. MEGGERS *describe these festive pygmy-size people as they found them, sharing their daily rounds. Turning the coin to reveal a contrasting culture,* LUIS MARDEN, *National Geographic writer-photographer, shows the numerous Indians of Guatemala living for church and market and perpetuating ancient arts and crafts.*

## THE WAI WAI OF GUIANA

**BY CLIFFORD EVANS and BETTY J. MEGGERS**

FAR BENEATH OUR DC-3 British Guiana's dense green jungle unrolled. Skimming above it, we could not help feeling that we were flying backward in time—back to that mysterious age before white men set foot in the New World.

Suddenly our plane lurched to a stop on Gunn's Landing Strip, a dirt runway scratched from the wilderness in the Crown Colony's far south, almost on the Equator. Looking out, we caught our first glimpse of the Indians. They stood by the runway, their light-brown skins glistening with red paint.

Short and stocky, they were as small as Central Africa's pygmies. In their simple breechclouts and aprons, and carrying long bows, they would not have seemed out of place to Columbus save for the strings of glass trade beads girdling necks, legs, and arms.

These were the Wai Wai we had traveled so far to study. Carib-speaking aborigines, they are the only uncivilized people left in British Guiana. Beside them stood two American missionaries, come to welcome us and lend a hand as interpreters. Soon we were pushing through the "big bush," then up the Essequibo to the missionary settlement.

At dawn several days later we loaded a dugout and set out on our first exploratory trip upriver. Our guide was Charlie, a civilized Wapishana Indian from the savanna who had married a Wai Wai. His English words were few, and conversation was limited.

Charlie was good-natured and willing, but a poor provider. Civilization had robbed him of the art of silently stalking game in the forest. Whenever he went off hunting, distant shots would raise our hopes. Nearly always he returned to camp empty-handed.

"What happened?" we would ask.

"Me shoot monkey," he would answer gloomily. "Him stay, hang by tail."

Provisions began to run low, so we looked for a Wai Wai hunter. Yukuma, a young stalwart, took on the job, and

we arranged to pick him up at his village. We arrived hours late, but Yukuma had made no preparations. After all, what is time in the jungle?

The delay gave us a chance to visit. A single thatched, cone-shaped hut housed the whole community of ten people. Inside, feather ornaments, gourds of palm oil, and baskets hung everywhere. Cassava cakes and smoked meat were piled on racks. The ceiling itself bristled with dozens of 6-foot arrows.

Lean dogs lay tethered on special platforms along the walls. Later we were amazed to find that Wai Wai often take their pets out on leash, walking them regularly like apartment dwellers.

The hut contained no partitions. Each family occupied the space between two roof posts. Every compartment had its hearth for cooking and night warmth, smoke drifting through a roof opening.

Native hospitality demands that food be offered visitors no matter when they arrive. At Yaka Yaka, a woman dressed in bead apron, necklaces, and arm and leg bands quickly laid a mat for us, first beating it on a dog to shake out loose dirt. Before us she placed a large bowl of cassava starch and palm fruit, another of wine made from *cara* (a potatolike tuber), a steaming pot of pepper broth, and cassava bread.

The broth set our mouths afire. Fortunately, the starch drink quenched the flames, though it was about as appetizing as flour paste. The wine proved mild and sweet, but the bowl's lip curved inward, so the liquid flowed more easily into the nose than the mouth.

We noticed sleeping hammocks draped between the hut's posts. A woman's was always slung beneath her husband's we learned, for it is her duty to

**Village in the Round**

A barking dog challenges visitors to Yewara, in the remote rain forests of British Guiana. Dr. Betty Meggers and her Indian companions pause before the pole-and-thatch hut housing the entire village, one of four in Wai Wai land. Custom prescribes that they wait for a formal invitation to enter. Once inside the communal dwelling, they will immediately be offered food and drink.

On other expeditions the authors found their privacy to resemble that of the proverbial goldfish under the curious stares of primitive peoples. Not so among the Wai Wai. When Drs. Evans and Meggers first hung their hammocks under a lean-to at Mawika, not even the smallest tots came to stand and stare. Jungle etiquette on the upper Essequibo is strict.

KODACHROME BY CLIFFORD EVANS

keep the fire going all night. Among the Wai Wai labor is sharply divided between the sexes. Men build the communal house, hunt and fish, clear land, plant, and sometimes help dig crops. They weave all hammocks, baskets and cloth. Women cook, chop firewood, tend children, fetch water, weave bead aprons, spin cotton, and make cassava graters. The graters are essential, for one of the most important of woman's tasks is processing cassava from its poisonous root state to a kind of bread (page 355).

Eventually Yukuma was ready. He piled the dugout high with cooking pots, bread, sugar cane, his hammock, two bows, stacks of arrows, and shotgun. Yukuma was proud of his gun, earned by working for the missionaries. But ammunition is scarce and gun blasts frighten off the game. For daily use he relied on silent and deadly arrows. No longer did we want for fish or game. Yukuma's bow and arrow seldom missed (page 344). With dawn, when the dripping jungle rang with melodies of waking birds, we would hear him imitate a call, to which a feathered creature replied. Soon he returned with the too-talkative bird for breakfast, and a monkey to add its rich, sweet flavor to the evening stew.

Food problem solved, we rode along the broad river highway through lonely jungle. In all this vast tangle of southern British Guiana there are only the missionaries and 60 Wai Wai. These few natives live in four villages close to the Essequibo, travel by water, and seldom penetrate the jungle except to hunt. Across the Brazilian border, on headwaters of the Mapuera River, live another 60 or 70 Wai Wai of similar ways.

Paddling along, we could see a bright-blue morpho butterfly glimmering overhead. Here a pale-green spider crouched on his web of golden silk. There, high in the trees, we spotted an ant nest, a lavender orchid, an oriole's cocoonlike nest. Bats clustered on the underside of a dead branch. Now and then along the bank appeared a slide where tapirs—largest land animals in the South American jungle—came to drink.

A heron, gleaming white in a universe of green, stood on a granite outcropping, eyeing a little fish skittering over the water's surface. Flights of gaudy macaws scolded incessantly.

Swirling rapids added spice to our journey. Often we wished we understood Wai Wai, or that Charlie knew more English, as we listened to our companions debate each passage. Gestures marked the argument, while the rough stretch loomed closer. Decisions were always reserved for the last moment.

One rapid barred our way three times on a certain trip. We were relieved when first and second tries succeeded. Imagine our horror, the third time, when we found that Charlie and Yukuma had grown bored and sought a new passageway. Again we were off on a tilt with disaster. That we came through safely is a tribute to the Indians' skillful maneuvering, not to their caution.

As we worked our way upstream, we investigated sites of long-abandoned villages the Wai Wai chief recalled from his boyhood. Our pottery finds from some 30 diggings were unspectacular and relatively recent. But this was significant, for it refuted previous theories that the region might be the original source of tropical forest culture like that of the Wai Wai.

Having neither time nor words to teach Charlie and Yukuma archeological technique, we did most of the work. We sent the men hunting; otherwise they waited. At such times the contrast between the Indian who lives off the jungle and one exposed to civilization was

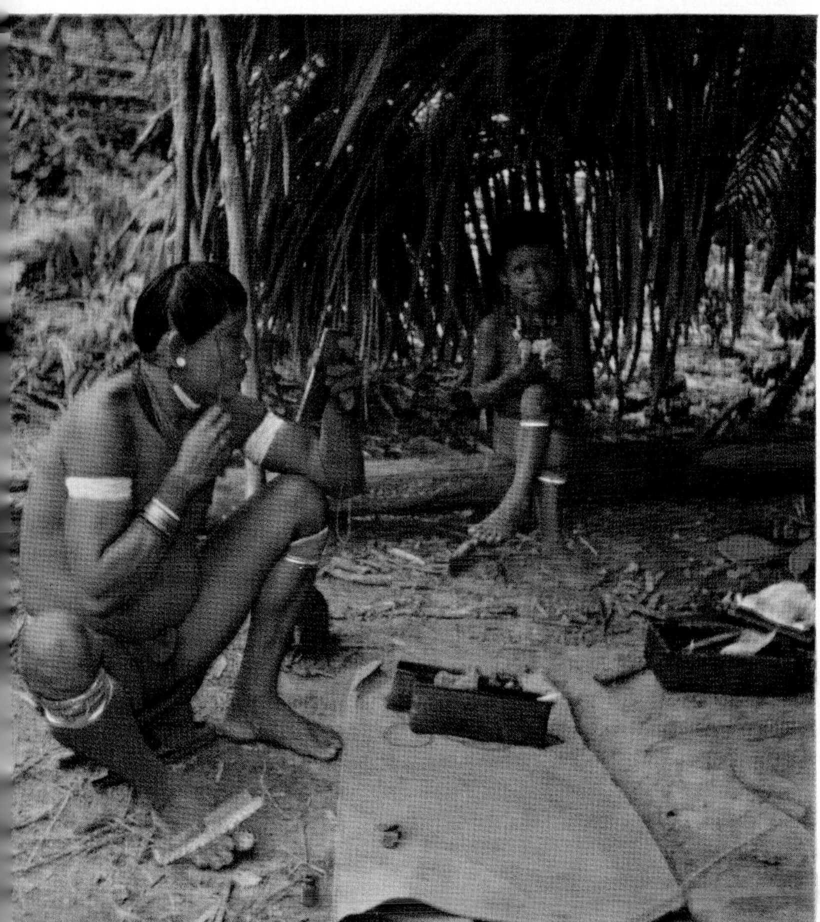

**Morning Make-up** starts a man's day right. Comb on foot, "vanity case" open before him, this Wai Wai paints shaved eyebrows, draws red designs on cheeks with tiny wooden paddle as a too-young spectator watches.

In the time-consuming daily routine, long jet-black hair must be combed and dressed heavily with palm-nut oil, then fashioned into a tight pigtail and adorned with feathers or encased in a long cane tube that hangs to the hips. Bodies are daubed red; eagle down is sprinkled on bangs. Earrings are never removed.

With white beads for arm bands, blue and white for legs, red for necklaces, the fastidious Wai Wai feels fully clothed. The women pay less attention to daily make-up.

**Primitive Artist** contrasts pot black and seed red in decorating his canoe paddle. The Wai Wai lavishly smear red on their bodies, implements, and dogs because they believe evil spirits cannot see anything painted that color. For red pigment they use the coating of the urucú seed; for black, soot mixed with cassava starch. The mixing can at the artist's knee was a contribution from civilization—eight days away by foot and canoe. His bracelets are seamed ends of smaller tin cans.

Wai Wai seldom probe the trackless jungle except to hunt. For them the Essequibo is a broad highway despite its menacing rapids. They measure distances in paddling time, or by the number of bends in the river. The Essequibo is also a handy larder. Fish abounding in the river and its backwaters are taken by poisoning, angling with steel hooks, and shooting with arrows. Harpoon heads attached to strong lines are used in the brawling rapids.

KODACHROMES BY CLIFFORD EVANS AND BETTY J. MEGGERS

striking. Charlie simply sat and watched or wandered about. Yukuma made baskets of palm leaves, sharpened the wooden points of his arrows, cleaned his gun, or practiced bird and animal calls—never at a loss for things to do.

Frequent stops for hunting and fishing delayed us. We became annoyed at what looked like overstocking. But a jungle Indian knows that lean days follow good ones. Yukuma had a special interest in hunting. His consumption of food was enormous. One day we kept record: a large bird, several pounds of smoked fish, half a huge cake of cassava bread, half a monkey, two long sticks of sugar cane, six plantains, and large quantities of pepper-pot broth!

The Wai Wai have a keen sense of humor and even enjoy a joke on themselves. Yukuma was no exception. Late one afternoon we returned to camp to find that a hawk had helped himself to our cache of smoked fish. Our provider doubled up with laughter. What a joke! To think a mere bird had outwitted the great hunter Yukuma!

Often pitching our camp near Wai Wai settlements, we found tribal courtesy shown in many ways. One of the most welcome was the privacy they allowed us. But failure to pry reflected no lack of interest. When the time seemed proper, they delighted in looking us over.

One of our camps was perched on the riverbank. Daily, women trooped by to bathe or fetch water, each carrying on her hip a child or a puppy. Often they

stopped to marvel at our camping equipment. One woman was fascinated by our canvas bucket; every trip she lingered, full of unbelief, to see if it still held water. Our Primus stove captivated another aboriginal housewife. She often appeared at mealtime to watch it perform. Once she brought her husband; from her sound effects we could tell she was describing just how it worked. All the Wai Wai enjoyed looking through the ground-glass focusing plate in our camera. They never tired of seeing people upside down drinking out of a bowl and not spilling a drop.

The Indians were much impressed by our size. One of them cut a straw the length of Cliff's foot and entertained his fellows hugely by comparing it, in clowning fashion, with his own. They were especially amused when we inadvertently copied their customs. Once we were forced by steep terrain and lack of suitable trees to hang our hammocks one above the other, native style. That sent the village into gales of laughter; everyone turned out to see that Betty's hammock was correctly placed at the bottom.

One morning we noticed something under way at a near-by pond. Investigating, we found Wai Wai poisoning fish. The fishermen had gathered quantities of a vine, one of a hundred-odd poisonous plants that South America's Indians know. Beaten to a pulp, the vines were

**Jungle Farmers** slash and burn to clear land for communal crops. Even with steel axes, felling hardwood trees is heroic work. Men burn off smaller growth, spend days chopping branches from fallen giants. Limbs, dense and wet after drying several months, must be fired repeatedly.

In a stump-strewn field, trunks lie everywhere like giant jackstraws (opposite). Hoe-wielding Indians plant cassava, sugar cane, bananas, pineapples, and tubers helter-skelter among them; further clearing would be waste time and effort, since the land will soon be abandoned. Almost never do Wai Wai return to a previous site.

Perhaps because their tillable land is so hard-won, the Indians can never understand why missionaries bother to grow flowers. The Wai Wai have no words for individual flowers, but can name every animal, bird, and fish.

Upper right: well-dressed Wai Wai's pigtail sports toucan and curassow feathers. Monkey teeth dangle at belt.

placed in a palm-leaf basket and sloshed vigorously through the water, leaving a wake of milky sap. Hardly had the Indian passed with his basket of death when small fish began to pop, gasping, to the pond's surface, for the sap paralyzes gill action. Then the excitement began. If someone tried to grab a fish, it showed sudden vigor and evaded capture. So the Indians set about with machetes and butcher knives, stunning their prey. Charlie muttered, "No good," in typical sportsman's reaction. But the Wai Wai found the tiny fish a welcome addition to their evening pepper pot.

Near our work's end, the village of Yewara, finding itself overstocked with cara, decided to convert the tubers into wine and invited the other three villages and us for a celebration. On the appointed day we heard shouting downriver. Soon dugouts streamed into the Yewara landing. Piling ashore with dogs, children and gear, the visitors set up camp. To our surprise, guests and hosts ignored each other. Yewaras came down to the river and filled their water jars as if the crowded bank were empty. By Wai Wai custom the time had not yet come to greet the guests.

Amid the hanging of hammocks and kindling of cooking fires, men busied themselves weaving long capes of palm leaves and shoulder fringes of yellow fronds. Both sexes applied fresh paint and sprinkled white eagle down on well-oiled bangs. Much testing of bark horns,

KODACHROMES BY CLIFFORD EVANS AND BETTY J. MEGGERS

**Costumed Wai Wai Hold Marathon Dance**

Party finery ranges from palm-frond capes to bright feather headdresses. Pendants in one young man's necklace are Brazilian census tags. Guests from other villages join their Yewara hosts in a festival lasting the better part of three days and nights. A shuffling, circling dance that fills waking hours is punctuated by shrill whistles and howls and frequent pauses for drinking tuber wine.

Like children everywhere, two small boys entering hut (lower left) have fun shrouding themselves in fathers' discarded capes. Heel of one betrays camouflage. Through all the intermittent din of pounding feet and primitive noisemakers, babies sleep in hammocks or in bark slings draped across mothers' shoulders.

KODACHROMES BY CLIFFORD EVANS AND BETTY J. MEGGERS

**Young Man With a Horn Tunes Up for the Festivities.** Shrill reed flutes, rattles, occasionally a harmonica add to the racket.

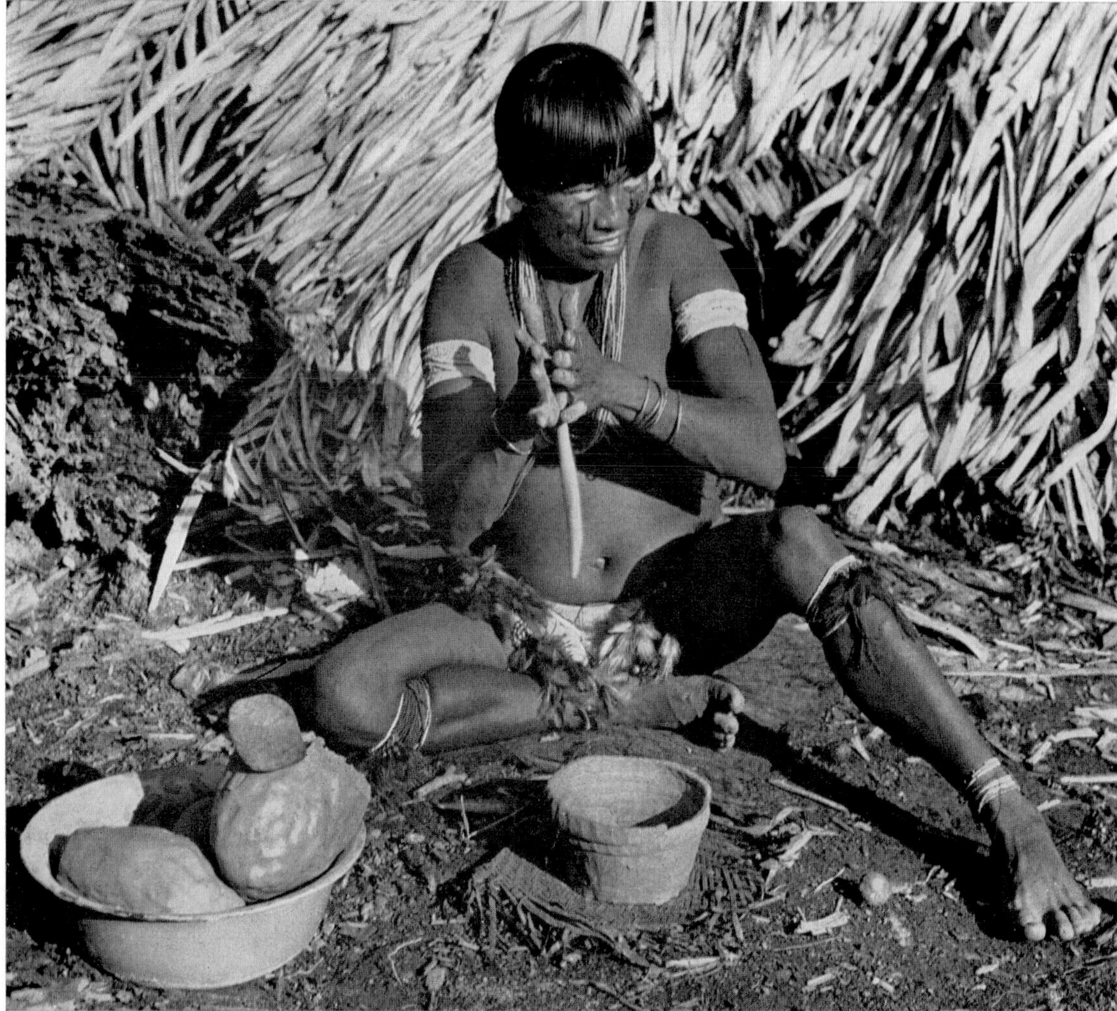

made for the occasion, filled the air with raucous counterpoint.

Dusk fell. Preparations complete, the visitors sallied forth to call on their hosts. Returning in the dark, they donned dance costumes and again climbed the village path. We crouched with them at the edge of the clearing where the men of Yewara, togged in fancy feather headdress, streamers, and leg and arm bands, were already circling single file in the fire's dim light.

Finally came the sign: the dancers stopped in front of the communal hut and stood in a line facing the clearing. Our party filed out in two lines, one for men, one for women, and amid the blaring horns the dance was on. It lasted

**Practiced Hands Make Pottery and Graters**

Like other American Indians, Wai Wai lack the potter's wheel. They coil Essequibo clay in layers, shape with fingers, smooth with a piece of gourd, and bake it in an open fire.

The woman opposite makes a cassava grater by driving stone chips into a spongy board. Later she will apply a coat of milky latex to hold the chips in. Grating is first step in turning the brown-skinned, poisonous root cassava, or manioc, into food. Stuffing the white pulp into a flexible sausagelike basket hanging from a house pole, the woman stretches the basket down with a long lever, squeezing till the deadly prussic acid juices stream out. The flour is baked on a griddle into thin, crisp cakes.

Cassava is staff of life to the tropical lowland Indian. British Guiana's savanna Indians have lost the art of making graters, so the primitive Wai Wai swap theirs with the "outsiders" for beads, knives, and other trade items.

CLIFFORD EVANS AND BETTY J. MEGGERS

three days, with the big bowl of purple wine passed frequently, and time out only for celebrators to sleep off their exhaustion.

On this festive note we left the Wai Wai to return to Georgetown, capital of British Guiana. We had come to the upper Essequibo in an hour and a half by air. It took us eight days by foot and dugout to reach civilization again. As we ended our excursion into the past, we could still echo the words of English explorer Robert Harcourt, who wrote in 1613: "The naturall inhabitants of that Countrey are a loving, tractable, and gentle people . . . with those barbarous people we may live in safety, without suspicion of trechery, or dread of danger. . . ."

But what of their future? Are the Wai Wai waging a losing fight against extinction or absorption? Smallpox or measles could wipe them out, as it did their predecessors, the Taruma. And even though they maintain their slim numbers, they can scarcely avoid influences from the outside world. Already the pottery vessel is giving way to white man's enamelware; an oil tin replaces the time-honored earthenware griddle. Few men in years ahead may see the Wai Wai as we saw them.

# TO MARKET IN GUATEMALA

**BY LUIS MARDEN**

IN THE GUATEMALA HIGHLANDS, where dark pines and lichen-covered oaks clothe the hillsides and wet gray mist swirls up from the valleys, I once met an Indian on his way to market. He was bowed under a top-heavy load of bulbous clay pots, but his dignity was unimpaired.

"Señor," he said, pointing to his thick-soled leather sandals, "you see these *caites?* Well, in the pictures, God and all the saints wear the same things. That proves Indians are the children of God."

The speaker was a living symbol of the two main concerns—religion and market—that mold the lives of the "naturals," as Guatemala's Indians call themselves. Their whole existence revolves around the religious calendar, with its feast and saints' days. When they speak to their God, prayers resemble conversation with a friend. In low-voiced monologue they talk to Him of poor crops, of family illness, and other troubles. Sometimes supplicants gesticulate fiercely, as if to say, "God, you make everything come out all right—or else!"

Going to market offers a welcome occasion for social exchange, church visiting, perhaps dancing to the sound of marimbas, besides buying and selling everything from pigs to incense, chickens and chile peppers and skirts to ceremonial masks, flutes, drums—and the inevitable tortillas, corn, and beans.

One woman, asked by a priest whether she would rather go to market or heaven, unhesitatingly chose the market.

Each highland village has its own market day. Most offer a specialty: Momostenango for blankets; Totonicapán for ribbons, belts, and Conquista-dance costumes; Chinautla for pottery. Some market centers are "empty towns"; Indians live in the surrounding countryside and gather there only for market or a fiesta.

Along roads that seem to tilt up into the sky, Indians trot under heavy loads piled on a four-legged wooden frame that hangs from a tumpline around their heads. With a metal-tipped staff to help them set down the load and to rise again, and a rolled-up palm-leaf raincape, rush sleeping mat, tin lamp, and battered coffeepot hanging to the outside, the villagers jog tirelessly along, stopping wherever night overtakes them.

So overdeveloped do bearers' calf muscles become that their short lower legs bulge like inverted brown tenpins. Some are bald from the rubbing of the tumpline. Loads of their produce or their wives' handicrafts sometimes exceed a hundred pounds, and they go 20, 30, even 50 miles to market. But no complaint, for the Guatemalan Indian is first and foremost a trader.

Pure-blooded Indians make up more than half of Guatemala's 3,800,000 population. Not for them the humid jungle that reaches north to the Mexican border or the hot coastal strips on both sides of the country. Their thatch-roofed villages of stone or adobe perch on the edges of ravines or nestle in valley hollows in the lofty region of cold blue lakes and sleeping volcanoes. From their deep forests comes the tangy smell of resin and charcoal fires.

In the 250-odd villages a race that was old when Cortés came to the New World carries on the traditional Maya pottery

**All Saints' Day in Chichicastenango.** Firecrackers pop and sizzle as St. James rides a tightrope from the belfry of Santo Tomás church. The effigy wears a necklace of 300-year-old pieces of eight; firecrackers explode in basket under his horse. On the crumbling church steps Indians rest, trade, kneel, and burn the copal incense their Maya ancestors burned to pagan gods.

KODACHROME BY LUIS MARDEN, NATIONAL GEOGRAPHIC STAFF

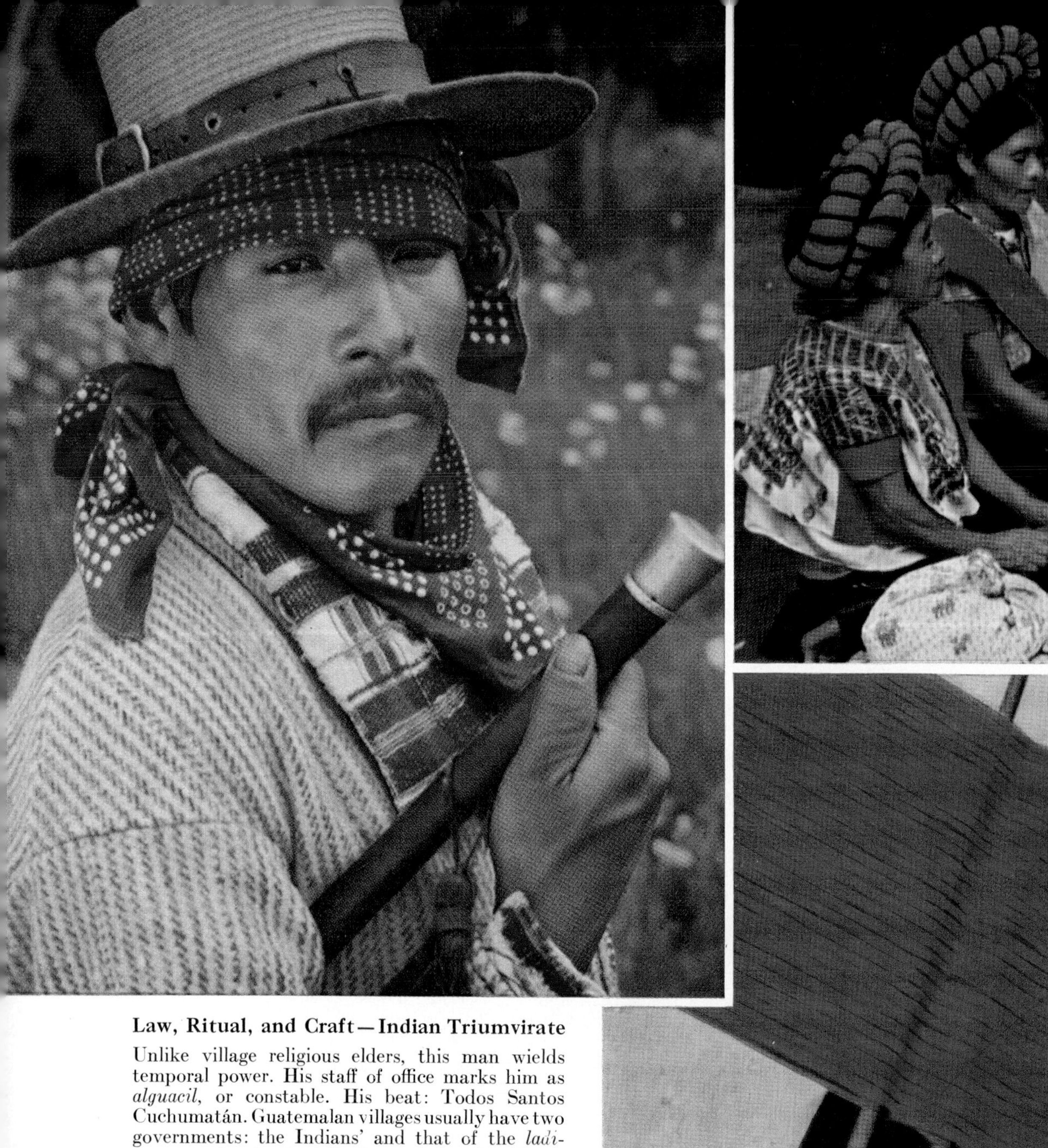

**Law, Ritual, and Craft—Indian Triumvirate**

Unlike village religious elders, this man wields temporal power. His staff of office marks him as *alguacil*, or constable. His beat: Todos Santos Cuchumatán. Guatemalan villages usually have two governments: the Indians' and that of the *ladinos*—people of mixed Indian and Spanish blood.

Women of a Palín religious group (upper right) meditate before partaking of a ceremonial meal.

Chichicastenango weaver (lower right) carries on Guatemala's famous art with ancient "hip" loom—two end sticks with warp threads stretched between. One is tied to an immovable object, the other to weaver's waist to permit adjustment of thread tension. Weavers seldom use a pattern; they work symbolic designs into fabric from memory, may weave in their initials as artists sign paintings, and leave a blank to show man's imperfections and so avoid envy of the gods. As 20th century penetrates the highlands, hand-weaving grows scarcer and villages tend to mix designs.

KODACHROMES BY LUIS MARDEN, NATIONAL GEOGRAPHIC STAFF

## Antonio Proudly Directs a Rite

Religious ceremony plays a large part in the life of this village elder, whose worship blends ancient beliefs with Roman Catholic teachings. "Our Indians want to be on good terms with God, and on not-too-bad terms with the Devil," a village padre told the author.

"It is true," the priest continued, "that they secretly pay homage to their idols, and pray to their supreme native deity, Nim Ajau, God World. He is all-pervading, everywhere, and he brings good crops and keeps a man from evil.

"Every village has its witch doctor. He pretends to deliver them from the evil designs of Ajau Juyú, the Lord of the Forest."

On a hill above Momostenango the author walked among mounds of smoke-blackened pottery fragments, the burning places or altars of God World. Through blue clouds of incense smoke he saw droning men and women kneeling before flickering flames, observing a holy day in the *tzolkin*, the 260-day Maya calendar. On the day of Eight Thread, or Eight Monkey, some 15,000 Indians come down from the hills to pray and make offerings at the burning places.

**Market Day at Nebaj** finds red-skirted women in majority. These Indians have trudged all night under loads of their specialties. Food, pottery, even coffins are sold in open market at this apple-growing center. Bargaining goes on in low tones; no one shouts his wares.

It's "business as usual" during baby's lunchtime in Sololá market (left). Behind nursing mother, men wear Sololá's traditional costume. Roosters and turkeys inspect hand-woven garments in vendors' baskets. Odor of garlic and onions reminds of the region's special produce.

Homeward bound from San Juan Sacatepéquez, women walk in "Indian file" (right). Baby rides mother's back; purchases fill baskets. Guatemalan Indians rarely walk abreast. Men wear sandals; women go barefoot.

KODACHROMES BY LUIS MARDEN, NATIONAL GEOGRAPHIC STAFF; GILES GREVILLE HEALEY (ABOVE); HELEN S. WILLIAMS (LEFT)

making, wood carving, and other handicrafts. Their hand-woven textiles have become world famous. Spaniards introduced the use of wool; before the conquest, Indians had worked only cotton. Dyes are indigo for blue, cochineal for red, brazilwood for purple, mixed chips of campeche and yellow wood for green.

Prominent in the textiles of many villages is the double-headed Hapsburg eagle of Charles V of Spain. Horsemen are represented as centaurlike beings with the man's torso sprouting directly from the horse's back. This practice stems from the early Indian belief that horse and rider were one strange animal.

Old dress remains much the same; colors run through the spectrum from deepest reds through saffron yellow to blue and violet. The woman wears a wraparound saronglike skirt, the *huipil* (a loose blouse), and shawl and headdress. Men's trousers are often striped or plaid, and topped with a gay sash or wraparound knee-length skirt. Each area, sometimes each highland village, has its own colors and costumes, and oldtimers in the Republic can tell where an Indian comes from by the way he dresses.

**Members of a Cofradía** at San Antonio Palopó appear with their patron saint before Lake Atitlán. Like other *cofradías*, this religious brotherhood cares for the church and stages festivals to honor its saint, whose image is kept in home of the chief *cofrade*. At rites they quaff a pungent ceremonial drink from a gourd, carry the saint's image outside, and dance for him, playing on drums, marimbas, and the thin-voiced *chirimía*, a sort of snake charmer's musette.

Opposite: In the clear waters of volcano-rimmed, mile-high Lake Atitlán, the hand-hewn boat seems suspended in air over vari-colored depths. The fisherman gingerly grasps one of several crabs clinging to the stale-fish bait on his trotline. Tying pincers with green rushes, stringing the crabs on a stalk, he will carry them alive to market across the 1,500-foot-deep lake.

In Guatemala City, most metropolitan of Central American capitals, brightly dressed Indians carrying loads of handicrafts or vegetables to the great mart trot unconcernedly past plate-glass windows displaying products of the machine age; in the highlands, amid the wailing of flutes and thumping of drums, kneeling Indians intone Maya chants. Guatemala today furnishes living proof that white settling of the New World did not inevitably mean extermination of the native Indian and that the two races and cultures can exist side by side in peace.

KODACHROMES BY LUIS MARDEN, NATIONAL GEOGRAPHIC STAFF

KODACHROME BY JUSTIN LOCKE

San Lorenzo Girls Rinse Corn at the Village Fountain, Favorite Tarascan Rendezvous

# CHAPTER 18

# MEXICO'S TIMELESS INDIANS

*MODERN MEXICO THROBS a song of the 20th century. Yet almost within the shadow of the capital's steel-and-glass skyscrapers, the heirs of lost civilizations live out hard, humble lives to the rhythm of an age-old refrain. No one needs a time machine to cut back through the centuries. Writer-photographer* JUSTIN LOCKE *turned off the Guadalajara-Mexico City highway to explore remnants of the Tarascan Indians' once-golden empire. He met a proud, friendly people who still hunt with prehistoric throwing sticks, fish from primitive dugouts, and kidnap brides. Entraining to remote Otomi villages northeast of the capital, Swedish anthropologist* HELGA LARSEN, *long a resident of Mexico, witnessed the perilous flying pole dance of pagan days.*

## THE TARASCANS OF LAKE PÁTZCUARO

**BY JUSTIN LOCKE**

THE PAST IS NEVER FAR AWAY in Mexico's Michoacán State, where Tarascan Indians and strange pagan gods ruled supreme before the white man came.

An aged, throbbing bus deposited me on the shore of Lake Pátzcuaro, seat of the golden empire that once stretched to the Pacific Ocean and rivaled in power the Aztec domain in pre-Hispanic Mexico. Today Tarascan country extends a scant 40 to 60 miles between western Sierra highlands, home of the volcano Paricutín, and the lake where I stood.

A hardy, 85-year-old fisherman agreed to take me to Janitzio, one of several islands that loomed through the dawn mist. His primitive, shallow-draft boat snaked through thick grass. Beyond us, a solitary hunter guided his boat toward a thousand tiny dots.

"Gallareta," said the old fisherman, pointing to a drifting flock of coots.

Cautiously the hunter rose. He catapulted his spear in a swift, high arc. Birds whirred into the air, wings flashing in the sun-flecked haze. But the hunter had made his kill. The *atlatl,* his highly effective spear thrower, I recalled, predates the bow.

Our boat nosed now toward Janitzio's shore, along with stragglers of the island's fishing fleet returning from the early morning catch. Misty sunlight washed the tan adobe buildings, the pitched roofs of tile, the balconies overhanging narrow, winding streets.

Big seines were being stretched to dry as I walked down a cobbled path to the home of Salvador Fermín (page 367), a fisherman whom I had met on an earlier visit. Through the open doorway I called into Fermín's terra-cotta kitchen, where bright-colored pottery decorated the red earthen walls.

A young Indian girl flipped tortillas above an open fire. The glare brightened her dark eyes, flashed from her silver earrings, tinted her sparkling yellow blouse. She wore a necklace of coral from the distant sea and a heavy wool skirt that extended to her bare feet.

**Island Fires Need Highland Fuel**

These Tarascans loading their dugouts live on Janitzio, a volcanic island denuded of wood. Their Sierra cousins, rich in forest products, catch no fish. Each Sunday forest and lake people meet in Erongarícuaro to exchange wares. Donkeys plod back to the mountains with fish; canoes (lower right) are pushed off to return across Lake Pátzcuaro with a week's firewood. The dugouts themselves are custom-made in the Sierra, borne to the lake by oxcart. Hewed from single pine logs, the flat-bottom craft appear awkward and bulky but can be paddled at surprising speed.

Tarascan women, celebrated for lustrous skin and long dark hair, let braids hang to their knees. They wear hand-loomed black wool skirts or red ones hung in pleats, topping them with aprons and blouses in a rainbow of hues. Drying nets (below) provide a filmy backdrop as Janitzio girls banter on a rocky path. One steps down to the lake front to wash dishes; her friends go to the market.



KODACHROMES BY JUSTIN LOCKE

"My father is hanging his nets with his crew, but my mother soon will be back from the store," she said shyly.

I sat by the door to wait. The room contained a wooden chest, nets, water jugs, *petates* or sleeping mats woven of tule just as they were five centuries ago. A far corner of the room shadowed an altar decorated with figurines and pictures of saints. A vase of paper flowers stood beside two receptacles for copal incense. These would be lit at sundown, a simple ritual recalling sacred bonfires pagan Tarascans lighted to their gods.

Tarascan Indians, I knew, had not always lived as humbly and obscurely as my friends, the Fermíns. Displacing or absorbing earlier nomadic and farming tribes in the 14th century, the Tarascans built an empire whose might was felt throughout west-central Mexico. Summoned by high priests in richly feathered capes, the warriors, naked bodies tattooed and painted red and black, sallied forth behind feathered banners, led by officers in jeweled vestments.

Tarascan craftsmen turned out copper tools that were widely sought, multicolored feather "paintings," brilliant gold and lacquer work, and idols carved from stone or molded of *pasta de maiz,* ground pith of cornstalks.

Powerful were the Tarascans until two related twists of fate. Hernán Cortés set foot on Mexican soil, and Tarascan chief Zuangua refused to join the Aztec emperor Montezuma in common cause against the invaders. The Tarascan empire in turn fell to the Spaniards, and the notorious Nuño de Guzmán, avid for gold, sealed its fate forever. The natives fled to the mountains.

While I daydreamed at the cottage door, Fermín's wife came up the street, bearing an earthen jar. From it she drew five glistening white fish, the prized *pescado blanco,* wrapped them in clean, wet grass, and gave them to me.

In following days, I watched Tarascans catch minnowlike *tiru* with their graceful *mariposa* nets—huge webbed "butterflies." In a bowered patio on Jarácuaro, "island of hatters," I listened to delicate, pensive Tarascan tunes, then boated to Erongarícuaro on the western shore for Sunday market, magnet for Tarascans everywhere.

On Saturday night burro trains laden with firewood thread down through pine forests from Sierra heights. Wrapped in colorful serapes, the foresters bed down beside their stacks of wood to await sunrise when islanders swarm ashore with baskets of fish to barter.

Dust swirls from bare feet in the village square. Laughter mingles with haggling. Wives from near and far inspect chickens, beans, sugar cane; chirimoyas, a tree-grown fruit. Vendors arrive with clay pots, palm-leaf raincoats, twig brooms. Boys sell garlic buds plucked from vegetable necklaces; hatters stack merchandise in tiers on their heads. A merchant from Guadalajara tempts passers-by with jewelry, ribbons, and toys.

Breezes whip men's baggy muslin pants as islanders shove off laden dugouts by noon to avoid late afternoon squalls.

On the opposite shore lies Tzintzuntzan or "Place of the Humming Bird," once-proud capital of the empire, now a sleepy village with 400-year-old olive trees. Tzintzuntzan on fiesta days throngs with satin-clad Tarascans and overalled Spanish-Indian mestizos who clamber to the tops of ancient ruins to enjoy views of village and lake.

Here and elsewhere I heard tales of remote, unexplored ruins. In Tarascan hands I often saw stone idols, copper bells, clay pipes, knives fashioned from tough volcanic glass, and other relics. I heard of the golden cow of Cerro el Zirate; of the dreaded *miringua,* malevolent spirit of the Sierra; and of buried treasure by the ton. I was asked in all seriousness: "Have you heard that the

KODACHROME BY JUSTIN LOCKE

Amid Drying Nets, Tarascan Fisherman Salvador Fermín Shows Off a Flavorsome Catch

## Fish by Sixes, Pots by the Pound . . .

"I offer my last six fish," island girl tells forester, "for another load of your firewood." These choice *pescado blanco* (white fish) share 6,671-foot-high Lake Pátzcuaro with tiny *tiru* caught in the famous butterfly nets, miniatures of which the dark-eyed Janitzio girls sell at lower right. Black bass, introduced into the lake, gobbled up so many tiru that the graceful, winglike nets fell into disuse until the fish made a limited comeback. Tata (father) Domingo, the octogenarian below, is too old to fish but young enough to make nets.

The Tarascan empire's once-great copper industry survives only in Santa Clara (below). Some 30 smiths fashion *casos* (kettles) from flat copper sheets, working with charcoal and antique hand bellows. Sold by weight, the pots are popular throughout Mexico. Tarascans once knew the secret of tempering the metal, legend says. But the conquerors levied a tribute in copper, seized the mines, and sapped the industry that had produced fine axes, hoes, pincers, awls, ornaments.



KODACHROMES BY JUSTIN LOCKE

KODACHROMES BY JUSTIN LOCKE

*Americanos* are draining the lake so as to reach the golden pillars that uphold Janitzio?"

Actual gold I found in the *tierra caliente* (hot country) to the south, once gold-working center of the empire. Goldsmiths still ply their craft in half a dozen villages, one appropriately on the Rio de Oro—River of Gold.

Trekking into the western Sierra on horseback, I climbed to Cherán, a hamlet clinging like lichens to a volcanic slope. The streets were deserted and cold; it was a rainy December day. Clouds scudded toward the valley, an unearthly place where cinder cones rise 800 feet above cultivated fields.

Bare-limbed willow trees framed a group of Cherán *trojes,* those baffling Tarascan log houses of obscure origin.

**Masks Off! Pranksters Feast After Fiesta**

Tarascans love to dance, not ballroom fashion but in teams at religious festivals, masquerading as saints or devils, hermits or buffoons. A favorite number is *Viejitos* (Little Old Men) in which youths masked as bearded, wrinkled patriarchs burlesque the infirmities of age. The highland swains above danced in disguise at the Fiesta of the Three Kings. Then, like Halloween pranksters, they serenaded girl friends and bearded prospective fathers-in-law. Home again, they shed camouflage, give way to laughter and a hearty meal of beans, tortillas, chile, and atole, a thin corn gruel. Pranks are gleefully recalled. "Did you see her face when I . . .?"

Opposite: The soft pat-pat of tortilla making seldom stops during daylight hours in this Janitzio Island home. As a welcome change for festivals, mother bakes sweetened wheat cakes in the beehive-shaped adobe oven. Content without refrigerator, vacuum cleaner, washer, or table, she loves to ornament walls with her pottery. Copper kettles, baskets, wooden trays come from Tarascan villages specializing in those wares. Bedroom, parlor, shrine, and kitchen share this clean-swept, chimneyless room.

Protruding shake roofs give the dwellings an Oriental look. A group of boys, faces solemn and dreamy, huddled beneath the eaves. Their bright woolen serapes provided the only touch of color.

To my surprise, I found an American couple teaching in Cherán. Mrs. Maxwell D. Lathrop, a linguist like her husband, told me: "Tarascan has no known kinship with any other Indian tongue.

"Written Spanish baffles Tarascan children, though their IQ is high. Learning to read their own language, they assimilate in six months what it takes three years to learn in Spanish."

At the village of San Lorenzo, near the cornfield where Paricutín rose like an evil genie to rain lava and ash on Tarascan lands, I stopped for Christmas.

By the village fountain, maidens washed corn for the holiday dishes (page 364). Guitar sound sparkled in the air. As I lingered, a guide gently chided me. "Be careful," he said. "Wells and public fountains, you know, are the scene of many courtships. Unless you plan to steal a girl to be your bride, let us be on our way."

He had a point. As in the days of the Spanish conquest, Tarascan youths frequently kidnap a mate—with the happy cooperation of the bride-to-be, of course.

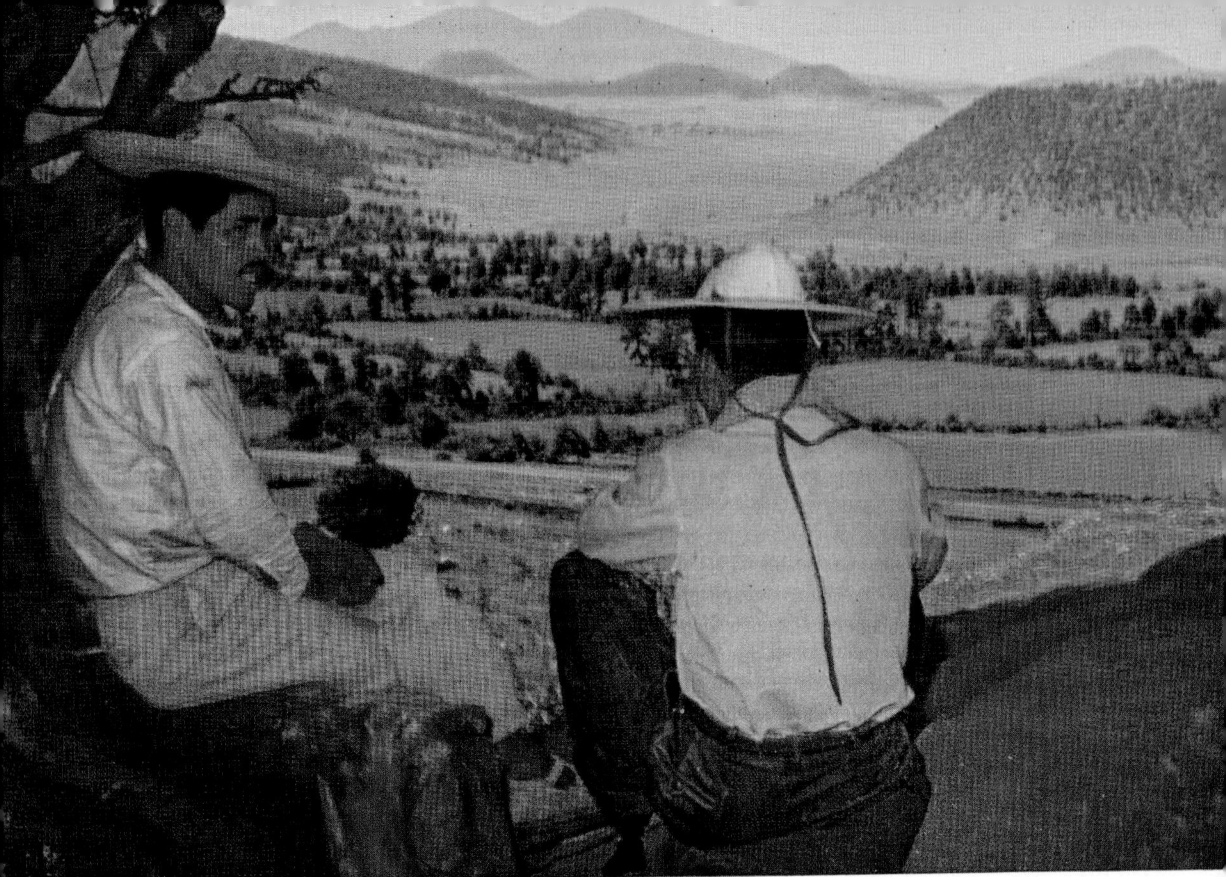

After a great hue and cry that is all part of the fun, the marriage is formalized.

About 10 o'clock on Christmas Eve, a confusion of sounds awakened the night. Entering the chapel courtyard, I saw musicians gathered around a small fire tuning their instruments. Tarascan women, faces covered by dark-blue shawls, entered the church to kneel before a portable shrine of the Virgin Mary.

Young girls, dressed as shepherdesses in blue and white and wearing flowered straw hats, shouldered the shrine, bearing it toward a village home honored with safeguarding the Christ Child's image during the year.

The musicians fell in behind and struck up an air. Villagers followed in silent procession. Pine flares began to appear in the darkness. When the Virgin was placed next to the Christ Child, the flickering tongues of fire revealed a strange dance before the sacred images. The shepherdesses sang softly as they glided about. Abruptly, devils in sparkling black-and-red costumes rushed in.

"I guard the Holy Child," shrieked a tiny winged angel and bravely stood her ground. Defiantly claiming their power over man, the demons nonetheless retreated. Masked hermits in conical hats and gray robes jumped upon them and struck them with whips of twine.

Bells summoned the villagers back to church. As the images were carried to the altar, prayers rippled through the church; hundreds of candles seemed to glow at once in the darkness.

To the strum of guitars, eight masked "negrito" dancers approached the center of the nave, clapped and danced. Candlelight shone softly on the bells, mirrors, and beads of their richly embroidered costumes. As the service ended, women sang a muted song, children blew faint whistles to imitate bird song.

In the doorway stood three devils in flashing costumes. Wrapping our blankets tightly about us, we gave them wide berth as we walked into the night.

## Ghosts of Dead Volcanoes Knob the Valley of Cherán

In this weird wonderland, not far from mighty Paricutín, "angry god of the Sierra," a farmer sowing corn may reap a live volcano. "I heard a low rumble, as if something had growled," said the plowman who witnessed Paricutín's incredible birth in 1943. "I looked; there was nothing. Then, just behind my furrow, I saw a spiral of white smoke." His cornfield erupted that night. Within a week the fiery cone grew to 500 feet; then to 1,500 feet—9,100 feet above sea level. Paricutín buried entire Tarascan villages, forcing Indians to flee across black seas of surging ash.

Mexico's belt of fire, overlying a reservoir of molten rock, has erected hundreds of cinder cones in the Tarascan highlands. Trees cover some ancient piles; other forlornly naked cinder heaps appear unchanged since their fires died. Farmers like these climb Juanchan (center) and till the crater bed.

Playing volcano, below, Tarascan boys start an eruption by puffing through an embedded pipe. The toy cone is shaped of ash spewed from near-by Paricutín, now a sleeping giant.

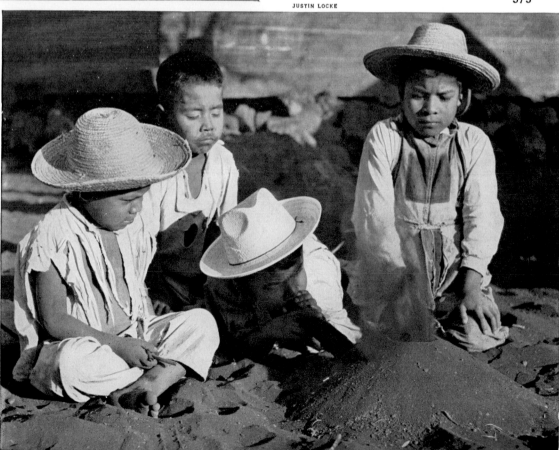



JUSTIN LOCKE

# MEXICAN FLYING POLE DANCE

**BY HELGA LARSEN**

DEFYING DEATH in a pagan rite, Indians of the eastern Sierra still erect poles as tall as masts and hurtle to earth on long, unwinding ropes. The dangerous dance of the *voladores* (flyers) survives in certain remote hamlets northeast of Mexico City although its symbolism has been almost entirely forgotten in the course of centuries.

Few outsiders had seen this spectacle, hitherto virtually unrecorded. So when I heard that the Otomi Indians were going to fly at Pahuatlán, I hastened there by train and horse.

When I arrived the flying pole already stood in the bustling plaza, a magnificent spar towering almost 70 feet. A live turkey, candles, chocolates, cigarettes and other offerings had been placed in the deep hole to nourish the pole and make it strong.

Three Indians climbed to the top, finding footholds in a thick vine twisted about the pole. They carried six long ropes and a short tree section hollowed out and smeared with pink soap. They fitted this cylinder over the pole top, like a thimble free to revolve.

The uneven top of the thimble was the "dance floor." It measured exactly 24 inches in diameter! Below it hung a framework of sticks and ropes—the aerial carrousel intended to hold the flyers. Over this frame the Indians passed their six long ropes, wound spool-like around the top of the pole, leaving the ends dangling in air.

The whole structure is so frail a flyer will tell you frankly, "We are helpless if anyone loses his balance." To muster courage, voladores often get drunk. Some villages have banned the dance because of fatal accidents.

Old Spanish chronicles mention four as the number of flyers. Dressed as birds, the men represented the four sacred



BODIL CHRISTENSEN; RODNEY GALLOP (RIGHT)

RODNEY GALLOP

birds guarding the cardinal points of the compass. The four flyers made 13 rounds before reaching the ground. Thus the rite symbolized the Indian "century"—four 13-year periods making up a 52-year cycle.

Pahuatlán has increased the number of daredevils to six. "Six is more elegant," natives told me.

The Indians climbed down the pole, now ready for the extraordinary dance. Excitement mounted in the plaza. Suddenly someone cried, "Los voladores!" Six gaily dressed flyers paraded into the plaza and approached the pole. The team wore bright red costumes, with two bandannas crossing in the back to suggest wings. All were men. The chief, 63 years old, had flown for 35 years. Five were dressed in breeches, the sixth in billowing skirts. This was Malinche, or Man-Woman, portrayed in nearly all Mexican dances and believed to represent the Indian girl who befriended Cortés.

One by one the flyers climbed up, Malinche hampered by her skirts. They seated themselves in the flimsy frame, bracing feet against the pole. They looked like rag dolls.

Then a volador climbed to the tiny platform and began to dance. The others shook rattles; one played flute and drum.

The music floated down as the tiny figure whirled and leaped. My heart surged into my throat; one false step, one slight loss of balance, and he would plunge to death at my feet.

The other flyers took turns at breath-taking acrobatics. Malinche's dance, to four different tunes, was the most spectacular. Spectators stiffened and gasped when she leaned recklessly from the little perch and enfolded each of the others with a large bandanna. Then she eased back into her place in the frame.

Now the voladores tied the rope ends around their waists. With a piercing cry, they hurled themselves backward into space.

For one breathless moment they dangled from the summit, five flyers head down—only Malinche flies feet first. The ropes started to unwind, slowly at first, then faster and faster as the voladores swung in ever widening circles.

Round and round the mast they flew, slim bodies stretched along taut ropes gripped with their feet—down to the red-tiled rooftops now, down to the balconies, down to the arcades, coming closer and closer to the sea of tense, upturned brown faces.

RODNEY GALLOP

The music had changed to a livelier rhythm; hollow instruments throbbed furiously. Even when it seemed the aerialists' heads would scrape the ground, one still played his pipe and drum, the others shook gourd rattles. Suddenly, as the crowd roared and broke like a surging wave around the voladores, the heroes righted themselves gracefully and landed—safe at last—on their feet.

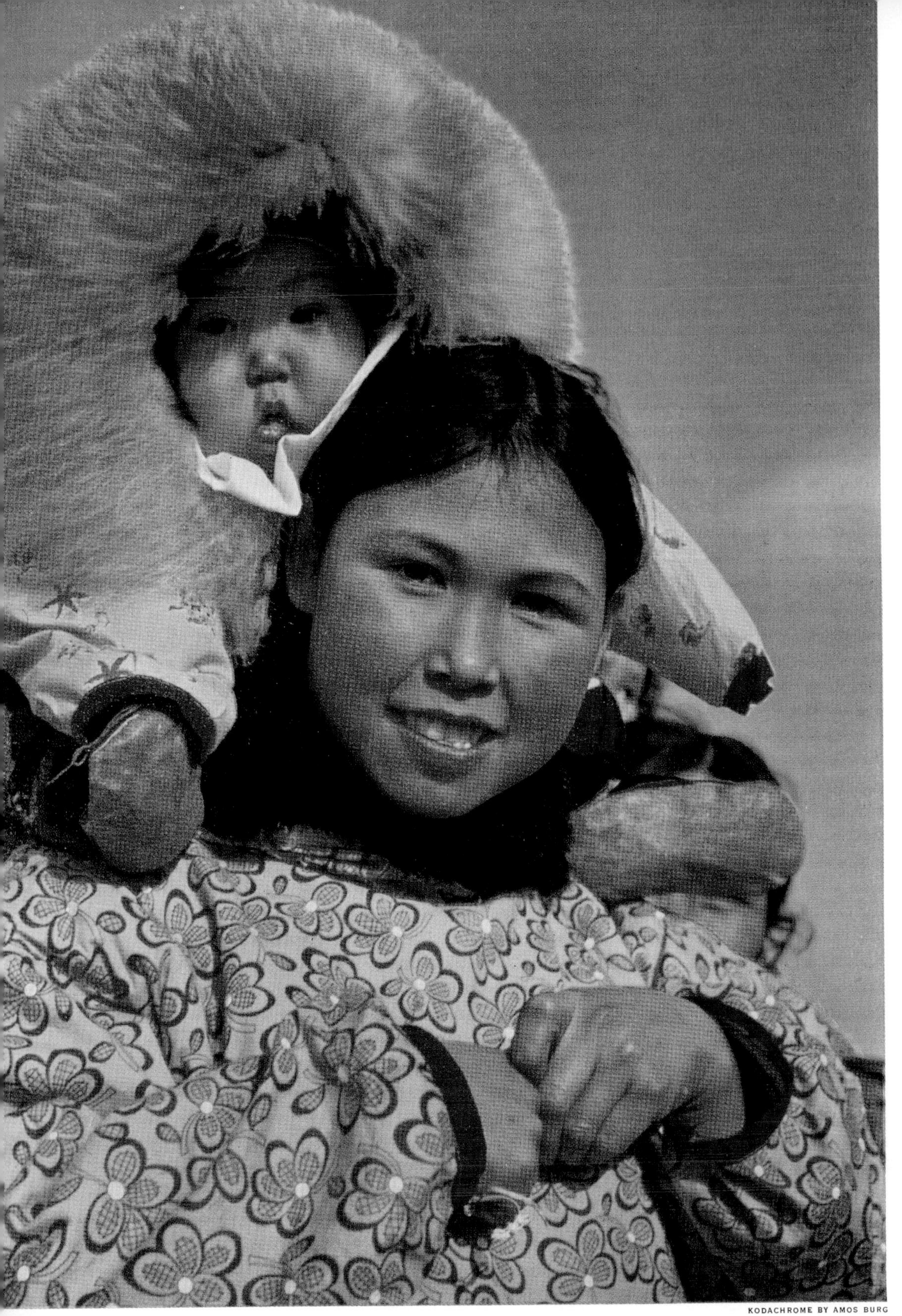

KODACHROME BY AMOS BURG

**A Fast-changing World Faces This Eskimo Mother and Her Solemn, Fur-framed Hitchhiker**

# CHAPTER 19

# NORTHLAND LIFE

TRANSPOLAR PLANES DRONE *through Arctic skies, weather and radar stations dot northland shores, yet the Eskimo remains master of a vast top-of-the-world domain. Numbering less than 40,000, this resourceful people draws on a 2,000-year-old culture, survives using ingenious gear adapted to a merciless environment. Central Eskimos have followed a rhythm of migration as unvarying as that of the birds—moving inland to fish and hunt game in summer, back to winter on the ice, realm of sea mammals and polar bears. One group, the Padlermiut, for some reason remained inland. Passing centuries obliterated maritime ties; caribou became focus of their existence.* DONALD B. MARSH, *Anglican Bishop of the Arctic, describes these unique Caribou Eskimos as he knew them in days before the airplane accelerated change in the northland. At Point Hope, Alaska, anthropologist* FROELICH G. RAINEY, *Director of the University Museum in Philadelphia, joins the colorful—and crucial—annual whale hunt of the Eskimo villagers of Tigara.*

## CANADA'S CARIBOU ESKIMOS

**BY DONALD B. MARSH**

THEY CALL themselves Padlermiut, People of the Willow Thicket. White men have dubbed them Caribou Eskimos, and with good reason. Fifty years ago these people depended upon one animal, the caribou, for life itself. Men, women, and children dressed in skins of caribou, which they hunted with bows and arrows. Caribou meat fed them. Caribou bones and antlers were their tools.

Though they lived on Canada's Northern Plains, only slightly west of Hudson Bay, theirs was an inland culture. Unique among Eskimos, they possessed no traditions of the sea. They spoke a language like that of Greenland Eskimos, yet they knew nothing of hunting sea mammals, Greenland's basis of life. Seal, walrus, polar bear were unfamiliar, salt water and tides mysteries. They had no seal-blubber lamps, trade-mark of Eskimos all over the North.

Today the Padlermiut depend as much on traders as on caribou. They hunt with guns instead of bows. Within a lifetime they have emerged from the past; modern times stare them in the face. As a missionary, in summer I have shared their smoky caribou-skin tents; in winter, their freezing crudely built igloos. For 20 years I watched them struggle with the elements and with advancing civilization.

When I first set sail from Churchill, seat of a small Church of England mission, I scarcely knew what to expect at Eskimo Point, 160 miles north. Even then, changes had already overtaken the Padlermiut. For one thing, those I met were camped beside salt water.

As the anchor dropped, I saw against a background of conical skin tents a group of men with long flowing hair and wrinkled, seamed, but smiling faces. All were clad in caribou skins; much of this clothing was so dirty and greasy as to look the color of the earth. They stooped slightly as they walked, so many winters

## Padlermiut Life: a Tuft of Moss, a Roof of Snow, and for Dining, an Ax

A village crone (below) returns from day-long rounds scraping snow from clumps of reindeer moss and stunted willows. "People of the Willow Thicket" lack seal or walrus oil, feed cooking fires with twigs. Amid littered furs and equipment (right) she will carry her load down steps to the rock-topped snow bench that forms the family hearth. Smoke drifts from porch and snow chimney. Crudely built, often roofed with caribou hide and raftered with summer's tent poles, these igloos chill to below zero when fires die. Awaiting a feast of cooked meat, tea-drinking men (below right) hack hors d'oeuvres from a frozen caribou carcass.



KODACHROMES BY DONALD B. MARSH

A. W. F. BANFIELD

had they huddled over feeble caribou-fat lamps; yet theirs was the dignity and poise of men who are sure of themselves. The women, hair matted and straggly and skin clothes greasy, also greeted me with friendly smiles. The young men and lads stood off by themselves. Their appearance gave me a shock. Surely these were not Eskimos! Most wore sweaters, many with encircling bands of color. The crowns of their heads were close-cropped, tonsure fashion.

So this was the new mode of the North!

Food dominates the thoughts of the Padlermiut. They often do not know where the next meal is coming from. When they have caribou, they eat one big feast of cooked meat each day. For an appetizer a haunch of frozen raw caribou, together with an ax, is provided. Anyone really hungry may chop off a portion. Most wait for the heaping, steaming pot of boiled meat.

The sight of a fire roaring on a snow bench within snow walls has never failed to astonish me. Smoke swirls, as if feeding on the snow itself. It blackens the cook's face and reddens her eyes, then drifts upward to a snow chimney. Handful by handful, she tosses twigs to the insatiable fire. In two or three hours the meat is done.

Nowadays the meat boils in a gasoline drum or washtub. In old days she would have used a polished stone vessel. For communal meals one woman usually cooks for the men and another for her sisters. Men and women feast separately.

The family dinner platter is a wooden tray four feet long, a foot wide, and two inches thick. Carved from a tree trunk, such a tray is an heirloom to be handed down from generation to generation—or to be buried with its owner for use in the next world.

When dinner is ready, the host invites the guests to fall to, but politeness demands some show of reluctance. Then, eyes lighting up, each man grasps his favorite portion—tongue, fat breast meat, steak. Sinking his teeth in one end, he shears off the remainder with a stroke of a butcher knife, just missing his nose and chin. Sinew, cartilage, fat, or flesh—all are grist for powerful jaws. Boiled head is a prime delicacy, as is rendered back fat stuffed sausagelike into caribou intestines.

No one talks, but silence does not reign! When the meat is devoured, the bones are cracked and the marrow extracted with special bone implements. Horns are sometimes eaten when in the velvet. At one time liver, head, and lungs were taboo, even to the dogs, but now only the lungs go uneaten.

Tea, black, strong, and bitter—and sometimes boiled from re-used leaves—is consumed in enormous quantities. Formerly the meat's cooking water was

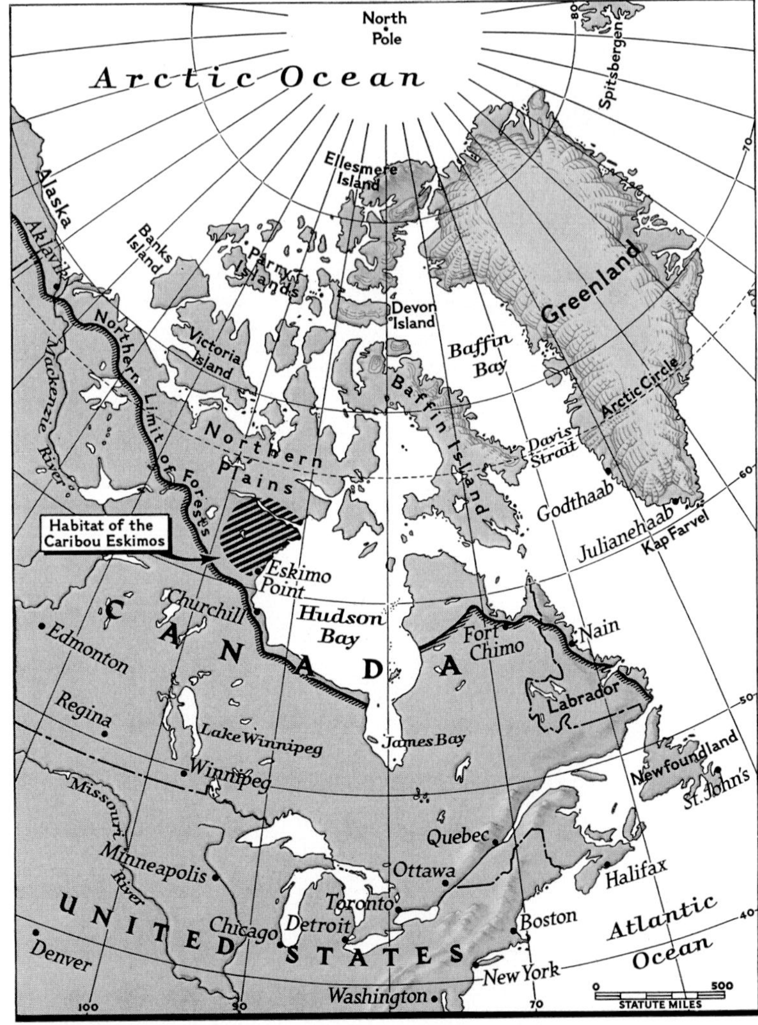


**Land of the Caribou—** and the Caribou Eskimo. In April and May, along the edges of the Arctic tree line, caribou mass for their great migration toward the lichen-rich tundra. First the does, heavy with fawns, then bucks with velveted antlers, emerge from the scrub, mill about on frozen lakes, and head north in mighty herds (left).

At defiles and oft-used crossings, Eskimos and Indians lie in wait with rifles, as their fathers once did with bows. Lookouts give cry. Downwind floats the clicking of the caribou's heel bones, the grunt of the loping herd, and its rank, distinctive odor.

Suddenly the dun-gray horde bursts into sight. Steel-jacketed bullets thud into leaping flesh. Behind the firing line, women and children ravenous for the season's first fresh meat bring kettles to boil. Later they cure the hides for clothing, cache the meat, remove sinews for sewing.

NATIONAL GEOGRAPHIC MAP DRAWN BY THEODORA PRICE AND IRVIN E. ALLEMAN

the standard drink. When I first visited the Padlermiut, they bought tea put up in lead-covered packages, melting down the metal in frying pans to make bullets.

In times of abundance a man may be invited to a succession of caribou banquets. I saw one man stagger out of his fourth en route to his fifth. Not knowing other meals were to follow, he had done his utmost at each to see that nothing was wasted. On a later occasion he had to slit his coat front and back in order to complete his rounds!

In early times, if the camp had meat, no one went hungry. When caribou were scarce, the successful hunter gave away most of his kill, happily boasting, "To me has fallen the privilege of providing for the camp." Today the rule applies only to native food. White man's food obeys white man's laws. Flour, lard, and meat bought at the store with fox pelts are not given away lightly. Men sit all day splitting matches to make them go three times as far.

As a shopper, the Caribou Eskimo cannot understand fixed prices. If his need is great, he is eager to pay more than the trader asks. One man offered three fox pelts for a snow knife, explaining that he was unable to hunt without the knife. Why the trader refused his offer baffled the Eskimo. Another man offered seven pelts for the trader's only razor—but the trader didn't want to grow a beard.

Gifts they undervalue to the point of seeming ingratitude. By their philosophy, if the donor had any use for the object, he wouldn't give it away.

Reading, writing, and arithmetic are comparative newcomers to the Eskimo's curriculum of life. Several decades ago the Reverend E. J. Peck, who spent 40 years among the Baffin Islanders, adapted Cree Indian characters to the Eskimo tongue. Now most Eskimos in the eastern Arctic can read their own language. For history, however, they have never needed the written word. A marvelous tribal memory serves them faithfully. Across the Arctic the centuries-old folklore is almost word for word the same, even among the most isolated tribes.

Custom rules life in the community. Timeless custom backed by strict taboos. One decrees that no woman in her fertile years may eat eggs. A wolf hunter, having wounded his prey by gunshot, killed it with an ax. In doing so he broke one of the wolf's bones—violation of a rigid taboo. He died soon after—and his fellows knew why!

An *angakok*, or shaman, may be either man or woman. Each has his or her own familiar spirit for consultation. Some witch doctors have performed such unbelievable feats that they have acquired a virtual life or death power over their fellows. Men have committed suicide on orders from an angakok.

Such a powerful wizard lived among inlanders of the Northern Plains. His people swear they saw him grow walrus tusks from his jaws. At his initiation into shamanship, he was reported to have buried himself in a lake freezing over. Three days later he was chopped out, none the worse, the Eskimos said.

Wearing charms comes as naturally to the Eskimo as his belief in shamans. I have seen some so smothered in tokens that they appeared to be in rags. Little bags may contain a fish heart, a piece of sealskin to give strength, weasel skin to impart hunter's cunning, or a cloth strip token from a well-wisher.

Many times I have witnessed the barbaric drum dance of the Caribou Eskimos. Inside a double-size tribal skin tent on an arctic evening, when darkness suspends the taboo against drum beating, a man steps past the outer circle of men into the tight inner ring of women squatting shoulder to shoulder. He taps the rim of his huge one-faced drum with a stubby clublike stick and the sound reverberates like an African tom-tom beat. His body sways rhythmically. He looks up, as if trying to remember his song. Then his knees bend until his caribou-skin coattails sweep the ground. With short steps he hops around the ring. A candle's flickering flame throws his shadow in grotesque shapes and highlights the onlookers' intense faces. Chanting women sway to and fro, closing their eyes as if in a trance.

This same dance they danced in the Stone Age. Yet many of their customs are changing. I remember one old man shaping a block of iron into a harpoon head with a toothless file. His task already had taken two days; he expected to take three more. He was in no hurry; what did time mean in the Arctic? With his new harpoon he would hunt seals so that he might have blubber in which to dip his raw caribou meat next winter. He was learning the ways of shoreline Eskimos.

**Alaskan Eskimos Face the Sea**

Ukivok village, perched on King Island's rocky southern slope, winters 150 Eskimos oriented to fog-shrouded Bering Sea life. Walrus-hide umiaks, now powered by outboard motors, serve the cliff-dwelling hunters and provide a link with mainland Alaska, 30 miles east (page 154). This fisherwoman chiseled a hole in the ice, kept it clear with long-handled scoop, lured bullheads with bright toothbrush handle. Barbless hooks enable mittened Eskimos to remove catches without exposing fingers to bitter cold. With no level land, boys play baseball on sea ice.

# ESKIMO WHALE HUNT

BY FROELICH G. RAINEY

WHEN THE SUN RETURNS in spring to glare down upon the wilderness of pack ice, the wives of the Tigara whaling captains begin preparations for their men to go out to hunt the largest of all living creatures, the great bowhead whale, Agavik.

Up to a generation ago, the Eskimo women prayed to the moon for success. They were not impressed by Sukunuk, the sun, regarded as female, but waited for the male moon, Alignuk, on whom depended their family security and the prestige of their kin.

In March, Alignuk would draw back the trap door in the floor of his house, and a faint silver crescent would appear in the night sky. Then each captain's wife would take her special little wooden bowl and fill it with clean, clear water from a certain lagoon.

After the dogs had quieted for the night, she stole out through the long entrance tunnel of her house and held her bowl up toward the moon, calling: "Alignuk, drop a whale into this pot so that we can kill one this spring!"

If she had obeyed all the rules and if the water was clear, her voice and the glimmer of light in the bowl reached up to Alignuk. He would send a whale.

**Red-stained Sea and Ice Spell Full Larders**

Shot in mass attacks as they ride north on floating ice pans, walrus provide King Islanders with meat, hides, oil, and ivory. The hunters above have had a good day: they butcher two huge carcasses, have another tethered to the ice, and drag a 200-pound calf from the water.

Below, women pare blubber from a sealskin with broad steel *ulu* blades shaped like pie wedges, as a hungry dog stands watch. Their splitting boards are heirlooms. They will soften the skin by chewing to make supple, water-resistant boots; use the carcass as food; burn the oil in lamps. The women wear cloth covers over caribou-skin parkas. Hunters wear white canvas jackets for camouflage on ice, hunt from October to June. When the last ice goes out, the entire King Island village leaves for Nome, 85 miles distant, for summer jobs or to sell walrus-ivory carvings.



Tigara clings to the very tip of a long ribbon of sand that curves out into the Arctic Ocean 200 miles north of Bering Strait. A strong northward sea current strikes this spit, known as Point Hope, and swings out toward the northwest. At certain times current and wind combine to force a lead, or opening, in the pack ice. In April, May, and early June, bowhead whales migrate northward along the open lead, heading for Point Barrow and the Arctic Ocean.

The lead along Point Hope usually opens under a north wind and closes under a south wind. The old men watch the weather closely to decide when the boats shall be taken out across the ice to open water. If the bitter male northeast wind blows, the lead will open, but great pans of shore ice may break off and be driven out to sea, carrying with them boats and crews. The ice may be crushed into a seething mass over which a boat cannot be dragged and through which no boat can be driven.

But that spring the day of launching was beautiful, dazzling bright, with only a breath of air from the north. Umigluk's team of nine dogs was hitched to a light sled and a line run from that to the boat sled. Each member of our crew also was in harness. We moved off through the piles of ice and pressure ridges, pulling not only the umiak but also a great pile of extra fur clothing, guns, and all manner of gear to be used on the ice. We would not return to shore until the lead closed, perhaps many days later.

All whaling gear must be clean and, if possible, new. The Eskimos believe the whale cannot easily see bright and shining gear, but if he does, it pleases

him. It promises sharp cutting knives and spades which will not hurt in the butchering. You see, the whale does not die, he only "has his parka removed"—painlessly, if knives are sharp—and returns to sea to report on his treatment by the Eskimos.

Umigluk's father had supervised the refitting of our fragile 20-foot umiak—half the length of the whales we were to attack in it. Old crones of the village, paid in tobacco and meat, had sewn skins of the bearded seal into a new cover for it. Umigluk's mother-in-law had purified it spiritually by an ancient ceremony on the ice.

The crew scraped clean all eight spruce paddles, the harpoon shafts, the great cutting lance shafts, the boat hooks. New sealskin floats were made and tested, new lines made fast. Harpoon bombs were refilled with fresh black powder, fuses reset, caps tested.

I knew from my crew mates, although he never told me himself, that Umigluk had retired the night before to sing his charm song, almost inaudibly, lightly tapping his tiny whaling captain's drum. This song had been taught him by his grand-

**Whaling, Eskimo Style!** In paddled boats, with hand harpoons and guns 50 years old, Tigara hunters pursue their Moby Dick, Agavik. Flukes flip skyward (top) as a wounded whale sounds. Sealskin float bobs in foreground. Blubber slab (center) goes to one crew as another (below) hacks gill bone away beneath baleen, the horny material from the mouth. Only the skull, representing the whale's spirit, returns to the sea.

FROELICH G. RAINEY; MERL LA VOY (BOTTOM)

father, a great medicine man, and no one must hear it.

Our crew, following tradition, had eaten a piece of whale caught the year before—black rubbery skin, yellow blubber, red meat, all raw and ripe. But there had also been an evil portent.

At Easter, in the centuries-old masked whaling dance, Kuwana had spun a wooden top, out of which rose goose feathers arranged like turnip leaves. If it had whirled smoothly and the feathers had sailed off into the air, the whaling would be a success. If it did not, some one present would die.

The top had spun smoothly for a moment, then caught and slid along the stage, scattering its feather plume. There was some laughter and joking when the moment of suspense was over, but I had watched old Nashugruk's drawn face as she sat staring at the top.

Three weeks later Poyuruk, the jovial dancer with the beaming smile, died with pieces of an exploded bronze shoulder gun embedded in his intestines, Kunuknoruk was badly wounded by another explosion, and two other antique guns—bought from American whalers more than 50 years before—had blown up as well.

Now, however, we were just beginning the spring hunt. Only a few minutes after we reached open water, someone shouted "Agavik!" There, half a mile off, a great black hulk surfaced to blow a fine puff of steam from its bow, then submerged.

Half an hour later we heard a harpoon gun fire to the east. Suddenly a boat shot out from behind the ice, then lay still, its crew waiting and watching.

Kunuknoruk rose in the stern of his boat, held out his arms over bowed heads, and prayed in a loud clear voice to Our Father, "Apapta" in Eskimo. In the old days his harpooner would have sung the Avituksiun, a prayer to hold the harpoon fast in the whale.

I asked old Qoqoq later why he prayed to Jehovah instead of to Alignuk, the moon, as he had during much of his life. He said it was not until the missionaries came that he knew Jehovah controlled the whales.

The prayer finished, we headed off toward where Umigluk thought the whale would blow next. After a long, hard pull, we heard the cry, "Avituk!" Again we drove our boat forward, racing the other crews toward a small dark sealskin float (avituk) fastened by 14 fathoms of line to the embedded harpoon iron. When the float appears it is a sign the whale is rising.

Each boat at the scene of a kill gets a portion of the whale, but what part depends upon the order of arrival, hence the race, which has every paddler exerting all his strength. After some two miles of chasing the elusive float most of us had the taste of blood in our mouths.

Ours were all young men; we soon drew into the lead. Suddenly the float broke the surface a hundred yards off our bow. We redoubled the stroke; our boat surged forward like a whale in full flight.

Then beneath us we felt a huge boiling movement of the water; the boat rocked crazily, and directly under the bow rose the great black bulk of the whale. There was a deep and unforgettable blast, something like the exhaust of a locomotive stopping at a station, as the whale blew steam into our faces.

Umigluk at the stern swung us about, and with one terrific stroke of our paddles we drove the boat up the glistening slope of the whale's back. Melik, the harpooner, rose, held the harpoon shaft high above his head, then drove it straight down through three feet of quivering skin, blubber, and flesh.

A mighty shudder passed from the whale through our flexible skin boat. A deep muffled thud followed as the harpoon bomb exploded in that mass of flesh; then came a convulsion that threw the boat off on its side. A cry from Umigluk warned us to clear away the sealskin floats attached to the line, which now was running out with the whale's sounding. In a moment line and floats disappeared. With all my heart-pounding excitement I yet remember the sweat-streaked, beaming faces of the crew, each shouting and laughing.

The nine boats now formed a wide circle. All of us watched for the float. At last it bobbed up, dark and agitated like a female bearded seal rising far out of the water, waving her flippers to lead you away from her pup.

As we closed in, the whale rose, spouting a mist of steam and blood. Kunuknoruk's boat swung in, and young Stephen leaned over the bow, brandishing a ten-foot steel-headed lance. The boat slid up over the whale's flippers until only the stern remained in the water. Stephen thrust downward, then raised himself over the lance like a pole vaulter, forcing it down through probably six feet of flesh.

Two other boats rushed to the kill, other lances searched for vital spots. In a few minutes it was finished. A black hulk floated quietly, with only an oil slick and swirls of bloody water to remind us of its death struggle.

Not until that moment did I realize it was snowing hard. The ice pack was no longer in sight, and the other boats seemed ghostly in the gray light.

As we began to tow the carcass in the blinding snowstorm, the "joy shout" went up, a short repeated barking sound like the cry of a sea lion. The cooks on the ice would hear this, and carry word to the village that the first kill of the spring had been made.

The whale was hauled onto the ice by pulleys, the flukes were cut away and carried to the village at once. They belong to the captain whose crew made the first strike, but are given to the community, symbol of the hunter's relation to supernatural forces, to the village, and to the spirit of the whale himself. Formerly, a piece was borne to the captain's wife on a staff, announcing success. She then came out on the ice with her little ceremonial bowl to give the whale a drink of fresh water. All sea mammals are forever thirsty, the Eskimos say.

Old men marked each boat crew's traditional share by cutting long gashes in the black skin. The last boat wins a "booby prize"—a strip the size of the captain's foot, cut completely around the whale just below the navel.

We worked all day and all night cutting up the whale. Dog teams raced back and forth from the edge of the ice to storage pits ashore, hauling the tons of meat. Sea gulls screamed overhead or dived for titbits in the water. The ice for yards around became slippery with blood and fat. A long, winding red trail marked the course of sleds across the ice to the shore. Clothing was soaked, greasy, but no one cared, for the butchering is a time of joy and feasting.

The hunt continued for many weeks. We waited long days and nights at the edge of the ice, raced through vast fields of drifting floes in pursuit of whales, or sat quietly far out in the lead while herds of white belugas broke the night silence with their puffing.

Once the pack ice began to break up unexpectedly, to grind and crash and move seaward. It was the only time I ever saw Eskimos really terrified. With only eight boats, in an hour of feverish work, more than 100 villagers, including women and children, were ferried across three ice-jammed channels to safety on shore. Later, when the ice reformed, they all went right back out on the pack.

When the sun began to circle the sky without setting, the ice again became restless. Big cracks appeared, pools of water collected on the smooth pans where our boats lay, and we could feel ourselves rising or falling as the ground ice prepared to move north. The season was over. We had struck 13 bowheads, killed five, cached meat from four.

We came off the ice for good one day early in June, dragging our boats across the last of the ice to the sand spit where bumblebees already had found the first spring flowers. It was time for Nalukatuk, the whale feast which begins the day after the boats reach shore and lasts for three days. Now appear such delicacies as raw whale kidneys, tongue, hearts, skin; "ice cream" made from beaten reindeer fat, bits of meat, and berries; and boiled flour-and-seal-oil soup.

Games of strength and endurance, dancing, singing, and drumming renew appetites. But the climax is Nalukatuk, the performance that gives the feast its name. This glorified tossing-in-the-blanket is both a delight and a terror.

FROELICH G. RAINEY

From four whale-jaw tripods, a large walrus hide is stretched by ropes three or four feet above the ground. Forty or fifty people grasp its edge by special rope handgrips, and together toss some courageous victim as high as 15 or 20 feet at each bounce.

Some Eskimos are skilled enough to keep their feet for minutes, "dancing in the air" to drumming and singing. But the novice has a bad time. He lands just at the wrong moment, his knees buckle, he soon sprawls on his face or back and tumbles through the air amid shouts of laughter, completely at the mercy of the tossers. Such is the Nalukatuk, high spot in the Tigara year!

KODACHROMES BY AMOS BURG

**Old or Young, Eskimos Grin at Life**

Good-natured and self-assured, the Eskimo meets life happily—from a great-grandmother, past 90, weaving a basket of beach grass, to a demure young coquette in hand-me-down dress. "Perhaps they laugh," one writer suggests, "because their parka fur tickles them all the time!"

Looking like a huge necktie rack, split red salmon dry in wind and sun (above) behind boy untangling his fish net. At Point Lay, where the Arctic Circle lies "down south," sod-covered frame house (left) resembles American prairie homes of a century ago. Storage wing needs neither turf overcoat nor glass windows.

KODACHROME BY JACK BREED

**Ute Mothers Tuck Sleepy Infants in Sunshaded Cradleboards** and strap them on their backs. These women belong to the Wiminuche branch, still nomadic, still chary of visitors to their southwestern Colorado reservation. The tribal council voted special permission to make this picture.

## CHAPTER 20

# THE AMERICAN INDIAN CITIZEN AND NEIGHBOR

ONCE MASTER OF THIS LAND, *the Indian is assuming a new role in the United States community. A citizen since 1924, he votes in State and Federal elections, adopts more and more of his white neighbor's ways. The 20th century penetrates even the remote land of the Havasupai, reports* JACK BREED. *The Indian offers his heritage of talents to the Nation.* DOROTHY DUNN, *founder of Santa Fe's School of Indian Painting, tells of a resurgence of native American art—no longer on rocks and buffalo hides but on the easel's paper and canvas—and presents paintings to reveal its vitality and impact. National Geographic staff writer* ROBERT L. CONLY *shows Mohawk daring at work building "Big Town" skyscrapers. But the clash of cultures, the tug of the past still have effect. In the Indian's changing world depicted by* MATTHEW W. STIRLING, *young veterans weigh their hopes of success in white society against tribal security on the reservation*

## CONTEMPORARY INDIAN PAINTERS

**BY DOROTHY DUNN**

NEAR TODAY'S ATOMIC CITY of Los Alamos, an archeological field unit from the Museum of New Mexico was digging in long-abandoned cave dwellings. The year was 1917. Young Crescencio Martinez from San Ildefonso Pueblo was at work as a laborer. One day he overheard archeologists praise pictographs and mural paintings on a cave's blackened walls.

"I can paint, too," he volunteered.

Crescencio got his chance. Given paper and paints, he produced surprising water colors. Soon he was painting dances of his pueblo's summer and winter festivals. With simple reverence he pictured singers, drummers, and dancers of corn, eagle, buffalo, and deer ceremonials. The series was almost complete when he died of influenza in 1918. Others carried on the work. Among them was Crescencio's nephew, Awa Tsireh.

In those days, incredible as it now seems, the Bureau of Indian Affairs banned native painting in Indian schools. Despite official disapproval, three talented youths—Ma-Pe-Wi of Zia Pueblo (page 399) and two Hopi boys, Fred Kabotie and Otis Polelonema, were given supplies by a sympathetic superintendent at the Indian school in Santa Fe and encouraged to paint on their own.

Meantime San Ildefonso was becoming an art center, sparked by a renaissance in pottery making brought about by Maria and Julian Martinez with their now famous matte-on-gloss black ware (page 117). Inspired by the new creative spirit, young men of San Ildefonso and near-by pueblos began painting. Interested Santa Fe people sponsored exhibitions as far as Madrid, Prague, Venice.

In 1932 a change in Indian Bureau policy led to the opening of art classes in the school at Santa Fe. Young people flocked to enroll—Pueblo, Navajo, and Apache from New Mexico and Arizona; Sioux from the Dakotas; Cheyenne, Arapaho, Kiowa from Oklahoma.

Every painter evolved a personal style within the tribal character. One artist specialized in old Plains abstract designs, another in everyday views, others in hunting scenes or the fantasy of tribal mythology. This they have in common: The Indian painter poses no models, follows no color theory, gauges no true perspective. Often he leaves background to imagination. By omitting nonessentials, he produces abstract symbols for plants, animals, earth, and sky. Yet he can convey mood or action with a few lines.

The contemporary movement now has extended to centers in Oklahoma, Utah, and Montana, with frequent exhibitions elsewhere in the country. Some 40 Indian artists today devote substantial time to painting. Three pioneers—Ma-Pe-Wi, Kabotie, and Polelonema—still are painting. Only middle-aged, they are known as the "old masters" of contemporary Indian painting. So spectacular has been this art development that the public sometimes forgets its roots are old.

Painting was already an ancient tribal activity when Spanish conquistadores forded the Rio Grande. For centuries aboriginal artists had expressed reactions to their native land in pictures carved in rock, engraved on bone, painted on hides, wood, pottery, plaster, cloth—even drawn in colored sand. Before white settlers took over the Great Plains, nearly every buffalo-hide tepee, robe, and shield bore vivid figures of horses and men in battles, hunts, and contests (page 53). Such decorations were emblems of prowess. Every man was an artist.

When buffalo herds and tribal lands disappeared, uprooted Indians, longing for self-expression, turned to makeshift materials. Army commissary books, traders' ledgers, lengths of cloth were filled with pencil and crayon drawings, and paintings done with

**Ma-Pe-Wi Paints a Buffalo Dance.** At home in Santa Fe, an "Old Master" of modern Indian painting gives pointers to his son; his Pueblo wife tends garden. The work on his easel later won high honors at the Santa Fe Fiesta exhibit. The French Government awarded him a medal in 1954 at the Inter-Tribal Indian Ceremonial at Gallup, New Mexico.

WESTERN WAYS FEATURES

brushes and ready-made colors. Subject matter also changed. Art became a nostalgic rendering of childhood reminiscences, youthful exploits, tribal wars of bygone days, and new battles with "long knives," the white men.

Indians in prison won vicarious victories and regained wishful freedom through their paintings. One Cheyenne, escaped from prison, went into battle with his book of drawings strapped to his side. A bullet pierced it, killing him. Later the work turned up in New York's American Museum of Natural History.

This new personal Plains style was the first attempt at art distinct from tribal needs. It recalled the grand days of the buffalo hunt. Religious rites long had

honored the mighty beast that fed, clothed, and sheltered the tented tribes —Sioux, Cheyenne, Crow, Kiowa, and others. Though the earth-shaking herds are gone, they live on in paintings not only of the Plains people, but of Southwest tribes that had little contact with the buffalo (page 404).

"I want to realize the glory of portraying the life of the Indian for the eyes of the people who do not know," says F. Blackbear Bosin, Kiowa-Comanche artist whose "Prairie Fire" retains the spirit and verve of traditional Plains works, though his technique is more naturalistic (page 402).

Unlike the 19th century Plainsmen, the Pueblo Indians and Navajo of the Southwest carried on their native arts as in the past. Tempera paint was made of earth pigments mixed with water or milk, brushes were the chewed ends of yucca leaves, mouths were atomizers. Few artists tried new materials.

One Navajo youth, fascinated by puffing locomotives of the 1880's, made colored-crayon sketches on wrapping paper at a trading post. Later the first known drawings of Navajo ceremonial figures on paper were discovered by an artist-archeologist working at Pueblo Bonito.

As he entered a trading post, he saw some crude but vigorous pictures penciled on cardboard box ends. Their creator, he learned, was Api Begay, who lived in a hogan off toward the horizon.

"What does he do for a living?"

"He don't do anything; he's an artist," someone quipped.

Eventually the archeologist found Api and asked him to do some drawings.

"What will you give me?" asked Api.

"A dollar and this box of colored pencils."

Api was so delighted that he quickly finished several drawings of mythical figures from Navajo rites.

The Navajo are primarily shepherds and horsemen, while the Pueblos live by the soil. Yet contemporary Navajo painters have adopted much in technique from their Pueblo neighbors, whose painting is precisely patterned, rhythmic, and symbolic, the natural expression of a people whose scheme of life is set by the solstices and ordered by the seasons.

In a region of capricious climate, Pueblo painters often express yearning for rain (page 406). Many Navajo paintings reflect the even more brutal water shortage in their barren grazing lands. But Navajo artists also portray cheerful themes as shown in Harrison Begay's girl with sheep (opposite). Charmingly simple, even in subject, is the Pueblo artist Garcia's painting of wild horses going into corral (page 407).

Navajo sand paintings to ward off evil spirits present impressive abstract designs matured through centuries of religious evolution (page 408).

The road traveled by Indian artists has not been easy. Discouragement has plagued many. Punishment and ostracism have been imposed by some communities that frowned on painting shared with outsiders. Indian art is just beginning to be known by the public at large, yet connoisseurs hail it as making valuable and unique contributions. Its influence on non-Indian artists and decorators shows in the striking sand-painting motifs that decorate a lounge of the liner *United States*.

And to the artist comes an occasional unexpected reward.

Pablita Velarde, outstanding Pueblo painter who has struggled most of her life against poor eyesight, lost her mother when she was three years old.

Recently she received a letter from an English woman who had followed her career. "I think," said this writer, "you may like to have this copy of a photograph I took of your father and mother on their wedding day in 1910."

It was the first photograph of her mother that Pablita had ever seen.

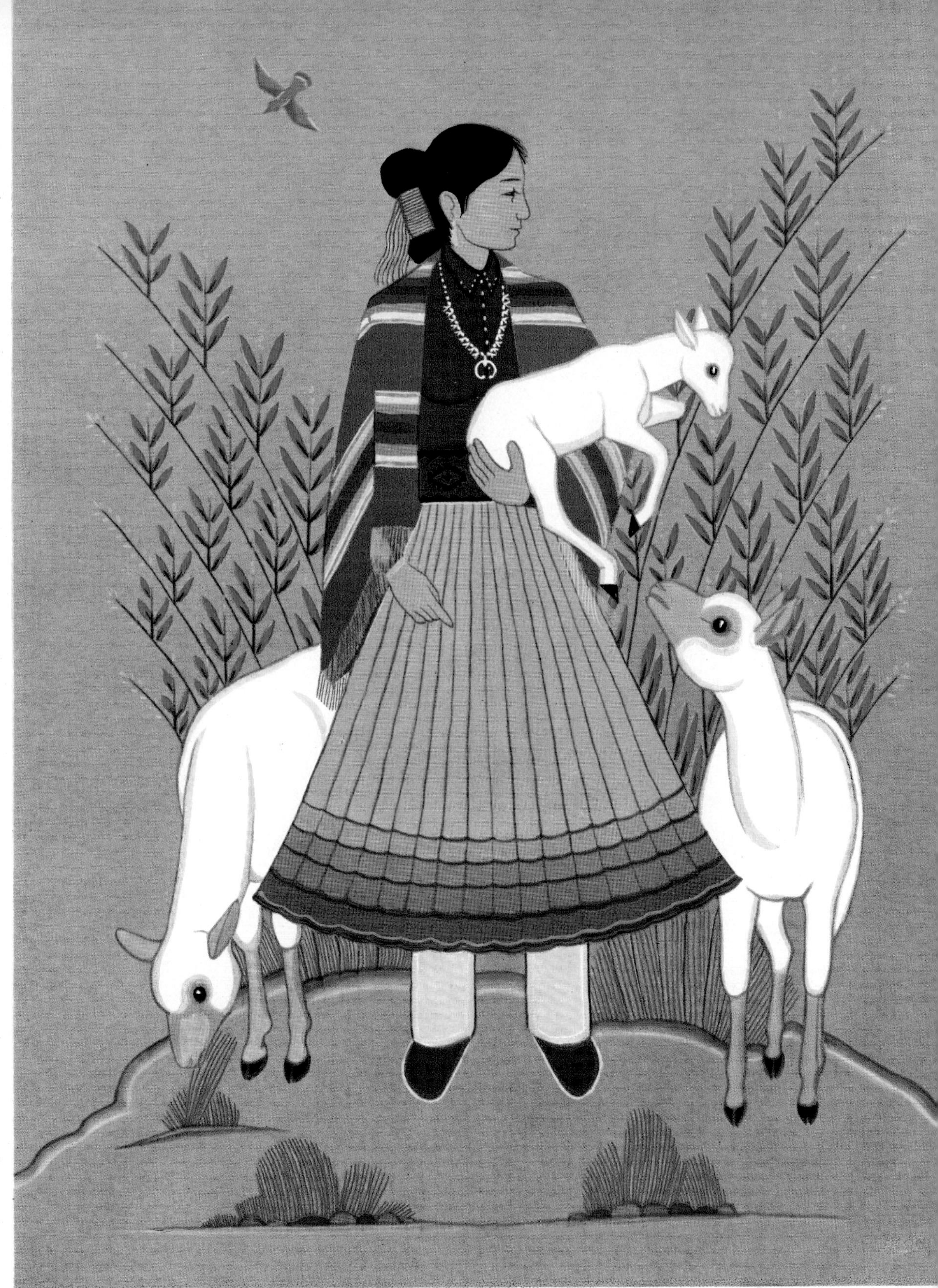

PAINTING FROM THE COLLECTION OF MRS. CHARLES H. DIETRICH

**Navajo Girl with Sheep** by Harrison Begay. Lovely girl in tribal dress reveals how well her people have treasured flocks introduced by the Spaniards. Idealized sheep, high-spirited horses, well-dressed people typify the decorative, analytic style of this noted Navajo artist, largely self-taught.

**Prairie Fire** by F. Blackbear Bosin. Searing waves of flame leap into the sky. Antelopes and wolves, their feuds forgotten, join mounted Indians in headlong flight across the drought-stricken Plains. Such is the artist's skill that his animals convey a sense of fright; even the grasses reflect foreboding.

PAINTING FROM COLLECTION OF THE PHILBROOK ART CENTER, TULSA, OKLAHOMA

Bosin, 34-year-old Kiowa Comanche, reveals the fury of life triumphing in the face of disaster. Speed and action are hallmarks of Plains art, modern and traditional. But in a concisely painted buffalo-robe history of a hundred years ago such an event would have been noted by a single symbol.

**Creek Ball Game** by Noah Deere. Graceful Eastern Woodlands athletes with plumed tailpieces and roached headdresses suggest a procession of youths around a classic Greek vase. But here noses and heads are bloody, for the game is *tokonhon* (stick ball), rough-and-tumble forerunner of lacrosse (page 22). Players may not touch the ball with their hands; they catch and throw it with a racket laced with thongs. Though the immediate object was to drive a stuffed deerskin ball through the opponents' goal post, the long-range aim was to test a man's endurance, honor, team spirit, and potential war valor. Often contests were ceremonial.

Noah Deere was 21 and a student at Bacone College when this painting won him a prize at Tulsa's Philbrook Art Center in 1950.

**Buffalo Hunt** by Ma-Pe-Wi. Indian hunters, racing under the abstract light of a geometric sun, drive a herd before them in such furious action that hoofbeats fairly pound across the page. The massive bulk of slain and stampeding animals contrasts sharply with the arrow's thin line. Even though they live outside the beasts' former range and lack its hunting tradition, Pueblo Indians cherish memories of bison. Hopi and Rio Grande pueblos still stage buffalo dances.

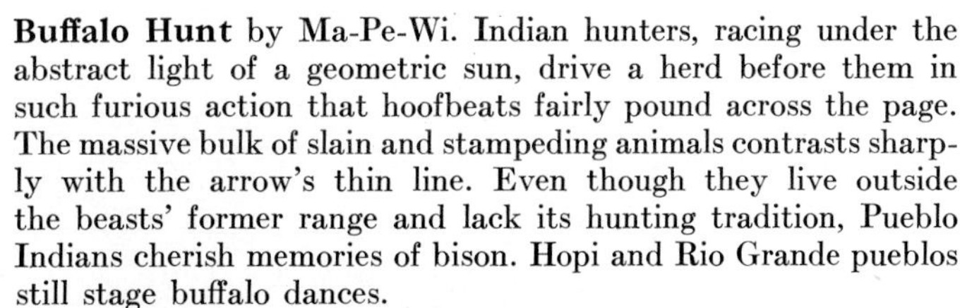

A Pueblo artist who has left his Zia home, Ma-Pe-Wi (Red Bird) here uses ancient symbols of his people. His clouds resemble those on weather charts. His Zia sun, rising above stylized mountains, today rides New Mexico's automobile tags, shines on State flag. Yuccas and piñons, or nut pines, long a source of Indian food, grow between triangular hills. *Buffalo Hunt*, an early work, displays the artist's characteristic grace. Even when portraying impending death, his art pulses with the joy of living.

The horizon detail in both these paintings is unusual in Indian works. Noah Deere (above) stylizes figures against a natural background; Ma-Pe-Wi employs realistic figures in an abstract setting.

PAINTINGS FROM THE COLLECTIONS OF THE PHILBROOK ART CENTER, TULSA, OKLAHOMA (ABOVE) AND THE INDIAN ARTS FUND, SANTA FE, NEW MEXICO

**The Delight Makers** by Fred Kabotie. As masked Kachina dancers swish sashes and shake rattles in rhythmic appeal to the rain spirits, Hopi clowns enliven the ceremony by climbing a ladder upside down.

"Delight Makers" is an anthropologist's name for all Pueblo clowns. In this happy scene they make spectators laugh as the sun smiles above a cloud chorus; even the doll grins. Three girls, hair worn in maiden style, peep from blankets. The tasseled pranksters—like other clowns somber beneath their paint—play more serious roles in secret rites.

**Horses Going into Corral** by Lorenzo Garcia (below). The artist has caught his motley, wild-and-woolly subjects on the border line of fact and fancy, as if elfin steeds were prancing from some unearthly pasture into the reality of work and saddle, unmindful of their fate. Only the roundup rider and his mount seem somewhat real. But he turns his face away, for his Santo Domingo Pueblo—also Garcia's home—frowns on reproductions of the human form.

PAINTINGS FROM THE COLLECTIONS OF MR. AND MRS. CHARLES DE YOUNG ELKUS (RIGHT) AND DOROTHY DUNN

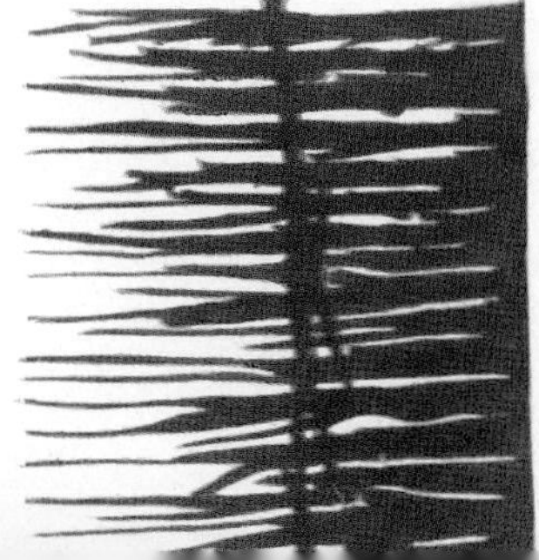
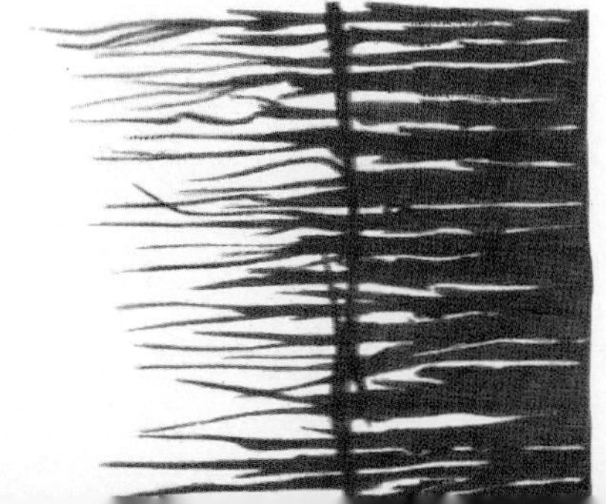

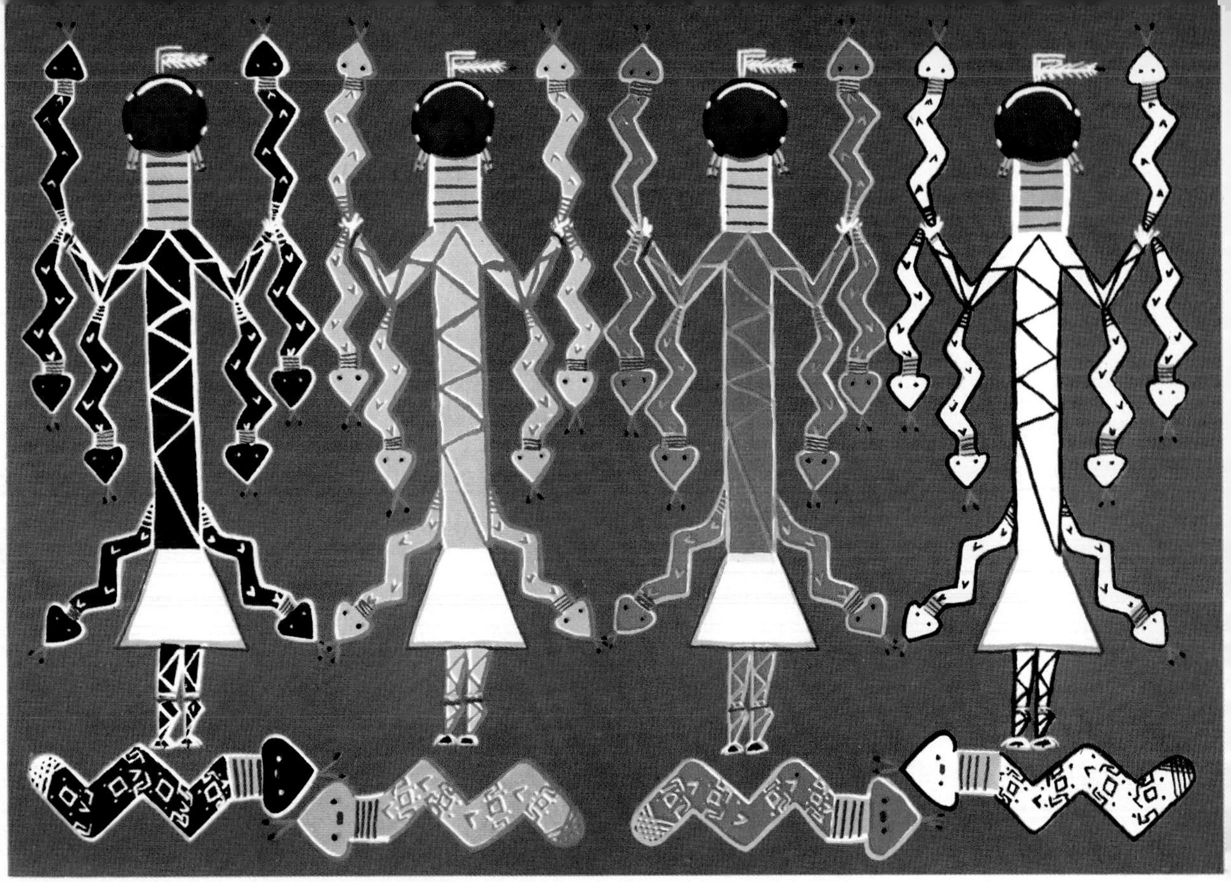

**Wind Way** by Bennie Tilden. Four long-necked healing spirits, holding snakes marked with deer tracks, derive from Navajo sand painting used in curing rites (pages 112, 119). Taboos forbid tribal artists to copy exactly the design of the original. At ceremony's end it is swept up and cast to the winds.

**Bear Hunt** by Joe H. Herrera. Tracks of man and bear chart hunt across abstract universe. As if sighting his quarry, hunter finally crouches on all fours. Bear prints cross squint-eyed sun, from which red-tipped clouds unfurl like sails. Horned moon looks down from upper right; ball below is a near-by planet. Symbolic rain falls in dots, mountains zigzag, triangle with seed is fertility symbol. Herrera's modern Pueblo art recalls the ancient forms.

PAINTINGS FROM THE SOUTHWEST MUSEUM, LOS ANGELES (ABOVE) AND THE MILLICENT A. ROGERS FOUNDATION COLLECTION

# THE HAVASUPAI

**BY JACK BREED**

AT HAVASU HILLTOP the Topocoba Trail begins a corkscrew descent into the land of the Havasupai, deep in a side gorge off the Grand Canyon of the Colorado. My leathery-faced, whistling Indian guide—"Joe Jones my name!"—casually spurred his horse over the edge and around the first of 29 switchbacks on a thousand-foot slope of slippery rock. As I followed, I did my best to forget his happy retort a few minutes before when I asked why horses rather than mules were used on the dizzy trail.

"You train horse early, he good as mule," Joe said, "but faster."

I swallowed hard and hung on. We dropped seemingly within minutes from the gray and buff limestone of the rim to the brilliant red sandstone of the inner gorge walls. Then we were in a meandering canyon, little more than a dry wash, that was to lead us 12 miles.

For three hours, from the rear, I had ample chance to study my companion. His was no traditional Indian garb; rather he wore sweat shirt, heavy boots, cotton socks, and, to top it all, a baseball cap! His tanned, round face, framing keen brown eyes, reminded me of a Hopi. But his gray hair was neatly cut and parted in barbershop style.

Gradually the red-walled ravine widened. Lush groves of cottonwoods and willows began to appear. Suddenly from the canyon wall came the rush and bubble of Havasu Creek, born of cold-welling springs—water as crystal-clear as any I had ever seen.

We crossed and recrossed the creek, riding between neatly fenced fields. Untethered horses looked up from their munching. Still I had seen neither Indians nor dwellings. Then, from a rise where the dusty trail cut between a boulder outcrop and the canyon wall, I saw, sprawled below, the lovely land of the Havasupai. Fields green with new corn bordered the sparkling stream. Orchards and rich brown, freshly turned earth surrounded quaint hogans and wooden cottages painted yellow, green, and blue.

At this point Havasu Canyon widens to about a quarter mile. Red walls rise hundreds of feet straight up (page 108). Two red pinnacles, ancient gods to the Indians, stand like sentinels. Legend says that when they tumble, doom will come upon the tribe.

Cottonwoods shade Supai village's "main street" leading to a white clapboard schoolhouse, with tiny steeple for the traditional bell, and playground of seesaws and swings—straight out of New England. Indians, busy over crops or chatting around a hogan, paused to wave to Joe, or just to stare at me.

Such is the home of the "People of the Blue-green Water." No automobile enters their hidden valley; the cold war seems far away.

At headquarters of Noble Guthrie, then Indian subagent on this remotest of United States reservations, I found electricity at the flip of a switch, hot and cold running water, refrigerators, innerspring mattresses, a radio transmitter, telephones, and a piano!

"Everything came in by horseback or by drag, down the trail you came," he said. "The old wagon road across the canyon hasn't been usable in years."

Mail comes in twice a week, and with it come cowboy boots, guitars, groceries, and most heavy provisions. It is much cheaper to mail goods to Supai than to hire a private pack horse.

When I was there, 35 Indian families lived in Havasu Canyon. They averaged four children each. Mr. Guthrie told me the reservation can support comfortably few more than 200 persons. A recent census showed 368, but many are away at any one time, working in Grand Canyon tourist centers or in towns near by.

For centuries the entire tribe moved out to gather seeds and track deer, antelope, and rabbit on the canyon rim in winter, farming their valley in summer. This semi-annual migration is now a thing of the past. Required school attendance for children through eighth grade is one obstacle. And few elders really want to leave their Shangri-La valley; they know a good thing when they have it.

No one here works harder than he has to. And since an implement company donated a tractor, packed in disassembled for use by the entire tribe, there's been even more time for horseback gallops along the canyon, rodeos, card games, and festivals. Almost as soon as they can walk, children learn to swim and ride. No elder tells them nay, for Havasupai believe that harsh words or punishment shrivel a child's soul.

If any one worries, it may be the older generation, remembering uneasily the terrible flash floods—the worst in 1911—that have roared down the valley to sweep the village away, while the Indians clung to the cliffsides. Perhaps they deplore, too, the coming of modern ways. Some had been loath to give up their primitive mud and brush hogans, like those of the Navajo. But most families now lived in small wood cottages brought in on mules by the Agency some years ago after a flood.

Joe Jones, I found, had only gone halfway. He and his wife still lived in a dark and smelly hogan—their cottage they used as an oversize closet! Inside I saw at least nine pairs of trousers. Joe's previous visitors had left him amply endowed with white man's pants, his pride and joy.

Cooking and much other household life of the canyon still goes on outdoors. I had hoped that hand-shaped pottery and coiled baskets might still be in use, but I was too late. Modern sheepherder stoves, aluminum and porcelained pots and pans have replaced them.

Older women still make fine Supai baskets for sale at the Agency. And I noticed, drying on fences and rooftops, the deer hides for which Havasupai are famous. They tan skins by hand with deer's brains and marrow, working them immaculately white and soft.

Today, as always, Havasupai are outstanding farmers. After each flood they have rebuilt their elaborate irrigation

**Heads Up! Bronc Loose!** Havasupai scatter before wild hoofs as a thrown rider, in red chaps, scrambles from the dust. Bred to the saddle, the Blue-green Water People hold an all-Indian rodeo and harvest festival each summer in their remote cliff-walled valley. Walapai and Mohave come from the West, Hopi and Navajo from the east, some riding as far as 165 miles to compete.

KODACHROME BY WILLIAM BELKNAP, JR

dams and ditches, and replanted their 175 acres of rich bottom lands, growing corn, beans, and squash as staple crops. From neat orchards come peaches, apricots, melons, and figs.

After hot work in the fields, the amazing Havasupai like to get even hotter, relaxing in steam baths. They parboil themselves in low tarpaulin-covered sweat lodges, half in and half out of the ground, by pouring water over fire-hot stones. Between periods of steaming—usually as long as it takes to sing four songs—they let sand dry on their bodies. They do this four times, then leap into the cold creek.

Havasupai still have a medicine man to shake his rattles over the sick. But they have a volunteer nurse who sees that seriously ill patients receive more modern treatment as well.

The populace turns out en masse for the movies shown in the schoolhouse. Western pictures are top favorites. Cheers and boos reverberate; next day youthful braves gallop through the valley, playing "cowboys and Indians."

Superb horsemen, the Havasupai leap on a mount even to go next door, rather than walk. It is a common sight to see four or five Havasupai on one horse, a father in the saddle and his youngsters hanging on tightly fore and aft.

Reluctantly I climbed on a horse myself one morning and started back up the 14-mile trail to Hilltop. Joe Jones whistled and shouted to move his pack horses along. At parting I asked him, "Is there anything you'd like me to send you, Joe? Something you need?"

"I like your pants, thank you very much," said Joe, eyeing my Navy khakis.

He was shouting happily at his horses again as I watched him disappear down the trail, my trousers *and* shirt tied neatly to the back of his saddle!

# THE INDIAN'S CHANGING WORLD

BY MATTHEW W. STIRLING

A BATTERED PICKUP TRUCK rattles away from South Dakota's Pine Ridge Indian Reservation. John Red Dog, full-blooded Dakota, drives to work for a rancher—a step toward answering his urge "to live like a white man."

Born in a meager frame house, Red Dog heard old men's wistful tales of buffalo hunts and battles with cavalry. Placed on the reservation, Red Dog's grandfather had scorned the plow offered him and remained bewildered by a life he had never known. The boy's father, lacking incentive, loafed about.

School meant little to Red Dog. Why study? His few ventures off the reservation taught him the bitter lesson of intolerance. He feared white men, was happy to return to strong family ties.

World War II's draft plunged Red Dog into a violent world. Gone was the warm security of his clan. In barracks no one cared. But gradually he learned self reliance, found he could make friends with white soldiers. He grew proud of his infantry unit, and of himself. A crack shot, he earned respect overseas on night patrols probing German positions. On furlough he saw London, Paris, Cannes. Shipped home, he spent a week visiting a white buddy in New York.

Return to the reservation after four years jolted him. Houses looked ramshackle, tribal leaders were sad old men clutching dreams. He found the ceremonies silly, snapped angrily at an elder who chided him. His family was hurt, but he didn't care. Listlessly, he worked his family's protected, tax-free acres. The scrawny cattle, the poverty depressed him. He talked with other Indian veterans, many bitter, more often drunk than sober. "Nuts," he would say in GI jargon, "I'm going over the hill."

Instead he married and raised a son. He managed to keep his family in food and clothing, and saw that his son studied hard at the Government school. Red Dog's wife, placid, contented, couldn't understand his restlessness. She had her man, her child, her home and chores. What else was there?

Red Dog pictured his son facing the same drab, pointless life. Letters from army friends in Los Angeles and Chicago made him grumble with envy.

The agent found him a job outside—if he could supply a truck. To get money, he asked the council's permission to sell tribal cattle. No law kept him on the reservation; as citizen he could come and go. But cattle rate as lengthy a harangue as tribal uranium deposits.

Red Dog got his truck, and his family soon joined him off the reservation. Some 240,000 United States Indians have taken Red Dog's way to assimilation in the white man's world. The remaining 285,000 dwell on 205 Federal reservations —a home the Indian can always return to. They too face change.

Ojibwa in Minnesota and Michigan woodlands act as guides to city sportsmen. Eastern Cherokees live the mountaineer-farmer lives of their North Carolina neighbors. Tradition-proud Pueblos see their young men take jobs with atom scientists. Navajo elders debated hiring a professional rainmaker complete with airplane and dry ice. Apaches have prospered farming New Mexico land; some bid for tourists with motels. Osage and other Oklahoma tribesmen hold public office, enter professions, often drive up in Cadillacs to inspect tribal oil wells.

Common to all areas is the impact of 25,000 World War II Indian veterans hastening the change. Still, tradition shows in timeless ceremonies and crafts, as the following pages illustrate.

KODACHROME BY JUSTIN LOCKE

**Girded with Jingling Bells, a Plumed Teen-ager Performs a Ritual Dance at Taos Pueblo**

KODACHROMES BY JUSTIN LOCKE

**Pueblo Ceremonies Strike an Old Refrain,** but the furniture is Grand Rapids. With rattles and sacred wand, San Ildefonso Indians seek rain for crops of corn. Mellowed adobe walls at Taos (left) recall pagan doorless days when ladders were drawn up to bar invaders. In the Cochiti apartment above, a crucifix looks upon a family supping on the linoleum, washing down tortillas with coffee from an enamel pot.

JOSEF MUENCH

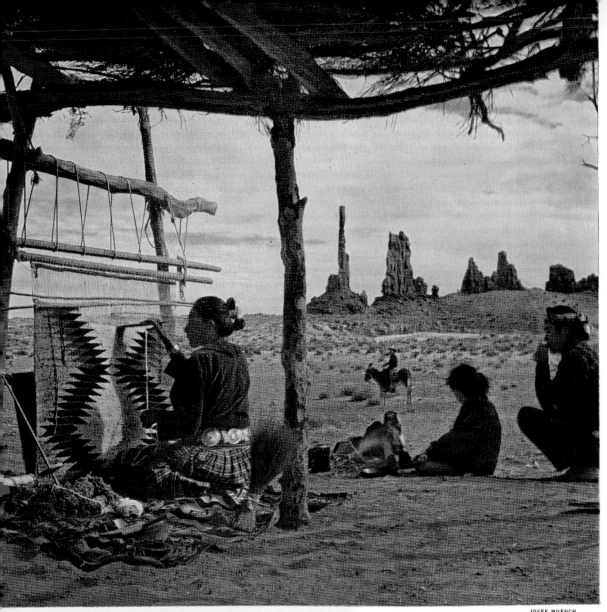

**Navajo Summer in the Open.** Amid towering sandstone pillars of mile-high Monument Valley, athwart the Arizona-Utah line, this family has quit winter's log-and-mud hogan for an arbor open to the breezes. Mother weaves a rug on a loom such as her people borrowed from ancient Pueblos.

Carding raw wool from flocks watched by son on donkey, she twists it into yarn on wooden spindle at her left, colors it with aniline dyes. Opening the warp threads on her upright loom with a stick, she inserts the colored weft threads, packs them down with toothed batten. A borderless geometrical pattern emerges; she seldom pictures men or animals. Left: Milking a balky Navajo goat is a fore-and-aft job!

ALFRED M. BAILEY AND FRED G. BRANDENBURG

**Birth of a Buckle.** Prize-winning silversmith Tom Burnsides finishes a shiny belt buckle at Arizona's Pine Springs Trading Post, center of Navajo silver casters. He cut his mold, entirely from imagination, in chalky volcanic tuff hacked from a desert outcrop. Here he chisels away excess silver from the cast, and files it smooth before polishing. All scrap goes into later melts.

The finished buckle (lower right) has center post and tongue soldered on. Just above, as it came from the mold, the cast still has branching channels and extra crossbars for even flow of molten silver from the pouring hole. Needles shooting out from edges indicate small passages punched in the mold to allow air to escape.

The artist adapted his bracelet from the leather bow guard of old-time Navajo archers. He wears a belt of silver concha disks, as does the woman weaver opposite, and turquoise ring and necklace. From boyhood, Navajo males wear bright headbands.

JACK BREED

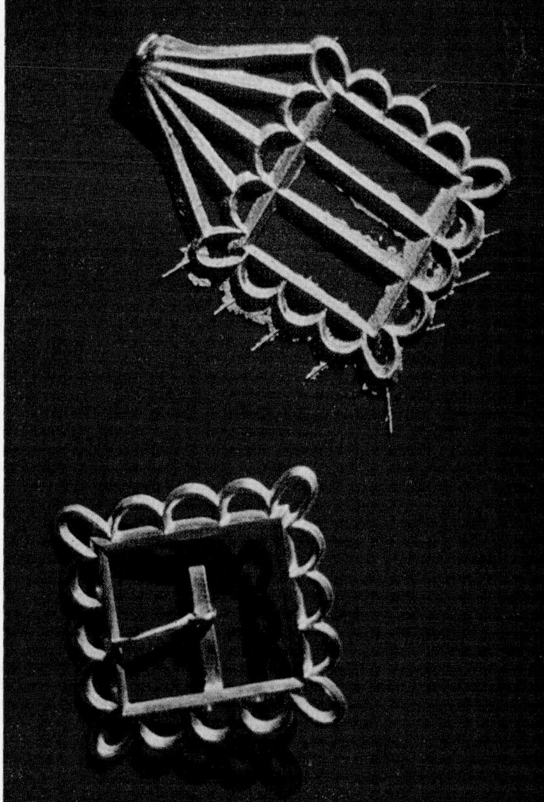

**Youthful Grins Tell a Success Story in Apache Town.** Bylas, a town straddling U.S. Highway 70, is home to 700 Apaches of Arizona's San Carlos Indian Reservation. Fathers of these children own radios, their mothers run powered washing machines. Neat frame houses replace brush wickiups of nomad days, pickup trucks supplant old buckboards. The neighboring town—Geronimo—recalls the fierce tribal reputation (page 115). Geronimo's raiding Chiricahua band, finally rounded up in 1886, were "prisoners of war" until 1913; recalcitrant young-'uns were carted to school, feet bound to prevent their leaping from wagons. But Apaches, like other Indian groups, now value education. These Bylas youngsters enjoy classes, sports, play trophy-winning basketball.

Most young Indians attend regular public schools. The U.S. Indian Service also maintains 189 day schools on reservations, as well as 74 boarding schools, mostly for the increasing Navajo. A Government fund aids college training. Many graduates enter the Indian Service as teachers, stenographers, may rise to become school or agency superintendents. Others have discovered the tourist-attracting value of traditional dances like that at right. When afternoon shadows deepen in Grand Canyon, Indians from the near-by Hopi reservation perform their feather dance on the canyon rim.

WESTERN WAYS FEATURES; JUSTIN LOCKE (OPPOSITE)

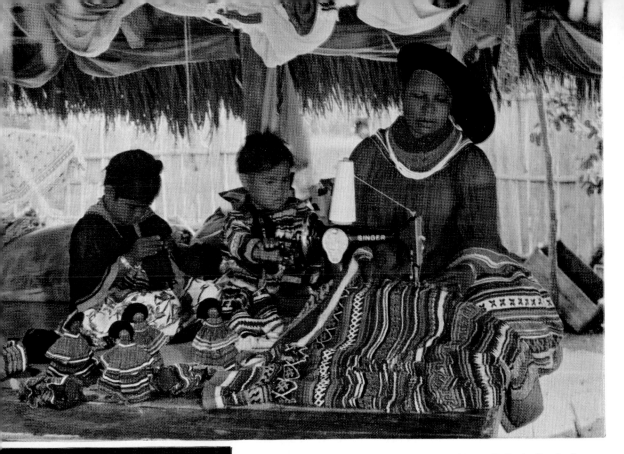

**Sewing Machines Conquer Where Soldiers Failed.** Seminole seamstress, helped by youngsters, descends from warriors who never surrendered, hung on in Florida after troops moved other Seminoles to Oklahoma (pages 68–71). Self-reliant Florida Indians cherish old ways, but accept white man's inventions and schooling, as earnest young faces show below. Seminole hunt and raise cattle on two reservations near Lake Okeechobee, or make livings outside, farming, lumbering, selling handicrafts.

Some Cherokees, too, resisted transfer west, stayed in North Carolina. Woman, left, one of the State's 5,200 Cherokees, strings green beans for winter fare. Dried, they are "leather britches."



NATIONAL GEOGRAPHIC PHOTOGRAPHERS
WILLARD R. CULVER AND ROBERT F. SISSON

# MOHAWKS SCRAPE THE SKY

BY ROBERT L. CONLY

THE LAST PLACE you'd expect to meet a Mohawk Indian is atop the towering steel skeleton of a New York City skyscraper. Yet many a Mohawk earns a living 500 to 1,000 feet in the air, where one misstep means death. I saw them catfooting along narrow girders, and wondered at this modern tribal occupation, more perilous than any warpath.

Mohawks helped build the lofty UN buildings, the Metropolitan Life Tower, Woolworth Building, RCA Building, and, outreaching all, the quarter-mile-high Empire State Building.

Tom Lahache, tall, dignified, with typical high Indian cheekbones and deep-set eyes, got his first job in "high iron" some 30 years ago when he was 17.

"You don't pay much attention to how tall a building is," he said. "If you slip, 50 feet is as bad as 500 feet."

With Tom in the riveting gang I watched were Tom Jacobs, Mike Tarbell, and Mickey Snow, all Mohawks, all veteran iron workers. Munching sandwiches and swigging soda pop, they explained how they operate; lunch over, they demonstrated.

Mickey heated rivets in a stove on the girders, then tossed each red-hot rivet to Mike, who caught it in a bucket, and with tongs thrust it into place. Lahache held it firm with a dolly bar while Tom Jacobs flattened the end with a rivet gun. Simple—as long as nobody stepped back into empty air.

These men are among some 400 Mohawks living in an old section of Brooklyn. A few own houses; the rest rent walk-up apartments. Some have cars; most have television sets on which they favor Western programs—about Indians.

Their migration to Brooklyn dates from the late 1920's. The origin of their hazardous talent goes back further still. After the American Revolution, the exiled Mohawks (page 26) settled in Canada on reservations like Caughnawaga on the St. Lawrence River. For nearly a century they farmed, trapped, piloted fur-laden canoes through the rapids. Then in the '80's a bridge company spanning the river from Caughnawaga to Lachine promised Mohawks jobs as laborers in return for use of their land.

As fast as the bridge went up, so did the Mohawks, swarming out on its narrow beams. Hardened riveters, working on the span's dizziest heights, would find Indians peering curiously over their shoulders to see what was going on.

Impressed, an engineer taught some to rivet. Men willing to crawl around girders were hard to find in those days. When the builders moved on, full-fledged Mohawk ironworkers went too—with brothers, cousins, and friends.

Why did Mohawks take so eagerly to this spine-chilling work? In 1714, John Lawson, surveyor and traveler, noted a puzzling Indian characteristic: "They will walk over deep Brooks, and Creeks, on the smallest Poles, and that without any Fear or Concern. Nay, an Indian will walk on the Ridge of a Barn or House and look down the Gable-end, and spit upon the Ground, as unconcerned, as if he was walking on Terra firma."

Joining construction gangs all over Canada, Mohawks followed jobs into the United States. Manhattan of the 1920's, its skyscrapers sprouting like beanstalks, was a happy hunting ground. Early to settle in Brooklyn was Tom Jacobs. His first job was almost his last.

"I was working on a corner 200, maybe 300, feet up," he told me. "My foot slipped, and all of a sudden there was nothing under me but the ground, so far away I could hardly see it. When I felt

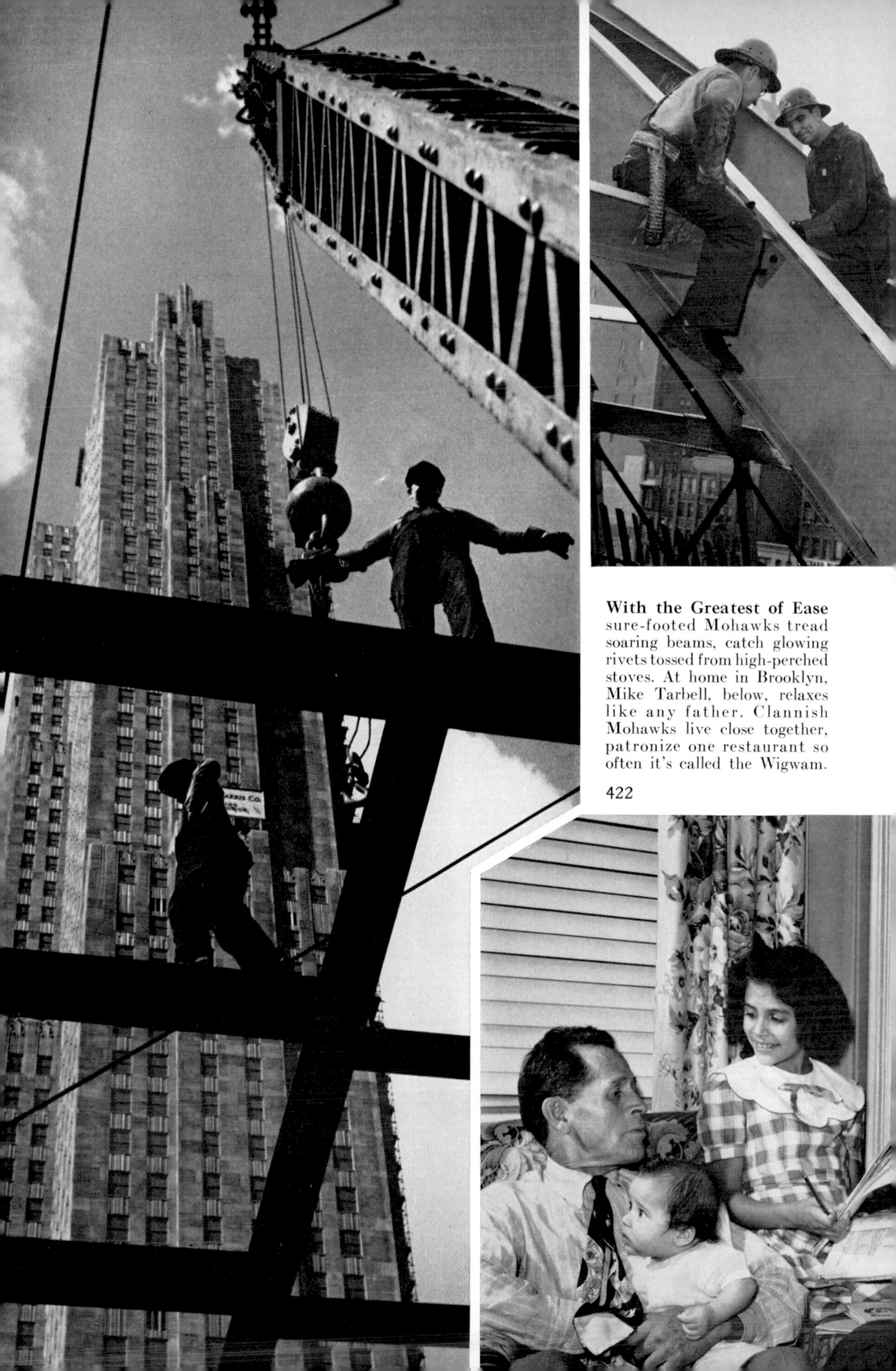

**With the Greatest of Ease** sure-footed Mohawks tread soaring beams, catch glowing rivets tossed from high-perched stoves. At home in Brooklyn, Mike Tarbell, below, relaxes like any father. Clannish Mohawks live close together, patronize one restaurant so often it's called the Wigwam.

**Standing on Air,** 1,472 dizzy feet above New York's 34th Street, Mohawk riveters erect the 222-foot television tower atop the Empire State Building, which they also helped build. For this breath-taking work, Indians collected $3.25 an hour. "Whatever they get," said an onlooker, "it isn't enough!"

NATIONAL GEOGRAPHIC PHOTOGRAPHER B. ANTHONY STEWART



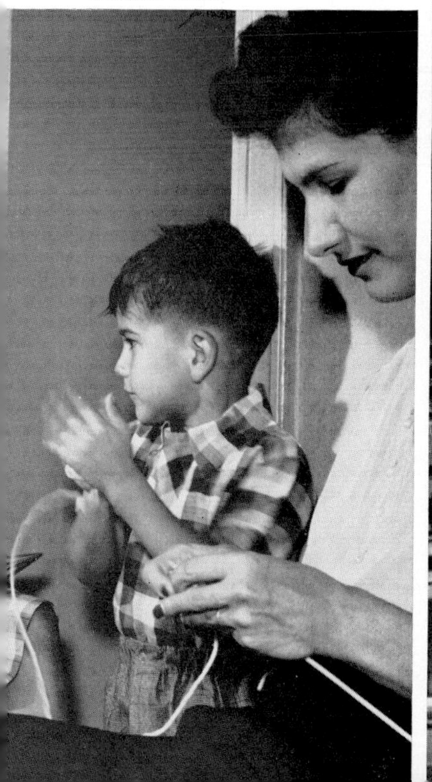

NATIONAL GEOGRAPHIC PHOTOGRAPHER B. ANTHONY STEWART

**Brooklyn Born Is Linda "Holding an Apple," but Blood of Mohawk Warriors Runs in Her Veins**

myself falling, I stuck out my arm, and it caught a beam. I just hung there, swinging in the wind. The other men shouted, 'Tom, what are you going to do?' What a question!

"I chinned myself on that beam, got a leg over it, and climbed up. I sat there for a while to get my breath, then went back to work."

Mohawks have adapted themselves well to Brooklyn, though elders frown on marriages between Indians and non-Indians (which happen anyway). Most are bilingual. Children go to public schools. Boys play baseball in streets and parks.

At Cuyler Presbyterian Church, when services were held in Mohawk, families would sing such old stand-bys as *Ni-io ta-tia-ta-nons-tat* ("Rock of Ages"). And after an "Indian show," complete with tepees, tomahawks, and a "campfire" made of sticks around a light bulb, they give hearty voice to their favorite song, *Ka-na-wa-ke te-tsi-te-we* — "Let's Go Back to Caughnawaga."

# • INDEX